'Tony Lane is a masterful teacher. From his co[...] of the history of doctrine he distinguishes the essentials of orthodoxy from debatable secondary matters. He has a knack of writing epigrammatic sentences that instantly clarify an issue. He has a gift for accurately apt illustrations. Just when things might be getting a little dull, he throws in a joke or even a cartoon. Ideal for anyone who wants to understand the basics.'

Richard Bauckham, Emeritus Professor of New Testament Studies
University of St Andrews, Scotland

'Engaging in style, evangelical in spirit, ecumenical in atmosphere, and eclectic in its use of resources, *Exploring Christian Doctrine* presents in concise and readable form some of the ripe fruit of Tony Lane's career-long ministry as a teacher of theology. In a well-conceived format, he lays out the big questions, offers his own perspective (always indicating the alternatives in the major issues) and on occasion, tantalizingly, leaves the reader to work through the issues independently. *Exploring Christian Doctrine* will delight students looking for a textbook that is clear and informative, never overbearing but always challenging.'

Sinclair B. Ferguson, Professor of Systematic Theology
Redeemer Theological Seminary, Dallas, Texas

'What does the Church believe? What does the Church's faith have to do with prayer and worship, and life in the everyday world? Why don't all churches believe the same thing? In this useful primer, Tony Lane addresses these basic questions and more, demonstrating again and again how the evangelical faith is grounded in Scripture and related to the Church's grand tradition. He charts his own path, to be sure, but all along the way he also shows why faithful Christians can look at some issues from different perspectives. Students, especially, will find this a welcome guide.'

Joel B. Green, Associate Dean for the Center for Advanced
Theological Studies, Fuller Theological Seminary, California

'Tony Lane's survey of Christian belief is accessible and engaging. Alive to historical debates and to contemporary challenges, his focus nonetheless remains on offering a clear and thorough account of the essential points of Christian doctrine from a broadly evangelical perspective. The structure of the book will help readers to engage and to go deeper where they wish. Anyone wanting to understand what Christians believe and why will find this an extremely helpful guide.'

Steve Holmes, Senior Lecturer in Theology
University of St Andrews, Scotland

'This is a simply outstanding introduction to doctrine; I know nothing like it. The product of decades of classroom experience, it is rooted in the Bible, answers a barrage of questions and objections, and is enlivened by cartoons and humour. If you think doctrine is dull and boring, think again.'

Robert Letham, Director of Research and Senior Tutor in Systematic
and Historical Theology, Wales Evangelical School of Theology

'This book does exactly what its title promises: it conducts beginning students of broadly evangelical theology on a search for buried treasure (the wealth of Christian tradition) and "risen" treasure (the wisdom and knowledge hid in Jesus Christ (Colossians 2:3)) by traversing the length and breadth of Christian doctrine. As with all successful journeys, this one comes with a map, compass and, most importantly, a knowledgeable and trustworthy guide. The book's structure is appetizingly laid out in a series of initial questions, positions taken, objections raised, errors to avoid and Lane's own succinct answers – all framed by credal and confessional bounds and set within the context of worship. As with all good travel, this exploration is also educational, broadening the mind, and Lane works hard to ensure that the traveller will not return home unchanged: in addition to the "answers", Lane suggests practical applications. This is only fitting, for the ultimate purpose of doctrine is to serve discipleship and doxology.'

Kevin J. Vanhoozer, Research Professor of Systematic Theology
Trinity Evangelical Divinity School, Illinois

EXPLORING CHRISTIAN DOCTRINE

Anthony N. S. Lane (DD, University of Oxford) is Professor of Historical Theology at London School of Theology. He is the author of a number of books, including *A Concise History of Christian Thought* (previously *The Lion Concise Book of Christian Thought*), *The Lion Christian Classics Collection*, *John Calvin: Student of the Church Fathers* and *Justification by Faith in Catholic–Protestant Dialogue*. This book is based on an introductory Christian Doctrine module that he has taught for many years. He is married and has two children and two grandchildren.

EXPLORING CHRISTIAN DOCTRINE

Tony Lane

First published in Great Britain in 2013

Society for Promoting Christian Knowledge
36 Causton Street
London SW1P 4ST
www.spckpublishing.co.uk

British Library Cataloguing-in-Publication Data
A catalogue record for this book is available from the British Library

ISBN 978–0–281–06449–6
eBook ISBN 978–0–281–07160–9

Typeset by Graphicraft Limited, Hong Kong
First printed in Great Britain by Ashford Colour Press

eBook by Graphicraft Limited, Hong Kong

CONTENTS

INTRODUCTION

WHAT IS THE PURPOSE OF THIS BOOK?

This book originated as a series of lectures for a first-year undergraduate Christian Doctrine Survey module. It is designed to be used by students at that level, either on their own or as a textbook for a whole cohort. It is also written to be accessible to the educated lay person who has had no formal theological training.

In writing the book I have sought to achieve a number of objectives:

1 to provide a basic account of Christian beliefs – the primary objective;
2 to give, as appropriate, a very brief account of the history of particular doctrines, showing how doctrines have developed historically and need to be understood contextually;
3 to illustrate particular doctrines with key historical texts, especially credal statements;
4 to show how different groups differ over particular doctrines;
5 to point to the interconnections between different doctrines, such as the person and work of Christ;

6 to show how particular doctrines relate to the contemporary scene – both Church and culture.

SPECIAL FEATURES

Each chapter contains a number of different types of material:

- **Aims of this chapter**: questions that the chapter sets out to answer.
- **What do you think? The question**: a question that can be considered there and then by the individual reading the book or by the group using it together.
- **What do you think? My answer**: having posed the question, later in the chapter I offer my own answer to it, deliberately not called 'The answer'.
- **Sceptic's corner**: a common objection, with my answer.
- **Credal statement(s)**: extract(s) from a creed, confession or similar document, some of these being contemporary.[1]
- **Error(s) to avoid**: way(s) in which the doctrine has been misunderstood *or*, more rarely:
- **Tension to hold**: two sides of the truth which need to be held in tension.

1

- **Speculation**: occasionally I have indulged in speculation.
- **Worship**: an extract from a hymn, a worship song or a liturgy, which relates to the topic.
- **Prayer**: usually from a historical source, especially the collects of the Anglican *Common Worship*, most of which originated in the Book of Common Prayer as it evolved from 1549 to 1666.

The inclusion of these last two items is deliberate, for two reasons. There is an ancient principle which is summarized in the Latin slogan *lex orandi lex credendi*, literally translated 'the law of prayer [is] the law of belief.' In other words, how we worship affects (sometimes effects) how we believe. It is probably true that most Christians learn as much from the liturgy, hymns or songs that they repeatedly hear, say or sing as they do from all of the sermons that they sleep through. This can be a good or a bad thing, depending on how good the material is. Worship is far too important to be left to musicians.

The second reason for including these items is that the purpose of theology is not just to inform us about God but to lead us to encounter him as the object of our worship. The *Athanasian Creed defines the Catholic faith as 'that we *worship* one God in trinity and trinity in unity'. *Calvin described the gospel as:

> a doctrine not of the tongue but of life. It is not apprehended by the understanding and memory alone, as other disciplines are, but it is received only when it possesses the whole soul, and finds a seat and resting place in the inmost affection of the heart. (*Institutes* 3:6:4)

*Bernard of Clairvaux described five different reasons for the pursuit of knowledge. To seek it for its own sake is curiosity; to seek it for fame is vanity; to seek it to gain money or honours is profiteering; to seek it to benefit oneself is prudence; to seek it to be of service to others is love (*Sermons on Song of Songs* 36:3). There is a legitimate role for all five motives – students can rightly be concerned about obtaining good grades and finding a good job after their studies. But to study theology without the desire to benefit oneself and others is to miss the point of it.

For these reasons, I have also included practical application within the book. To present theology as if it were purely about abstract ideas and not about truths that should lead to worship and to discipleship is to misrepresent it. It is possible, of course, to study theology (and to read this book) as a purely academic exercise, as an outside observer, but those who do so should always bear in mind that this is not the prime purpose of the discipline. Someone who is tone deaf could analyse a symphony mathematically but would be missing the most important feature of the symphony.

- **Question(s) to answer**: one or more questions which should be answered in *no more than 100 words*. Sometimes people are asked to set out their views at length, with the opportunity to prepare in advance – e.g. when giving a talk. On other occasions, we may be asked a question for which an answer is expected on the spot. The questioner will not be satisfied with the offer of a 2,000-word essay in a month – what is required is a brief answer there and then. These 100-word answers are preparation for that situation. For convenience these questions are all listed together at the end of the book.

- **Resources**: further reading on the topic. The word 'Resources' indicates that this is not a 'reading list' of items that the reader is expected to read. It is a list of useful resources should you want to go deeper into any of the topics at a later date. I have also referred in many places to my own writings on different topics. This is not because I think my own writings are necessarily the best available (at least I am not prepared to admit to thinking that!) but because they serve to explain more fully points that I am trying to make in a brief concise account.
- **Technical terms**: theology has acquired a certain number of technical terms and there is a glossary at the end of this book offering a brief definition of those that have been used.

CROSS-REFERENCES IN THE TEXT

- There are many references in the text to figures from the past and most of these are described in my *Concise History of Christian Thought*,[2] which previously went through four editions as *The Lion [Concise] Book of Christian Thought*.[3] Where such a figure (or council or creed) is mentioned an asterisk (*) indicates that they can be found in this work. This is done only for the first mention in each chapter. The Nicene Creed is found under 'Council of Constantinople (381)'; Gregory of Nazianzus and Gregory of Nyssa are found under 'Cappadocian Fathers'; the Westminster Catechisms are found under 'Westminster Confession of Faith'.[4]
- The *Catechism of the Catholic Church* (= CCC), published in 1994, offers a succinct summary of authoritative Roman Catholic teaching.[5] Throughout the book

I give references to this so that those readers interested in knowing the Roman Catholic position on any topic can easily access it. There is much in the *Catechism* that can be affirmed by all orthodox Christians and I have from time to time cited it under 'Credal statement(s)'.

- One unusual feature of this book is that most of the time I *quote* biblical passages rather than simply give references. There are two reasons for this. First, the degree of biblical literacy is considerably less than it once was and one cannot assume when mentioning Romans 8:28, e.g., that most readers will know what is being referred to. Second, the reality is that it is very rare for people to look up a reference to see what it says.[6] I have chosen to use the English Standard Version of the Bible (ESV) because it manages to keep closer to the original than almost any other translation while remaining readable.

APPROACH

This book takes an orderly, structured approach to Christian doctrine rather than offering a 'system'. The contents page indicates the basic structure. After some introductory chapters the book is based on the framework of 'Creation' – 'Sin and evil' – 'Redemption' – 'Future glory'. Getting the framework right is very important, just as the foundations are important for a house. In that sense this is an orderly, structured account. On the other hand, I am opposed to the 'big idea' approach, the idea that there is a single 'central dogma' or 'controlling principle' for theology. For example, (some) Lutherans see the doctrine of justification by faith in this way; (some) Calvinists see doctrine of the sovereignty of God similarly; *Karl Barth explicitly made

Christology the controlling principle for his theology; some today try to fit all doctrine into the category of 'relationships' or of 'narrative'. These different perspectives all shed light on theology. For example, much of the Bible is in the form of narrative and interpreting it from that perspective can be helpful – but does not, however, have much light to shed on the book of Proverbs. When one particular doctrine or approach or principle is set up as the key to the whole of the Bible or to the whole of Christian doctrine it always ends up bringing distortion.

*Augustine described the task of theology as 'faith seeking understanding', drawing on the Greek Septuagint translation (the one used by the New Testament writers) of Isaiah 7:9: 'If you do not believe, neither shall you understand.' *Anselm picked up on this theme, entitling one of his works *Faith Seeking Understanding*. This book likewise aims to make sense of theology, to help us to understand it. It will not succeed totally in this task, for two reasons. Paul states that here and now we only 'see in a mirror dimly' (1 Cor. 13:12), for more on which see Chapter 3. We can hardly expect to understand God fully if he is the eternal Creator and we are his creatures. Indeed, Martin Rees, the Astronomer Royal, points out that we cannot expect fully to understand even the created order: 'Some aspects of reality – a unified theory of physics or a full understanding of consciousness – might elude us simply because they're beyond human brains, just as surely as Einstein's ideas would baffle a chimpanzee.'[7] Apart from the doctrine of God there are other aspects of Christian teaching that I cannot claim to have explained fully, both for the reason just given and because of my own personal

shortcomings. The fact that I cannot offer a totally watertight system does not cause me to doubt my faith. Atheism has far more serious shortcomings. It fails to offer any ultimate meaning to life and undercuts the rational process itself, as will be argued in Chapter 4. It also undercuts human dignity by teaching that human beings are merely the accidental outcome of a blind process of evolution, as will be argued in Chapter 6.

My stance can be described as 'eclectic' rather than 'confessional'. I write as an Evangelical Christian, but I draw upon a wide range of Christian traditions – Reformed, Baptist, Lutheran, Catholic, etc. – without being tied to any specific one. I do not regard one of these as right and all the others as wrong, but all of them as more or less accurate portrayals of the truth, for more on which, see Chapter 3. The credal statements tend especially to be Reformed, but that is because they have produced so many! For the same reason, many of the prayers are Anglican. The eclectic nature of the work can be seen from the frequency of citation. The authors most cited are (in descending order): Augustine (early Catholic), Calvin (Reformed), *Luther (Lutheran), the *Wesleys (Methodist), C. S. Lewis (Anglican), *Irenaeus (early Catholic), *Moltmann (modern Reformed) and Barth (modern Reformed). The documents most cited are (in descending order): *Common Worship* (Anglican), *Westminster Confession of Faith* (Reformed), the Book of Common Prayer (Anglican), *Catechism of the Catholic Church* (Roman Catholic),[8] *the Nicene Creed (early Catholic), the *Chalcedonian Definition* (early Catholic) and the *Second Vatican Council (Roman Catholic).

I write as an Evangelical but this does not stop me from occasionally being critical of

Evangelical traditions in places where I think they have strayed from Scripture, Scripture rather than Evangelical tradition being my norm. I have sought to be Bible-based, which is why there are so many scriptural quotations. I hope that this book will be of interest and value to those who would not consider themselves to be Evangelical, as well as those who do.

The challenge of theology is not just to get the doctrines right but also to get them in the right proportion. A portrait might portray the hands and the head completely accurately, but if the former are twice the size of the latter the result is distortion. For example, there is just one passage in the Bible (Rev. 20:1–7) that refers explicitly to a Millennium, a 1,000-year rule of Christ on earth. Despite this, there are some Christian groups for whom this is a major preoccupation and a test of orthodoxy. That is to lose all sense of proportion. Again, as we shall argue in Chapter 12, one aspect of the work of Christ is Penal Substitution, the idea that Christ on the cross bore our punishment. For some people, however, this has become not just one aspect of what Christ has done but the sum total of it.[9] This is a failure to hold the doctrine in the right proportion. As Colin Gunton put it, 'To seek "balance" as a primary end in theology is to court boredom, if not disaster; yet imbalance can also be catastrophic.'[10]

Studies of Christian doctrine mostly focus on points that are disputed and sometimes the impression can be given that Christians disagree on everything. That is not true. There is a considerable amount of common ground, which is generally accepted, but the greatest attention is given to those *relatively* few areas that are disputed. Politicians agree that there should be income tax and that it should be higher for higher earners, but all the debate is focused on the border disputes of just *how* high this or that rate should be. Theology likewise focuses on areas of dispute. One of the benefits of heresy is that it forces the Church to sort out her beliefs, as with the doctrine of the Trinity in the fourth century. G. A. Boyd and P. R. Eddy's *Across the Spectrum* offers a helpful account of where Evangelicals differ on a range of doctrines.[11] I have provided cross-references to this in the notes.

Also to be mentioned are the series of 'Four Views' books in which four (sometimes two, three or five) different views are expounded and critiqued in turn by their opponents. The pioneering volume was R. G. Clouse's *The Meaning of the Millennium*, published in 1977 by IVP (USA). Since then many others have been published by IVP, by Zondervan (generally of a lesser quality) and more recently by B & H Publishing and others. Usually they provide an excellent introduction to a controversy. At the last count there were over 70 such volumes. The relevant ones are given in the list of resources at the end of each chapter.

There are places in the book where I express my views clearly and forthrightly –

on the deity of Christ, for example. There are others where I set out the rival views side by side, sometimes in such a way that the discerning reader can see where my sympathies lie, sometimes not. My aim has been to steer a middle course between telling people what to believe on every issue and sitting on every fence. I hope readers will think that I have struck a reasonable balance in this. Also, while I am firmly convinced about core beliefs like the love of God or the resurrection of Christ, there are other disputed areas where I find it harder to make up my mind. The study of theology can bring greater conviction in some areas but in other areas it can serve to strip away unfounded dogmatism.

ACKNOWLEDGEMENTS

This book is based upon a Christian Doctrine Survey module that I have taught to first-year students at London School of Theology since 2006. As it has moved from lecture notes to a full-blown book I have received assistance from a variety of my students:

- Ian LaRiviere kindly gave me an electronic copy of his excellent notes, which formed the basis for writing up the chapters. He also proof-read the finished product with painstaking care.
- Helena Cantrell and Ruth Gookey each contributed substantially to the writing up of the text as their second-year practical placement.
- Kirsty Gardner, when taking the module, checked my written copy and helpfully made a note of all the places where I embellished it during the lectures.
- Charlie Comerford and Sophia Davies each supplied me with a list of thought-

provoking questions, comments and objections, which have left their mark on the final product in many ways.

I am very grateful to these six for those specific tasks, especially to Ian, Helena and Ruth. The book also owes a lot to the stimulus provided by the eight cohorts who have taken the module from 2006 to 2013. Accordingly, this book is dedicated to all of them. I hope that those who complained that I didn't answer all their questions will be more satisfied by the book!

I am also grateful to my former colleague Bob Letham for reading the whole and making helpful comments. Also to a number of colleagues who have provided assistance on specific points, including David Peacock, Conrad Gempf, Jean-Marc Heimerdinger, Steve Motyer, Steve Walton and Rob Cook.

Naturally, none of the above is to be held responsible for the remaining defects of the book.

Since the scope of the book, like the module, is 'God, the universe and everything', I have derived ideas from a wide range of sources too numerous to mention or even to remember. During the final six months I have more often than not returned from church with ideas of something to add or to change or of a fresh way to state something.

In the process of delivering the lectures and of interaction with my assistants there was continuing banter between myself as a cat-lover and some of them as (for some strange reason) dog-lovers. I have left some of this in the volume to lighten what can at times be a heavy subject.

ABBREVIATIONS

*	A person, document or gathering featured in my *Concise History of Christian Thought*.
ATS	G. A. Boyd and P. R. Eddy, *Across the Spectrum* (Grand Rapids: Baker, 2002 and 2009). Chapter numbers change so ch. m/n means Chapter m in the first, Chapter n in the second edition. The second edition adds an Appendix.
CCC n	Catechism of the Catholic Church, paragraph n.

NOTES

1 For a small library of historic creeds and other statements of faith, see J. H. Leith *Creeds of the Churches*. Louisville: Westminster John Knox, 1982, third edn. For a collection of Evangelical statements, see J. I. Packer and T. Oden *One Faith: The Evangelical Consensus*. Downers Grove: IVP, 2004.

2 *A Concise History of Christian Thought*. London: T & T Clark (Continuum) and Grand Rapids: Baker, 2006.

3 *The Lion Concise Book of Christian Thought*. Tring: Lion, 1984, revised reprint 1986; *The Lion Book of Christian Thought*. Oxford and Batavia, Illinois: Lion, 1992; *The Lion Concise Book of Christian Thought*. Oxford: Lion, 1996; *The Lion Concise Book of Christian Thought*. Oxford: Lion, 2002. There have been other American editions as well as translations into about a dozen other languages.

4 For a similar work, which focuses on 100 classical texts, see my *Lion Christian Classics Collection*. Oxford: Lion, 2004.

5 There are various printed and online editions, such as <http://www.vatican.va/archive/ENG0015/_INDEX.HTM>.

6 In my experience faulty references on lecture handouts can remain unchallenged for many years.

7 <http://www.dailymail.co.uk/sciencetech/article-1286257/Limitations-human-brain-mean-understand-secrets-universe.html>.

8 Not counting all of the references to it in brackets on every issue.

9 A good test here is to look at the content of the hymns and songs about the work of Christ that are sung in church.

10 C. Gunton *Act and Being*. London: SCM Press, 2002, 20.

11 G. A. Boyd and P. R. Eddy *Across the Spectrum*. Grand Rapids: Baker, 2002 and 2009.

Part A

METHOD

Chapter 1

KNOWING GOD

Aims of this chapter

In this chapter we look at the sources of theology, asking:

- How can we know God?
- How much of God can we know from nature and reason?
- Do we need tradition or is the Bible all that we need?
- What is the value of tradition?
- What is the role of the Holy Spirit in doing theology?

THE KNOWLEDGE OF GOD AND OF OURSELVES

*Calvin starts his *Institutes* with an oft-quoted statement:

> Nearly all the wisdom we possess, that is to say, true and sound wisdom, consists of two parts: the knowledge of God and of ourselves. (*Institutes* 1:1:1)

He goes on to state that knowledge of God and knowledge of ourselves are interlinked. We know God not as someone remote and irrelevant but as he relates to us. Likewise, we cannot know ourselves properly except as related to God – as created, fallen, redeemed and destined for glory. This book is structured around these four points.

Secular science and psychology can teach us a lot about ourselves. So can literature and I personally have benefited greatly from the profound insights into human nature found in C. P. Snow's novels, in particular his 'Strangers and Brothers' series. We can and should learn from all that is true in secular thought, but we need to place it within the framework of a Christian perspective. Biology and brain science can teach us much about ourselves, but without the understanding that we are created in God's image such knowledge is partial and one-sided. To understand ourselves properly we need to see ourselves as related to God.

So how *do* we know God? First, we must consider whether/to what extent God can be known from nature and reason alone.

NATURAL THEOLOGY (CCC 27–49)

Natural Theology refers to what can be known about God outside of Judaeo-

Christian revelation – through the study of nature (both the universe as a whole and humanity in particular) and through reason. Some Christians have claimed that through Natural Theology God's existence can be proved. In his hugely influential *Natural Theology, or Evidences of the Existence and Attributes of the Deity* (1802), William Paley used the analogy of a watchmaker. If you were walking in the country and came across a watch on the ground you would deduce, from its complexity and design that there must have been a watchmaker who created it. Likewise, nature manifests a complexity and design that points to a Creator. This argument was answered later in the century by Charles Darwin, whose theory of evolution offered an alternative explanation for the design. (Ironically, not only did Paley and Darwin both study at Christ's College, Cambridge, but they actually, in their respective times, occupied the same set of rooms there.)

Paley's argument has fallen out of favour, but are there other rational, philosophical grounds for affirming the existence of God? Generally Christians have said that to *some* extent there are, but that philosophy on its own is not sufficient to lead us to a true knowledge of God. *Augustine, referring to his conversion in AD 386, stated that the *Greek philosophers had taught him that 'In the beginning was the Word and the Word was with God, and the Word was God' (John 1:1), but that they could not teach him that 'the Word became flesh and dwelt among us' (John 1:14) (*Confessions* 7:9). *Thomas Aquinas, in the thirteenth century, was even more confident about Natural Theology, writing a book entitled *Manual Against the Heathen*, which expounded theology on the basis of reason alone. He offered five proofs for the

existence of God, known as the 'Five Ways', and philosophers today still debate their validity. Thomas maintained that philosophy can establish the existence of God and some of his attributes (such as his love, wisdom and omnipotence), but that it is only by God's revelation that we can know the gospel, and Christ in particular.

However, not all Christians have favoured Natural Theology. Around AD 200 *Tertullian wrote against those who made use of philosophy in their theology, arguing that philosophy was the parent of heresy, not a preparation for the gospel.

> What indeed has Athens [philosophy] to do with Jerusalem? What concord is there between the Academy [of Plato] and the Church? What have heretics to do with Christians? Our instruction comes from the porch of Solomon [as opposed to the Stoic Zeno], who himself taught that the Lord should be sought in simplicity of heart. Away with all attempts to produce a Stoic, Platonic and dialectic [Aristotelian] Christianity. (*Prescription of Heretics* 7)

Despite this rousing rhetoric Tertullian was quite prepared to make use of philosophy when it suited his purposes. A more principled and thorough rejection of Natural Theology came from the Swiss theologian *Karl Barth, especially in the 1930s when he was opposing those within the German Church who sought to blend Christianity with the ideology of the Nazi party. In 1934 Barth, together with others in the 'Confessing Church', which opposed the influence of Nazi ideas upon the Church, drew up the *Barmen Declaration*. The first article of this states:

Jesus Christ, as he is testified to us in the Holy Scripture, is the one Word of God, whom we are to hear, whom we are to trust and obey in life and in death.

Barth held that nothing can be known about God except through Christ. He denied that there is a 'point of contact' between the gospel and non-Christian thought. The gospel does not scratch where it itches; it brings its own itch with it. The gospel comes to the world not like an aircraft seeking an existing landing strip but like a bomb, which creates its own crater when it arrives.

Barth was more opposed to Natural Theology than any other major theologian in the history of the Church. While he may be right about the dangers of letting the world set the agenda, most theologians would not agree that it is either desirable or indeed possible to insulate theology from non-Christian thought to the extent that Barth describes.

There are passages of Scripture that point towards revelation through creation. Psalm 19:1–6:

The heavens declare the glory of God, and the sky above proclaims his handiwork. Day to day pours out speech, and night to night reveals knowledge. There is no speech, nor are there words, whose voice is not heard. Their voice goes out through all the earth, and their words to the end of the world. (19:1–4)

What can be known about God is plain to them, because God has shown it to them. For his invisible attributes, namely, his eternal power and divine nature, have been clearly perceived, ever since the creation of the world, in the things that have been made. So they are without excuse. (Rom. 1:19–20)

Paul, standing in the midst of the Areopagus, said: 'Men of Athens, I perceive that in every way you are very religious. For as I passed along and observed the objects of your worship, I found also an altar with this inscription, "To the unknown god." What therefore you worship as unknown, this I proclaim to you.' (Acts 17:22–23)

This can be understood differently according to whether it is read 'What therefore *you worship* as unknown' or 'What therefore you worship *as unknown*'.

SPECIAL REVELATION (CCC 50–73)

'Special revelation' (sometimes referred to as the 'Judaeo-Christian revelation') is contrasted with God's 'general revelation' through creation. God revealed himself specifically to Abraham and then to Israel, through Moses, the prophets, etc., and in his mighty deeds (such as the Exodus). After many centuries of revelation to the people of Israel, God's supreme revelation comes through Jesus, his Son. The letter to the Hebrews expresses this well:

Long ago, at many times and in many ways, God spoke to our fathers by the prophets, but in these last days he has spoken to us by his Son, whom he appointed the heir of all things, through whom also he created the world. (1:1–2)

Jesus is the Word made flesh. 'In the beginning was the Word, and the Word was with God, and the Word was God.' This same eternal Word 'became flesh and dwelt among us' (John 1:1, 14). God's supreme revelation is not merely a prophet (such as Moses) nor a book (like the Qur'an) but the Word himself who became one of us.

How do we know of what he has done and said? This is through Scripture, the written word, which is there to point us to Christ, the living Word. 'You search the Scriptures because you think that in them you have eternal life; and it is they that bear witness about me' (John 5:39). In the next chapter we will consider the nature of the Bible.

SOLA SCRIPTURA?[1]

It is popularly supposed that *sola scriptura* (i.e. 'Scripture alone') was one of the slogans of the sixteenth-century Reformation. In fact the slogan emerged at a later date, but it can be seen as encapsulating a key idea of the Reformation. What was that idea? The Reformers certainly did not see the Bible as the sole source or resource in doing theology. They made considerable use of earlier teaching, such as that of Augustine. They did not regard the Bible as the sole authority since they were very ready to draw up new confessions of faith which had authority in their churches. The key point, though, was that all of these resources and authorities were subordinate to the authority of Scripture and were to be tested by it.

In all of this we must not lose sight of the goal, which is that we come to know God as he is revealed to us, supremely in Christ. The Bible is not a 'paper pope' but the means through which God speaks to us by his Spirit, with the goal of pointing us to his Son.

Credal statement

The supreme judge by which all controversies of religion are to be determined, and all decrees of councils, opinions of ancient writers, doctrines of men, and private spirits, are to be examined, and in whose sentence we are to rest, can be no other but the Holy Spirit speaking in the Scripture. (*Westminster Confession of Faith (1647), 1:10)

*John Wesley, the great eighteenth-century revivalist and founder of Methodism, held that our theology should be based on Scripture, which is to be interpreted with the help of reason and tradition and in the light of our experience: i.e. Bible, experience, reason and tradition – which makes the mnemonic 'Bert'. This has come to be called the 'Wesleyan Quadrilateral'. These are not four equal authorities but three aids to the understanding of an authoritative Scripture.

There are two other factors to be borne in mind. First, the task of theology is not a purely individual matter but is to be pursued within the Church, the Christian community. Second, the Christian faith is not timeless but always finds expression within particular cultural settings. This is true of the Bible itself and of the person of Christ, each of which comes in the context of particular cultures. The task of theology is to relate Christian revelation to the culture of the time, to ask 'if that was said in the first century, what does it mean for us in the twenty-first century today?'

What do you think? The question

Can we read the Bible without tradition?

TRADITION (CCC 74–100)

The Christian faith was not invented last year nor has the Bible recently been discovered for the first time. We are the heirs of nearly 2,000 years of reading the Bible and living the Christian life since the time of Christ and the apostles. During that time the Church has explored the Christian faith and expounded it in many contexts, with the help of the Holy Spirit. The faith has been passed down from generation to generation, as is described in 2 Timothy 2:2: 'what you have heard from me in the presence of many witnesses entrust to faithful men who will be able to teach others also.' Paul handed the faith to Timothy, who was to hand it on to others. This process of passing on the Christian faith from person to person is what is meant by 'tradition'. Tradition is the sum total of what has been handed down to us, our Christian heritage.

Tradition is hugely influential. The overwhelming majority of Christians are introduced to the faith by tradition. They are raised in a Christian home, they hear about Christ from a friend, they are taught about Christianity at school, they read a book about it, etc. A very very tiny number become Christians through reading a Bible with no previous knowledge of the faith – but even then the Bible will have been translated and that is a further aspect of the process of tradition. When our new convert begins to read the Bible for himself, tradition is still there. When he reads 'In the beginning, God created . . .' what does he understand by the word 'God'? This will have been learnt from tradition. We don't approach the Bible with an empty mind waiting to be filled, but with an open mind ready to be corrected. We cannot read the Bible without tradition, but we can allow the Bible to correct that tradition. We then return to reading the Bible with that corrected tradition and the process proceeds. This is sometimes called the 'hermeneutical spiral'.

Tradition is hugely influential. Most Christians remain in the tradition in which they were raised or converted. We learn from reading the Bible, but most of the time we see there what our tradition points out to us. Protestants read Romans and see a doctrine of justification by faith alone, but what they see there was by and large not seen by people who read Romans before the Reformation. My point is not that the doctrine is not there, but that we see it because others have seen it before us. It is *very* rare for someone to see something in Scripture that no one has seen before – something true, that is!

There are two sorts of Christians. Not those who are influenced by tradition and those who are not, but those who are aware of the influence and those who are not. The most powerful influences are those of which we are unaware. Think of two people in canoes on a river, being carried downstream towards a waterfall. One is aware of this, the other not. Both are subject to the same influence; one of them is in a position to do something about it.

What do you think? My answer

Can we read the Bible without tradition? My answer to this question is 'No' and 'Yes', in that order. No, we cannot read the Bible without being influenced by tradition – that influence being mainly but not entirely positive. Yes, in the sense that the Bible stands over against tradition to test and correct it.

Errors to avoid

There are two opposite errors to avoid when it comes to tradition.

- One is to despise tradition, our Christian heritage. This is to insult the Holy Spirit, who has been at work in the Church since New Testament times. It is also arrogant. The implication is that God has had nothing worthwhile to teach Christians over the last two millennia but has chosen to reveal the truth now to me. It is also dangerous. Those who despise tradition often end up re-inventing the earliest heresies of church history. Some of the sixteenth-century Anabaptists and some of the early Brethren in the nineteenth century thought that they did not need tradition. Both groups returned to the crude second-century heresy that Mary was merely the host mother of Jesus.[2] In the words of George Santayana,

'Those who are ignorant of history are condemned to repeat it.' Of course, to affirm the value of tradition is not the same as saying that nothing can ever be changed or improved. As Jaroslav Pelikan put it, 'Tradition is the living faith of the dead; traditionalism is the dead faith of the living.'[3]

- The opposite error is to treat tradition as infallible and to be unwilling to question it or to adapt it for changed situations. We need to respect tradition without being in bondage to it. Karl Barth expressed this well when he affirmed the authority of Church and tradition, seeing them both in the light of the Fifth Commandment, to honour our father and mother. This authority is real but limited, in that both are subject to the word and therefore to Scripture. They are open to be reformed and corrected, while Scripture is not.[4]

THE VALUE OF TRADITION

Four specific examples can be given.

1 It has been said that the one page of the Bible that is not inspired is the Contents page! How do we know which books should be included in the Bible? (CCC 120–27) The canon of the New Testament (i.e. the list of books) emerged gradually over many centuries. By the end of the second century there was agreement about the four Gospels, Acts and the letters of Paul. Concerning the remaining nine books (Hebrews to Revelation) there was controversy for some time, with different lists being put forward, though most of these lists were very close to ours. By the fourth century there was widespread agreement except over Hebrews (which

was questioned in the Latin western half of the Roman Empire) and Revelation (which was questioned in the Greek eastern half of the Roman Empire). This difference was resolved with both books being accepted.

So we receive our New Testament canon from tradition. Does this mean that the Church is the higher authority because it made these books scriptural? No. The Church confesses that Christ is God but it is not therefore the Church that makes him God. The fact that the Church confesses the deity of Christ does not make her a higher authority than Christ. Likewise the Church acknowledges that Galatians, say, is the word of God; she does not thereby *make* Galatians God's word.

2 The New Testament contains the raw materials for a doctrine of the Trinity,

but does not itself work out that doctrine. The classical doctrine of the Trinity emerged after some 300 years of debate, answering questions and, especially, excluding false solutions. This tradition is of immense value for understanding the doctrine, as we shall see in Chapter 16. The development of the doctrine of the Trinity was not an addition to the teaching of the New Testament but rather a clarification, a making sense of what is there in the New Testament. The same can be said for other doctrines, such as the person of Christ (Christology) or the work of Christ.

Not all development is benign, though. The Roman Catholic teaching on Mary (Mariology) has also developed from the New Testament, but it has led to doctrines that go far beyond anything taught there – such as the belief that Mary was conceived without original sin (the Immaculate Conception, defined in the 1854 papal bull *Ineffabilis Deus*) and was assumed into heaven (the Assumption, defined in the 1950 apostolic constitution *Munificentissimus Deus*). These doctrines, together with the beliefs that she is the Queen of Heaven and that we should pray to her, are in no way 'a making sense of what is there in the New Testament'.

3 Tradition can be described as vicarious experience. An old proverb states that 'experience is the wisdom of fools'. This may appear to be counter-intuitive, but the point is simple. Fools learn from experience that fire burns your fingers; wise people learn this by heeding what they are taught – and by observing fools! The biggest fools do not learn even from their own experience. As the saying goes, there is not much to learn from the second kick of the mule. There is no need to reinvent the wheel in every generation. When it comes to Christian doctrine we can learn from the great thinkers and debates of the past – and this book will make reference to many of these. As Bernard of Chartres put it in the twelfth century:

> We are like dwarves sitting on the shoulders of giants [the ancients]. We see more than them and things that are further away – not because our sight is better than theirs, nor because we are taller than they were, but because they raise us up and add to our stature by their enormous height. (Quoted by John of Salisbury, *Metalogicon* 3:4)

Isaac Newton also described his relation to earlier scientists as 'standing on the shoulders of giants' and these words are written round the rims of some British £2 coins. The difference is that while Bernard was most definitely a dwarf relative to the ancients, Newton completely dwarfed all who had gone before him.

4 Tradition hands down to us many creeds and confessions. There are the creeds from the Early Church, the so-called *Apostles' Creed and *Nicene Creed. There are early confessions like the Definition of the *Council of Chalcedon and the so-called *Athanasian Creed. There are statements produced by councils of the Church. At the Reformation there were many different confessions of faith. These all have value, though like all tradition they are subject to the teaching of Scripture. They appear throughout this book under the heading of 'Credal statements'.

Credal statement

Wherefore we do not despise the interpretations of the holy Greek and Latin fathers, nor reject their disputations and treatises concerning sacred matters as far as they agree with the Scriptures; but we modestly dissent from them when they are found to set down things differing from, or altogether contrary to, the Scriptures. Neither do we think that we do them any wrong in this matter; seeing that they all, with one consent, will not have their writings equated with the canonical Scriptures, but command us to prove how far they agree or disagree with them, and to accept what is in agreement and to reject what is in disagreement. (*Second Helvetic Confession* (1566), ch. 2, written by *Bullinger)

EXPERIENCE

*Luther and Calvin both recognized the important role that experience plays in the theological task. Luther's theology was forged on the anvil of his personal struggles,[5] and he stated this in a typically graphic way:

It is by living, indeed by dying and by being damned that one becomes a theologian – not merely by understanding, reading and speculation. (*Lectures on Psalms* 5:11)

Calvin's was also a theology of experience. He repeatedly appeals to experience, often using traditional refrains such as 'experience teaches'. When expounding his doctrine of the inner witness of the Spirit, Calvin claims that he speaks 'of nothing other than what each believer experiences within himself' (*Institutes* 1:7:5).

One way that experience functions is as a test of doctrine. For example, some have argued that Christians should never suffer from ill health. Such beliefs may spring up from time to time, but they always fade away in the light of experience. The same can be said for the belief that it is possible to live without sin.

Worship

Oh, make but trial of his love!
Experience will decide
How blest are they, and only they,
Who in his truth confide.
(Nahum Tate and Nicholas Brady, 'Through all the changing scenes of life')

THE 'INNER LIGHT' (CCC 66–67, 73)

Throughout church history there have been groups claiming to have received direct revelation from the Holy Spirit as an *alternative* to Scripture, in *opposition* to Scripture. This is sometimes referred to as the 'Inner Light'. An early example of this came in the Montanists, a second-century group based in modern-day Turkey who claimed that the Spirit was changing some of the instructions of the New Testament (such as permission for the widowed to remarry) on the grounds that the End was about to happen. Many such groups have followed them. Their record is not a good one,[6] and J. S. Whale once commented that 'belief in the Inner Light may be the shortest road to outer darkness'.[7] If tradition (which is relatively fixed) needs to be tested by Scripture, how much more does the 'Inner Light' (which can lead anywhere) need such a test?

Belief in the Inner Light is found among groups claiming special revelation, but it can also be found in a more subtle way in some Liberal thinkers. Geoffrey Lampe, for example, appealed to the 'Christ-Spirit' as a ground for rejecting the teaching of Jesus on hell, as found in Matthew.[8] For 'Christ-Spirit' here, read 'spirit of modern

God's told me that we should get married.

Well, He's not mentioned anything to me.

© Miriam Kendrick 2013 www.miriamkendrick.co.uk

Western Liberalism'. Such an approach leads many today to reject those parts of the Christian faith that they find uncongenial.

Calvin devotes a chapter of his *Institutes* to refuting those who set fresh revelation from the Holy Spirit *against* Scripture (1:9). He argues that it is the Holy Spirit who inspired the Scriptures and that he will not encourage us to despise them, nor will he speak contrary to them. Any alleged manifestation of the Spirit today is to be tested by Scriptures that he inspired. Paul ordered that the utterances of prophets should be tested (1 Cor. 14:29).

Sceptic's corner

Is this not to subject the Spirit to a book?

Answer: No. If someone claims to have discovered a new Rembrandt painting, a key test will be to compare it with the undoubted paintings by Rembrandt. The doubtful is tested by the certain.

When I present my credit card my signature is sometimes compared with that on the back of the card. I do not complain that I am being subjected to a piece of plastic. Those who complain about the Spirit being subjected to a book are usually complaining about their own utterances being tested by the Word of God.

Calvin emphasizes the unity of the Word and the Spirit. The role of the Spirit is to seal our minds with the truth of the Gospel. This unity is well expressed by two modern aphorisms: 'The Spirit without the word is dangerous; the word without the Spirit is deadly; the word with the Spirit is dynamite.' Or, more succinctly, 'Too much word – dry up; too much Spirit – blow up; word and Spirit – grow up!'

The *Second Vatican Council (1962–65) warned against seeking revelation beyond the revelation that we have in Christ:

> The Christian economy, therefore, since it is the new and definitive Covenant, will never pass away; and no new public revelation is to be expected before the glorious manifestation of our Lord Jesus Christ. (*Divine Revelation* 1:4, quoted in *CCC 66)

The key word here is 'public'. There is no room for further revelation, whether in the form of the Qur'an, the Book of Mormon or Sun Myung Moon's *Exposition of the Divine Principle*. This does not preclude prophetic utterances which do not claim to be further public revelation and it does not preclude guidance to individuals as they face important decisions.[9] God speaks today, though not normally as dramatically as was recently experienced by one preacher!

'Speak to me, God. Speak to me.' [These were the words of] Don Hardman, preaching at First Baptist Church in Forest, Ohio, immediately before being struck by lightning through his microphone. Unhurt, he continued preaching for 20 minutes before discovering that the steeple was on fire.[10]

PRAYER

Now to him who is able to strengthen you according to my gospel and the preaching of Jesus Christ, according to the revelation of the mystery that was kept secret for long ages but has now been disclosed and through the prophetic writings has been made known to all nations, according to the command of the eternal God, to bring about the obedience of faith – to the only wise God be glory for evermore through Jesus Christ! Amen. (Rom. 16:25–27)

Question to answer

- What role do reason, tradition and experience have in theology?

NOTES

1 See A. N. S. Lane, 'Sola Scriptura? Making Sense of a Post-Reformation Slogan' in P. E. Satterthwaite and D. F. Wright (eds) *A Pathway into the Holy Scripture*. Grand Rapids: Eerdmans, 1994, 297–327.
2 Melchior Hofmann was an Anabaptist who held this view; see G. H. Williams *The Radical Reformation*. Kirksville (Missouri): Sixteenth Century Journal Publishers, 1992, third edn, 490–95. For the early Brethren, see F. F. Bruce 'The Humanity of Jesus Christ'. *Journal of the Christian Brethren Research Fellowship* 24 (1973) 5–10.
3 J. Pelikan *The Vindication of Tradition* New Haven: Yale University Press, 1984, 64.
4 K. Barth *Church Dogmatics* I.2. Edinburgh: T. & T. Clark, 1956, 585–86; *The Humanity of God*. London: Collins, 1967, 10.
5 See P. Althaus *The Theology of Martin Luther*. Philadelphia: Fortress Press, 1966, 55–63, 173–78.
6 For an unsympathetic account, see R. Knox *Enthusiasm*. Oxford: OUP, 1950.
7 Quoted by S. Neill *Christian Holiness*. London: Lutterworth, 1960, 29.
8 G. Lampe *God as Spirit*. London: SCM Press, 1983, 113.
9 On that issue, see D. S. Huffman (ed.) *How Then Should We Choose? Three Views on God's Will and Decision Making*. Grand Rapids: Kregel, 2009.
10 *Christianity Today*, September 2003, 23.

RESOURCES

S. B. Cowan (ed.) *Five Views on Apologetics*. Grand Rapids: Zondervan, 2000.

J. I. Packer *Knowing God*. London: Hodder & Stoughton, 1983, esp. Chapters 1–4.

D. Thorsen *The Wesleyan Quadrilateral*. Lexington: Emeth Press, 2005, revised edition.

D. H. Williams *Evangelicals and Tradition*. Grand Rapids: Baker, 2005.

THE BIBLE

Aims of this chapter

In this chapter we look at the Bible, asking:

- Who is/are the author(s) of the Bible?
- What is meant by 'word of God'?
- *Why* should we regard the Bible as God's word?
- Does the Bible contain any mistakes?
- How should we use the Bible?

THE AUTHORSHIP OF THE BIBLE

Traditionally Christians have seen the Bible as the inspired word of God, but in the last 200 years or so this has been questioned. Today many see the Bible as just a collection of fallible human writings by people with some degree of religious insight – the Liberal position.

THE BIBLE AS THE WORD OF GOD
(CCC 101–41)

The Bible is God's word, 'breathed out by God', as stated in 2 Timothy 3:16: 'All Scripture is breathed out by God and profitable for teaching, for reproof, for correction, and for training in righteousness.' This means that the biblical writers wrote

Tension to hold

On the one hand, Christians accept the Bible as God's word. On the other hand, when they read it they encounter problems. For example, Psalm 75:3 states: 'When the earth totters, and all its inhabitants, it is I who keep steady its pillars.' No one today thinks that the earth rests on pillars. So how do we resolve the tension between our beliefs about Scripture and some of what we find in it? The key is to take *both* of these seriously.

This tension can be expressed in terms of the dual authorship of Scripture. The Bible is 'the word of God in the words of men' – blending divine authorship and the role of genuine human authors, not just scribes. The key to a correct view of Scripture is to hold fast to both sides, recognizing the tension between them.[1]

what God wanted them to write, that the Bible is God's word or message to us. *B. B. Warfield (d. 1921) argued at length for this view, his claim being that 'what the Bible says, God says'. Warfield showed that in the New Testament 'Scripture says' and 'God says' are equivalent. This is sometimes referred to as '*verbal* inspiration', the point being that what God inspires is the *wording* of Scripture, the text itself.

In thinking about biblical inspiration we need to distinguish between two different issues: *what* the Bible is (the word of God) and *how* any particular portion of Scripture came to be written (which will vary considerably). For this variety one can consider the ways in which the following books came to be written:

- An Old Testament prophet like Isaiah or Jeremiah receives and records oracles from God.
- Paul receives news from Galatia and promptly writes to the Galatians expressing his displeasure (1:6–9).
- David prays for forgiveness in Psalm 51.
- Luke engages in careful historical research in order to write his Gospel (Luke 1:1–4).

These all came to be written in very different ways, but they are all part of the word of God.

Worship

Powerful in making us wise to salvation,
witness to faith in Christ Jesus the Word;
breathed out for all by the life-giving Father –
these are the Scriptures, and thus speaks the Lord.

Prophecy, history, song and commandment,
gospel and letter and dream from on high;
words of the wise who were steered by the
   Spirit –
these are the Scriptures on them we rely.
(Christopher Idle)

Break thou the bread of life, dear Lord, to me,
As thou didst break the loaves beside the sea;
Beyond the sacred page I seek thee, Lord;
My spirit pants for thee, O living Word!

Oh send thy Spirit, Lord, now unto me,
That he may touch my eyes, and make me see;
Show me the truth concealed within thy Word,
And in thy Book revealed I see thee, Lord.
(Mary Lathbury and Alexander Groves)

WHAT IS MEANT BY 'WORD OF GOD'?

It is not just the Bible that is God's word and we need to place this description of the Bible in a wider context:

- **The eternal Word** who was with God in the beginning and indeed was God (John 1:1). 'The Word' is a title for the eternal Son of God, the second person of the Trinity.
- **The incarnate Word**. The eternal Word became flesh and dwelt among us (John 1:14).
- **The written Word**. The Bible is God's written word, pointing to the incarnate Word (John 5:39).
- **The preached word**. Proclaiming the message of Scripture is also, in a derivative way, the word of God. In the words of the *Second Helvetic Confession* of 1566, written by *Bullinger, 'the preaching of the Word of God is the Word of God'.
- **Visible words**. The sacraments of baptism and Holy Communion have since *Augustine been referred to as 'visible words' since they present the message of the gospel in a visible (and tangible and edible) way.

WHY SHOULD WE REGARD THE BIBLE AS GOD'S WORD?

The 'we' in this question refers to believing Christians, not to unbelievers. This is not an attempt to persuade non-Christians that the Bible is God's word, which would be to put the proverbial cart before the horse. Normally

"How can I be sure this is inerrant?"

people come to faith in Christ and *then*, to use *Luther's phrase, believe the Scriptures for Christ's sake. It *can* happen differently of course, especially where people have been brought up from childhood to respect the Bible as God's word, but the normal pattern is for faith in Christ to come first.

There are four reasons why Christians should regard the Bible as God's word:

THE TEACHING OF JESUS

First, Jesus regarded the Old Testament (the extent of Scripture at that time) as the authoritative word of God that must be fulfilled and that stands over against human tradition. The evidence for this is found in many places in the Gospels. For example:

- Matthew 19:4–5: 'Have you not read that he who created them from the beginning made them male and female, and said, "Therefore a man shall leave his father and his mother and hold fast to his wife, and they shall become one flesh"?' The words of Genesis 2:24 are attributed to him 'who created them from the beginning', i.e. God.
- Mark 7:13: '. . . thus making void the word of God by your tradition that you have handed down. And many such things you do' – the word of God has priority over human tradition.
- John 10:35: 'If he called them gods, to whom the word of God came – and Scripture cannot be broken . . .'
- When he was tempted, Jesus responded to Satan by appealing to Scripture (Matt. 4:1–10 = Luke 4:1–12).
- Mark 12:24: 'Jesus said to them, "Is this not the reason you are wrong, because you know neither the Scriptures nor the power of God?"'

It is noteworthy that such teaching is found in all of the different strands of Gospel tradition – in all four Gospels, in 'Q' and in all other strands of tradition that have been identified. B. B. Warfield in a number of his writings demonstrated this very clearly. He showed how the belief in Scripture as God's word is based not (as is sometimes alleged) on one or two isolated proof texts but on a mass of biblical evidence, which he cites.

> The effort to explain away the Bible's witness to its plenary inspiration reminds one of a man standing safely in his laboratory and elaborately expounding . . . how every stone in an avalanche has a defined pathway and may easily be dodged by one of some presence of mind. We may fancy such an elaborate trifler's triumph as he would analyse the avalanche into its constituent stones and demonstrate of stone after stone its pathway is definite, limited and may easily be avoided. But avalanches, unfortunately, do not come upon us stone by stone, one at a time, courteously leaving us opportunity to withdraw from the pathway of each in turn – but all at once, in a roaring mass of destruction. Just so, we may explain away a text or two which teach plenary inspiration, to our own closet satisfaction, dealing with them each without reference to its relation to the others – but these texts of ours, again, unfortunately do not come upon us in this artificial isolation. Neither are they few in number. There are scores, hundreds of them – and they come bursting upon us in one solid mass. Explain them away? We should have to explain away the whole New Testament. What a pity it is that we cannot see and feel the avalanche of texts beneath which we lie hopelessly buried as clearly as we may see and feel an avalanche of stones!
> (*The Inspiration of the Bible*, 119–20)

THE TEACHING OF THE NEW TESTAMENT WRITERS

Second, the view of the Bible as God's word is common to all of the New Testament writers. The best-known and the most explicit passages are 2 Timothy 3:16 (quoted above) and 2 Peter 1:20–21: 'No prophecy of Scripture comes from someone's own interpretation. For no prophecy was ever produced by the will of man, but men spoke from God as they were carried along by the Holy Spirit.' But these verses simply state explicitly what is implicit throughout the New Testament. Mostly this teaching is found in incidental, passing comments, showing that it was uncontroversial. A few examples will suffice:

- Hebrews 3:7: 'Therefore, as the Holy Spirit says, "Today, if you hear his voice"' (quoting Psalm 95:7).
- 1 Peter 1:10–12 refers to revelation given to the prophets.
- Acts 1:16: 'the Scripture had to be fulfilled, which the Holy Spirit spoke beforehand by the mouth of David concerning Judas'.

I invite those who do not believe that the New Testament writers held that 'what the Scripture says, God says', to read through the New Testament carefully observing the way in which the writers regard the Old Testament.

The passages reviewed so far all refer to the New Testament use of the Old Testament, which establishes the Old Testament, but what is the basis for believing in the New Testament Scriptures? First, if God chose to provide an authoritative written interpretation of his revelation to the people of Israel, one would hardly expect him to do less for his supreme revelation through his Son (Heb. 1:1–2).

Second, it has been argued that the New Testament writers (or at least some of them) saw themselves as writing Scripture and deliberately modelled their writing on Old Testament patterns. Finally, 2 Peter 3:16 refers to 'some things in [Paul's letters] that are hard to understand, which the ignorant and unstable twist to their own destruction, as they do *the other Scriptures*'. This indicates that Paul's letters are already being viewed as Scripture, that parallel to the existing Old Testament Scriptures there is a new body of New Testament Scripture. That simply leaves the question of *which* books belong to the New Testament, the extent of the New Testament canon, on which see the previous chapter.

Sceptic's corner

The argument so far uses the Bible to prove that the Bible is the word of God, which is a blatantly circular argument.

Answer: The argument is not circular. It starts by turning to the Gospels for evidence of Jesus' beliefs and argues that there is overwhelming evidence that he regarded the Old Testament as the word of God. This argument does not require any prior belief about the accuracy of the Gospels and *Rudolf Bultmann, who was extremely sceptical about their reliability, nonetheless regarded it as clear that Jesus held such a view.[2] Thus the argument is not 'believe the Bible because the Bible says so' but, 'believe the Scriptures for Christ's sake'. The quotations from the rest of the New Testament demonstrate that the apostles did just that.

TRADITION AND EXPERIENCE
Third, that the Bible is the inspired and infallible word of God was all but universally held until the nineteenth century. The Liberal view that then emerged is a relative novelty. This does not necessarily prove it to be wrong, but the burden of proof lies upon those who choose to reject the consensus of all previous Christian belief. Also experience shows that *as a general rule* Liberal churches decline and lack spiritual life, while those with a vigorous belief in Scripture as God's word are more likely to thrive and grow. This trend is recognized by secular sociologists. In other words, God is still committed to his Scripture even if some churches are not.

WITNESS OF THE HOLY SPIRIT
Fourth, *Calvin (*Institutes* 1:7) asks how we can be *sure* that Scripture is God's word and how we can know this with a firm conviction of faith. His answer has been very influential. He acknowledges that there is a legitimate place for rational apologetic arguments and indeed writes a chapter setting some of these out (*Institutes* 1:8). He also acknowledges that the Church has an important role in bearing witness to Scripture. My belief that the Bible is God's word is not merely a personal opinion. But the *primary* basis for our certainty is that the Holy Spirit himself bears witness by speaking to us through the Bible and by opening our eyes to see that it is the word of God.

Credal statement

We may be moved and induced by the testimony of the Church to an high and reverent esteem of the Holy Scripture. And the heavenliness of the matter, the efficacy of the doctrine, the majesty of the style, the consent of all the parts, the scope of the whole (which is, to give all glory to God), the full discovery it makes of the only way of man's salvation, the many other incomparable excellencies, and the entire perfection thereof, are arguments whereby it does abundantly evidence itself to be the Word of God: yet notwithstanding, our full persuasion and assurance of the infallible truth and divine authority thereof, is from the inward work of the Holy Spirit bearing witness by and with the Word in our hearts. (*Westminster Confession of Faith* (1647), 1:5)

. . . IN THE WORDS OF MEN

The Bible has genuine authors. Scripture is the word of God – but it is also the words of Isaiah, Mark, Paul, etc. These are *real* authors, not just scribes taking dictation. The Bible has a divine author and genuine human authors. This does not mean that the Bible is *partly* God's word and *partly* human words. It is not that some parts are from God, and others from human beings. Nor is it the case that God provided the ideas and the human authors the words. The words are also from God: Paul stated that he taught 'in words not taught by human wisdom but taught by the Spirit' (1 Cor. 2:13). At the same time, it is *all* human. Jeremiah's 'oracles' are from God yet are also in Jeremiah's own style. Paul and John each have their own distinctive theology – complementary, but not identical. At the same time, it is *all* the word of God – even a very 'human' book like Ecclesiastes. It is not only the 'Thus says the Lord' passages that are the word of God. This can be seen from the way in which the New Testament writers treat the Old Testament.

So the Bible is not partly human and partly divine, but wholly human and wholly divine. In the same sentence Luke refers to the 'Law of Moses' as the 'Law of the Lord' (Luke 2:22–23). The book of Jeremiah is 'the words of Jeremiah . . . to whom the word of the LORD came' (Jer. 1:1–2). Warfield uses the word *concursus* to describe this dual authorship. There is a 'running together', a cooperation of the human and the divine. To use a feeble illustration, in a three-legged race two people cooperate and run together. A better comparison is with the work of the Holy Spirit in our conversion: he moves us and we believe – both are fully involved (Phil. 2:12–13). So the whole Bible is God's word, even the most 'human' parts, and the whole Bible is written by human beings, even the divine oracles.

> **What do you think? The question**
>
> Does the Bible contain any mistakes?

INFALLIBLE, INERRANT OR . . . ?[3]

Evangelical scholars generally agree that the Bible is the word of God, but differ when it comes to the implications of this. There is a spectrum of views:

- Some insist that Scripture contains no errors at all, that it is *inerrant*. The *Chicago Statement on Biblical Inerrancy* (October 1978)[4] propounds a strict, but carefully defined inerrancy.
- Others allow for minor blemishes that do not affect the overall picture – for example, some of the discrepancies between the different Gospels. Such people often prefer to use the word *infallible*, emphasizing that the message of the Bible is trustworthy. Sometimes people distinguish between what the Bible *teaches* and what it *touches* (in passing). Theological matters fall into the first category; scientific into the second. But what of history? It is there that most of the alleged errors are found, yet historical events (such as the resurrection) lie at the heart of the Christian faith.

Both of these views are found over the centuries, though the first was more common. More recently there has been considerable dispute over this matter, especially since the 1970s in the USA. In the UK there is less polarization, with the acceptance of variety within limits. This is not unhealthy. The key to this doctrine is the tension between the divine and human aspects of Scripture and where there is a tension there will always be the scope for differences. The most important point is whether one maintains the tension between the two sides rather than the exact point on the spectrum that one holds. The problem with strong terms like 'inerrancy' is that they need to be qualified to allow for the hyperbole, approximation and imprecision that we see in Scripture. It may be simpler just to say that what the Bible teaches is true.

Also, statements about the truth/infallibility/inerrancy of Scripture do not resolve the question of what it means. For example, the strongest affirmations of the reliability of Genesis 1 tell us nothing about whether or not the six 'days' are to be interpreted as 24-hour periods. Augustine believed in the total truthfulness of Scripture but regarded the six days as figurative.

What do you think? My answer

Does the Bible contain any mistakes? The answer to this question depends on what counts as a mistake. For instance, 2 Chronicles 4:2 implies that π, the relation of circumference to diameter, is 3, rather than 3.141... Is 2 Chronicles mistaken? If it had stated that $\pi = 5$, that would be a mistake; $\pi = 3$ is an approximation. The Synoptic Gospels locate the cleansing of the Temple at the end of Jesus' ministry; John 2:13–22 locates it at the beginning. Is John mistaken? Only if he claims to be presenting the ministry of Jesus in chronological order. I would see it as wrong to describe either book as 'mistaken'. What each teaches is true, given the limitations of what they set out to do, which was neither to give a precise definition of π nor to present a chronological account of Jesus' ministry. I would not want to talk of 'errors' in the Bible but, like *John Stott, I am not persuaded that 'inerrant' is a helpful term.[5] Calling 2 Chronicles 4:2 inerrant creates the impression that one is claiming a greater degree of precision than is there found. One might say of a portrait, for example, that it was a true and faithful representation of the subject, but it would be inappropriate to call it inerrant. Parts of the Bible are like that.

Paul and James present very different accounts of justification, as will be seen in Chapter 20. Some Liberal scholars take the line that these are incompatible and that one of them (probably James) is mistaken. Such an approach is wrong and I will argue in Chapter 20 that while James' teaching clearly differs from Paul's, they are complementary and we do not need to, and ought not to, choose between them.

It is sometimes claimed that the biblical authors speak 'with a single voice'. Such a description does not fit what we see with Paul and James, for example. A much better illustration would be a choir where the singers sing with different voices but in harmony. This points to an acceptable meaning of 'harmonization' – not forcing the different authors to say the same thing but seeing an ultimate unity and harmony behind the very different things that they say, each from their different perspective.

Errors to avoid

This chapter started with the tension that exists between the affirmation of Scripture as God's word and the problems that we meet in the text itself. There are two opposite errors to avoid, which come from denying or underestimating one or other of the sides of this tension.

1   The Liberal error comes from denying, explicitly or implicitly, that the Bible is God's word. Instead it is seen as a collection of fallible human writings by people with some degree of religious insight. Where the teaching of Scripture is unpalatable this can be dismissed as mistaken. Such an approach makes it very difficult for the Church to make a clear stand against contemporary culture. Those holding it often regard themselves as speaking prophetically, but the prophetic message is usually one that derives from (parts of) the surrounding culture.

2   The fundamentalist error comes from belittling (rarely actually denying) the role of the human authors. God speaks to us supremely by his Son becoming one of us, a human being. In Scripture he speaks to us through human words and human authors. In the next chapter we will consider some of the implications of this.

Credal statements

We affirm the divine inspiration, truthfulness and authority of both Old and New Testament Scriptures in their entirety as the only written word of God, without error in all that it affirms, and the only infallible rule of faith and practice. (*Lausanne Covenant*, art. 2 from *Lausanne Congress (1974))

Since therefore all that the inspired authors or sacred writers affirm should be regarded as affirmed by the Holy Spirit, we must acknowledge that the books of Scripture firmly, faithfully, and without error teach that truth which God, for the sake of our salvation, wished to see confided to the Sacred Scriptures. (*Divine Revelation* 3:11 from the *Second Vatican Council (1962–65), quoted in *CCC 107)

BIBLE READING (CCC 131–33)

One of the distinctive marks of Evangelicals has been not just a 'high' doctrine of Scripture (which was held by all Christians until the nineteenth century) but also an emphasis upon individual Bible reading. That has, of course, been possible for most Christians only since the invention of printing and high rates of literacy. The Roman Catholic Church often discouraged Bible reading in the past, but with the Second Vatican Council in the 1960s the Church changed direction on this and started to encourage all Catholics to read the Bible.

The Church 'forcefully and specifically exhorts all the Christian faithful . . . to learn the surpassing knowledge of Jesus Christ, by frequent reading of the divine Scriptures. "Ignorance of the Scriptures is ignorance of Christ."' (*CCC 133, quoting from *Divine Revelation* 6:25)

In 1967 *Joseph Ratzinger commented that in previous Roman Catholicism, 'private reading of Scripture played no important role and even for meditation and for preaching was not considered of prime importance . . . It is fair to say that Catholic piety has still largely to discover the Bible properly.'[6] As Pope Benedict XVI he sought to rectify this. In October 2008 he launched a week-long Bible-reading marathon on Italian television[7] and preached to the Synod of Bishops on the importance of the Bible in the life of the Church and the indispensable need for *a robust and credible pastoral promotion of the knowledge of Sacred Scripture* to announce, celebrate and live the Word in the Christian community'.[8]

USING THE BIBLE

The Bible is the word of God, but this does not mean that any point can be settled just by quoting one text in isolation from the rest of Scripture, by which method one can prove almost anything. *Dietrich Bonhoeffer, in a helpful analogy, compared the use of Scripture to walking on thin ice. When doing that it is important not to remain stationary at one point, if we do not want to fall through, but to move around. In this book I aim to follow his advice, by appealing to the range of biblical teaching on each topic, not just to isolated passages. In places we will see the importance of holding in tension complementary truths, as in Chapter 21, for example. The biblical teaching on a particular topic is not what is said by one or two verses taken in isolation but what is taught by the biblical canon as a whole. So, for example, Proverbs teaches that those who lead a righteous life are rewarded, Job and Ecclesiastes protest that this is not always so, and the New Testament squares the circle with the idea of rewards in the Age to Come.

It must also be remembered that the purpose of the Bible is not just to inform us. As we have seen, 'all Scripture is breathed out by God' with the aim that it

should be 'profitable for teaching, for reproof, for correction, and for training in righteousness' (2 Tim. 3:16). As we read it we should remember that 'this is the one to whom I will look: he who is humble and contrite in spirit and trembles at my word' (Isa. 66:2).

PRAYER

Blessed Lord, who caused all holy Scriptures to be written for our learning: help us so to hear them, to read, mark, learn and inwardly digest them that, through patience, and the comfort of your holy word, we may embrace and for ever hold fast the hope of everlasting life, which you have given us in our Saviour Jesus Christ, who is alive and reigns with you, in the unity of the Holy Spirit, one God, now and for ever. Amen. (*Common Worship*, Collect for the Last Sunday after Trinity)

Questions to answer

- Who is/are the author(s) of the Bible?
- *Why* should we regard the Bible as God's word?

NOTES

1 This was argued by J. I. Packer 'Hermeneutics and Biblical Authority', *Churchman* 81 (1967) 7–21, reprinted in *Themelios* 1:1 (Autumn 1975) 3–12, and found at <http://www.biblicalstudies.org.uk/article_herm_packer.html>.
2 R. Bultmann *Jesus and the Word*. London: Collins, 1958, 51–53.
3 ATS ch. 1.
4 Available online, e.g. at <http://www.bible-researcher.com/chicago1.html>.

5 J. Stott *Evangelical Truth*. Leicester: IVP, 1999, 73–74.

6 H. Vorgrimler (ed.) *Commentary on the Documents of Vatican II*, vol. 3. London: Burns & Oates; New York: Herder and Herder, 1968, 270, a translation of the 1967 German original.

7 <http://www.bbc.co.uk/worldservice/learningenglish/newsenglish/witn/2008/10/081006_pope_bible_marathon.shtml>.

8 <http://www.vatican.va/holy_father/benedict_xvi/homilies/2008/documents/hf_ben-xvi_hom_20081026_conclusione-sinodo_en.html>.

RESOURCES

P. Adam *Written for Us: Receiving God's Words in the Bible*. Nottingham: IVP, 2008.

A. T. B. McGowan *The Divine Spiration of Scripture: Challenging Evangelical Perspectives*. Nottingham: IVP, 2007.

D. J. Tidball *The Bible*. London: Monarch, 2003.

B. B. Warfield *The Inspiration and Authority of the Bible*. Phillipsburg, New Jersey: P&R, 2012.

N. T. Wright *Scripture and the Authority of God*. London: SPCK, 2005.

Chapter 3

SPEAKING ABOUT GOD

Aims of this chapter

In this chapter we consider the status of our religious language, asking:

- How can finite human beings speak about God? We will review three different ways in which theologians have sought to answer this question:
  - the contrast between the positive and negative ways of talking about God,
  - the concepts of analogy and metaphor,
  - the concept of accommodation.
- Is God male?
- What is the status of our theological models?

HOW CAN FINITE HUMAN BEINGS SPEAK ABOUT GOD? (CCC 39–43, 48)

When we consider the gulf that exists between the eternal, infinite, pure Creator, and ourselves as puny, short-lived, sinful creatures, it is easy to see that there is a problem. How is it possible for us accurately and meaningfully to speak of God?

Theology, derived from the words *theos* and *logos*, means to talk about God. It refers to something that is done by *all* Christians, not just those who might think of themselves as

'theologians'. Indeed, this takes place whenever any human being talks about God.

POSITIVE AND NEGATIVE WAYS

There are two different ways of talking about God:

1 **The positive way** (*via positiva* in Latin, also known as the *cataphatic* way, from the Greek). This speaks of what God *is*: for example, God is Love, God is Creator,

I'm upholding a traditional cataphatic theology.

No you're not. You're just being dogmatic.

© Miriam Kendrick 2013 www.miriamkendrick.co.uk

God is Saviour. (I always found it difficult to remember whether 'cataphatic' referred to the positive or negative way until I realized that *cat*-aphatic must be positive!)

2 **The negative way** (*via negativa* in Latin, also known as the *apophatic* way, from the Greek). This states what God *is not*. Such an approach serves to emphasize God's transcendence, the fact that God's ways are not our ways. Scriptural examples of this include:

For my thoughts are not your thoughts, neither are your ways my ways, declares the LORD. For as the heavens are higher than the earth, so are my ways higher than your ways and my thoughts than your thoughts. (Isa. 55:8–9)

Oh, the depth of the riches and wisdom and knowledge of God! How unsearchable are his judgements and how inscrutable his ways! (Rom. 11:33)

For now we see in a mirror dimly, but then face to face. Now I know in part; then I shall know fully, even as I have been fully known. (1 Cor. 13:12)

My favourite passage for this idea is Ezekiel 1:28:

Like the appearance of the bow that is in the cloud on the day of rain, so was the appearance of the brightness all around. Such was the appearance of the likeness of the glory of the LORD. And when I saw it, I fell on my face, and I heard the voice of one speaking.

Ezekiel did not see the Lord, he did not see the glory of the Lord, did not even see the likeness of the glory of the Lord. All that he saw was 'the appearance of the likeness of the glory of the LORD'. The prophet was in no danger of confusing the visible image with God himself.

It is the Eastern Orthodox tradition that places the strongest emphasis on the apophatic way. Some Orthodox theologians even go as far as claim that it is the *only* legitimate way. Such an approach leads to a heavy emphasis upon mystery – which manifests itself in Orthodox church buildings and in Orthodox liturgy.

By contrast, *some* Evangelicals are in danger of going to the opposite extreme, of overplaying the positive way and forgetting the need for the negative way. For some there is no mystery because they understand it all!

Which of the two ways do we find in Scripture? Most of what the Bible states about God is positive, though there are the occasional negative qualifications, as in the passages quoted above. This is a healthy balance. An example of the need for balance can be seen in the idea of God's wrath. Scripture makes positive statements about this, but we must always remember that there are important differences between our all-too-imperfect human anger and the purity of God's displeasure against sin. We will consider this further in Chapter 7.

Credal statement

God transcends all creatures. We must therefore continually purify our language of everything in it that is limited, image-bound or imperfect, if we are not to confuse our image of God – 'the inexpressible, the incomprehensible, the invisible, the ungraspable' – with our human representations. Our human words always fall short of the mystery of God. (*CCC 42)

Errors to avoid

We need both ways for balance. Either way on its own is dangerous:

- The positive way taken on its own can lead to idolatry, equating God with our human concepts or with something created. It can lead to an over-familiarity with God, to thinking of him simply as a larger version of ourselves. It can also lead to a 'know-it-all arrogance'. The proclamation of the gospel should be with confidence, but also with humility, with a recognition that we do not know it all, with a recognition that God infinitely transcends our understanding of him, even our biblically based understanding of him. We must not lose sight of the dimension of mystery.
- The negative way taken on its own can lead to agnosticism – agnosticism not about whether there is a God but about what he is, an inability to state anything positive about him. The result is a lack of knowledge about God. This danger is illustrated by the title of a late fourteenth-century mystical work – *The Cloud of Unknowing*.

He who is eagerly pursuing the nature of the self-existent [God] will not stop at saying what he is not, but must go on beyond what he is not and say what he is. For it is easier to take in some single point than to go on disowning point after point in endless detail, in order both by the elimination of negatives and the assertion of positives to arrive at a comprehension of this subject.

One who states what God is not without going on to say what he is acts much in the same way as someone who being asked how many twice five make answers, 'Not two, nor three, nor four, nor five, nor twenty, nor thirty, nor in short any number below ten, nor any multiple of ten', but does not answer 'ten', nor settle the mind of his questioner upon the firm ground of the answer. For it is much easier, and more concise, to show what a thing is not from what it is, than to demonstrate what it is by stripping it of what it is not. (*Gregory of Nazianzus, *Theological Orations* 2:9)

Worship

Immortal, invisible, God only wise,
In light inaccessible hid from our eyes,
Most blessèd, most glorious, the Ancient of Days,
Almighty, victorious, thy great name we praise.

Great Father of Glory, pure Father of Light,
Thine angels adore thee, all veiling their sight;
All laud we would render, O help us to see:
'Tis only the splendour of light hideth thee.
(Walter C. Smith)

ANALOGY AND METAPHOR

*Thomas Aquinas (d. 1274), one of the greatest theologians of all time, discusses the role of analogy and metaphor in his *Sum of Theology* 1:13:1–6. His account is very helpful and has been highly influential. He discusses different types of statement about God.

Negative statements about God are relatively straightforward; they can be simply and literally true. One can, for example, state without any reservations, that 'God is not a tomato'. Positive statements, however, are more complex. Take the statement 'God is Father' or 'God is love'. Are these statements simply literal truth? To unpack this further, Aquinas differentiates between two different sorts of positive statements about God: metaphorical and literal.

- **Metaphorical statements**, such as Psalm 18:2: 'The LORD is my rock and my fortress and my deliverer, my God, my rock, in whom I take refuge, my shield, and the horn of my salvation, my stronghold.' The words 'rock', 'fortress' and 'stronghold' apply primarily to physical things. The psalmist uses them of God only in a secondary, metaphorical way. God is *like* a rock, a fortress or a stronghold – in certain respects. Likewise, when the Frenchman calls his lover 'my little cabbage' ('*mon petit chou*') he is not commenting on the colour of her leaves.
- **Literal statements**, such as 'God is good' or 'God is love'. These statements are literally true of God. Most of our literal language about God consists of anthropomorphisms, referring to God in human terms to which we can relate. God is love; we also love; God is Father; so also am I. We use the same words of God and of ourselves. Do the words mean the same when they refer to us and to God? Thomas sets out three different possibilities:
  - The two meanings are *univocal*, i.e. there is no difference in meaning. When we say that an Alsatian is a dog and a terrier is a dog, we use the word 'dog' in exactly the same way. God's transcendence means that this cannot be the case when we talk about God. God is manifestly not Father in the same sense that I am a father.
  - The two meanings are *equivocal*, i.e. there is no shared meaning between the two. When we say that a dog has a bark and a tree has a bark, we use the word 'bark' in two totally different ways. Knowing what a dog's bark is like is of no help whatsoever in understanding what a tree's bark is like. If our use of words about God/ourselves is equivocal

that means that we actually know nothing at all about God.
  - The third possibility, for which Aquinas opts, is that the two meanings are *analogical*, by which he means 'somewhere between' univocal and equivocal. So when we state that God is love we are saying that there are important similarities between his love and ours (the *positive* way) but that his love also transcends ours (the *negative* way).

Words like 'rock' and 'fortress' apply primarily to physical objects, not to God. What about words like 'love', 'goodness', or 'father'? Do these apply *primarily* to God or to us? In our experience and understanding we are inclined to start with human love, goodness and fatherhood and move from there to understand God's love, goodness and fatherhood. But in reality the order is reversed. It is God's love, goodness and fatherhood that come first and ours derive from them as a pale reflection. This can be illustrated from two passages, cited by Thomas:

- Ephesians 3:14–15: 'For this reason I bow my knees before the Father, from whom every family [or fatherhood] in heaven and on earth is named.' It is *God's* fatherhood that is primary.
- Mark 10:18: 'Jesus said to him, "Why do you call me good? No one is good except God alone."' In other words, true goodness is found only in God (that is primary) and any goodness we might have is only a very imperfect reflection of his. So while human goodness helps us to understand God's goodness, it is God's goodness that is the source of any human goodness.

This relationship is summed up in *Moltmann's saying that 'The order of being

and the order of knowing are opposite.'[1]
The order of being is from the top down –
God is the source of goodness and love.
On the other hand, the order of knowing is
from the bottom up – we understand God's
goodness and love in the light of ours.

> Names applied to God and to other
> beings are not used either entirely
> univocally or entirely equivocally . . .
> They are used according to analogy . . .
> For, from the fact that we compare other
> things with God as their first origin, we
> attribute to God such names as signify
> perfections in other things. This clearly
> brings out the truth that, as regards the
> giving of the names, such names are used
> primarily of creatures, inasmuch as the
> intellect that gives the names ascends
> from creatures to God. But as regards
> the thing signified by the name, they
> are used primarily of God, from whom
> the perfections descend to other beings.
> (Thomas Aquinas, *Compendium of
> Theology* 1:27)

What do you think? The question

Why should human language have any validity in
talking about God?

ACCOMMODATION

Accommodation is the idea that
God tempers or accommodates his
communication with us to a form or
level that we can understand. He speaks
to us in ways far below his greatness. This
is similar to the way in which a primary
school teacher relates to small children by
speaking to them in language and concepts
that they can understand. Accommodation
does involve simplification, but what are

the alternatives? God could try to explain
it fully, rather like trying to explain
Newton's laws of physics to a 3-year-old,
or simply remain silent. Each of these is
a total failure to communicate.

The idea of accommodation was found in
the Early Church Fathers (of the second to
fifth centuries) and was especially used by
*Calvin, who stated:

> Who even of slight intelligence does not
> understand that, as nursing mothers
> commonly do with infants, so God is wont
> in a way to babble when he speaks to us?
> Thus such forms of speaking do not so
> much express clearly what God is like as
> to accommodate the knowledge of him
> to our slight capacity. To do this he
> must descend far beneath his loftiness.
> (*Institutes* 1:13:1)

Accommodation follows the basic principle
of the Incarnation. God speaks to us/reveals
himself to us by becoming one of us. 'The
Word became flesh and dwelt among us,
and we have seen his glory, glory as of the
only Son from the Father, full of grace and
truth' (John 1:14). Similarly in Scripture
God speaks to us in human language.
God is portrayed as Lord, Judge, etc., by
anthropomorphism, by using human terms.
This human language is true, because we
are made in the image of God, even though
it is not the *whole* truth. As Aquinas says, such
talk is *analogical*, not *univocal* or *equivocal*. It
needs to be qualified (*negative* way) because
God is different from us, but it is still true
(*positive* way) because we are made in God's
image, as we shall see in Chapter 6.

Our knowledge of God, our speech about
God, is true but not the whole truth, not
absolute or perfect truth. In Francis Schaeffer's

What do you think? My answer

The reason why human language has some validity in talking about God is that we are made in God's image. It is this that makes the Incarnation of Christ possible.

words, we have 'true truth' but not 'exhaustive truth'. Or, as Paul put it, 'Now we see in a mirror dimly, but then face to face. Now I know in part; then I shall know fully, even as I have been fully known' (1 Cor. 13:12). Paul wrote this at a time when mirrors were polished pieces of bronze and gave a far from perfect view of oneself.

Why is it that God needs to accommodate himself to us? There are a number of reasons for this.

- We have been created as intelligent beings in the image of God, yet in relation to God we are merely tiny mortal creatures. It is completely unrealistic to think we could ever understand God's communication to us unless it was accommodated.
- On top of this we are sinful creatures. Our capacity to understand God is affected by this sin, yet, as already stated, even without sin we would never understand God fully.
- We can also see that God's revelation of himself was progressive, not given all at once. God educated his people gradually, over many centuries. This explains why polygamy was tolerated for a time. God's gradual education of his people came to a culmination in the sending of his Son (Heb. 1:1–2). The central argument of the letter to the Hebrews is that the Old Testament revelation was incomplete

and that it points forward to more that is to come.

Sceptic's corner

Why didn't God simply explain everything at once? Why did he allow mistaken ideas and practices to remain for so long?

Answer: The key to this is to remember that God was not dictating an incomprehensible manual but seeking to educate his people. It would have been impossible and pointless to inform the early Israelites about the findings of modern cosmology, for example. It took centuries to get them to grasp a simple concept like the need to worship Yahweh alone and this lesson was not fully learned until after the Exile. If something so basic took so long to communicate we can see why God needed to be patient in unfolding his revelation.

IS GOD MALE?

The first point to note is that God is neither human nor sexual. We speak of him in human terms by analogy, because he has accommodated himself to us. This is possible because we are created in his image, and it is as male and female that we image God (Gen. 1:27). Very occasionally, in Scripture God is compared to a mother (Isa. 49:15, 66:13). By contrast, throughout the whole of Scripture God is referred to by male language: 'Lord', 'Father', etc. Furthermore, in both Testaments God's relation to his people is compared to that of bridegroom to bride (e.g. Isa. 62:5b; Rev. 19:7). I am not aware that anyone has ever suggested reversing that analogy. Does this language disadvantage women? That is a complex question, but it should be noted that today (the time when this issue is being raised) women significantly outnumber men in almost all churches. We will return to that in Chapter 24.

Credal statement

In no way is God in man's image. He is neither man nor woman. God is pure spirit in which there is no place for the difference between the sexes. But the respective 'perfections' of man and woman reflect something of the infinite perfection of God: those of a mother and those of a father and husband. (*CCC 370)

THEOLOGICAL MODELS

Where does all this leave our theology, our talk about God? We have truth about God, or the things of God, but not truth with mathematical precision. In arithmetic there is only one correct answer. If the answer is 42, 43 is wrong. Theology is not always so precise. Theologians (like the Bible) use different models to describe the work of Christ, as we shall see in Chapter 12. This can be compared to the way in which we use 2D drawings used to represent 3D realities. An example of this can be seen in the two world maps below and overleaf.

With world maps a curved surface is represented on a flat piece of paper – which can be done in different ways with different projections. Likewise, there are also different ways of representing God, none of which portrays the whole truth.

Where we have different models we have to consider whether these are complementary or contradictory. Thus our two world maps are two different projections, each of which brings out different points. The second projection (Mercator) represents directions accurately (e.g. the line south-west of a

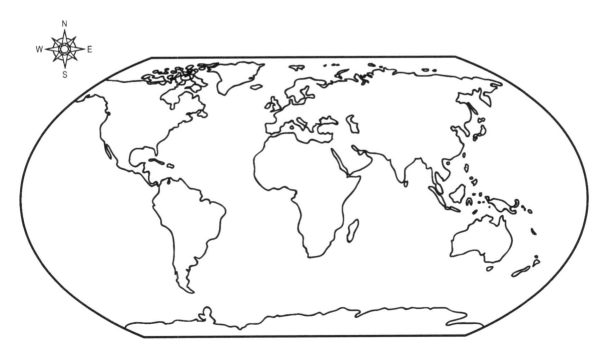

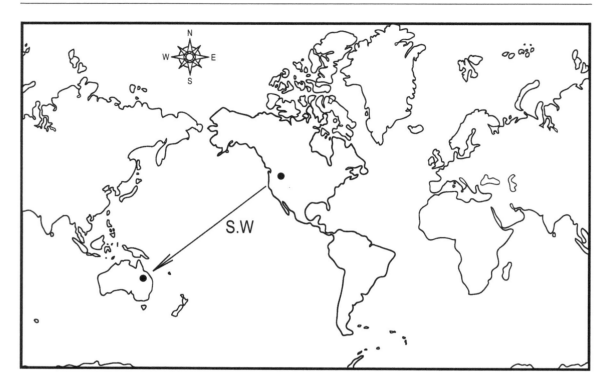

point) but, as can be seen, distorts regions near the poles, making Greenland appear to be huge. The first projection gives a more accurate representation of relative size, but not of directions. Neither projection is wrong, yet neither represents the reality perfectly. But that does not mean that 'anything goes'. One map shows the UK at the centre; the other has the USA at the centre. Here, clearly, the first is true and the second false! The second map involves cutting Asia in half, which is obviously wrong. This fact can even be recognized by someone living in America, as is shown by the cartoon on page 39:

Another illustration is different portraits of the same person. These will all be different and in principle they might each be true, although it is possible to produce a portrait that is untrue. All representations are limited, but some can actually misrepresent.

This is why we have four Gospels, each of which is partial but true. They are complementary, each one presenting a different aspect of the reality of Christ. John recognizes that the full reality of Christ is greater than he could portray: 'Now there are also many other things that Jesus did. Were every one of them to be written, I suppose that the world itself could not contain the books that would be written' (21:25). As well as the four canonical Gospels there are later gospels and other writings about Jesus which often present false pictures of him, especially denying that he was fully human. One suggests that Jesus did not really suffer on the cross;[2] another that he swapped places with Simon of Cyrene and laughed at him while he was crucified.[3]

So also, as with maps and with portraits, different theological models may be

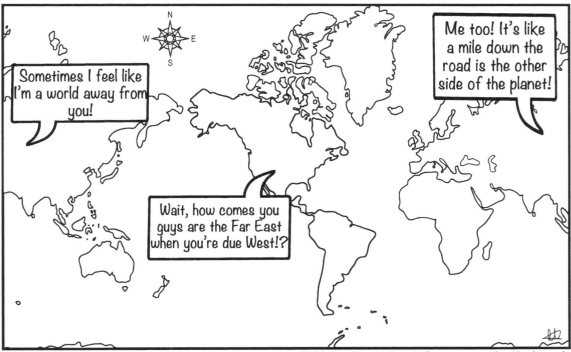

© Miriam Kendrick 2013 www.miriamkendrick.co.uk

complementary, but differences can also reflect that one or more are simply wrong.

PRAYER

O God, whose beauty is beyond our imagining and whose power we cannot comprehend: show us your glory as far as we can grasp it, and shield us from knowing more than we can bear until we may look upon you without fear; through Jesus Christ our Saviour. (*Common Worship*, Post Communion for Third Sunday after Trinity)

Question to answer

- How can finite human beings speak about God?

NOTES

1 J. Moltmann *The Trinity and the Kingdom of God*. London: SCM Press, 1981, 152–53; *The Way of Jesus Christ*. London: SCM Press, 1990, 77.
2 Gospel of Peter 4:10.
3 Second Treatise of the Great Seth 56. Cf. Irenaeus, *Against Heresies* 1:24:4.

RESOURCES

N. L. Geisler *Thomas Aquinas: An Evangelical Appraisal*. Grand Rapids: Baker, 1991, ch. 10, 'Analogy'.

D. R. Stiver *The Philosophy of Religious Language*. Oxford: Blackwell, 1996, chs 2, 6.

Part B

CREATION

Chapter 4

THE CREATION OF THE UNIVERSE

Aims of this chapter

In this chapter we look at the creation of the universe, asking:

- How did God create the universe?
- What are the implications of the doctrine of creation?
- Is creation a single event at the beginning or a continuing process?
- How should theology relate to modern science?
- Does modern science exclude the possibility of miracles?

CREATION *EX NIHILO* (CCC 296–98, 285)

Christian theology since the second century has claimed that God created the universe out of nothing (*ex nihilo*). While this exact phrase is not found in the Bible, it is the clear implication of biblical teaching:

- Genesis 1:3 presents the universe as called into being by God's word, hence the implication that the universe is not eternal but created: 'God said, "Let there be light," and there was light.'
- Psalm 33:6 also speaks of creation by God's word, 'By the word of the LORD the heavens were made, and by the breath of his mouth all their host.'
- Also, Hebrews 11:3: 'By faith we understand that the universe was created by the word of God, so that what is seen was not made out of things that are visible.'
- Romans 4:17 goes further than the idea of God creating by his word, coming close to the idea of creation *ex nihilo* ' . . . [God] who gives life to the dead and calls into existence the things that do not exist'.

The doctrine of creation *ex nihilo* is, therefore, a natural conclusion from what is said about creation in Scripture.

God created the universe by/through the pre-incarnate Christ:

- John 1:3: 'All things were made through him, and without him was not any thing made that was made.'
- Colossians 1:16: 'For by him all things were created, in heaven and on earth, visible and invisible, whether thrones or dominions or rulers or authorities – all things were created through him and for him.'

Worship

All things bright and beautiful,
all creatures great and small,
all things wise and wonderful
the Lord God made them all.

Each little flower that opens,
each little bird that sings,
he made their glowing colours,
he made their tiny wings.
(Cecil F. Alexander)

IMPLICATIONS OF THE DOCTRINE OF CREATION

The doctrine of creation has important implications both for our view of life and for our behaviour:

LIFE HAS A DEFINITE MEANING AND PURPOSE

If the universe is created by God, life has a definite meaning and purpose. If, however, it is the product of random chance, as atheists maintain, life has no ultimate meaning. Bertrand Russell's blunt statement of this is often quoted:

That Man is the product of causes which had no prevision of the end they were achieving; that his origin, his growth, his hopes and fears, his loves and beliefs, are but the outcome of accidental collocations of atoms . . . that all the labours of the ages, all the devotion, all the inspiration, all the noonday brightness of human genius, are destined to extinction in the vast death of the solar system, and that the whole temple of Man's achievement must inevitably be buried beneath the debris of a universe in ruins – all these things, if not quite beyond dispute, are yet so nearly certain that no philosophy which rejects them can hope to stand. Only

within the scaffolding of these truths, only on the firm foundation of unyielding despair, can the soul's habitation henceforth be safely built.[1]

Russell was thinking of the final extinction of the human race but the same can be said for the individual as well. Without God, life is just 'a tale told by an idiot, full of sound and fury, signifying nothing'.[2]

Atheism also undercuts reason itself. If our thought processes have evolved in order to ensure our evolutionary survival, they must be efficient at enabling us to survive and propagate, but there is no reason to suppose that they are reliable for philosophical discussion. Atheism and Theism compete not as truth claims but as strategies for passing on one's genes. Would we trust a computer if we knew that it was simply the product of a mindless and unguided process?[3] C. S. Lewis expressed this point well:

Supposing there was no intelligence behind the universe, no creative mind. In that case, nobody designed my brain for the purpose of thinking. It is merely that when the atoms inside my skull happen for physical or chemical reasons to arrange themselves in a certain way, this gives me, as a by-product, the sensation I call thought. But if so, how can I trust my own thinking to be true? It's like upsetting a milk-jug and hoping that the way the splash arranges itself will give you a map of London. But if I can't trust my own thinking, of course I can't trust the arguments leading to atheism, and therefore have no reason to be an atheist, or anything else. Unless I believe in God, I can't believe in thought: so I can never use thought to disbelieve in God.[4]

THE UNIVERSE IS NOT DIVINE

The universe is not divine, is not part of God. Hinduism and Eastern religions blur the gap between God and creation, seeing all things as part of God. Similar views are found in Western ideologies that have been influenced by them. This is known as Pantheism. By contrast, the Old Testament stresses that there is a clear divide between Creator God and his creation:

- Genesis 1:14–18 states that the sun was created by Yahweh, while it was worshipped as divine by some of Israel's pagan neighbours.
- Isaiah 40:21–31 emphasizes the transcendence of Yahweh over the whole of creation.

THE SOUL IS NOT DIVINE

Platonism and Neoplatonism, schools of *Greek philosophy around in the early Christian centuries, held that the soul was divine and the body relatively unimportant. This idea is also found in Gnosticism, a major movement of Christian heresy in the second century. Gnostics saw the soul as a divine spark, which needs to return to its heavenly home and leave behind the body in which it is entombed. The Bible, by contrast, has a lower view of the soul (not divine but created by God) and a higher view of the body (part of God's good creation). In the third century, through theologians like *Origen, a modified version of the Gnostic picture crept into Christian theology and the future hope was seen increasingly as going to heaven, with less and less emphasis upon the resurrection of the body. We will consider this more fully in Chapter 29.

THE MATERIAL CREATION IS GOOD

The Platonist and Gnostic belittling of the body arose from the belief that the physical universe was not created by the Supreme God but was the product of some lesser deity. Indeed, one Gnostic writer maintained that the universe emerged by accident as the result of a belch by a junior deity – not exactly a ringing endorsement of physical matter! The early Christians were influenced by this intellectual climate, leading to extremes of asceticism. So for example, according to *Athanasius, Antony (the first monk) ate in private because he was ashamed that he needed to eat. This shame arose from a practical belief that the physical is shameful, which is contrary to the Christian doctrine of creation. Antony (and those like him) would not have denied the doctrine of creation, but they were driven by ideas which were in fact diametrically opposed to it. False ideas from the surrounding culture can infect our practical beliefs without our ever formally accepting them. C. S. Lewis wrote, in opposition to such views, '[God] likes matter. He invented it.'[5] There is a type of 'other-worldliness' which belittles the physical creation and appears very 'pious' but reflects Platonist and Gnostic, rather than Christian, beliefs.

- 1 Timothy 4:4: 'Everything created by God is good, and nothing is to be rejected if it is received with thanksgiving.'

HUMANITY IS CALLED TO TAKE CARE OF THE WORLD

The physical world is God's creation and we are appointed by God to be stewards of it, to take care of it. One aspect of our creation in God's image is the command to subdue the earth:

Then God said, 'Let us make man in our image, after our likeness. And let them have dominion over the fish of the sea and over the birds of the heavens and over the livestock and over all the earth and over every creeping thing that creeps on the earth' . . . And God said to them, 'Be fruitful and multiply and fill the earth and subdue it and have dominion over the fish of the sea and over the birds of the heavens and over every living thing that moves on the earth.' (Gen. 1:26, 28)

This command to subdue creation has led ultimately to modern science and technology. These have given us huge benefits. I am writing this in a warm room, lit by electric lights, on a computer which I can see clearly thanks to good spectacles. At the same time such benefits have also led to massive pollution of the environment and to evils like nuclear weaponry. We may, in a sense, be the lords of creation, but we also need to see it as *God's* creation and ourselves as its tenants, as stewards called to act responsibly. If you own a house you can do with it more or less what you want; if you are renting it you cannot start knocking down walls. Adam was told to take care of creation as a gardener, not to use his dominion to abuse it, as an excuse for predatory exploitation. 'The LORD God took the man and put him in the garden of Eden to work it and keep it' (Gen. 2:15). There are some who have adopted the idea that the physical creation is divine as a basis for ecological concern. There is no need to do this as the biblical doctrine of creation and human stewardship already provides an adequate basis.

CONTINUING CREATION (CCC 301, 320, 421)

So far we have been considering God's initial creation, but that is not the end of his creativity. God is still at work in his creation: 'My Father is working until now, and I am working' (John 5:17).

He is preserving and sustaining the universe through his word and his Word:

- Colossians 1:17: 'in him all things hold together'.
- Hebrews 1:3: 'he upholds the universe by the word of his power.'

God did not simply create the universe and then leave it to run under its own steam:

- Job 34:14–15: 'If [God] should set his heart to it and gather to himself his spirit and his breath, all flesh would perish together, and man would return to dust.'

We should think of creation being not like Windsor Castle, which having been built survives without its builders, but more like a bouncy castle, which collapses the moment the electricity is turned off.

Deism emerged in the eighteenth century as a response to the then latest science, which compared the universe to a vast clockwork mechanism that runs according to rules. Deists saw God as the 'clock maker' who, having created the universe and wound it up, leaves it to run on its own. One might say that after creation he takes a 13.7-billion-year sabbatical. This is not the biblical view – and is based on a science that is now very out of date. Today, however, many Christians who think of themselves as orthodox actually hold to a modified Deism. They believe that the universe essentially runs on its own, but that God occasionally intervenes – to perform miracles, to become incarnate and to provide them with a parking spot when they pray. By contrast the biblical picture is that God is constantly upholding his universe.

God does not merely uphold the universe, but is also working out his purposes in history, through his providence. We will consider that further in Chapter 9.

God is working towards his new creation, the new heavens and new earth in which righteousness dwells (2 Pet. 3:13; Rev. 21:1). We will consider that further in Chapter 29.

What do you think? The question

Is the Christian doctrine of creation compatible with modern science?

CHRISTIANITY AND SCIENCE[6]
(CCC 283–85)

How to relate Christian faith to scientific discoveries is a vital issue, as most people today see science as the source of rational objective truth. So Christian theology in general and the doctrine of creation in particular must relate to it or else be seen as myth or a fairy tale. This issue is important especially for teenagers from Christian homes learning science at school, who are likely to ask how what they are taught as fact at school ties in with what they have learned of faith at home and at church. There are two dangers to avoid in handling this issue.

So how should theology relate to science? There is no question of either discipline supplanting the other, though some

Errors to avoid

1 The first is to treat the Bible as a science textbook. The biblical authors were not scientists and the questions that they were answering were not those asked by scientists today. Galileo stated that the Bible was written 'to teach us how one goes to heaven, not how heaven goes'.[7] So, for example, Scripture uses descriptive language in speaking about God's creation – e.g. speaking of the sun 'rising'. From a scientific perspective this statement is not true, but it describes accurately how things appear from our perspective. Scientists today still refer to sunrise and sunset, even though they believe that it is the earth's rotation that causes this effect.

2 The second error is not allowing the Bible to make any scientific claims at all. It is true that the Bible was not intended to be a science textbook, but that does not mean that it teaches nothing of relevance to modern science. In particular, it does teach about how both the universe and life came into existence, albeit in a non-scientific way. For example, it teaches that the universe is not eternal but was brought into being by God 'in the beginning'. Science and theology have different interests, but they are describing the same reality and this means that their claims will at times overlap. So while Christian theology has no stake in most of the claims of modern science, the two disciplines are not completely unrelated and theology does have an interest in some scientific claims. The one single reality is being explored from two different perspectives, with two different sets of questions, albeit with some common interests. The Bible and Christian faith refer to the meaning and purpose of life, which fall outside the scope of science, even if individual scientists may choose to express opinions about it.

fundamentalist atheists talk as if this were the case, as do some fundamentalist Christians. Nor should the relationship between the two disciplines be too close. The relationship should remain at the level of a tentative alliance, because scientific ideas are constantly changing. As has been said, 'Religion must learn to live with whatever cosmology, whatever theory, science provides: but on no account must it ever marry any of them.'[8] In this instance cohabitation is preferable to marriage! Dean Inge famously warned that whoever marries the spirit of this age will find himself a widower in the next. Deism embraced eighteenth-century science too closely, ending with a defective theology allied to what is now seen as defective science. Modern science is not infallible, but it is the best that we have at this stage and theology needs to coexist with it, without necessarily accepting every single claim made by scientists. Science advances by progressive approximations to the truth and does not offer us final, absolute truth.

*Augustine in the fifth century, who had a very high view of biblical authority, warned about the danger of Christians pontificating from ignorance on scientific matters:

> Usually, even a non-Christian knows something about the earth, the heavens, and the other elements of this world, about the motion and orbit of the stars and even their size and relative positions, about the predictable eclipses of the sun and moon, the cycles of the years and the seasons, about the kinds of animals, shrubs, stones, and so forth, and this knowledge he holds to as being certain from reason and experience. Now it is a disgraceful and dangerous thing for an infidel to hear a Christian, presumably giving the meaning of Holy Scripture, talking nonsense on these topics; and we should take all means to prevent such an embarrassing situation, in which people show up vast ignorance in a Christian and laugh it to scorn. (*The Literal Meaning of Genesis* 1:19:39)

He did not regard the 'six days' of Genesis 1 as literal 24-hour periods.

According to science the universe began some 13.7 billion years ago with the 'Big Bang', which was followed by a process of expansion, development and evolution. There are now more than a hundred billion galaxies in the universe and the average galaxy contains more than a hundred billion stars. So how does this relate to Christian doctrine?

Creation *ex nihilo* can be referred to the beginning of the universe. Science has no explanation of what caused the Big Bang, God's initial creation. Indeed, Francis Collins, the head of the Human Genome Project, put it very strongly:

> The Big Bang cries out for a divine explanation. It forces the conclusion that nature had a defined beginning. I cannot see how nature could have created itself. Only a supernatural force that is outside of space and time could have done that.[9]

The subsequent development of the universe can be seen as God's continuing creation. Consequently the modern scientific picture of the origins of the universe need cause no problem for the Christian doctrine of creation. How to interpret Genesis 1—2 is a separate issue.[10]

Scientists from 2288 discuss using their newly developed time machine.

© Miriam Kendrick 2013 www.miriamkendrick.co.uk

What do you think? My answer

In my view, the Christian doctrine of creation is compatible with modern science. That is not to say that the modern scientific explanation is infallible or that it will not change further with time, only that there is no need for Christians to oppose it on theological grounds.

Sceptic's corner

Surely modern science teaches us that miracles (such as Jesus' Virgin Birth and resurrection) are not possible.

Answer: This has been claimed by sceptics since the eighteenth-century Enlightenment. Some Liberal theologians have mistakenly adopted this argument and have produced drastically pruned theologies that exclude God from intervening in his universe. There is a fundamental error in this approach. First-century people were not stupid. They were well aware that virgins do not conceive and the dead do not rise. The early Christians believed in the Virgin Birth and the resurrection not because their science was defective but because they believed in a God who was active within his universe. The contrast is not between ancient and modern science but between a purely Naturalist philosophy, which claims that nothing exists apart from the material universe, and a philosophy (or theology) that acknowledges the active existence of God. Both views are found in the first century and both views are found among twenty-first-century scientists.

God's upholding of the universe includes its running in a regular way. We can only do science and technology, and indeed conduct our everyday lives, because of the regularity of nature. On rare occasions, however, God acts beyond (rather than against) the regular operation of the universe, supremely in the Incarnation when the divine Word became one of us.

Credal statement

We believe that the Father, by the Word – that is, by his Son – created of nothing the heaven, the earth, and all creatures, as it seemed good unto him, giving unto every creature its being, shape, form, and several offices to serve its Creator; that he doth also still uphold and govern them by his eternal providence, and infinite power for the service of mankind, to the end that man may serve his God. (*Belgic Confession of Faith* (1561), art. 12)

PRAYERS

Praise the LORD! Praise the LORD from the
  heavens; praise him in the heights!
Praise him, all his angels; praise him, all
  his hosts!
Praise him, sun and moon, praise him, all
  you shining stars!

Praise him, you highest heavens, and you
  waters above the heavens!
Let them praise the name of the LORD! For
  he commanded and they were created.
And he established them for ever and
  ever; he gave a decree, and it shall not
  pass away.   (Ps. 148:1–6)

Bless the LORD, O my soul! O LORD my
God, you are very great! You are clothed
with splendour and majesty, covering
yourself with light as with a garment,
stretching out the heavens like a
tent . . . You cause the grass to grow for the
livestock and plants for man to cultivate,
that he may bring forth food from the earth
and wine to gladden the heart of man, oil to
make his face shine and bread to strengthen
man's heart . . . O LORD, how manifold are
your works! In wisdom have you made them
all; the earth is full of your creatures. Here
is the sea, great and wide, which teems
with creatures innumerable, living things
both small and great. (Ps. 104:1–2,
14–15, 24–25)

Questions to answer

- What are the implications of the doctrine of
  creation?
- How should theology relate to modern science?

NOTES

1 B. Russell 'A Free Man's Worship', in
  A Free Man's Worship and Other Essays.
  London: Unwin, 1917.
2 Shakespeare, *Macbeth*.

3 A point made by John Lennox in
  <www.bbc.co.uk/news/science-
  environment-19997789>.
4 *The Case for Christianity*. New York:
  Macmillan, 1975, p. 32.
5 *Mere Christianity*. London: Fontana,
  1955, p. 62.
6 ATS ch. 4.
7 S. Drake *Discoveries and Opinions of
  Galileo*. New York: Doubleday Anchor
  Books, 1957, p. 186.
8 D. MacLeod, 'Creation and Scientific
  Explanation', *SJT* 36 (1983), 306,
  quoting P. Carvin.
9 F. S. Collins, *The Language of God:
  A Scientist Presents Evidence for Belief*.
  London: Simon & Schuster, 2007, p. 67.
10 H. Blocher, *In the Beginning* (Leicester:
  IVP, 1984) is an excellent example of
  how to do this.

RESOURCES

R. J. Berry (ed.) *The Care of Creation*.
Leicester: IVP, 2000.

H. Blocher *In the Beginning*. Leicester:
IVP, 1984.

S. Bouma-Prediger *For the Beauty of the
Earth*. Grand Rapids: Baker, 2001.

R. F. Carlson (ed.) *Science and Christianity:
Four Views*. Downers Grove: IVP, 2000.

P. Copan and W. L. Craig *Creation out
of Nothing*. Grand Rapids: Baker, 2004.

R. D. Geivett and G. R. Habermas (eds) *In
Defence of Miracles: A Comprehensive Case for
God's Action in History*. Leicester: IVP, 1997.

J. Houston *I Believe in the Creator*. London:
Hodder & Stoughton, 1979.

Chapter 5

THE SPIRIT WORLD

Aims of this chapter

In this chapter we look at the spirit world, asking:

- What did God create apart from the physical universe?
- What and where is heaven?
- What is the role of angels?
- What are Satan and demons?
- What place should the spirit world hold in our beliefs?

As we saw in the previous chapter, Genesis 1 and 2 speak clearly of God creating the universe by his word, but the universe is not God's sole creation. The *Nicene Creed, the one truly ecumenical creed used by East and West alike, begins with an affirmation of the dual character of God's creation. God is the maker not just of earth and visible things but also of heaven and invisible things:

> We believe in God, the Father almighty, maker of *heaven* and earth and of all things visible and *invisible*.

What do you think? The question

What and where is heaven?

HEAVEN (CCC 325–27)

In both Testaments the word 'heaven(s)' can refer to the skies and the 'heavenly' bodies:

- Genesis 1:1: 'In the beginning, God created the heavens and the earth.'
- Psalm 19:1: 'The heavens declare the glory of God, and the sky above proclaims his handiwork.'
- James 5:18: '[Elijah] prayed again, and heaven gave rain.'

Elsewhere in the Bible, though, heaven refers to a realm beyond the physical universe that transcends it, the abode of God. For example:

- Deuteronomy 26:15: 'Look down from your holy habitation, from heaven.'
- Matthew 6:9: 'Our Father in heaven'.
- Acts 1:11: 'This Jesus, who was taken up from you into heaven . . .'
- Revelation 4:1: 'Behold, a door standing open in heaven!'

This does not mean that God was seen as dwelling in the higher reaches of the universe, even in Old Testament times.

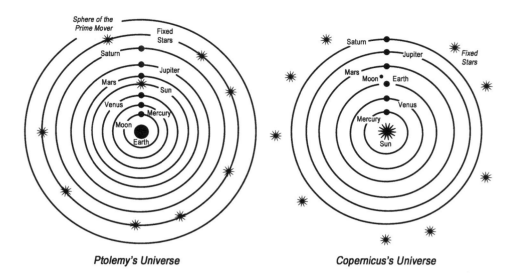

Ptolemy's Universe   Copernicus's Universe

'Behold, heaven and the highest heaven cannot contain you' (1 Kings 8:27). God transcends his creation.

Having established that there is a heaven, the next question is *where* is it? The Greek writer Ptolemy (d. *c*. AD 168) believed the earth was stationed at the centre with the sun, moon, planets and stars all rotating around it in concentric circles. Heaven lay beyond these, as the fiery place where God lives. In 1543, however, the astronomer Nicolaus Copernicus proposed a rival model with the sun, not the earth, at the centre and the earth as just one of the planets revolving round the sun. Copernicus was speculating without hard evidence, but this changed when Galileo (d. 1642) made a telescope and observed that Jupiter had moons. That proved that not all heavenly objects rotate around the earth. As a result Galileo got into trouble with the Roman Inquisition – more because he undermined the ruling Aristotelian view (of Ptolemy) than because of any conflict with Scripture. This illustrates the maxim that if you marry the spirit of the age (Ptolemaic astronomy)

you will find yourself a widower – though in this case it came after 1,500 years of happy marriage!

So, in the light of Copernicus and Galileo, where *is* heaven? Modern Western Christians have not always found heaven easy to comprehend. Many have absorbed heaven into God, with heaven being just another way of saying 'wherever God is'. For many, if not most, reality in practice reduces to the physical universe (as viewed by secular modern science) with God added on. This worldview leaves no room for

What do you think? My answer

Heaven is a realm that transcends the physical universe. It is described in various ways in the Bible, but this is an area where we need to heed the warnings of Chapter 3. The biblical account is accommodated to our ability to understand, and any positive statements that we make need to be balanced by negative statements as to how heaven transcends our understanding.

such biblical entities as angels, demons, principalities and powers. The trouble with such a truncated concept of creation, as *Moltmann observes,[1] is that God does not really fit and is easily squeezed out. The biblical picture is much richer than this, with spiritual beings, angels and fallen angels. The Bible, like the Nicene Creed, affirms the dual character of God's creation.

ANGELS (CCC 328–36, 350–52)

God by Christ created not just human beings and animals, but also angels:

- Colossians 1:16: 'By him all things were created, in heaven and on earth, visible and invisible, whether thrones or dominions or rulers or authorities – all things were created through him and for him.'

Angels are an embarrassment to many Western Christians today and are often explained away or ignored. In Scripture, by contrast, they play a significant role, being mentioned over 100 times in the Old Testament and over 160 times in the New Testament. However, Scripture tells us relatively little about them. We are only told on a need-to-know basis, which leaves us with many unanswered questions. For example, do angels occupy space? This was the reasoning behind the alleged medieval debate about how many angels can dance on a pin-head.[2] Such speculation is a waste of time; we do not know or need to know. We do know, however, that there are ranks of angels – angels and archangels, cherubim and seraphim.

Scripture mentions three main roles of angels:

WORSHIPPERS

Angels are worshippers of God. For example:

- Isaiah 6:1–3:

  In the year that King Uzziah died I saw the Lord sitting upon a throne, high and lifted up; and the train of his robe filled the temple. Above him stood the seraphim . . . And one called to another and said: 'Holy, holy, holy is the LORD of hosts; the whole earth is full of his glory!'

- In Daniel 7:9–10, and Revelation 4—5 we see large numbers of angels devoted to worshipping God.

This has practical relevance. If we are worshipping in a church with a very small congregation it can be a great encouragement to remember that we are joining in with something much bigger – the angelic worship. This is expressed in some liturgies:

Worship

Therefore with angels and archangels, and with all the company of heaven, we proclaim your great and glorious name, for ever praising you and saying: Holy, holy, holy Lord, God of power and might, heaven and earth are full of your glory. Hosanna in the highest. (*Common Worship*, Communion Service)

Some years ago part of a service at the church I belonged to was broadcast by the BBC World Service. There was a red light and we were told that while that was lit we were being joined by over a million people. I can still remember the sense of loneliness that I felt when the light went out. The congregation had become 'only' the 300 people physically present. But in fact, when it comes to joining with the angelic congregation the red light is always lit; there is no reason to feel that we are 'only' 8, or 80, or 800 . . .

MESSENGERS
Angels serve as messengers of God – God's flunkeys, one might say. Indeed, the Greek word *angelos* means 'angel' or 'messenger'. In Luke 1:19, 26 the angel Gabriel has important messages to bring to Zechariah and to Mary. In Daniel and Revelation angels reveal the future.

PROTECTORS
Angels are protectors:

- Psalm 34:7: 'The angel of the LORD encamps round those who fear him, and delivers them.'
- Psalm 91:11: '[God] will command his angels concerning you to guard you in all your ways.'
- Matthew 18:10: 'See that you do not despise one of these little ones. For I tell you that in heaven their angels always see the face of my Father who is in heaven.' This passage has led many to the idea that we each have a guardian angel, for which Acts 12:15 is also cited.

Angelic protection is not something that we are normally aware of. There is a revealing story in 2 Kings 6. The king of Syria had sent an army to seize Elisha and when Elisha's servant awoke he saw that they were surrounded by horses and chariots. Naturally he is terrified, but Elisha assures him that 'those who are with us are more than those who are with them'. Elisha then prays, 'O LORD, please open his eyes that he may see.' At that point his servant sees that

'the mountain was full of horses and chariots of fire all round Elisha' (6:15–17). There was a spiritual reality that the young man could not see until Elisha prayed for his eyes to be opened.

Today there are people who give accounts of being rescued by angels. We certainly do not need to believe *all* of these. Some people are gullible and, sadly, some deliberately sensationalize things. On the other hand, we should not start with the assumption that they are all wrong. We need to be critical in the sense of discerning, while allowing that some at least may be true.

Furthermore, listening to the news, there are many cases where people seem to enjoy a 'lucky escape'. For example, on 17 January 2008 an aircraft coming in to land at Heathrow lost power and only just avoided crashing. Pilot John Coward commented that 'All the crew did their job absolutely brilliantly but I think some thanks has to go to the Man Upstairs for giving us that little lift at the end.'[3] One cannot be dogmatic about any individual case, but in principle it is possible that God in his mercy occasionally intervenes

Speculation

Purely as speculation, I wonder whether such angelic intervention may not be more common than we realize. Putting it differently, if God confined his upholding of the universe purely to maintaining the 'laws of nature', might there not be far more tragedy than we actually see in our world? Clearly, though, God does allow massive tragedies to occur and we will consider that issue more fully in Chapters 9 and 10.

to avert tragedy. Clearly, however, such escapes do not always happen and we must be careful not to present a picture that ignores the tragedies that do happen in this life.

HISTORY OF VIEWS ON ANGELS

Views on angels have changed over history. As we have seen, Old and New Testaments both refer to them. Greek Platonist philosophy also included belief in angels. Philo, a first-century Jew, fused together the Jewish and Greek understandings of angels and his ideas were subsequently taken over in the Early Church.

Around AD 500 a Syrian monk wrote a very speculative work on angels entitled *The Celestial Hierarchy*, in which he describes nine ranks of angels. The author claimed to be Paul's disciple Dionysius the Areopagite, described in Acts 17:34, though no one believes that claim today and he is now known as *'Pseudo-Dionysius'. In the Middle Ages, however, his claim was believed and his works were therefore treated with huge respect. As a result the Middle Ages saw rich speculation about angels and their role. The sixteenth-century Reformers, however, sought to curb this and bring beliefs about angels back to sober biblical limits, eliminating later speculation. The eighteenth-century Enlightenment went further and questioned the very existence of angels, regarding them as mere flights of fancy. Twentieth-century theology has, however, taken them more seriously again. *Karl Barth devoted over 250 pages of his *Church Dogmatics* to angels – though given the size of that work 250 pages is a modest amount! Jürgen Moltmann, another key theologian of the twentieth century, has also taken them seriously.

FALLEN ANGELS (DEMONS)
(CCC 391–95, 414)

Satan and demons are clearly referred to in Scripture. Mark's Gospel devotes considerable attention to Jesus' battle against them. Satan tempted Jesus after his baptism and on later occasions (Luke 4:1–13). The Hebrew name 'Satan' means 'accuser'. Paul and Peter both highlight our struggle against Satan and demons:

- Ephesians 6:12, 16:

  For we do not wrestle against flesh and blood, but against . . . the spiritual forces of evil in the heavenly places . . . Take up the shield of faith, with which you can extinguish all the flaming darts of the evil one.

- 1 Peter 5:8: 'Your adversary the devil prowls around like a roaring lion, seeking someone to devour.'

Why would there be evil spirits in God's good creation? There are indications in Scripture that Satan and demons are angels that have fallen into sin, angels that did not keep to their proper bounds:

- 2 Peter 2:4: 'For if God did not spare angels when they sinned, but cast them into hell and committed them to chains of gloomy darkness to be kept until the judgement . . .'
- Jude 6: 'The angels who did not stay within their own position of authority, but left their proper dwelling, he has kept in eternal chains under gloomy darkness until the judgement of the great day.'

They are angels who fell because they rebelled against God.

In addition to these two passages, in the Old Testament two kings are talked about in such cosmic terms that theologians have traditionally seen a reference not just to earthy rulers but to Satan himself:

How you [the king of Babylon] are fallen from heaven, O Day Star, son of Dawn! . . . You said in your heart, 'I will ascend to heaven; above the stars of God I will set my throne on high . . . I will make myself like the Most High.' But you are brought down to Sheol, to the far reaches of the pit. (Isa. 14:12–15; 'Day Star' is translated 'Lucifer' in the King James Version)

You [the king of Tyre] were the signet of perfection, full of wisdom and perfect in beauty. You were in Eden, the garden of God . . . You were blameless in your ways from the day you were created, till unrighteousness was found in you . . . You were filled with violence in your midst, and you sinned; so I cast you as a profane thing from the mountain of God . . . Your heart was proud because of your beauty; you corrupted your wisdom for the sake of your splendour. (Ezek. 28:12–19)

The strongest argument that Satan and demons are fallen angels is theological. All that God creates is good, so they must have turned from an original goodness. It is unacceptable to say either that they were not created by God or that he created them evil. Traditionally all angels were seen as having a period of probation during which they once for all chose whether to obey God or to sin. We must, however, beware of over-confident speculation. Milton's *Paradise Lost* is a great work of literature and its basic outline is biblical but it also goes far beyond the scanty information found in Scripture.

The infernal Serpent; he it was whose guile, stirred up with envy and revenge, deceived the mother of mankind, what time his pride had cast him out from Heaven, with all his host of rebel angels, by whose aid aspiring to set himself in glory above his peers, he trusted to have equalled the most High, if he opposed; and with ambitious aim against the throne and monarchy of God raised impious war in heaven and battle proud with vain attempt. (Milton, *Paradise Lost*, Book 1, lines 34–43)

Credal statement

[God] also created the angels good, to be his messengers and to serve his elect; some of which are fallen from that excellency, in which God created them, into everlasting perdition; and the others have, by the grace of God, remained steadfast and continued in their primitive state. (*Belgic Confession of Faith* (1561), art. 12)[4]

The twentieth century, thanks especially to modern media, has brought home the reality of evil. As a result, there is an increased willingness to talk of the demonic, but not necessarily to see this in personal terms. Moltmann sees demons as impersonal forces of destruction, at work in social systems, for example. Since the 1950s there has been a new interpretation of the 'principalities and powers' referred to by Paul (Rom. 8:38; Eph. 3:10, 6:12; Col. 1:16, 2:15). It is proposed that these should be seen not (or not only) as heavenly beings but as social, economic and political structures.

This interpretation has proved very popular, for a variety of reasons. It takes seriously the reality of evil. It offers a rational interpretation of passages that appeared obscure and mythological. It also provides a biblical basis for talking about social structures, a modern preoccupation about which the Bible has little to say. One problem, though, is that the references are so general that these passages become like a blank cheque in that they can be used to denounce the pet dislikes of the interpreter, whether that be socialism, capitalism or whatever. The idea that the forces of evil work through social systems is certainly sound, but the attempt to interpret all of the biblical teaching on the demonic as impersonal is not convincing.

Sceptic's corner

*Bultmann famously wrote, in a 1941 essay, that 'it is impossible to use electric light and the wireless and to avail ourselves of modern medical and surgical discoveries, and at the same time to believe in the New Testament world of spirits and miracles'.[5]

Answer: Where miracles are concerned Bultmann was clearly wide of the mark. There are many top scientists who unreservedly believe in such miracles as the literal resurrection of Jesus Christ. When it comes to the spirit world, however, Bultmann's charge is much closer to the mark. It is indeed hard to hold together an ancient view of the spirit world and a modern Western scientific worldview. Christians can operate in effect with a worldview which includes God and the universe but no 'spirit world', resulting in what Paul Hiebert calls 'the excluded middle'.[6] This happens either by actually denying the existence of the spirit world or, more commonly, by according only formal recognition of its reality.

Osadolor Imasogie, in his discussion of African theology, makes this last point very lucidly. The nineteenth-century Western missionaries who brought the gospel to Africa, he argues, maintained a formal belief in the spiritual realm because it is found in the Bible. But for them such entities as heaven, angels, Satan and evil forces had become mere 'cultural clichés'. Their belief in the spirit world was not a dynamic reality but rather an 'afterglow of the biblical worldview'. As traditionalists they affirmed the spiritual realm, against the surrounding deistic culture, but this belief was largely theoretical.[7] As with the Cheshire cat, the reality had gone.

Western Christianity has largely forgotten the dimension of heaven and the spirit world, but this is still very much a reality in much Asian and African Christianity. The greatest challenge is how to relate it to the modern scientific worldview – e.g. with relation to the causes and cure of disease.

Exorcism is a rather extreme approach Mrs Watson. Next time you have a headache I suggest you just take some paracetamol.

© Miriam Kendrick 2013 www.miriamkendrick.co.uk

Errors to avoid

Today there is in the West a modest revival of interest in the spirit world. But has the Western Church learned to handle the topic adequately? There are, as C. S. Lewis warned,[8] two errors to avoid. On the one hand there is the danger of neglect; on the other hand there is the opposite danger of an unhealthy preoccupation with the topic.

The challenge for Western Christians is to recover this dimension of thought, but without becoming neurotic and seeing demons everywhere. In its extreme this can become murderous. A few years ago the BBC reported the burning alive of elderly people in Africa on suspicion of witchcraft.[9] Similar abuses have taken place in the immigrant population in the UK.

PRAYER

Everlasting God, you have ordained and constituted the ministries of angels and mortals in a wonderful order: Grant that as your holy angels always serve you in heaven, so, at your command, they may help and defend us on earth; through Jesus Christ our Lord. (*Common Worship*: Collect for Saint Michael and All Angels)

Questions to answer

- What did God create apart from the physical universe?
- What place should the spirit world hold in our beliefs?

NOTES

1 J. Moltmann *God in Creation*. London: SCM Press, 1985, 175–82.
2 For an account of the origins of this story, see <http://en.wikipedia.org/wiki/How_many_angels_can_dance_on_the_head_of_a_pin%3F>.
3 <www.dailymail.co.uk/news/article-509325/I-thank-Man-Upstairs-says-Heathrow-crash-hero-John-Coward.html>.
4 The continuation of the 'Credal statement' from the previous chapter.
5 R. Bultmann 'New Testament and Mythology' in H. W. Bartsch (ed.) *Kerygma and Myth* vol.1. London: SPCK, 1964, second edn, 5.
6 P. Hiebert 'The Flaw of the Excluded Middle', *Missiology* 10 (1982) 35–47.
7 O. Imasogie *Guidelines for Christian Theology in Africa*. Achimota, Ghana: African Christian Press, 1983, 51–53.
8 C. S. Lewis *The Screwtape Letters*. London: Fontana, 1955, 9.
9 <http://news.bbc.co.uk/1/hi/world/africa/8119201.stm>.

RESOURCES

J. K. Beilby and P. R. Eddy (eds) *Understanding Spiritual Warfare: Four Views*. Grand Rapids: Baker, 2012.

O. Imasogie *Guidelines for Christian Theology in Africa*. Achimota, Ghana: African Christian Press, 1983, chs 3 and 4.

A. N. S. Lane (ed.) *The Unseen World. Christian Reflections on Angels, Demons and the Heavenly Realm*. Carlisle: Paternoster, 1996.

J. Moltmann *God in Creation*. London: SCM Press, 1985, ch. 7.

P. S. Williams *The Case for Angels*. Carlisle: Paternoster, 2002.

Chapter 6

HUMANITY

Aims of this chapter

In this chapter we look at humanity, asking:

- What is the image of God in which we are created?
- How do human beings differ from animals? Or from computers?
- Should we think of ourselves as composed of body, soul and spirit, or as body and soul, or simply as a unity?
- How should we react to modern scientific theories of evolution?
- What about extra-terrestrial intelligence?

Then God said, 'Let us make man in our image, after our likeness. And let them have dominion over the fish of the sea and over the birds of the heavens and over the livestock and over all the earth and over every creeping thing that creeps on the earth.' So God created man in his own image, in the image of God he created him; male and female he created them. And God blessed them. And God said to them, 'Be fruitful and multiply and fill the earth and subdue it and have dominion over the fish of the sea and over the birds of the heavens and over every

living creature that moves on the earth.' (Gen. 1:26–28)

Then the LORD God formed the man of dust from the ground and breathed into his nostrils the breath of life, and the man became a living creature. (Gen. 2:7)

THE IMAGE AND LIKENESS OF GOD
(CCC 355–61, 380–81)

Do the words 'image' and 'likeness' (Gen. 1:26) refer to the same thing, or to two distinct things? From the second century many theologians have drawn a distinction between them. The image of God is essential to our humanity, and cannot be lost, while the likeness consists of righteousness, being without sin, which can be lost. However, this distinction is bad exegesis. Genesis 1:26 is an example of Hebrew parallelism, found throughout the Old Testament, where something is repeated using different words. Here 'image' and 'likeness' are not two different things but are synonymous, two different ways of saying the same thing.

If image and likeness are synonymous, can it/they be lost? We find two different

59

answers to this in the Bible. Genesis 9:6 mandates the death penalty on the grounds that 'God made man in his own image'. By contrast, the New Testament teaches that Christ came to restore the image of God, which implies that it has been lost:

- Romans 8:29: 'For those whom he foreknew he also predestined to be conformed to the image of his Son.'
- Colossians 3:10: 'you . . . have put on the new self, which is being renewed in knowledge after the image of its creator'.

There is a tension here. In some sense the image is lost, in another it is not. The traditional distinction between image and likeness may be poor exegesis of Genesis 1:26, yet it is good theology in that it does capture the two sides to the question found in Scripture.

What do you think? The question

How do human beings differ from animals?

© Miriam Kendrick 2013 www.miriamkendrick.co.uk

HUMANS VERSUS ANIMALS

In many ways we *are* animals, and there is much that we can learn about ourselves from animals. Animals are used for medical research and the testing of drugs because we have so much in common with them. Animals are also used for psychological research, and the bad news is that the animals selected are rats, because of their psychological similarity to humans!

We share some 98.5 per cent of our DNA with chimpanzees. That may sound impressive until we learn that we also share 50 per cent of our DNA with trees. Even the tree huggers may be surprised to learn that! Also, the differences in DNA between all humans amount to well under 0.1 per cent – vastly less than the 1.5 per cent difference from chimpanzees.

Because we have so much in common with them I can empathize with cats and I understand that there are even some people who can empathize with dogs. To some extent we can appreciate and understand the emotions of our pets. By contrast, it is much harder to empathize with flies, say. Indeed, until a few years ago no one even knew for sure whether they slept. (They do.) But while we have so much in common with some animals, we are not just super-animals; we have the added dimension of the image of God.

IMAGE OF GOD[1]

Genesis 1 refers to the creation of animals, insects, birds and fish, but it is only human beings that are described as being created in God's image. This sets apart us from animals, and makes us *like* God. But what is this image? We find the answer not just in Genesis 1:26–28 but from the *whole* of scriptural teaching about what it is to be human. So what is it that marks out human beings, rather than animals, as being in the image of God? There are a number of answers to this question:

1 **Reason**. Reason has traditionally been seen as part of the image of God. The ability to reason is seen as a human distinctive. 'Be not like a horse or a mule, without understanding, which must be curbed with bit and bridle, or it will not stay near you' (Ps. 32:9). We are able to reason things out. Although today we understand that some animals are smarter than was previously thought, the ability to reason still remains an

"It says on your résumé that you were created in God's image. Very impressive."

area where human beings are distinctive. Language and speech are human distinctives which image the God who reveals himself as Word. Some animals can be taught very basic language, but not language as we know it. There is the joke about the man who taught his dog to play poker. When someone said how clever the dog was, he replied that she was not that smart as she always wagged her tail when she had a good hand!

2 **Will**. Will is another area that has traditionally been seen as part of the image of God. We have free will (albeit spoiled by sin) and moral responsibility. This is something assumed of humanity throughout Scripture, yet never taught of animals. Animals do not face a coming judgement day! Mark Twain observed that 'Man is the only animal that blushes. Or needs to.'[2]

Human responsibility is qualified by the fact that we are all greatly influenced both by *nature* (our genetic inheritance, what we are born with) and by *nurture* (our social and psychological conditioning, what we are trained into).[3] Some light can be shed on the respective roles of these two by the study of identical twins, especially those separated at birth. What we become is affected not just by nature and nurture but also by the choices that

---

Tension to hold

Genesis brings out well the two sides of this issue about humanity and God's image. On the one hand, we are made in God's image (1:26) and have God's breath (2:7); on the other hand, we are formed from the dust of the ground (2:7). There is a tension between these two aspects, between the divine breath and the dust of the ground. Those who have the second point, seeing humanity as the accidental result of a blind process of evolution but lacking the idea of creation in God's image, undermine human dignity. In his 1991 encyclical *Centesimus Annus*, Pope John Paul II based his social teaching and his opposition to atheistic Communism on the human dignity, rights and responsibilities, which flow from creation in God's image: 'God has imprinted his own image and likeness on man (cf. Gen. 1:26), conferring upon him an incomparable dignity' (1:11).

we make along the way, which are involved in moulding our personality and character. Nature and nurture both influence us, but not to the extent of eliminating all personal responsibility. For the Team GB medal winners at the 2012 Olympics three factors came into play. First, they needed the innate ability that came from nature; second, they needed the nurture that was provided by the investment in training programmes, amounting to £4 million per medal; finally, none of this would have been any use apart from their personal dedication and commitment to the task.

3 **Spirituality**. Spirituality is another human distinctive. We have a capacity to worship – whether we worship God, idols or pop idols.[4] We also have a sense of eternity. '[God] has made everything beautiful in its time. Also, he has put eternity into man's heart, yet so that he cannot find out what God has done from the beginning to the end' (Eccles. 3:11). Unlike animals, we are able to relate to God. We were made to worship God and to enjoy him (see 'Worship', opposite):

> What is the chief end of man? Man's chief end is to glorify God and to enjoy him for ever. (*Westminster Shorter Catechism* (1647), q. 1)

4 **Authority**. Human beings are entrusted with authority over creation as God's stewards. A minority in the Early Church understood this to be the meaning of the image of God, drawing on Genesis 1:26, 28 and on Psalm 8:6–8: 'You have given him dominion over the works of your hands; you have put all things under his feet, all sheep and oxen, and also the beasts of the field, the birds of the heavens, and the fish of the sea, whatever passes along the paths of the seas.' As we have seen in Chapter 4, this is relevant for our understanding of and attitude towards ecology today.

5 **Creativity**. God is creative and we image him by being creative – though with the important difference that, unlike God, we don't create out of nothing, even though magicians may sometimes try to make us think that they can. We have the ability both to create and to enjoy art, music, literature, etc.

6 **Community**. We image God not just as individuals but also together, in relationships, in community. We see this especially in Genesis 1:26–27, where it is as male and female that we bear God's image. Again, the God whose image we bear is a trinity of Father, Son and Holy Spirit.

Worship

Almighty God, you have made us for yourself, and our hearts are restless till they find their rest in you: pour your love into our hearts and draw us to yourself, and so bring us at last to your heavenly city where we shall see you face to face; through Jesus Christ our Lord. (*Common Worship*, Collect for Seventeenth Sunday after Trinity, echoing the words of *Augustine)

Credal statement

We confess and acknowledge that our God has created man, i.e., our first father, Adam, after his own image and likeness, to whom he gave wisdom, lordship, justice, free will, and self-consciousness, so that in the whole nature of man no imperfection could be found. (*Scots Confession* (1560) by *John Knox, ch. 2)

What do you think? My answer

These are all ways in which we image God and which distinguish us from the animals. We must not make the mistake of reducing the image of God to any one of these on its own. Theology, like clothes styles, is subject to fashion and the fashion today is to understand everything in terms of relationships and community. This is indeed part of what it means to image God – but not the whole. Ants, bees and computers in a network all exemplify community and relationships. On the other hand, a human being stranded on a desert island is still human. After the war one Japanese soldier remained on his own, hiding in a jungle for many years before discovering that the war was over. He was still a human being in God's image.

We image God in all six of these ways, but we must also remember that in each and every one of them the image has been spoiled by sin, as we will see in the next chapter. Christ came to restore this image.

HUMANS VERSUS COMPUTERS

We are not just super-animals and nor are we just super-computers, biological computers, as some secularists claim. Computers can perform very complex tasks and some can beat Grand Masters at chess. But at heart all they are doing is adding up 0s and 1s very quickly. It is possible to draw parallels between computers and the human brain, but a human being is much more than just a calculating machine. Unlike us, computers do not have self-consciousness. I have self-consciousness and I am prepared to give other people the benefit of the doubt when they tell me that they have it. There

is no reason to suppose that a computer has it or indeed ever could have it. We can feel joy and pain, but a computer cannot – though it is relatively easy to programme a computer to *say* 'Ouch' when you hit it.

BODY–SOUL–SPIRIT[5] (CCC 362–68, 382)

There has been a long-running dispute between those who say that human nature is twofold, i.e. body and soul (dichotomy), which has been the majority view, and those who say that it is threefold, i.e. body, soul and spirit (trichotomy), the minority view. The latter view has often been allied with a distinctive stance on sanctification. More recently some have rejected both views and seen human nature as a unity (monism).

There are a few passages in the New Testament that are quoted to support a trichotomist view:

- 1 Thessalonians 5:23: 'Now may the God of peace himself sanctify you completely, and may your whole spirit and soul and body be kept blameless at the coming of our Lord Jesus Christ.'
- 1 Corinthians 15:44: 'It is sown a natural body; it is raised a spiritual body. If there is a natural body, there is also a spiritual body.' 'Natural' in the Greek is the adjective from the noun 'soul'.
- Hebrews 4:12: 'For the word of God is living and active, sharper than any two-edged sword, piercing to the division of soul and of spirit, of joints and of marrow, and discerning the thoughts and intentions of the heart.'

This is a flimsy basis for making a sharp contrast between soul and spirit. In Mark 12:30 we are told to love God with all our heart, soul, mind and strength. This doesn't mean that these are the four parts of which we are composed. They are to be seen as *aspects* rather than an inventory of items.

The Bible (especially the Old Testament) stresses our unity. It does not teach the type of dualism found in *Greek philosophy, whereby we are a soul, a divine spark that just happens to be living (or even trapped) in a body. Dualists sometimes even compare the body to a suit of clothes. The real 'me' is the soul. This was the view of the Gnostics, who referred to the body as a tomb in which the soul is trapped. This implies a very low view of the body. The biblical view is not that we are souls that just happen to be living in a body. Indeed, it would be true to say that the Old Testament views us as *animated bodies* (Gen. 2:7) rather than *incarnate souls*.

The Bible does not support a Greek dualism that suggests we are souls that just happen to be living in a body; nor does it support a pure monism. Even in the Old Testament dead people continue to exist in Sheol after the decay of their bodies. While the New Testament does not teach a Greek dualism it does allow a distinction between body and soul. Human nature cannot be reduced to the bodily or physical. Sometimes the Greek word 'soul' simply means 'person' – as in Acts 27:37: 'We were in all 276 persons in the ship.' But sometimes the soul is contrasted with the body, as in Matthew 10:28: 'Do not fear those who kill the body but cannot kill the soul.'

This is not just theoretical speculation. It becomes crucially relevant when we ask what happens when we die. Monists hold that we cease to exist at death and that God will reconstitute us at the final resurrection. There is sufficient evidence in the New Testament, however, to indicate something of us survives between death and resurrection, as we will see in Chapter 29.

HUMAN ORIGINS

How does the Bible relate to modern scientific theories of evolution? Modern science talks of a process of evolution, which gave rise to *homo habilis* some two to four million years ago, which led to further evolution towards *homo sapiens*. Some 10–12,000 years ago there was the rise of agriculture, which made civilization possible.

How accurate is this picture? I do not know. It is based on very fragmentary evidence and it is likely that it will be revised in due course. How does it cohere with Genesis 1—2? These chapters are to be seen neither as literal scientific history nor as myth, but rather as an account of human origins in figurative language.[6] What matters for Christian doctrine is that there is a decisive point at which human beings in the image of God come into being. Chimpanzees are not made in God's image; we are. When did the change occur? How did it happen? Was there special intervention by God? Such questions may be of interest but they are not crucial for the doctrine of creation. Personally I am happy to remain agnostic on such details.

Sceptic's corner

The whole idea of evolution is clearly contrary to the Christian faith and it is not possible to believe in evolution and be a Christian.

Answer: There are many issues involved here. Some have questioned how the 'survival of the fittest' is compatible with Christianity, but that this is how nature functions is beyond dispute. Others claim that the Bible blames all of the evil in the world on human sin, which is awkward if humanity has only appeared recently in cosmic history. We will consider that further in Chapter 8. It is worth noting that *Augustine, expounding Genesis in the light of the science of his day, taught an instantaneous creation *ex nihilo* of a universe containing 'seedlike principles' which contain the potential for the later development of living things.[7] This suggests that were Augustine to be living today he would not find it hard to accept the theory of evolution.[8]

Speculation

Does extra-terrestrial intelligence (ETI) exist? If it does, how should Christians react to it? Christian theologians have been discussing this issue for some 700 years. I see no reason to exclude the possibility of ETI existing though I think it highly unlikely, given the distances and timescales involved, that we will have a meaningful encounter with it (or them). Christians already believe in the existence of a form of ETI, namely angels. The Bible makes no mention of ETI elsewhere in the universe – but nor does it mention America. Genesis 1:26–27 affirms that humanity, as opposed to animals, is created in God's image; it does not deny that elsewhere in the universe there may be other beings also in God's image. Such beings may or may not have sinned. If they have, God will have devised a way in which to effect their salvation.[9]

PRAYER

Eternal Father, you said, 'Let us make mankind in our image and likeness.' Thus, you were willing to share with us your own greatness. You gave us the intellect to share your truth. You gave us the wisdom to share your goodness . . . It was love which first prompted you to create us; and it was love which caused you to share with us your truth and goodness. Out of the same love that caused you to create us, you have now sent your only Son to save us. He is your perfect image and likeness, and so through him we can be restored to your image and likeness. (*Catherine of Siena)

Question to answer

- What is the image of God in which we are created?

NOTES

1 ATS ch. 5.
2 *Following the Equator* (1897).
3 For a blistering attack on views that deny the role of nature, see S. Pinker *The Blank Slate: The Modern Denial of Human Nature.* London: Penguin, 2002, ch. 19. While he affirms the role of genetic inheritance, he emphasizes the role of fate, rather than free will (397–98). For a balanced account of the roles of nature, nurture and our own choices, see F. S. Collins *The Language of God: A Scientist Presents Evidence for Belief.* London: Simon & Schuster, 2007, 257–63.
4 One of my research assistants argued that 'unlike cats, dogs also have the capacity to worship', but I would see this only as a precedent for idolatry.
5 ATS ch. 6/Appendix 4.
6 For an excellent account of this, see H. Blocher *In the Beginning.* Leicester: IVP, 1984.

7 Augustine *The Literal Meaning of Genesis*, as expounded by A. E. McGrath, *A Fine-Tuned Universe: The Quest for God in Science and Theology*. Louisville: Westminster John Knox, 2009, 101–108.

8 For more on this issue, see Collins *The Language of God*, 145–211.

9 I have dealt with this more fully in 'Is the Truth Out There? Creatures, Cosmos and New Creation', *Evangelical Quarterly* 84 (2012) 291–306; 85 (2013) 3–18.

RESOURCES

D. Alexander *Creation or Evolution: Do We Have to Choose?* Oxford: Monarch, 2008.

H. Blocher *In the Beginning*. Leicester: IVP, 1984.

F. S. Collins *The Language of God: A Scientist Presents Evidence for Belief*. London: Simon & Schuster, 2007.

J. Green and S. Palmer (eds) *In Search of the Soul: Four Views of the Mind–Body Problem*. Downers Grove: IVP, 2005.

J. P. Moreland and J. M. Reynolds (eds) *Three Views on Creation and Evolution*. Grand Rapids: Zondervan, 1999.

C. Sherlock *The Doctrine of Humanity*. Leicester: IVP, 1996.

T. Smail *Like Father, Like Son: The Trinity Imaged in our Humanity*. Milton Keynes: Paternoster, 2005.

SIN AND EVIL

Chapter 7

SIN

Aims of this chapter

In this chapter we look at sin, asking:

- What is sin?
- How has the doctrine of sin been sidelined?
- Are all people *equally* sinful?
- Is sin purely individual?
- What are the effects of sin?

This and the next chapter inevitably have a negative tone, for we are focusing on the disease from which everyone is suffering. The purpose is not to focus on the bad news for its own sake but as a prelude to the good news that follows. The Christian faith is centred on the cure that God has provided to counteract sin. The cure is very drastic, namely God sending his own Son to die for us. The extremity of the cure shows us just how serious the disease is.

THE NATURE OF SIN (CCC 386–87)

Scripture uses many different words to describe sin, involving the following ideas:[1]

- failure or missing the mark;
- going astray, trespass, transgression;
- rebellion against God, ungodliness;
- breaking God's laws, disobedience;
- perversity, wickedness, iniquity;
- unrighteousness, injustice;
- lust, evil desire.

Sin is a disease to which there are many sides. We must avoid the 'one size fits all' approach which seeks to reduce it to just one thing. Some have mistakenly tried to trace all sin back to a single principle, be that unbelief (*Luther), pride (*Augustine), selfishness, lack of self-esteem or . . .

Sins of omission are as important as sins of commission.

- James 4:17: 'Whoever knows the right thing to do and fails to do it, for him it is sin.'
- In Matthew 25:41–46 the lost are condemned for what they did *not* do:

I was hungry and you gave me no food, I was thirsty and you gave me no drink, I was a stranger and you did not welcome me, naked and you did not clothe me, sick and in prison and you did not visit me.

Whether we sin by doing or by not doing we sin simply because we are sinners. Sin manifests itself most obviously as specific deeds or 'sins', but these are the outward manifestation of a deeper reality. Sin starts as orientation of our lives, as a disposition of the heart, which leads to sinful desires, which lead to sinful thoughts, which lead to sinful deeds. The sin in our lives may be compared to the ground elder in a garden, which manifests itself all over the place and is extremely hard to eliminate. Tackling its visible manifestation above the surface is no more than a holding operation. Similarly with sin, we need to fight it vigorously and concertedly, but we will never be able to get rid of it completely in this life.

NEGLECT OF THE DOCTRINE

The doctrine of sin is undoubtedly unpopular. Most people prefer to hear about innate human goodness. But as with any disease, correct diagnosis is necessary if we are to identify the cure. Doctors do their patients no favours by telling them that they are well when they are not. I suffered for a while from a dentist who did just that, with dire consequences. The comforting diagnosis that he offered to me, as to his other patients, was 'Leave well alone, old boy/girl.' Unfortunately we were confronted, when he retired, with a long list of neglected problems.

The cure, as previously stated, is God sending his own Son to die for us. Jesus' very name indicates what his role was to be: '[Mary] will bear a son, and you shall call his name Jesus, for he will save his people from their sins' (Matt. 1:21). The fact that God needed to send his Son indicates how serious the disease is.

Today sin is often excused on genetic, social (bad upbringing) or psychological (dropped on the head as a child) grounds. All three of these factors are real, but not so as to eliminate the element of personal choice, except in the most extreme of examples.[2]

Taking a low view of the seriousness of sin has been characteristic of Liberal theology since the nineteenth century. Typically, this low view of sin leads to a low view of the work of Christ (limiting his role to that of example and teacher), which in turn leads on naturally to a low view of the person of Christ (reducing him merely to a good man). Today the marginalization of the doctrine of sin can even be found in much of Evangelicalism. Evidence for this can be seen in modern choruses and worship songs, the majority of which emphasize themes like glory and power, with relatively little mention of sin and its cure. Again, it is not uncommon to hear comments like 'God loves us just as we are, because that's how he made us.' This completely ignores the fact that sin has turned us into something very different from what God intended. It would not be legitimate to argue that 'God loves me just as I am, because that's how he made me – a serial killer.' (For the record, I am not a serial killer!) For most of the nineteenth century Evangelicalism was the dominant force in British church life, yet by the end of the century it had been largely eroded by Liberalism. Currently, Evangelicalism is arguably the strongest element in British church life, but there is no automatic guarantee that it will not again suffer the fate of its nineteenth-century ancestor.[3]

Take away the alarmed conscience and you may close the churches and turn them into dancing-halls. (*Søren Kierkegaard)

Worship

Almighty and most merciful Father; We have erred, and strayed from thy ways like lost sheep. We have followed too much the devices and desires of our own hearts. We have offended against thy holy laws. We have left undone those things which we ought to have done; And we have done those things which we ought not to have done; And there is no health in us. But thou, O Lord, have mercy upon us, miserable offenders. Spare thou them, O God, which confess their faults. Restore thou them that are penitent; According to thy promises declared unto mankind in Christ Jesu our Lord. And grant, O most merciful Father, for his sake; That we may hereafter live a godly, righteous, and sober life, To the glory of thy holy Name. Amen. (Book of Common Prayer, General Confession)

What do you think? The question

Are all people *equally* sinful?

THE UNIVERSALITY OF SIN

Sin is a disease from which we all suffer. Scripture repeatedly states that all have sinned in one way or another; no one is exempt. In Romans 1:18—3:20 Paul develops an argument for the universality of sin, reaching the conclusion that 'all have sinned and fall short of the glory of God' (3:23). We sin not just from time to time, but consistently throughout our lives. We cannot escape from it and the whole of human nature is affected by sin:

- **Our reason**. Ephesians 4:17: 'Now this I say and testify in the Lord, that you must no longer walk as the Gentiles do, in the futility of their minds.'

- **Our will**. John 8:34: 'Jesus answered them, "Truly, truly, I say to you, everyone who commits sin is a slave to sin."'
- **Our emotions**, feelings and every other part of our makeup are affected by sin.

This is the original meaning of the potentially misleading term 'total depravity' – not that there is no goodness left in people, nor that we are as bad as we could possibly be, but that every part of us is to some extent spoiled and tainted by sin.

So serious is the situation that what we need is a heart transplant: 'I will give you a new heart, and a new spirit I will put within you. And I will remove the heart of stone from your flesh and give you a heart of flesh' (Ezek. 36:26). The drastic nature of the cure indicates the seriousness of the disease. The root of sin lies in the heart, yet we conceal it both from others and from ourselves. 'The heart is deceitful above all things, and desperately sick; who can understand it?' (Jer. 17:9). There is a science fiction story in which an invention brings it about that everyone can read everyone else's mind. The result is that no two people can bear to be with each other and the human race faces extinction. More mundanely, how many people could face the world if all of their thoughts from the last 24 hours were publicly broadcast?

Psychology confirms this capacity of the heart, showing that the majority of mental life is subconscious. What we are aware of is only the tip of the iceberg, the 10 per cent that is above the surface. From time to time nasty things rise up into our conscious minds. Sometimes we find ourselves thinking or even saying things that shock us and are inclined to ask, 'Where did that come from?' The things that we do spontaneously can serve to reveal to us the reality that lies beneath the surface. As Jesus put it, 'From within, out of the heart of man, come evil thoughts, sexual immorality, theft, murder, adultery, coveting, wickedness, deceit, sensuality, envy, slander, pride, foolishness' (Mark 7:21–22). I can vouch for the accuracy of this.

This shows us what the fallen human heart is really like. The same point is made in a secular psychology book by Robert Simon, entitled *Bad Men Do What Good Men Dream*[4] – and the bad news for women is that he is using 'man' in the inclusive sense of human being, not just males! In a much quoted passage, Stephen Pinker describes how he came to reject a naïve view of human goodness.

> When law enforcement vanishes, all manner of violence breaks out: looting, settling old scores, ethnic cleansing, and petty warfare among gangs, warlords and mafias. This was obvious in the remnants of Yugoslavia, the Soviet Union, and parts of Africa in the 1990s, but can also happen in countries with a long tradition of civility. As a young teenager in proudly peaceable Canada during the romantic 1960s, I was a true believer in Bakunin's anarchism. I laughed off my parents' argument that if the government ever laid down its arms all hell would break loose. Our competing predictions were put to the test at 8:00 A.M. on October 17, 1969, when the Montreal police went on strike. By 11:20 A.M. the first bank was robbed. By noon most downtown stores had closed because of looting. Within a few more hours, taxi drivers burned down the garage of a limousine service that had

competed with them for airport customers, a rooftop sniper killed a provincial police officer, rioters broke into several hotels and restaurants, and a doctor slew a burglar in his suburban home. By the end of the day, six banks had been robbed, a hundred shops had been looted, twelve fires had been set, forty carloads of storefront glass had been broken, and three million dollars in property damage had been inflicted, before city authorities had to call in the army and, of course, the Mounties to restore order. This decisive empirical test left my politics in tatters (and offered a foretaste of life as a scientist).[5]

In the UK there was a similar experience with the riots that took place in the summer of 2011.

Credal statement

> If anyone denies that it is the whole person, that is both body and soul, that was 'changed for the worse' through the offence of Adam's sin, but believes that the freedom of the soul remains unimpaired and that only the body is subject to corruption, he is deceived by the error of Pelagius. (*Council of Orange (529), canon 1)

Fallen human nature has a bias to sin and is enslaved to it. We are in bondage to sin:

- Romans 8:7–8: 'The mind that is set on the flesh is hostile to God, for it does not submit to God's law; indeed, it cannot. Those who are in the flesh cannot please God.'
- John 8:34: 'Everyone who commits sin is a slave to sin.'

We cannot avoid sin – it is not something that we can just give up for Lent. This is not to say that one cannot resist particular temptations, just that we are not capable of avoiding sin altogether. After all, even the alcoholic can sometimes decline a drink. The three traditional sources of temptation are the world, the flesh and the devil. All three are named in Ephesians 2:1–3:

> You were dead in the trespasses and sins in which you once walked, following the course of *this world*, following *the prince of the power of the air*, the spirit that is now at work in the sons of disobedience – among whom we all once lived in *the passions of our flesh*, carrying out the desires of the body and the mind.

As the final phrase indicates 'flesh' indicates sinful human nature, whether or not physical.

Many of our natural desires have become inordinate (excessive) or disordered (wrongly directed). The desire for and enjoyment of food is a good gift of God's creation; gluttony is a perversion of this into an inordinate desire. The desire for and enjoyment of sleep is a good gift of God's creation; sloth is a perversion of this into an inordinate desire. The desire for and enjoyment of sex is a good gift of God's creation; sexual immorality/paedophilia is the perversion of this into an inordinate/disordered desire. Without these natural desires we would be in danger of starving, dying of exhaustion or failing to propagate ourselves, but unfortunately in our present sinful state these desires have become inordinate and disordered. The fact that we need to wear clothes in public is testimony to the inordinate nature of our desires. One profession that knows all about human lusts is the advertising industry, which knows how to exploit them to sell products.

We are not all tempted by the same sins. As someone once put it, some men have no more desire to sleep with another man's wife than to brush their teeth with his toothbrush! We are all to some extent enslaved to particular lusts, to inordinate and disordered desires. The classic trio is money, sex and power. Each of these is valid and necessary in its proper place. After all, you would not be reading this book without sex – that is, unless your parents had indulged! Many people suffer from some sort of addiction – whether to drugs, alcohol, pornography, chocolate, work, shopping . . . Some of these (such as chocolate) are 'respectable' and people can even boast of their addiction; others (such as pornography) are not respectable and people go to pains to hide their addiction.

It is important to distinguish between natural desires (which are good, God-given and proper) and lusts or inordinate desires. *Calvin contrasts the inordinate lusts of the ungodly with the manner in which the godly may seek the same things:

> Although the faithful also desire and seek after their worldly comforts, yet they do not pursue them with immoderate and irregular ardour; but can patiently bear to be deprived of them, provided they know themselves to be objects of the divine care. (*Commentary on Psalms* 4:7)

One might say that our desires become inordinate and lustful when we seek ultimate satisfaction outside of God.

Tension to hold

We need to hold in tension two different truths taught in Scripture. On the one hand, Scripture teaches that we are all sinners, we have all fallen short of the glory of God (Rom. 3:23). If we forget this truth we can easily become arrogant, like the Pharisee in the parable in Luke 18:11–12:

> The Pharisee, standing by himself, prayed thus: 'God, I thank you that I am not like other men, extortioners, unjust, adulterers, or even like this tax collector. I fast twice a week; I give tithes of all that I get.'

On the other hand, Scripture distinguishes between the righteous and sinners, as for example in Psalm 1:1, 5–6:

> Blessed is the man who walks not in the counsel of the wicked, nor stands in the way of sinners, nor sits in the seat of scoffers . . . Therefore the wicked will not stand in the judgement, nor sinners in the congregation of the righteous; for the LORD knows the way of the righteous, but the way of the wicked will perish.

It is important to maintain both sides of this tension. Without the first point (the universality of sin) the righteous are tempted to look down on 'sinners' and despise them. But without the second point (the contrast between righteous and sinners) we end up with a moral relativism, where there is nothing to choose between a Stalin and a Mother Teresa. As someone once put it, 'We are all of the same mould, but some are mouldier than others!'

What do you think? My answer

Are all people *equally* sinful? All equally, without exception, have sinned, but that does not mean that all have sinned equally, to the same extent. All are sinners, but there remains a distinction between the righteous and sinners. Furthermore, not all sin is equal before God and the Bible contains many distinctions between different types of sin. For example:

- unintentional sin versus defiant sin (Num. 15:27–31);
- sins of ignorance versus deliberate sins (Luke 12:47–48);
- light versus grave sins (John 19:11);
- sins that do not lead to death versus those that do (1 John 5:16–17);
- different sins leading to differing degrees of judgement (Mark 12:40).

In the Sermon on the Mount Jesus compared lust to adultery: 'You have heard that it was said, "You shall not commit adultery." But I say to you that everyone who looks at a woman with lustful intent has already committed adultery with her in her heart' (Matt. 5:27–28). He similarly compared anger to murder (5:21–22). It is important to be clear what Jesus is saying. Lust in the heart is sinful, but clearly to go on to commit the deed is worse. If anyone really believed that to commit murder was no worse than to be angry with someone, you would do best not to meet with that person without a bodyguard! There are those who deny this and say that the deed is no worse than the thought. It may be significant that one person I knew who argued for that view subsequently went on to commit the deed of adultery, presumably encouraged by the thought that this was no worse than his previous sin of lust.

CORPORATE SIN

Sin is not solely individual, but is also corporate. Scripture often refers to national sin and the guilt that flows from it:

- Ezra confesses and associates himself with the sins of the nation (9:6–15): 'O my God, I am ashamed and blush to lift my face to you, my God, for our iniquities have risen higher than our heads, and our guilt has mounted up to the heavens' (v. 6).
- Isaiah in the presence of God identifies himself with the sins of the nation: 'Woe is me! For I am lost; for I am a man of unclean lips, and I dwell in the midst of a people of unclean lips' (6:5).

So also today, the sins of nations can lead to judgement. Sin can be found in the structures of society as well as in individuals. One only has to think of the slave trade, the Holocaust, Communism, Apartheid or the abortion industry. During the 'troubles' in Northern Ireland there was much violence including murder. As someone put it, it was not that Ulster had been hit by a crime wave. People were caught up in rival causes and those who might otherwise have led law-abiding lives indulged in violence. This was the action of individuals, but they were not merely making personal choices: they were involved in a system. Reducing all sin to personal individual choices is an error of Western individualism. While there has of late been a relative neglect of the doctrine of sin among Evangelicals, one positive change is a greater willingness to take seriously the corporate and social dimension of sin, rather than viewing it in purely individual terms. Just as there is a corporate dimension to sin, the same is true of sanctification, as we shall see in Chapter 21.

Sceptic's corner

Why is there so much judgement in the Bible?

Answer: Today many pride themselves that society has become non-judgemental. What they mean is that almost any sexual activity other than paedophilia is now regarded as acceptable. In other areas, though, we have become increasingly judgemental. Even factually correct statements can lay people open to the accusation of racism. In 2012 in the UK a gang of Asian men in Rochdale were finally convicted for sustained sexual abuse of underage white teenage girls. For some time the police had declined to act on this for fear of being accused of racism. Second, in 2005 Lawrence H. Summers, president of Harvard University, drew attention to the fact that in maths and science tests, more males earn the very top scores, as well as the very bottom scores. He merely suggested that further research was needed to determine whether this had a biological basis.[6] There was considerable opposition from the faculty and Summers was accused of sexism. The next year he resigned.[7]

Many today speak of a God who is loving and affirming but never condemns anyone. But God is our heavenly Father rather than Grandfather – the difference being that grandparents can spoil children whereas parents have the responsibility for discipline. 'God is love' (1 John 4:8, 16); but equally, 'God is light, and in him is no darkness at all' (1 John 1:5). It is because God loves righteousness that he cannot tolerate evil. In Romans 12:9 the command to 'Let love be genuine' is immediately followed by the command 'Abhor what is evil.' True love of the good must include the hatred of evil.

Sin has effects or consequences. 'Can a man carry fire next to his chest and his clothes not be burned?' (Prov. 6:27). The trouble is that people often do not want to hear this:

> They are a rebellious people, lying children, children unwilling to hear the instruction of the LORD; who say to the seers, 'Do not see,' and to the prophets, 'Do not prophesy to us what is right; speak to us smooth things, prophesy illusions, leave the way, turn aside from the path, let us hear no more about the Holy One of Israel' (Isa. 30:9–11).

EFFECTS OF SIN (CCC 399–401)

The effects of sin are manifest. Some examples are:

1 **Bondage**. We have already considered how sin leads to bondage to sin.
2 **Blindness**. Sin deceives us and blinds us to the truth. To commit sin is bad but to approve it as if it is good is worse. Paul concludes his (highly relevant to today) catalogue of the sins of the Gentile world in Romans 1:24–32 with 'Though they know God's decree that those who practise such things deserve to die, they not only do them but give approval to those who practise them.' Jeremiah refers to those who do not even know how to blush: 'Were they ashamed when they committed abomination? No, they were not at all ashamed; they did not know how to blush' (6:15 = 8:12).

This charge can be true of different sins in different societies. In the 1950s a top hotel in Nairobi had a sign saying, 'No dogs or blacks beyond this point'. Younger people today find it hard to believe that could have happened. By contrast, today almost any sexual activity is acceptable, in a way that would have disgusted most people in the 1950s.

3 **Guilt**. Sin makes us guilty and liable to punishment. The Suffering Servant of Isaiah 53 comes to make an offering for guilt (v. 10).
4 **God's wrath**. Sin provokes God's holy displeasure and indignation. Many query this today, but is it conceivable that God can view the rape and murder of a small child without any displeasure or indignation? If so, it would only prove that he did not care. The opposite of wrath is not love but indifference.[8] On the other hand, Scripture repeatedly affirms that God is slow to anger (e.g. Exod. 34:6). As *Luther pointed out, judgement is God's 'alien work' (Isa. 28:21), not something he enjoys, as with the parent forced to discipline a child. Also, God's wrath is pure, holy and loving, not like our human anger – we need here the 'negative way' described in Chapter 3.
5 **Judgement and punishment**. God hates sin and brings it into judgement, both now and at the End. In the Old Testament the prophets pronounced judgement on the nations and on the people of God. Both Israel and Judah were sent into exile. There is also judgement on individuals, such as David after Bathsheba (2 Sam. 12:1–14) and Ananias and Sapphira (Acts 5:1–11). Finally there will be judgement at the End, on which see Chapter 28.
6 **Death**. 'The wages of sin is death' (Rom. 6:23), both as a natural outworking and as a punishment imposed by God. Sin leads to physical death, to spiritual death (alienation from God) and to eternal death (final separation from God).

7 Alienation. In Genesis 3 we see the different ways in which sin alienates us:

(a) from God: 'And they heard the sound of the LORD God walking in the garden in the cool of the day, and the man and his wife hid themselves from the presence of the LORD God among the trees of the garden' (3:8);

(b) from one another: 'The man said, "The woman whom you gave to be with me, she gave me fruit of the tree, and I ate"' (3:12);

(c) from ourselves: 'Then the eyes of both were opened, and they knew that they were naked. And they sewed fig leaves together and made themselves loincloths' (3:7), introducing the idea of shame;

(d) from creation: 'Cursed is the ground because of you; in pain you shall eat of it all the days of your life' (3:17–19) – back to the ground elder!

PRAYER

Almighty God, our heavenly Father, we have sinned against you and against our neighbour in thought and word and deed, through negligence, through weakness, through our own deliberate fault. We are truly sorry and repent of all our sins. For the sake of your Son Jesus Christ, who died for us, forgive us all that is past and grant that we may serve you in newness of life to the glory of your name. Amen. (*Common Worship*, Holy Communion)

Question to answer

- What are the effects of sin?

NOTES

1 Cf. T. D. Alexander et al. (eds) *New Dictionary of Biblical Theology*. Leicester: IVP, 2000, 781–88.

2 For one such extreme example, see <http://news.bbc.co.uk/1/hi/health/2345971.stm>.

3 For a warning of the danger of this, see A. McGrath *Evangelicalism and the Future of Christianity*. London: Hodder & Stoughton, 1994, 190–92.

4 R. I. Simon *Bad Men Do What Good Men Dream*. Washington, DC: American Psychiatric Press, 1996.

5 S. Pinker *The Blank Slate: The Modern Denial of Human Nature*. London: Penguin, 2002, 331.

6 <http://www.boston.com/news/education/higher/articles/2005/01/19/harvard_womens_group_rips_summers/?page=full>.

7 <http://en.wikipedia.org/wiki/Lawrence_Summers#President_of_Harvard>.

8 For more on this, see A. N. S. Lane 'The Wrath of God as an Aspect of the Love of God' in K. Vanhoozer (ed.) *Nothing Greater, Nothing Better*. Grand Rapids: Eerdmans, 2001, 138–67.

RESOURCES

T. D. Cooper *Sin, Pride & Self-Acceptance*. Downers Grove: IVP, 2003.

D. R. Davies *Down Peacock's Feathers*. London: Centenary Press, 1942.

A. N. S. Lane 'Lust', *Evangelical Quarterly* 78 (2006) 21–35.

C. Plantinga *Not the Way It's Supposed to Be: A Breviary of Sin*. Grand Rapids: Eerdmans, 1995.

Chapter 8

THE FALL AND ORIGINAL SIN

Aims of this chapter

In this chapter we examine the doctrines of the Fall and original sin, asking:

- Where does sin come from?
- What is original sin?
- Do we have free will?
- Are children innocent?
- Does Genesis 3 describe an actual event?

PROCEDURE

You may ask why in the last chapter we started with the fact of sin and are only now considering original sin and the Fall. Surely the reverse order (Fall, original sin, sin) would make more sense as this keeps to both the chronological and the logical order, moving from cause to effect. For this reason, starting with the Fall has been the traditional order of proceeding, found both in works of theology and in credal statements, but I would suggest that it is the wrong order (especially today), for three reasons:

1 Scripture frequently proclaims the fact of human sin, but says relatively little about the origin of sin in the Fall. Genesis 3 and Romans 5 are the main passages that speak of the Fall and apart from these there are only a few isolated statements. Even in Romans, Paul first, at some length (1:18–3:20), establishes the universality of human sin and only later, in the context of Christ's work, turns to the origin of sin in Adam's Fall (5:12–21). In Scripture the fact and universality of sin are the primary concern while the doctrines of the Fall and original sin are relatively secondary and rarely mentioned. To start with the fact of sin before moving on to the Fall and original sin is, therefore, to follow the emphasis of Scripture.

2 The reality of sin is clear in everyday life, while the doctrines of the Fall and original sin are less evident. *Pascal aptly described original sin as a great mystery:

> Nothing jolts us more rudely than this doctrine [of original sin], and yet, but for this mystery, the most incomprehensible of all, we remain incomprehensible to ourselves. The knot of our condition was twisted and turned in that abyss, so that it is harder to conceive of man without this mystery than for man to conceive of it himself. (*Pensées*, 131)

It is a sound principle always to work from that which is plain to that which is obscure, not the other way round. Following this principle it makes sense to start from the doctrine of sin, which is relatively plain, and to move on to examine the more obscure doctrines of the Fall and original sin.

3 The first two reasons apply in any generation, the third relates to the last 150 years in particular. The twentieth century produced ample evidence for the fact of human sin. This was partly because of the evils perpetuated in that century and partly because, unlike previous centuries, so much of it was recorded on film and broadcast on TV. Americans experienced the horrors of the Vietnam war in their own living rooms, while most civilians in the First World War had no idea of what was happening in the trenches. The idea of original sin, that we are all born with a bias towards sin, is much more plausible today than it once was. But since Darwin and the idea that humanity is the product of a process of evolution over millions of years, the concept of a Fall has become more problematic.

Accordingly, having considered the universality of sin in the previous chapter we will now move on to consider next the doctrine of original sin and then, finally, the question of the Fall.

PART I: ORIGINAL SIN (CCC 388–89, 402–409, 415–19)

The doctrine of original sin proclaims that babies are born not morally pure or neutral but with an inbuilt bias to sin. Sin is not purely an individual matter but the human race corporately has taken a wrong turn.

Pelagius, a fifth-century monk from the British Isles, denied this, arguing that babies were born pure, without any bias towards sin, learning to sin from their environment and by example. Against this *Augustine maintained that we all fell in Adam, that we all sinned in him and that as a result children are born in bondage to sin and to lust. It should perhaps be pointed out that Pelagius was an unmarried monk, whereas Augustine had experience of parenthood! Augustine was the first to expound the doctrine of original sin at length, though he did not invent the doctrine. Pelagius's teaching is regarded as heresy by almost all churches.

> All who deny this, call it 'original sin,' or by any other title, are but heathens still in the fundamental point which differences Heathenism from Christianity. (*John Wesley, *Sermon on Original Sin* 3:2)

Augustine's teaching or variants of it were held in the West until the eighteenth century. Then the Enlightenment seriously

© Miriam Kendrick 2013 www.miriamkendrick.co.uk

challenged the idea of original sin and an 'optimistic' view of human nature emerged, that children were not born with sin in their nature. There was no major war in Europe between the exile of Napoleon in 1815 and the outbreak of the First World War in 1914 (though Europeans were busy fighting elsewhere in the world and the French and Prussians had a brief spat) and it was easy to imagine that humanity had progressed to a higher level. Nineteenth-century Liberal theology also had little concept of the inherent sinfulness of fallen human nature. These denials of original sin were of course strengthened by the rise of Darwinianism, which offered an alternative explanation for the evil in the world. Nineteenth-century optimism took a hammering in the twentieth century and it has been said, with pardonable exaggeration: 'Our grandfathers in their simplicity found it hard, if not impossible, to believe in Original sin; it is not so with us; perhaps among the traditional dogmas this one alone can now be accepted as almost self-evident.'[1] As a result, the doctrine of original sin began to be taken seriously again, through the work of theologians such as *Karl Barth and *Reinhold Niebuhr, who spelt out the effects of sin on human culture and civilization. But whereas original sin has to some extent made a come-back, the idea of a historical Fall is still widely questioned in the light of evolutionary theory.[2]

Credal statement

It is also taught among us that since the fall of Adam all men who are born according to the course of nature are conceived and born in sin. That is, all men are full of evil lust and inclinations from their mothers' wombs and are unable by nature to have true fear of God and true faith in God. (*Augsburg Confession (1530), art. 2)

Sceptic's corner

Does it make any sense to talk of a baby being sinful?

Answer: Undoubtedly there is a *relative* innocence in children. They have as yet committed few personal sins and they are not yet hardened in sin, but they also have an inherent tendency to sin and before long this will bear fruit. We have an inbuilt tendency to be sentimental about the very young, but although baby scorpions may look cute they grow into adult scorpions. Likewise human babies are also baby sinners. Children may have a relative innocence but there is also (in boys in particular) an original brutality (leading to bullying, for example) that has to be trained out. I have personally had the experience of spending some time in a concentration camp (a boys' boarding school) and I have no doubt about the total depravity of all males! When I was about 5 years old my mother took me to see cowboy films and I remember how shocked I was to hear that the people who were shot had not really been killed – and how scandalized I was to hear that not even the Indians were killed! Steven Pinker summarizes it well:

The most violent age is not adolescence but toddlerhood . . . The question . . . we've been trying to answer for the last 30 years is how do children learn to aggress. [But] that's the wrong question. The right question is how do they learn not to aggress.[3]

The same point is made by William Golding in his classic novel *Lord of the Flies* (1954).

This has implications for child rearing and education. Until the Enlightenment, the goal was to curb evil; since then it has increasingly been to nurture the goodness inherent in human nature. Clearly this is not a simple either–or matter and there is a role for both sides – but whereas earlier generations may have overemphasized the negative side and neglected the positive, there is no doubt that today the pendulum has swung heavily in the other direction.

> Ignorance of the fact that man has a wounded nature inclined to evil gives rise to serious errors in the areas of education, politics, social action and morals. (*CCC 407)

ORIGINAL SIN AS PARADOX

The doctrine of original sin can be stated in terms of a paradox. This can be expressed in various ways:

- Sin is inevitable; yet it is nevertheless our responsibility.
- We are enslaved to sin and in bondage to it; yet we choose it freely.
- Sin is universal; yet it is our personal choice.

FREE WILL?

People often boldly proclaim that the Bible teaches free will, but the term never appears in Scripture. Before deciding whether or not we have free will we need to distinguish between various different meanings of the term:

1 Most people assume that free will refers to indeterminacy or unpredictability, sometimes called 'libertarian' free will. With this type of free will we can go either way. Personally I like both cheesecake and Black Forest gateau and if offered a choice between these I cannot predict in advance which I would choose – it is unpredictable. This is how the situation of Adam and Eve before the Fall has traditionally been understood. They were able to sin and able not to sin. The outcome could not be predicted. As fallen sinners, by contrast, we cannot avoid sin completely. If unpredictability is what is meant by free will, God does not have it. We need not worry that tomorrow he might change his mind and become evil.

Tension to hold
ORIGINAL SIN AS PARADOX

Logically there is a problem with these pairs, but we cannot (or at least should not!) deny either side. Both are taught by Scripture. Furthermore, both accord with our human experience. Sin is a statistical certainty. When a baby is born we might ask, 'Is it a boy or a girl?' but we do not ask, 'Will she grow up to be a sinner?' We know the answer. Yet even though it is inevitable that we will all sin, we are also held responsible for our behaviour. This statistical certainty and our responsibility for sin are both clear in Scripture and both also accord with human experience.

Almost everyone would agree at least that other people fall short of what they should be. At the same time we treat people as responsible for their behaviour. The paradox accords with the complexities of real life. As a graffito once put it, 'Don't adjust your sets, the fault lies with reality.' Of course it is true that different people have different opportunities in life, but these do not fully determine our actions; we retain free will. Some academics may write against the reality of human responsibility, but it is unlikely that they will live their private lives according to this theory.

2 There is also the perfect freedom of being unchangeably good. God is free in this sense in that he is perfectly good. Clearly we do not yet enjoy this freedom, but we will have it in the Age to Come. Then there will be no more sin and no more danger of sin. Our union with Christ is 'so that we would no longer be enslaved to sin' (Rom. 6:6). The prayer of St *Chrysostom in the Anglican liturgy refers to God, 'whose service is perfect freedom'. To serve God, to be totally committed to the good, is the ultimate freedom.

3 According to the final meaning of free will, which we can call free choice, there are areas where our behaviour is not unpredictable but we still choose freely. Faced with a choice between a cat or a dog as a pet, I will inevitably choose a cat. It is a genuinely free choice, but also completely predictable. Likewise whenever curry is served at lunch I invariably go for the non-spice alternative. It is a free choice, but totally predictable. In the same way sinners sin inevitably, but voluntarily; it is of their own free choice, not because of external coercion. As fallen sinners we are in bondage to sin not in the way that a hostage may be held prisoner by terrorists against her will, but in the way that an addict is enslaved but still acts of his own choice. Sin controls us from within, not in the way that a puppet's movements are imposed externally.

As originally created Adam and Eve were able to sin and able not to sin. They had both free choice and indeterminacy. As fallen sinners we are not able not to sin; we have lost indeterminacy, but not free choice. While we can to some extent choose whether or not to commit *particular* sins, we cannot avoid sin completely. In the Age to Come we will attain the perfect freedom of being unchangeably good and will not be able to sin. This entails no loss of free choice because we will no longer *want* to sin. The inability to sin will not be like the inability of the smoker to smoke when deprived of cigarettes.

Credal statement

1 God hath endued the will of man with that natural liberty, that it is neither forced, nor by any absolute necessity of nature determined to good or evil.
2 Man, in his state of innocency, had freedom and power to will and to do that which is good and well-pleasing to God; but yet mutably, so that he might fall from it.
3 Man, by his Fall into a state of sin, hath wholly lost all ability of will to any spiritual good accompanying salvation; so as a natural man, being altogether averse from that good, and dead in sin, is not able, by his own strength, to convert himself, or to prepare himself thereunto.
4 When God converts a sinner, and translates him into the state of grace, He frees him from his natural bondage under sin; and, by His grace alone, enables him freely to will and to do that which is spiritually good; yet so, as that by reason of his remaining corruption, he does not perfectly, or only, will that which is good, but does also will that which is evil.
5 The will of man is made perfectly and immutably free to good alone, in the state of glory only.

(*Westminster Confession of Faith* (1647), ch. 9)

ORIGINAL GUILT

'Original sin' usually refers to the idea that we are born with a bias towards sin, a doctrine that is very widely held; 'original guilt' refers to the idea that we are born with some measure of guilt, a more controversial doctrine. Clearly the newborn are not guilty of any personal sins, but is there a corporate guilt of the human race? Another way of looking at this is to ask whether Christ died for all or only for those who reach a certain age. Did Christ die for the stillborn?[4]

What do you think? The question

Does it *matter* whether Genesis 3 describes an actual event?

PART 2: THE FALL (CCC 390, 396–98)

There are two ways of viewing Genesis 3:

- as a *mirror* in which we see what we now are;
- as a *window* through which we see the past cause of our present plight.

There is no doubt that Genesis 3 sheds light on how we are today tempted to sin, but to limit it to that is to miss out a major part of its significance within the narrative of Genesis. In chapters 1 and 2 we have a world which is good and indeed 'very good' (1:31). Yet by Genesis 4 we see brother killing brother. That is bad and very bad. So what has gone wrong?

The answer is to be found in Genesis 3. Adam and Eve turned away from God and for this there were consequences. It does not matter whether every detail (e.g. the snake) is taken literally. As previously stated, I would see these chapters neither as literal scientific history nor as myth, but rather as an account of human origins in figurative language.[5] What does matter is that this refers to an actual event where the human race turned against God. Paul sees it as pivotal in Romans 5:12–21 and 1 Corinthians 15:21–22: 'For as by a man came death, by a man has come also the resurrection of the dead. For as in Adam all die, so also in Christ shall all be made alive.' So Genesis 3 is not just a mirror but also a window onto something that happened in history.

There is another way to approach this question. Why is it that all people grow up to be sinners? What are the options?

1 **It is a coincidence**. But it is not credible that billions of people have all by coincidence made the same choice. The biblical and Christian doctrine of sin is not that by a strange coincidence all just happened to have sinned but that this is inevitable and predictable.
2 **God made us that way**. In that case we are not responsible. It is because of the way that we are created that we breathe and grow hair. That is not something for which we feel personally responsible – it is just how we are made. The responsibility is God's rather than ours. But sin is not like that.
3 **Sin is a hangover from our evolutionary origins**. This again removes our responsibility.
4 **God made us good but the human race turned away from God to sin** – as portrayed in Genesis 3. This establishes *human* responsibility rather than God's – but I can still object that it is not *my* fault. We can blame it on Adam and Eve. This objection is especially powerful in a culture imbued with modern Western individualism. It is worth bearing in mind that in many other cultures this is not seen as a problem. We cannot help the fact that we live in one particular culture, but we must not fall into the mistake of absolutizing this culture as if it were the final truth by which all else, including Christian revelation, must be judged.

Modern Westerners tend to see themselves as independent individuals, as if the human race were like a collection of stones on a beach. A better analogy might be to see ourselves like apples on a tree – clearly distinct from one another but inseparably interconnected. Paul describes Christians as organs in a body (1 Cor. 12:12–27). The Western emphasis upon individual rights and responsibilities has brought many benefits, but has also had negative effects on society. We need to recognize that there is a corporate as well as an individual side to sin and responsibility. There is such a thing as national guilt – as well as national pride. And if sin and guilt were totally individual, where would that leave Christ's death for our sins?

> No man is an Island, entire of itself; every man is a piece of the Continent, a part of the main . . . any man's death diminishes me, because I am involved in Mankind; And therefore never send to know for whom the bell tolls; it tolls for thee.
> (John Donne, *Meditation* 17)

Sceptic's corner

Surely modern science has ruled out the possibility of the Fall as an actual event?

Answer: There is a widespread traditional view that Adam and Eve were created morally perfect and immortal and lived in a perfect world. The Garden of Eden becomes like the lost city of Atlantis, the scene of a primitive culture of great value. Such a picture does indeed clash with modern science – but is it what the Bible teaches? In fact this view owes more to tradition than to Scripture.

We can consider the different points in turn:

1 The idea of a perfect world conflicts with Tennyson's portrayal of 'nature red in tooth and claw'.[6] But while Genesis portrays the world as very good (1:31), it does not say that it was perfect. Furthermore, there are hints in Genesis 3 itself that evil has entered God's good world. Eve was tempted by the serpent, who was clearly in opposition to God. Human sin was not the first rebellion against the Creator in the universe. The serpent is later identified as Satan, in Revelation 12:9, 20:2. Adam and Eve were expelled from the garden. Are we to understand by this that paradisal conditions were at that time confined to the garden? Genesis 2:8 and 3:23 could be taken to imply that. There are certainly no grounds for dogmatically stating that the whole world was at that stage perfect.

It is not the Bible that tells us that animals were pacifists and vegetarians before the Fall. Isaiah 11:6–9 and other passages present a picture of harmony and peace in the animal kingdom, but this is a vision of the End, not the beginning. Apart from *Origen, no Christian theologian of stature has fallen into the mistake of supposing that the End will simply be a restoration of the beginning. A comparison of Genesis 1—2 with Revelation 21—22 shows that the End far excels the beginning. The ability not to sin will be replaced by the inability to sin.

2 Before the Fall, Adam and Eve were not yet morally perfect. They were on trial. They had not yet sinned, but nor had they yet learned obedience. Their state was that of being able not to sin.

They had not reached the state of not being able to sin. Had they reached it, the Fall would have been impossible! It is therefore wrong to think of Adam and Eve as falling from a great moral height. Rather, they were setting out on a path of moral testing and at an early stage they took a wrong turn.

The serpent promised that Adam and Eve would become 'like God, knowing good and evil' (v. 5). This was no idle boast since according to the statement of God himself that is exactly what did happen (v. 22). What does this mean?[7] It cannot mean omniscience, as some interpreters suggest, since that was manifestly not the outcome of the Fall – as students taking exams know all too well. Nor can it mean the *experience* of doing both good and evil, since God does not have that. It must mean moral autonomy and independence, setting oneself up as one's own judge of what is right and wrong. This is precisely what Adam and Eve did. The serpent challenged them to become like God by setting themselves up as their own arbiters of good and evil, in opposition to God. This is the essence of sin – setting oneself up against God. Thus the first sin was a declaration of moral independence, a premature step into adult independence, a wrong turning which took us forward in the wrong direction rather than a fall from a state of perfection already achieved.

3 Were human beings immortal before the Fall? Genesis 3 and Romans 5 both blame death on the Fall. How can this be squared with an evolutionary account of the origins of life? It is important to note what Genesis does and does not say. Death is the penalty of sin, but it is not stated that Adam was immortal before

he sinned. Clearly he was not, since by definition an immortal being cannot die! Rather, he had access to the tree of life and this access was denied to him after his sin. What Adam and Eve had was the *potential* of *future* immortality, through the tree of life – and they lost this by sinning. It will be clear that this picture does not clash with an evolutionary picture of human origins. Immortality is portrayed by Genesis as something that was held before us, which we never attained. There is no need to postulate an immortal state of unfallen humanity. Genesis is at this point compatible with a picture of humanity emerging from a brutish origin.

4 Another issue is whether the whole human race is descended from a single pair, Adam and Eve. Traditionally Christians have argued that this is so and the Bible can easily be read this way.[8] On the other hand, Genesis 4 implies that Cain left his family to confront other people and refers to him building a city. The current scientific evidence supports the idea that the human population was low at certain stages, but not that the human race is descended from a single pair.[9]

What do you think? My answer

If we bear these four points (continued overleaf) in mind we have a picture of conditions before the Fall that are not in conflict with the scientific evidence. All that is necessary for the doctrine of the Fall is that human beings were created good but turned aside from God. It is hard to see how *any* scientific evidence could ever disprove that.

What about 1 Corinthians 15:22: 'as in Adam all die, so also in Christ shall all be made alive'? Adam's role has often been seen as 'federal headship', which does not necessarily involve our direct physical descent from him. And, clearly, there is no question of physical descent from Christ.

Worship

In Adam all must die,
forlorn and unforgiven;
in Christ we come alive,
the second Man from heaven.
(David Mowbray, 'Now lives the Lamb of God')

PRAYER

O Lord God, eternal and almighty Father, we acknowledge and sincerely confess before your Holy Majesty that we are miserable sinners, conceived and born in guilt and sin, prone to iniquity, and incapable of any good work, and that in our depravity we make no end of transgressing your commandments . . . Nevertheless, O Lord, we anxiously lament that we have offended you, and we condemn ourselves and our faults with true repentance, asking you to succour our wretchedness by your grace. Deign, then, O most gracious and most merciful God and Father, to bestow your mercy upon us in the name of Jesus Christ your Son our Lord.
(*Calvin, *Forms of Prayer for the Church in Geneva*)

Questions to answer

- What is original sin?
- Does Genesis 3 describe an actual event?

NOTES

1 A. G. Smith writing in 1954, quoted by J. H. Walgrave in T. F. Torrance (ed.) *The Incarnation*. Edinburgh: Handsel Press, 1981, 153.

2 Augustine's view that original sin is passed on by the lust involved in sexual intercourse has very little support today. Original sin should not be thought of as involving any change in DNA.

3 S. Pinker *The Blank Slate: The Modern Denial of Human Nature*. London: Penguin, 2002, 316, quoting R. Tremblay.

4 Augustine held that those who died in infancy would be lost unless they had been baptized, but there would be very few people today who would tie the salvation of infants so closely to baptism. See, e.g., CCC 1261.

5 For an excellent account of this, see H. Blocher *In the Beginning*, Leicester: IVP, 1984.

6 Tennyson, *In Memoriam A.H.H.* 56.

7 See Blocher, *In the Beginning* 126–33 on the meaning of the phrase. See also C. Westermann *Genesis 1–11. A Commentary*. London: SPCK, 1984, 240–48; V. P. Hamilton *The Book of Genesis Chapters 1–17*. Grand Rapids: Eerdmans, 1990, 163–66.

8 Contrary to many English translations, the Greek of Acts 17:26 does not say God made the nations from one *man*.

9 F. S. Collins *The Language of God: A Scientist Presents Evidence for Belief*. London: Simon & Schuster, 2007, 126, 206–10.

RESOURCES

H. Blocher *Original Sin*. Leicester: IVP, 1997.

A. Jacobs *Original Sin: A Cultural History*. London: SPCK, 2008.

B. Ramm *Offence to Reason: A Theology of Sin*. San Francisco: Harper & Row, 1985.

M. Shuster *The Fall and Sin: What We have Become as Sinners*. Grand Rapids: Eerdmans, 2004.

Chapter 9

PROVIDENCE

Aims of this chapter

In this chapter we examine God's providence, asking:

- Is God in control of human history?
- What are the benefits of believing in providence?
- How can the doctrine of providence be abused?
- What about free will?
- Does God will evil events?

DOES OUR GOD REIGN?[1]

Traditionally Christians have affirmed that God does indeed reign. This chapter will expound *Calvin's doctrine of providence, as set out in his *Institutes* 1:16–18, which is one version of the traditional doctrine, noting how it differs from other versions. At the end we will examine more briefly a recent radical alternative to this doctrine.

Does God reign? If so, why do tragedies occur, like the recent tsunamis in Asia (26 December 2004) and Japan (11 March 2011)? Were they God's will? Is he in control? We will consider these issues from two different perspectives:

- **Providence** (this chapter): the extent of God's control
- **Theodicy** (next chapter): *why* is there evil? The 'justification of God'.

GOD'S SOVEREIGNTY (CCC 302–305, 321–23)

God created the world and sustains it. He also governs it and works out his purposes through providence, to bring both blessing and judgement. God's providence is not capricious, as it is portrayed in Islam. It is God that reigns, as Scripture repeatedly affirms:

- Psalm 97:1: 'The LORD reigns, let the earth rejoice; let the many coastlands be glad!'
- Ephesians 1:11: God 'works all things according to the counsel of his will'.
- Proverbs 16:9: 'The heart of man plans his way, but the LORD establishes his steps.'
- Proverbs 21:1: 'The king's heart is a stream of water in the hand of the LORD; he turns it wherever he will.'
- Amos 3:6: 'Does disaster come to a city, unless the LORD has done it?'
- Romans 8:28: 'We know that for those who love God all things work together for good, for those who are called according to his purpose.'

As this tiny selection of passages shows, it is God that reigns, not fortune or chance. His control extends to human deeds and political events. Nothing happens outside of God's purposes. This was stated clearly by Calvin:

Not only heaven and earth and the inanimate creatures, but also the plans and intentions of men, are so governed by his providence that they are borne by it straight to their appointed end. (*Institutes* 1:16:8)

Differences emerge when we consider the question of permission. Calvin believed that everything that happens does so because God positively ordained it. He was consistent in extending this to include even Adam's sin – Adam fell because God ordained it. *Augustine, by contrast, held that God positively ordains some things, others (such as Adam's Fall) he allows or permits and then weaves into his plan.

THE BENEFIT OF THE DOCTRINE

Calvin stresses that this doctrine is given to us not for philosophical speculation, but for practical Christian living. If God is in control that means that nothing can hurt us *at random*, but only as God purposes. We should 'fear God and dread nought', a motto derived from the name of the first modern battleship, HMS *Dreadnought*.

Worship

Father, although I cannot see
the future you have planned,
and though the path is sometimes dark
and hard to understand,
yet give me faith, through joy and pain,
to trace your loving hand.
(John Eddison)

Fear Him, ye saints, and you will then
Have nothing else to fear;
Make you His service your delight,
Your wants shall be His care.
(Nahum Tate and Nicholas Brady, 'Through all
the changing scenes of life')

We should see all that happens to us as coming from God. There is biblical precedent for such an attitude:

- Job's response to disaster: 'And he said, "Naked I came from my mother's womb, and naked shall I return. The LORD gave, and the LORD has taken away; blessed be the name of the LORD"' (1:21).
- Joseph's response to being sold into slavery by his brothers:

  And now do not be distressed or angry with yourselves because you sold me here, for God sent me before you to preserve life. For the famine has been in the land these two years, and there are yet five years in which there will be neither ploughing nor harvest. And God sent me before you to preserve for you a remnant on earth, and to keep alive for you many survivors. So it was not you who sent me here, but God. (Gen. 45:5–8)

- Also in Genesis 50:20: 'As for you, you meant evil against me, but God meant it for good, to bring it about that many people should be kept alive, as they are today.'

A similar attitude was taken by some at least of the victims of the 2004 tsunami. This doctrine can be a great comfort to those who are suffering and to those who worry about the uncertainties of life. Nothing can happen to us outside the will of God. There is *no* guarantee that the thing that we most fear will not happen to us – but it will happen to us only if God purposes it. We may be terrified of being bitten by dogs but this will not happen unless God allows it.

Sceptic's corner

How can a good God will disaster?

Answer: We will consider the conflict between suffering and God's goodness further in the next chapter. Accepting disaster from the hand of God is not always easy and it requires faith. The phenomenon of suffering in this life is sometimes compared to a tapestry, of which we can currently see only the reverse side, which is full of loose ends and looks a complete mess. One day we will see the front, where there is a perfect picture, as illustrated in this poem:

THE PLAN OF THE MASTER WEAVER

My life is but a weaving
Between the Lord and me,
I may not choose the colours,
He knows what they should be.

For he can view the pattern
Upon the upper side

© 2013 Miriam Kendrick, www.miriamkendrick.co.uk

90

While I can see it only
On this, the under side.

Sometimes he weaves in sorrow,
Which seemeth strange to me;
But I will trust his judgement,
And work on faithfully;

'Tis he who fills the shuttle,
And he knows what is best,

So I shall weave in earnest,
Leaving to him the rest.

Not till the loom is silent
And shuttles cease to fly,
Will God unroll the canvas
And explain the reason why.

The dark threads are as needed
In the Weaver's skilful hand,

Error to avoid
THE ABUSE OF THE DOCTRINE

The fact that all things come from God should not lead us to neglect either our own role or the role of other people. For instance, it is God who provides for our needs – but he normally does so through our own choices and efforts. Normally it is through our having a job and earning our keep. Sometimes God provides through other people, in which case we should not neglect to be grateful to them. We give thanks to God before a meal – and thank the cook. We thank God for gifts – and thank the giver. Likewise, we should take sensible precautions. In the seventeenth century Oliver Cromwell told his soldiers before a battle to 'Trust God, and keep your powder dry.' This is evidence not (as some secular historians have imagined) of Cromwell's hypocrisy but of a biblical doctrine of providence. Nehemiah's response to the threat of attack was that 'we prayed to our God and set a guard as a protection against them day and night' (Neh. 4:9). Fatalism, the idea that because all is ordained there is no point in making any effort, is not a biblical approach and misunderstands the doctrine of providence.

I once visited the Isle of Lewis, in the Outer Hebrides, where I was told that many deep-sea fishermen cannot even swim. They could fall off their ships in harbour and drown. Apparently their attitude was, 'When it's my time to go, I'll go.' This is fatalism, not a belief in providence. I used to think that this was a consequence of the very strong Calvinism in the Isle of Lewis until I heard of similar attitudes among fishermen in other places – so maybe it is just an occupational hazard! We need to trust God and also do our bit. Planning, saving and insurance policies are all consistent with a trust in providence. It would be a mistake to think that we can abuse the environment as much as we like on the grounds that God will keep us from disaster.

There is the story of the elderly man whose house was threatened by rising floodwater. His neighbours came to take him to safety but he refused, saying, 'God will rescue me.' Later the police came and he gave them the same response. The waters rose and he went up to the first floor. A rescue boat arrived but he refused to go with them, saying 'God will rescue me.' The waters rose and he went onto the roof. A helicopter came to lift him off but he refused, saying, 'God will rescue me.' The waters rose further and he drowned. When he came into the presence of God he cried out, 'Lord, you promised to rescue me!' God replied, 'I sent your neighbours, I sent the police, I sent a boat, I sent a helicopter – what more should I have done?'

As threads of gold and silver
In the pattern He has planned.
(Anon.)

FREE WILL AND RESPONSIBILITY
(CCC 306–308)

God's providence does not undermine free will and responsibility. Providence does not imply that God manipulates us like a chess player moving pieces. We are free agents, not puppets. We can think of God as the perfect people-manager, persuading them to do what he wants them to do, not as a chess player moving inanimate objects. God's providence and our choice operate at different levels. As an illustration we can think of the relation between the author of a novel and the characters. The murderer cannot turn round to Poirot and protest that Agatha Christie made him do it. The author and the villain are operating at different levels. This is an imperfect analogy, not least because God appears in our story in a way that Agatha Christie does not appear in her novels, but it does illustrate how different causes can operate at different levels.

Sometimes in the Bible the same event is attributed to God, to Satan and to people, as with the final rebellion described in 2 Thessalonians 2:9–12:

The coming of the lawless one is by *the activity of Satan* with all power and false signs and wonders, and with all wicked deception for those who are perishing, because *they refused* to love the truth and so be saved. Therefore *God sends them* a strong delusion, so that they may believe what is false, in order that all may be condemned who did not believe the truth but had pleasure in unrighteousness.

All three are involved, but in different ways. Likewise, David's census of the nation is ascribed, as well as to David, to God (2 Sam. 24:1–2) and to Satan (1 Chron. 21:1–2). These should not be seen as alternatives; they can all be true on different levels.

God's will is the ultimate, primary cause of all things. But he works out his will through secondary causes. If I jump out of the window I will fall to the ground – thanks to gravity. God works through free human choices and even through random events: 'The lot is cast into the lap, but its every decision is from the LORD' (Prov. 16:33).

In British local council elections, with small numbers of people voting in each ward, it is not uncommon for there to be a dead heat, whereupon the result is decided by the toss of a coin, the drawing of lots or something similar. It sometimes happens that this determines the outcome not just for that individual seat but for control over the whole council for the next four years. From our perspective it depends on chance (Luke 10:31) but not from God's perspective.

Credal statement

God, the great Creator of all things, doth uphold, direct, dispose, and govern all creatures, actions, and things, from the greatest even to the least, by his most wise and holy providence, according to his infallible foreknowledge, and the free and immutable counsel of his own will, to the praise of the glory of his wisdom, power, justice, goodness, and mercy.

Although in relation to the foreknowledge and decree of God, the first cause, all things come to pass immutably and infallibly, yet, by the same providence, he ordereth them to fall out according to the nature of second causes, either necessarily, freely, or contingently.

God, in his ordinary providence, maketh use of means, yet is free to work without, above, and against them, at his pleasure. (*Westminster Confession of Faith* (1647), 5:1–3)

What do you think? The question

Does God will disasters?

GOD AND EVIL (CCC 312)

God's relation to events can be viewed at two different levels.

1 If God is in control and working out his loving purposes then all that takes place is willed by him, at least in the sense that he allows or permits it. A skilful child-minder will be in control not in the sense of determining all that happens but in the sense of having an overall strategy and making sure that nothing is permitted that is contrary to that strategy. The children are going to leave the house at 8.30, properly dressed with clean teeth and washed faces; on the way to that end there is room for manoeuvre concerning who plays with which toys at points where they are not otherwise engaged.

    Why would God even allow events like the tsunamis? One reason is that without tsunamis and earthquakes the earth's surface would eventually become flat and would all be covered by water. As human beings we have a vested interest in these events. God wills tsunamis at least to the extent of allowing them.

2 Some specific events are positively willed by God. This is clear from Scripture. Many times in the Old Testament we read of God bringing disaster as judgement on Israel or on the nations. In Isaiah, God states that he is sending Assyria to judge Israel:

(a) Isaiah 10:5–6: 'Ah, Assyria, the rod of my anger; the staff in their hands is my fury! Against a godless nation [Israel] I send him, and against the people of my wrath I command him, to take spoil and seize plunder, and to tread them down like the mire of the streets.' God was using Assyria as a tool of his judgement. They, however, were doing it for purely selfish and wicked reasons:

(b) Isaiah 10:7: 'But he does not so intend, and his heart does not so think; but it is in his heart to destroy, and to cut off nations not a few.'

They meant it for evil and were not at all reluctant to plunder Israel. It is not as if they were wanting to send food parcels to Israel but God forced them to devastate the land instead. God used their wicked intent to bring his judgement upon Israel. The supreme example of this is the cross of Jesus – clearly a wicked deed, but purposed by God for his plan of redemption:

(a) Acts 2:23: 'This Jesus, delivered up according to the definite plan and foreknowledge of God, you crucified and killed by the hands of lawless men.'

(b) Acts 4:27–28: against Jesus were gathered 'both Herod and Pontius Pilate, along with the Gentiles and the peoples of Israel, to do whatever your hand and your plan had predestined to take place'.

They all meant it for evil, but God used their actions to bring about our salvation.

GOD AT WAR

The great majority of Christians have held that God does reign, that he is in control and that nothing happens without at least his permission. In the modern West, however, this belief has been questioned and some have sought to excuse God from any responsibility for the evil in the world by denying that it happens with his permission.

Gregory Boyd, an Evangelical theologian, rejects the idea that God reigns now, claiming instead that he will not do so until the End.[2] We cannot say that God is reigning now, because people disobey his will, Boyd argues. In this present age there is conflict or warfare between God and Satan, between the kingdom of God and the kingdom of Satan. It is not yet true that God reigns.

This argument confuses two different senses of 'God's will':

1 God's will as his *commands*: what he tells us to do, such as love one another. In this sense we pray that God's will may be done on earth as in heaven (Matt. 6:10), but that has not yet happened. In this sense there is warfare between God and his enemies and it is not until God's final triumph that it will be true that his will is done.
2 God's will as his *purpose and plan*: the present situation of warfare is itself part of God's plan and is in his control. *Luther called Satan 'God's devil' to

make the point that God is working out his purposes through Satan.

In short, *both* things are true. In the Lord's Prayer we pray 'thy kingdom *come*' but also 'thine *is* the kingdom'. On the one hand, there is conflict between God and Satan and God's will will not prevail until the End. On the other hand, God is currently working out his purposes in history. Boyd is right to affirm the former, wrong to deny the latter. Arguably the greatest ever book written on the theme of 'God at war' is Augustine's *City of God*. In this work Augustine interprets the whole of history as a struggle between two cities or communities: the city of God and the city of Satan. But at the same time Augustine firmly believed in God's sovereignty as the one who was in control of the whole process. He saw no need to set one view against the other.

CONCLUSION

God does reign. He reigns here and now in that he is in control and working out his purposes; he will reign in a fuller sense in the Age to Come when his will shall be done on earth as in heaven. In affirming God's providence, however, we need to note two points.

1 **Realism**. Paul confidently affirmed that 'for those who love God all things work together for good' (Rom. 8:28). What he did not say is that 'all things work together for the *best*'. That would be manifestly untrue. When we disobey God we may well lose out on the best. I have seen many a promising ministry destroyed by an act of folly or by a fatal character flaw. What Romans 8:28 does mean is that even when things are grim God can bring some good out of the situation.

There is no guarantee that 'it' won't happen, whatever it is that we fear, but if it does happen, it will only be within God's will and he will bring good out of it.

2 **Permission**. Christians have overwhelmingly held that God does reign, here and now, but there are legitimate differences of opinion concerning what he positively ordains and what he allows by way of permission.

Worship

How lovely on the mountains are the feet of Him
Who brings good news, good news,
Announcing peace, proclaiming news of happiness:
Our God reigns, our God reigns!

Our God reigns!
Our God reigns!
Our God reigns!
Our God reigns!
(Leonard E. Smith, Jr)

PRAYER

O God, whose never-failing providence ordereth all things both in heaven and earth: We humbly beseech thee to put away from us all hurtful things, and to give us those things which be profitable for us; through Jesus Christ our Lord. Amen. (Book of Common Prayer: Collect for the Eighth Sunday after Trinity)

Question to answer

- Is God in control of human history?

NOTES

1 ATS ch. 2.
2 G. A. Boyd, *God at War: The Bible and Spiritual Conflict*. Downers Grove: IVP, 1997, followed by *Satan and the Problem of Evil: Constructing a Warfare Theology*. Downers Grove: IVP, 2001. For a thorough review of this, see D. Carson, *Journal of the Evangelical Theological Society* 42 (1999) 251–69.

RESOURCES

D. and R. Basinger (eds) *Predestination and Free Will: Four Views*. Downers Grove: IVP, 1986.

B. Farley *The Providence of God*. Grand Rapids: Baker, 1988.

P. Helm *The Providence of God*. Leicester: IVP, 1993.

D. Jowers et al. *Four Views on Divine Providence*. Grand Rapids: Zondervan, 2011.

T. Tiessen *Providence and Prayer: How Does God Work in the World?*. Downers Grove: IVP, 2000.

Chapter 10

EVIL AND SUFFERING (THEODICY)

Aims of this chapter

In this chapter we look at evil and suffering, asking:

- If God is all good and all powerful, why is there evil in God's universe?
- Where does evil come from?
- Are there reasons for the existence of evil and suffering?
- Where does Jesus fit into this?
- Is God the sovereign God of providence or the vulnerable God who suffers?

IF GOD IS ALL GOOD AND ALL POWERFUL, WHY IS THERE EVIL?
(CCC 309–13, 324)

This is the classic trilemma – three facts that appear to be incompatible with one another. It goes back to the ancient world and, according to *Tertullian, was put forward by the heretic Marcion:

> If God is good and foreknows the future and is able to avert evil, why did he permit man, the very image and likeness of himself . . . to be deceived by the devil, and fall from obedience of the law into death? For if God had been good, and so unwilling that such a catastrophe should happen, and prescient, so as not to be ignorant of what was to come to pass, and powerful enough to hinder its occurrence, that issue would never have come about, which should be impossible under these three conditions of the divine greatness. (*Against Marcion* 2:5)

I recently heard on television the repeated statement that the Bible tells us not to question God. The author obviously does not know much about the Bible since many Old Testament writers question God vigorously, crying out over the issue of evil and suffering. The supreme example is, of course, Job. The prophet Habakkuk also struggled with the prevalence of evil:

> Are you not from everlasting,
> O Lord my God, my Holy One? . . .
> You who are of purer eyes than to
>   see evil
> and cannot look at wrong,
> why do you idly look at traitors
> and remain silent when the wicked
>   swallows up
> the man more righteous than he?
> (Hab. 1:12–13)

Psalm 73 is written by someone who is envious of the prosperity of those who are arrogant and wicked. Other psalms are written out of the immediacy of suffering, such as Psalm 13:

Worship

How long, O LORD? Will you forget me for ever?
How long will you hide your face from me?
How long must I take counsel in my soul
and have sorrow in my heart all the day?
How long shall my enemy be exalted over me?
Consider and answer me, O LORD my God;
light up my eyes, lest I sleep the sleep of death,
lest my enemy say, 'I have prevailed over him',
lest my foes rejoice because I am shaken.
(Ps. 13:1–4)

There is no complete answer to this quandary and if I had found one I would have won the Templeton Prize and a Nobel Prize. But there are partial answers that can go some way towards an explanation, and that can provide a basis for thinking that it is not unreasonable to hold onto the trilemma in faith.

THEODICY

'Theodicy' means 'justification of God', in particular in the light of evil and suffering, and has since the eighteenth century been a hot issue in the West. The term was coined by the German philosopher Leibniz, who used it as the title of a book in 1710. Leibniz maintained that we live in 'the best of all possible worlds', in that any other world would suffer from greater defects. But in 1755 Lisbon was hit by an earthquake and a tsunami, causing thousands of deaths, and many people asked why there should be such suffering. The Deist philosopher Voltaire mocked the idea of 'the best of all possible worlds' in his novel *Candide* (1759).

Ironically, the issue of suffering has become most acute in the West, where we have modern technology, medicine, etc. Until recently, the death of a child was common and so was accepted as painful, but normal. Today in the West it is not at all common so on the rare occasions when it does happen it is viewed as scandalous. In the West a common reaction to the 2004 Asian tsunami was to see it as a reason for doubting God's existence, whereas in Asia a more common response was to pray. We have got to the stage where we think that life should be painless, because we have become used to having safety and comfort.

There are two opposite dangers to avoid as we consider this issue:

- Those who have not themselves suffered much are in danger of being insensitive to the pain of others. They are not upset by the problem of suffering because they are not the ones that are suffering. I remember hearing a moving testimony from a mother whose baby had suffered

© Miriam Kendrick 2013 www.miriamkendrick.co.uk

from a skin complaint. She frankly confessed that the issue of suffering had not previously bothered her because suffering had not affected her so directly.

- Some go to the opposite extreme and claim that it is obscene to discuss the problem of suffering in a logical, rational way when people are suffering so deeply. They are right that there is an insensitive way in which to seek an answer to the problem, wrong in seeking to ban all rational discussion of the issue. There is a place and a time to discuss the reasons for suffering – but such discussion can be profoundly unhelpful for people at the point of suffering.

We do need to be sensitive to those who are suffering, but that should not prevent us from discussing the topic in a rational way. After the trial of a criminal, the media love to ask the victims, or their relatives, whether they are satisfied with the verdict and the sentence. This makes for good television, but in an important sense those who are personally involved are the least competent to judge on that issue. If someone was on trial for murder, there is no way that relatives of the victim would be allowed to serve as a judge or jurors, for the simple reason that they could not assess the case fairly. In the case of suffering, those who are in the thick of it are not the best equipped to assess the situation. In discussing the question of suffering we need to strike a balance, discussing it in a rational way, but without losing our sensitivity towards those who may be suffering deeply.

Credal statement

The fact that God permits physical and even moral evil is a mystery that God illuminates by his Son Jesus Christ who died and rose to vanquish evil. Faith gives us the certainty that God would not permit an evil if he did not cause a good to come from that very evil, by ways that we shall fully know only in eternal life. (*CCC 324)

ORIGIN OF EVIL

Where does evil come from in God's universe? God did not create evil. In Genesis 1 the account of creation ends with the statement that 'God saw everything that he had made, and behold, it was very good' (1:31). His creation includes beings that were created good, but with free will, and so with the potential of turning from God and becoming evil. And it is not only human beings that have that capacity. Genesis 3 begins with a serpent, who tempted Eve. Later in Revelation this serpent is identified as Satan:

- Revelation 12:9: 'The great dragon was thrown down, that ancient serpent, who is called the devil and Satan, the deceiver of the whole world.'
- Revelation 20:2: 'And he seized the dragon, that ancient serpent, who is the devil and Satan, and bound him for a thousand years.'

So there was already evil in God's universe. Human sin was not the first sin. First came the fall of angels, as discussed in Chapter 5.

Since first Satan then Adam and Eve chose evil, does this mean that evil already existed for them to be able to choose it? If someone goes into a newsagent's and is tempted by a pornographic magazine, the magazine must already exist. The origin of evil is not like that. Evil is the corruption or spoiling of something that already exists as good.

Natural desires and pleasures become corrupted into lusts. Worship becomes idolatry; enjoying food becomes gluttony; the right use of God's creation becomes materialism, etc. Evil does not exist in its own right; it is parasitic on goodness.

> Wickedness, when you examine it, turns out to be the pursuit of some good in the wrong way . . . Goodness is, so to speak, itself: badness is only spoiled goodness. (C. S. Lewis)[1]

Darkness is the absence of light, not something that exists in itself; cold is the absence of heat, not something that exists in itself. Evil does not exist in its own right but the reverse is not true. Goodness can exist without evil.

So what God created is a world in which there was the possibility of evil, thus enabling his creatures to exercise free will.

REASONS FOR EVIL AND SUFFERING

What follows is not a full answer to this question, explaining all suffering. We have no such complete answer in this life, but there are some partial explanations which go *some* way towards explaining it and encourage us to think that it is not totally meaningless.

THE PRICE OF FREEDOM
If people are to have freedom this means that they must be able to hurt both themselves and others – whether wilfully (e.g. murder) or by accident (e.g. a car crash). Moral evil and pain are both part of the necessary price that we pay for freedom – our own and others'. People are free to act badly or irresponsibly. The alternative would be for us to be forcibly curbed – e.g. prevented from speeding. Some ask, 'Could there not be *less* freedom?' – but that question would continue to be asked however much our freedom were to be curbed. Although things are not fully as we would like them, nevertheless we still wish to continue to exist as free people. Human freedom accounts for much suffering, but not all. It does not explain natural disasters, like tsunamis. It does not account for situations where children are savaged by ferocious dogs.

Sceptic's corner

In Dostoyevsky's *The Brothers Karamazov*, one of the characters claims that no alleged good (e.g. an eternity of bliss in the future) can justify the torture of one child:

> I appeal to you – answer me: imagine that it is you yourself who are erecting the edifice of human destiny with the aim of making men happy in the end, of giving them peace and contentment at last, but that to do that it is absolutely necessary, and indeed quite inevitable, to torture to death only one tiny creature, the little girl who beat her breast with her little fist, and to found the edifice on her unavenged tears – would you consent to be the architect on those conditions? Tell me and do not lie! (287–88)

Answer: This sounds like a noble sentiment, especially in the context of the incident described in the book. But if it were true, the right course of action would be to bring about a nuclear holocaust and to terminate life on this planet, one of the features of which is the acute suffering of many little children. Anyone who chooses to bring a child into the world is in fact voting for the view that despite the risk of suffering it is better to exist than not.

CHARACTER BUILDING

This is another reason given for the existence of evil in the world, as is argued by *John Hick. Suffering is part of the 'soul-making process'.

> We do not act on the premise that pleasure is the supreme end of life; and if the development of these other values sometimes clashes with the provision of pleasure, then we are willing to have our children miss a certain amount of this, rather than fail to come to possess and to be possessed by the finer and more precious qualities that are possible to the human personality . . . If, then, there is any true analogy between God's purpose for his human creatures, and the purpose of loving and wise parents for their children, we have to recognize that the presence of pleasure and the absence of pain cannot be the supreme and overriding end for which the world exists. Rather, this world must be a place of soul-making.[2]

This echoes the poet John Keats, who described the world as 'the vale of soul-making'. Suffering builds moral character.

There is much truth in this idea. God trains us through suffering. 'The Lord disciplines the one he loves, and chastises every son whom he receives' (Heb. 12:6). Discipline is an essential part of the responsible raising of children. We all need discipline.[3] Hebrews contains the remarkable statement that even Jesus, who was without sin, learned obedience and was made perfect through suffering (5:8). It is not that he was previously disobedient – obedience is a positive quality, more than just the absence of disobedience. God uses our suffering to build a Christ-like character:

- Hebrews 12:11: 'For the moment all discipline seems painful rather than pleasant, but later it yields the peaceful fruit of righteousness to those who have been trained by it.'

We must acknowledge, though, that suffering can break a character as well as make it. Character building is not the complete answer to the question of suffering, but it is a partial answer. At least some good effects can come about through suffering.

GOD'S JUDGEMENT ON SIN

This is not a popular idea today, but *some* suffering can be seen as God's punishment of sin. Certainly much suffering is a direct (or indirect) consequence of our own bad behaviour. Drunkenness gives rise to hangovers and to sclerosis of the liver. But we must not fall into the trap of supposing that *all* suffering is due to this. Christians, unlike Hindus, do not regard suffering in this life as punishment for evil in a former life. The book of Job is all about a man whose suffering was not a judgement on his own sin, and Jesus says the same of the man born blind:

> As he passed by, he saw a man blind from birth. And his disciples asked him, 'Rabbi, who sinned, this man or his parents, that he was born blind?' Jesus answered, 'It was not that this man sinned, or his parents, but that the works of God might be displayed in him.' (John 9:1–3)

What this passage and the book of Job deny is that *all* suffering is due to sin. What the Bible and experience both teach is that much of our suffering *is* caused by sin. Evil has bad consequences which involve suffering, though not all sin is punished here and now, in this life. *Augustine expresses this well:

> If punishment were obviously inflicted on every wrongdoing in this life, it would be supposed that nothing was reserved for the Last Judgement; on the other hand, if God's power never openly punished any sin in this world, there would be an end to belief in providence. (*City of God* 1:8)

God's judgement on sin in this life mostly takes the form of judgement on society. We see this in the judgement against Israel and other nations in the Old Testament prophets. Paul argues likewise in Romans 1:18–32. Such judgement is a blunt instrument in that the innocent may suffer alongside the guilty. In 1945 Germany

reaped the consequences of its actions, but the suffering was shared by all Germans, not only by the guilty. The young girls who were raped by occupying Soviet soldiers in Berlin were reaping the consequences not of their own sins but of those of the German army that had invaded the Soviet Union.

JESUS CHRIST

THE SUFFERING GOD

Today it is increasingly popular to seek the answer to suffering in the fact God shares our suffering – which popularity does not make it right, but nor does it make it wrong. This approach is expounded well by *Jürgen Moltmann, especially in his *The Crucified God* (ch. 6). God is not remote and distant from us, not immune from suffering, but rather identifies with us and shares our suffering, in Christ. This is especially true in the cross. Jesus experiences rejection by God and by humanity. The Father suffers the loss of his Son. This does not explain *why* there is suffering, but shows us a God who cares, a God who shares our suffering, a God who understands and identifies with us in our suffering. A similar approach is also found in an anonymous story called 'The long silence':

> At the end of time, billions of people were seated on a great plain before God's throne. Most shrank back from the brilliant light before them. But some groups near the front talked heatedly, not with cringing shame but with belligerence. 'Can God judge us?'
> 'How can he know about suffering?' snapped a pert young brunette. She ripped open a sleeve to reveal a tattooed number from a Nazi concentration camp.

Errors to avoid

There are two opposite errors to be avoided when considering God's judgement on sin.

- The first is to deny that God acts in judgement in history. Such an approach is possible only by rejecting much of what the Bible teaches, in the New Testament as well as the Old.
- The opposite error is to be over-confident in discerning God's hand of judgement. In the light of September 11, 2001 (the attack on the Twin Towers) two different American theologians wrote books suggesting that it could be seen as God's judgement on the USA. The problem was that, putting it crudely, one of them saw it as God's judgement on American politics for having strayed too far to the left, the other for not having moved sufficiently far to the left. A good case can be made for seeing the incident as God's judgement, but care has to be exercised when stating *what* the judgement is for.

'We endured terror . . . beatings . . . torture . . . death!' In another group a Negro boy lowered his collar. 'What about this?' he demanded, showing an ugly rope burn. 'Lynched, for no crime but being black!' In another crowd there was a pregnant schoolgirl with sullen eyes: 'Why should I suffer?' she murmured. 'It wasn't my fault.'

Far out across the plain were hundreds of such groups. Each had a complaint against God for the evil and suffering he had permitted in his world. How lucky God was to live in Heaven, where all was sweetness and light, where there was no weeping or fear, no hunger or hatred. What did God know of all that man had been forced to endure in this world? For God leads a pretty sheltered life, they said. So each of these groups sent forth their leader, chosen because he had suffered the most. A Jew, a Negro, a person from Hiroshima, a horribly deformed arthritic, a thalidomide child. In the centre of the vast plain, they consulted with each other.

At last they were ready to present their case. It was rather clever. Before God could be qualified to be their judge, he must endure what they had endured. Their decision was that God should be sentenced to live on earth as a man. Let him be born a Jew. Let the legitimacy of his birth be doubted. Give him a work so difficult that even his family will think him out of his mind. Let him be betrayed by his closest friends. Let him face false charges, be tried by a prejudiced jury and convicted by a cowardly judge. Let him be tortured. At the last, let him see what it means to be terribly alone. Then let him die so there can be no doubt he died. Let there be a great host of witnesses to verify it.

As each leader announced his portion of the sentence, loud murmurs of approval went up from the throng of people assembled. When the last had finished pronouncing sentence, there was a long silence. No one uttered a word. No one moved. For suddenly, all knew that God had already served his sentence.

SUFFERING WITH AND FOR CHRIST

A major New Testament theme is that we are called to suffer with and for Christ. We are not promised an easy path to glory, with health, wealth and prosperity; on the contrary it is through suffering here and now, whether imposed upon us or voluntarily embraced. It is to this that we are called:

- Luke 9:23: 'If anyone would come after me, let him deny himself and take up his cross daily and follow me.'
- 1 Peter 2:18–25:

  Servants, be subject to your masters with all respect, not only to the good and gentle but also to the unjust. For this is a gracious thing, when, mindful of God, one endures sorrows while suffering unjustly. For what credit is it if, when you sin and are beaten for it, you endure? But if when you do good and suffer for it you endure, this is a gracious thing in the sight of God. For to this you have been called, because Christ also suffered for you, leaving you an example, so that you might follow in his steps.

- Philippians 3:10: 'that I may know him and the power of his resurrection, and may share his sufferings, becoming like him in his death'.

This suffering is the path to glory:

> We are children of God, and if children, then heirs – heirs of God and fellow heirs with Christ, provided we suffer with him in order that we may also be glorified with him. For I consider that the sufferings of this present time are not worth comparing with the glory that is to be revealed to us. (Rom. 8:16–18)

As I write these words I am sitting in a building site because of an extension being built on the back of our house. This is involving some three months of hardship, but that will fade into nothing by comparison with the glory that is shortly to be revealed, when the extension is complete. This relatively trivial example illustrates the manner in which hope for the future can help us to endure the sufferings of this life. Jesus cites the example of childbirth (John 16:21–22).

Suffering with Christ accounts for *some* suffering, but by no means all. It does not account for suffering due to ill health or to the bad after-effects of our own wrong actions.

What do you think? The question

Is God the sovereign God of providence or the vulnerable God who suffers?

PRAYERS

> Though the fig tree should not blossom, nor fruit be on the vines, the produce of the olive fail and the fields yield no food, the flock be cut off from the fold and there be no herd in the stalls, yet I will rejoice in the Lord; I will take joy in the God of my salvation. God, the Lord, is my strength; he makes my feet like the deer's; he makes me tread on my high places. (Hab. 3:17–19)

What do you think? My answer

Should we think of God as sovereign or as vulnerable? Fortunately, we do not need to choose between these two. Both are part of the revelation of God in Scripture. We see the two side by side in the book of Revelation. Christ is the Lamb that was slain, that suffered for us:

> And between the throne and the four living creatures and among the elders I saw a Lamb standing, as though it had been slain, with seven horns and with seven eyes, which are the seven spirits of God sent out into all the earth. (5:6)

But immediately before he is portrayed as a conquering lion: 'Weep no more; behold, the Lion of the tribe of Judah, the Root of David, has conquered, so that he can open the scroll and its seven seals' (5:5). Revelation also proclaims that the Lord God Almighty reigns: 'Then I heard what seemed to be the voice of a great multitude, like the roar of many waters and like the sound of mighty peals of thunder, crying out, "Hallelujah! For the Lord our God the Almighty reigns."' (19:6).

In the past the main emphasis was on God's sovereignty, and people hardly thought that he could suffer (on which, see Chapter 17). Nowadays the pendulum has swung the other way. In reality, both aspects are true.

Lord God, whose blessed Son our Saviour gave his back to the smiters and did not hide his face from shame: give us grace to endure the sufferings of this present time with sure confidence in the glory that shall be revealed; through Jesus Christ our Lord. (*Common Worship*, Post Communion for Fourth Sunday of Lent).

Question to answer

- If God is all good and all powerful, why is there evil?

NOTES

1 C. S. Lewis *Mere Christianity*. London: Fontana, 1955, 46.
2 J. Hick *Evil and the God of Love*. London: Collins, 1968, 294–95.

3 I know of an academic and his wife who resolved that they would never say 'No' to their child. Apparently she grew up to be disturbed.

RESOURCES

H. Blocher *Evil and the Cross*. Leicester: IVP, 1994.

S. T. Davis (ed.) *Encountering Evil: Live Options in Theodicy*. Edinburgh: T & T Clark, 1981.

S. J. Keillor, *God's Judgments: Interpreting History and the Christian Faith*. Downers Grove: IVP, 2006.

C. S. Lewis *The Problem of Pain*. London: Fontana, 1957.

M. Larrimore (ed.) *The Problem of Evil: A Reader*. Oxford: Blackwell, 2001.

U. Middelmann *The Innocence of God*. Milton Keynes: Paternoster, 2007.

REDEMPTION: GOD AND HIS WORK

Chapter 11

THE LAW AND THE OLD TESTAMENT

Aims of this chapter

In this chapter we look at the law and the Old Testament, asking:

- Is the Old Testament law binding on us today?
- What are the uses of the moral law?
- Is love all that we need for moral guidance?
- What is the role of law in the Christian life?
- How does the New Testament relate to the Old?

WHAT IS THE ROLE OF LAW IN THE CHRISTIAN LIFE? (CCC 1950–86)

GRACE AND LAW

Even in the Old Testament the law is seen as a response to God's grace. The Ten Commandments begin with an account of what God has done – 'I am the LORD your God, who brought you out of the land of Egypt, out of the house of slavery' (Exod. 20:2) – before moving on to what he requires of us. The law is not the way of earning God's favour but, rather, of responding to it. 'Theology is grace and ethics is gratitude.' Psychology teaches us that people work better from a basis of being accepted, rather than striving to be accepted. This is how God deals with us. We are unconditionally accepted in Christ – but that does not mean that obedience is optional or that there are no conditions once we are accepted.

IS THE OLD TESTAMENT LAW BINDING ON US TODAY?

In 2000 there appeared on the Internet a spoof letter seeking advice about how to apply various Old Testament laws today, including the following questions:

I would like to sell my daughter into slavery, as sanctioned in Exodus 21:7. In this day and age, what do you think would be a fair price for her?

Leviticus 25:44 states that I may indeed possess slaves, both male and female, provided they are purchased from neighbouring nations. A friend of mine claims that this applies to Mexicans, but not Canadians. Can you clarify? Why can't I own Canadians?

I have a neighbour who insists on working on the Sabbath. Exodus 35:2 clearly states he should be put to death. Am I morally obligated to kill him? Am I morally obligated to kill him myself?

107

My uncle has a farm. He violates Leviticus 19:19 by planting two different crops in the same field, as does his wife by wearing garments made of two different kinds of thread (cotton/polyester blend). He also tends to curse and blaspheme a lot. Is it really necessary that we go to all the trouble of getting the whole town together to stone them (Lev. 24:10–16)? Couldn't we just burn them to death at a private family affair like we do with people who sleep with their in-laws (Lev. 20:14)?

A humorous real-life example illustrating the problems of applying the Old Testament law is seen in the man who had Leviticus 18:22 (which denounces homosexual practice) tattooed on his arm, apparently unaware that Leviticus 19:28 prohibits tattoos! The fundamentalist atheists use such examples as a basis for rejecting Christian ethics.

There is a serious issue here. Are Christians committed to such laws? If not, why not? In my experience all Christians realize that they are not so obliged, but few are able to explain why not. Many suggest that it is because our culture is different, but were that the ground we could equally dismiss the teaching of Jesus on the ground that our culture is different from his.

There is a witty poster doing the rounds of Facebook:[1]

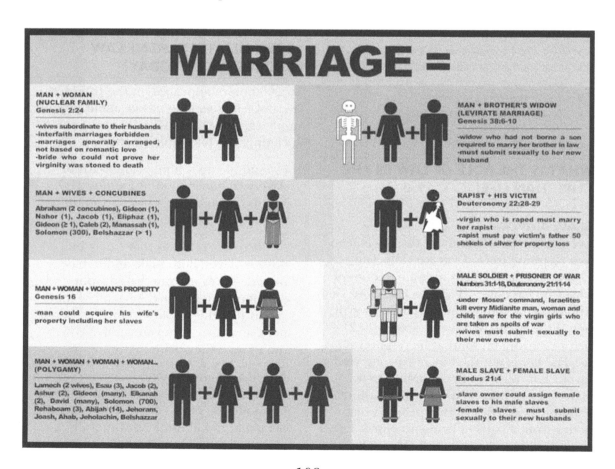

This is intended as a riposte to those who appeal to the 'traditional view of marriage' and the web address describes it as 'Marriage according to the Bible'. In fact it offers some Old Testament teaching on sexuality and completely ignores the teaching of the New Testament, which for the West has been the 'traditional view of marriage' for some 1,500 years.

There are two points to be made in response to such presentations.

1 The fallacy underlying them is that they ignore the transition from Old to New Testament/Covenant. The laws quoted there do not apply today, not because the Old Testament was written a long time ago, not because we live in a different culture, but because Jesus has come and changed the basis of our relationship to God, as we shall see shortly. (The 'spoof letter' was written in the context of Judaism, not Christianity, as presumably was also the poster, which is why they ignore the New Testament.)

2 Christians may not be subject to such laws, but those who accept the Bible as God's word still need to consider why such laws were *ever* commanded. *Calvin's teaching is quite illuminating on this point. He accepts without question that these laws were given by God, but at the same time does not hesitate to call some of them 'barbaric', such as the provision for the enslavement of Israelites. The reason for such barbarity is that God needed to accommodate his law to the barbarism of the people at that stage, to their hardness of heart (Mark 10:5), as he progressively led them through his prophets towards a truer understanding of the standard of behaviour he requires. For accommodation, see Chapter 3.

Sceptic's corner

What about Old Testament passages where they are told to exterminate their enemies, such as Deuteronomy 20:16–18; 1 Samuel 15:1–3?

Answer: This is a tricky question but there are three basic points that can be made:[2]

1 These commands are not for Christians. A good case can be made for the legitimacy of just wars, fought in the name of the state, but there is no place for a holy war, fought in the name of the Church or of the Christian faith. This is an important difference between Christianity and Islam. In short, we can take up arms for the United Kingdom, but not for the kingdom of God.

2 The comments just made about barbarity and accommodation apply.

3 The God of the Bible is not a pacifist. The End will bring judgement on specific groups. For example: 'So will Babylon the great city be thrown down with violence' (Rev. 18:21). The fate of those who remain opposed to God will be eternal death, on which see Chapter 28. It is true of the present age that 'God did not send his Son into the world to condemn the world, but in order that the world might be saved through him' (John 3:17), but this is a postponement of judgement, not a renunciation of it.

THREE TYPES OF OLD TESTAMENT LAW

Traditionally the laws given in the Old Testament (especially in the law of Moses) have been divided into three types:[3]

1 **The moral law**, which is eternal and unchanging. Murder, theft and adultery are always wrong. In different generations the Church will be pressured by the surrounding culture into giving way on different areas of the moral law. In today's Western culture the pressure is to adopt a libertarian view of sex, in which any consensual sexual activity is OK, whether pre-marital or extra-marital. Giving in to such pressures is always the easiest option, but the episodes of church history that we are most ashamed of include those where there was such capitulation.

2 **The civil law**, which was intended for the Jewish state, but contains abiding *principles*. For example, Deuteronomy 22:8: 'When you build a new house, you shall make a parapet for your roof, that you may not bring the guilt of blood upon your house, if anyone should fall from it.' This was given because people spent time on flat roofs and there was a safety issue. I have a flat roof without a parapet – but no one ever goes onto it except to repair it. An equivalent to the Old Testament command today would be to ensure that balconies are designed so that people will not fall off them. It can be seen as the principle underlying modern health and safety laws – which is certainly not to say that every modern bureaucratic regulation is justified! Likewise the establishment of cities of refuge (e.g. Num. 35:10–12) was intended to curb private vengeance – something that we do in a different way today by our criminal justice systems. In short, the principles of the Old Testament civil laws apply; the specific laws do not.

3 **The ceremonial law**, which was a preparation for Christ and is fulfilled in him. As Christians we, unlike Jews in Old Testament times, are allowed to eat bacon sandwiches. The Old Testament food laws no longer apply to us. Mark records Jesus' words: 'Do you not see that whatever goes into a person from outside cannot defile him, since it enters not his heart but his stomach, and is expelled?', and concludes, 'Thus he declared all foods clean' (7:18–19). We no longer offer animal sacrifices and Hebrews explains that these have been superseded by the one sacrifice of Christ (9:6—10:18).

This division of the Old Testament law into three is not *explicitly* biblical. In the Pentateuch all three types are found side by side without distinction. Nowhere in the New Testament is this sort of division set out. But although the division is in that sense not biblical, the conclusions that it reaches *are* biblical. Paul clearly expected his converts to refrain from theft, murder and adultery – the commands of the moral law are repeated time and again in the New Testament. Paul also vigorously opposed the idea that Gentile believers be told not to eat bacon sandwiches and he never suggested that Christians should seek to implement the provisions of the Old Testament civil law. To pick up our earlier example from Leviticus, the prohibition of homosexual practice (18:22) is reaffirmed in the New Testament, the prohibition of tattoos (19:28) is not.

While the division is very helpful, it does not resolve all issues. For example, the Sabbath command is among the Ten Commandments, but is a mixture of civil law (treatment of servants) and ceremonial law (observation of a particular day). The early Christians met for worship not on the Jewish Sabbath (Saturday) but on the Lord's Day (Sunday). There are abiding principles such as the need to rest, the proper treatment of employees and the need for regular times of corporate worship.[4]

What do you think? The question

Is love all that we need for moral guidance?

THREE USES OF THE (MORAL) LAW

The sixteenth-century Reformers taught that there were three uses of the law – i.e. three different functions or roles of the law. These apply to the moral law in general, whether this is found in the Old Testament, the New Testament, our conscience or the law of the land.

THE FIRST USE OF THE LAW

The First Use of the law is to convict us of sin, to show us our moral inability and our bondage to sin – and thus our need of Christ to rescue us. This is done by external commands, but most effectively by internal commands, such as 'You shall not covet' (Rom. 7:7–12) and, supremely, the command to love. Attending worship is relatively easy; loving God with all our hearts is a different matter. Abstaining from literal murder is not too hard for most of us; loving our neighbours as ourselves is rather harder. As Paul said, 'through the law comes knowledge of sin' (Rom. 3:20) – the law shows us what we are like. 'If it had not been for the law, I would not have known sin' (Rom. 7:7).

THE SECOND USE OF THE LAW

The Second Use of the law is to restrain the ungodly. In other words, people are kept from gross sin or crime by fear of the law, because they fear God's punishment. This may be a fear that God will judge us

directly, either here and now or at the End. More likely it is a fear of God's punishment through the state:

> Let every person be subject to the governing authorities. For there is no authority except from God, and those that exist have been instituted by God . . . [The ruler] is God's servant for your good. But if you do wrong, be afraid, for he does not bear the sword in vain. For he is the servant of God, an avenger who carries out God's wrath on the wrongdoer. Therefore one must be in subjection, not only to avoid God's wrath but also for the sake of conscience. (Rom. 13:1–5)

The Second Use of the law is vital for law and order – anarchy is a great evil. But it does not produce heart obedience; sin is restrained, not cured. Just as the brake lights all come on just before the speed camera, so also there is a cloud of exhaust fumes just after the camera as people accelerate away. The law restrains people from sin, but does not generally lead to a change of heart. In fact, laws can actually incite people to disobey them and every command can be seen as an invitation to sin. I remember once passing a shop window where there was a large sign which read 'Don't read this.' The effect was to make me stop in my tracks and turn to read it.

The essence of this Second Use is that sin and crime are curbed by fear of the consequences. The same result can be achieved by a fear of the natural consequence of sin, for example when people may be restrained by the fear of catching a sexually transmitted disease.

So to what extent should the government legislate for morality? How much this is

© Miriam Kendrick 2013 www.miriamkendrick.co.uk

desirable or possible will vary from context to context. The idea that the government should not legislate on moral issues is ridiculous. Should murder be legal? Or enslaving people? Those who argue against moral legislation usually mean that they want the greatest possible *sexual* freedom, though usually they will draw the line at

© Miriam Kendrick 2013 www.miriamkendrick.co.uk

paedophilia. Legislating contrary to public opinion can be counter-productive. The prohibition of alcohol in the USA between 1918 and 1933 did an immense amount of harm, facilitating the rise of gangsterism. On the other hand, legislation can help to change social attitudes, as has happened with racism and smoking.

THE THIRD USE OF THE LAW

The Third Use of the law is to guide and exhort the believer, to show us how to live. Psalm 119 expresses a delight in this role of the law – for example: 'How sweet are your words to my taste, sweeter than honey to my mouth! Through your precepts I get understanding; therefore I hate every false way' (119:103–104). For Calvin this was the 'principal use' of the law because it corresponds to its proper purpose, which is to bring about obedience. *Luther, however, saw things differently, arguing that law has no place in living the Christian life – except inasmuch as it points us back to Christ whenever we sin (First Use).

Luther took the line that he did because he was thinking of law in the sense of God's wrath against sin, the awareness of which was a key factor in his conversion. The prime motivation for Christian obedience is not to escape God's wrath, though that motivation may come into play when we go astray. The sheep that grazes in the centre of the field need not worry about the electric fence, but the sheep that seeks to stray outside the field will encounter it. This is how the Christian relates to the law, according to Luther.

There is an important truth in what Luther said. The Christian life is not primarily about obeying laws or keeping rules. God is looking not for reluctant outward conformity to a code but a willing obedience born of love, a free joyful obedience from the heart. The primary source of law for the Christian is God's law written on our hearts. The promise of the New Covenant is that 'I will put my law within them, and I will write it on their hearts' (Jer. 31:33). This is the work of the Holy Spirit: 'I will put my Spirit within you, and cause you to walk in my statutes and be careful to obey my rules' (Ezek. 36:27). The Holy Spirit gives us love for God and neighbour.

Love is the *motivation* for all true obedience:

> If I speak in the tongues of men and of angels, but have not love, I am a noisy gong or a clanging cymbal. And if I have prophetic powers, and understand all mysteries and all knowledge, and if I have all faith, so as to remove mountains, but have not love, I am nothing. If I give away all I have, and if I deliver up my body to be burned, but have not love, I gain nothing. (1 Cor. 13:1–3)

Indeed, I would argue, more controversially, that love is also the *content* of all true obedience. God asks nothing of us except what love dictates. Jesus and Paul both propound love as a summary of the law:

> You shall love the Lord your God with all your heart and with all your soul and with all your mind. This is the great and first commandment. And a second is like it: You shall love your neighbour as yourself. On these two commandments depend all the Law and the Prophets. (Matt. 22.37–39)[5]

Romans 13:8–10: 'The one who loves another has fulfilled the law . . . Love is the fulfilling of the law.'

What do you think? My answer

So can we say with *Augustine, 'Love, and do what you want' (*Homilies on 1 John* 7:8)? This is often quoted today; what is less often mentioned is that he used this principle in order to justify the coercion of heretics! That illustrates perfectly the reason why love is not enough, why we need the law to interpret to us what love actually means. Jesus said, 'If you love me, you will keep my commandments' (John 14:15). Consider the case of a little child crossing the road with his mother. Because he does not understand the dangers he needs to obey her commands and do what she says.

According to the Babylonian Talmud, a Gentile approached the rabbi Hillel and offered to convert if he could teach him the whole Torah while he stood on one foot. Hillel's answer was, 'That which is despicable to you, do not do to others. This is the whole Torah and the rest is commentary. Go and learn it' (*Shabbat* 31a).

The point of the story is not that we can dispense with the commentary. How often have we heard those who have abandoned their families justify it by saying, 'We did it for love' – meaning that they were driven by their hormones? All sorts of crimes have been committed in the name of 'love'. Those who wish to liberalize laws often do so by citing specific examples and appealing to love. Thus divorce laws should become lax, because this is loving for those who are unhappily married – but there is a price to be paid by abandoned spouses and children and by those whose marriages will fail in the future because of easy access to divorce. Euthanasia should be made available out of love for those who are suffering – but there will be a price to be paid by elderly folk pressurized to embrace it by greedy relatives. (As the quip goes, 'Where there is a will, there is a relative!')

113

This point is made by the heroine in Charlotte Brontë's *Jane Eyre*, who discovers at the altar that her husband-to-be is already married. 'Love' would have told her to go ahead with the wedding, but:

Laws and principles are not for the times when there is no temptation: they are for such moments as this, when body and soul rise in mutiny against their rigour; stringent are they; inviolate they shall be. If at my individual convenience I might break them, what would be their worth? They have a worth – so I have always believed; and if I cannot believe it now, it is because I am insane – quite insane: with my veins running fire, and my heart beating faster than I can count the throbs. Preconceived opinions, foregone determinations, are all I have at this hour to stand by: there I plant my foot.[6]

The relation between love and law can be compared to that between water and pipes. Without the pipes to channel and direct it, water can do more harm than good. On the other hand, the most perfect piping system in the world is of no use whatsoever unless there is water to flow through it. Likewise, the piping system of the law is useless without the water of love, while the latter can be dangerous when not directed by the former.

Worship

How can a young man keep his way pure?
    By guarding it according to your word.
With my whole heart I seek you;
    let me not wander from your commandments!
I have stored up your word in my heart,
    that I might not sin against you.
Blessed are you, O Lord;
    teach me your statutes!

With my lips I declare
    all the rules of your mouth.
In the way of your testimonies I delight
    as much as in all riches.
I will meditate on your precepts
    and fix my eyes on your ways.
I will delight in your statutes;
    I will not forget your word.
(Ps. 119:9–16)

OLD TESTAMENT VERSUS NEW TESTAMENT

How does the New Testament relate to the Old? This question might appear to be boring and theoretical, but in fact it is extremely practical. The way we answer it will affect our stance on many other issues, though most Christians are unaware of this. Such issues include the following: Should we be pacifists? Must we observe the Sabbath? Is it legitimate to have a state religion? Should babies be baptized? Clearly in the Old Testament the people of God fought wars, kept the Sabbath, lived in a 'theocratic' society and circumcised baby boys. How relevant is that in deciding what we should do today? Most Christians approach such issues without realizing that their judgements are largely determined by the view they are presupposing (usually without reflection) on the relation between Old and New Testaments.

First, we must note some important differences between Old and New Testaments/Covenants (the same word in Greek):

1 In the Old Testament the people of God form an elect nation; in the New Testament the elect people are composed of individuals from all nations.

2 The Old Testament has the shadow; Christ brings the reality (Heb. 8:1–6, 10:1–14):

For since the law has but a shadow of the good things to come instead of the true form of these realities, it can never, by the same sacrifices that are continually offered every year, make perfect those who draw near . . . By a single offering [Christ] has perfected for all time those who are being sanctified. (Heb. 10:1, 14)

3 Under the Old Covenant God's law was written on tablets of stone; under the New Covenant it is written on our hearts: 'You show that you are a letter from Christ delivered by us, written not with ink but with the Spirit of the living God, not on tablets of stone but on tablets of human hearts' (2 Cor. 3:3).

4 At Pentecost the Holy Spirit is poured out on 'all flesh':

In the last days it shall be, God declares, that I will pour out my Spirit on all flesh, and your sons and daughters shall prophesy, and your young men shall see visions, and your old men shall dream dreams' – as promised in the Old Testament. (Acts 2:17; see Joel 2:28)

Despite these differences, can we talk of there being *one* Covenant? In the Old Testament God makes a number of different covenants with his people:

- With Noah: 'I establish my covenant with you, that never again shall all flesh be cut off by the waters of the flood, and never again shall there be a flood to destroy the earth' (Gen. 9:11).
- With Abraham: 'On that day the LORD made a covenant with Abram, saying,

"To your offspring I give this land . . ."' (Gen. 15:18).
- With Moses: 'Behold the blood of the covenant that the LORD has made with you in accordance with all these words' (Exod. 24:8).
- With David: 'For does not my house stand so with God? For he has made with me an everlasting covenant, ordered in all things and secure' (2 Sam. 23:5, looking back to 7:12–16).
- Finally, the promise of the New Covenant:

Behold, the days are coming, declares the LORD, when I will make a new covenant with the house of Israel and the house of Judah, not like the covenant that I made with their fathers on the day when I took them by the hand to bring them out of the land of Egypt, my covenant that they broke, though I was their husband, declares the LORD. But this is the covenant that I will make with the house of Israel after those days, declares the LORD: I will put my law within them, and I will write it on their hearts. And I will be their God, and they shall be my people. And no longer shall each one teach his neighbour and each his brother, saying, 'Know the LORD,' for they shall all know me, from the least of them to the greatest, declares the LORD. For I will forgive their iniquity, and I will remember their sin no more. (Jer. 31:31–34).

Yet there is also a sense in which there is one underlying covenant of grace with Abraham, as Paul argues in Galatians 3:15–25:

This is what I mean: the law, which came 430 years afterward, does not annul a covenant previously ratified by God, so as to make the promise void. For if the inheritance comes by the law, it no longer comes by promise; but God gave it to Abraham by a promise. (3:17–18)

There is an underlying unity in all of God's dealings with his people.

Tension to hold

All Christians agree that there is some continuity between Old and New Testaments, and also that there is some discontinuity. To deny any continuity would be to follow the second-century heretic Marcion, who denied that the God and Father of Christ has anything to do with that nasty Old Testament God; to deny any discontinuity would be to remain in Judaism. On the one hand, both covenants are about the same God and about the covenant made with Abraham – Christ is the fulfilment of Old Testament promises. On the other hand, the outworkings in Old Testament and New Testament are very different.

Christians differ according to how much weight they put on continuity or discontinuity. Mennonites, for example, stress the discontinuity, emphasizing the newness of the New Covenant. They are pacifists, do not baptize babies, etc. The Reformed, by contrast, lay more stress on the continuity, baptizing babies and not generally being pacifists. Alec Motyer, a Reformed scholar, once referred to 'that cursed blank page between Malachi and Matthew', signifying his unhappiness with those who place too much stress on the discontinuity.[7] The most important point is to maintain the tension; there can be debate about the precise weight to be placed on each side of it.

Credal statement

The Old Testament is not contrary to the New: for both in the Old and New Testament everlasting life is offered to Mankind by Christ, who is the only Mediator between God and Man, being both God and Man. Wherefore they are not to be heard, which feign that the old Fathers did look only for transitory promises. Although the Law given from God by Moses, as touching Ceremonies and Rites, do not bind Christian men, nor the Civil precepts thereof ought of necessity to be received in any commonwealth; yet notwithstanding, no Christian man whatsoever is free from the obedience of the Commandments which are called Moral. (*Thirty-Nine Articles*, art. 7)

PRAYERS

Lord, you have taught us that all our doings without love are nothing worth: send your Holy Spirit and pour into our hearts that most excellent gift of love, the true bond of peace and of all virtues, without which whoever lives is counted dead before you. Grant this for your only Son Jesus Christ's sake. (*Common Worship*: Collect for Second Sunday after Trinity)

Almighty God, you have taught us through your Son that love is the fulfilling of the law: grant that we may love you with our whole heart and our neighbours as ourselves; through Jesus Christ our Lord. (*Common Worship*, Post Communion for Sixteenth Sunday after Trinity)

Questions to answer

- What is the role of law in the Christian life?
- How does the New Testament relate to the Old?

NOTES

1 <http://www.bilerico.com/2011/10/ marriage_according_to_the_bible.php>.

2 For a full discussion, see C. S. Cowles et al. *Show Them No Mercy – Four Views on Canaanite Genocide*. Grand Rapids: Zondervan, 2003.

3 On this division, see P. S. Ross, *From the Finger of God: The Biblical and Theological Basis for the Threefold Division of the Law*. Fearn: Mentor, 2010.

4 This is a controversial topic. See C. J. Donato (ed.) *Perspectives on the Sabbath: Four Views*. Nashville: B&H, 2011.

5 As Jesus says, these are two commandments, not three. The idea that we are also *commanded* to love ourselves is a recent aberration born of a therapeutic culture.

6 C. Brontë, *Jane Eyre*. London: J. M. Dent, 1950, 317.

7 As a student in the early 1970s I heard him make this comment. In a conversation in 2010 he vigorously reaffirmed it.

RESOURCES

G. L. Bahnsen et al. *Five Views on Law and Gospel*. Grand Rapids: Zondervan, 1996.

C. E. Braaten and C. R. Seitz (eds) *I am the Lord Your God*. Grand Rapids: Eerdmans, 2005.

C. J. H. Wright *Walking in the Ways of the Lord*. Leicester: IVP, 1995.

C. J. H. Wright *Old Testament Ethics for the People of God*. Leicester: IVP, 2004.

Chapter 12

THE WORK OF CHRIST

Aims of this chapter

In this chapter we look at the work of Christ, asking:

- What did Christ come to do for us? (In answering this we will outline four basic models that have been used.)
- How do these four models relate to one another?
- Is there a place for the doctrine of Penal Substitution?

INTRODUCTION

The New Testament has a range of material relating the question of what Christ came to do for us. This material can be arranged into four basic pictures or models: Christ as teacher, as victor over Satan, as Second Adam and as an atonement for sin. Each of these models is found both in the New Testament and in later theology and worship, and together they are seen to be complementary to each other; they are four angles on the same reality.

CHRIST AS TEACHER (CCC 516, 520)

This model responds to the fact that sinful humanity is ignorant of God and needs to be shown the way. Christ meets this need by showing us God and by his teaching and example.

CHRIST SHOWS US GOD

Jesus reveals the character and love of God by the quality of his own life. The cross in particular shows us God's love.

- John 1:18: 'No one has ever seen God; the only God, who is at the Father's side, he has made him known.'
- John 14:9: 'Jesus said to him, "Have I been with you so long, and you still do not know me, Philip? Whoever has seen me has seen the Father. How can you say, 'Show us the Father'?"'
- Romans 5:8: 'God shows his love for us in that while we were still sinners, Christ died for us.'
- 1 John 4:9–10:

In this the love of God was made manifest among us, that God sent his only Son into the world, so that we might live through him. In this is love, not that we have loved God but that he loved us and sent his Son to be the propitiation for our sins.

CHRIST'S TEACHING

The most famous example of this is found in the Sermon on the Mount (Matt. 5—7). Ironically, although this is probably the most admired, it is also the least practised of all Jesus' teaching. It impressed its original hearers: 'When Jesus finished these sayings, the crowds were astonished at his teaching, for he was teaching them as one who had authority, and not as their scribes' (Matt. 7:28–29). It has also impressed many down the ages, such as Mahatma Gandhi – though it did not persuade him to become a Christian.

CHRIST'S EXAMPLE

Jesus taught not just with words but by his very life – by specific actions, such as washing his disciples' feet (setting the example of a servant leader), by his Incarnation and by his cross:

- John 13:14–15: 'If I then, your Lord and Teacher, have washed your feet, you also ought to wash one another's feet. For I have given you an example, that you also should do just as I have done to you.'
- 2 Corinthians 8:9: 'For you know the grace of our Lord Jesus Christ, that though he was rich, yet for your sake he became poor, so that you by his poverty might become rich.'
- 1 Peter 2:21: 'For to this you have been called, because Christ also suffered for you, leaving you an example, so that you might follow in his steps.'

This is the least controversial of the four models and the easiest to grasp. But although it is an important part of the work of Christ, it is not the whole of it. Liberal theology since the nineteenth century, contrary to the almost unanimous tradition of the Church, has sought to reduce Christ's work to this aspect alone, arguing that our basic problem is ignorance and that Jesus simply came to teach us. Today there are people who argue that the essence of Christianity is the moral teaching of Jesus, the command to love one's neighbour, and that all talk of miracles or the deity of Christ is just superstition and a distraction from this. Clement Attlee said to his official biographer that he believed in the ethics of Christianity, but not the 'mumbo jumbo'.

Some seek to reduce Jesus' death on the cross to a demonstration of God's love. But in what way does the cross demonstrate love if there was no need for it? It would be like me torturing the cat and then telling you that I was doing it because I loved you. James Denney made this point well:

> If I were sitting on the end of the pier, on a summer day, enjoying the sunshine and the air, and someone came along and jumped into the water and got drowned 'to prove his love for me', I should find it quite unintelligible. I might be much in need of love, but an act in no rational relation to any of my necessities could not prove it. But if I had fallen over the pier and were drowning, and someone sprang into the water, and . . . saved me from death, then I should say, 'Greater love hath no man than this.' I should say it intelligibly, because there would be an intelligible relation between the sacrifice which love made and the necessity from which it redeemed.[1]

The role of Christ as teacher is an important part of the New Testament portrayal of his role, but it is only one part of it.

CHRIST AS VICTOR OVER SATAN ('CHRISTUS VICTOR') (CCC 538–40, 566)

This model responds to the fact that sinful humanity is in bondage to Satan and evil forces. Christ came to set us free from this bondage. 'He has delivered us from the domain of darkness and transferred us to the kingdom of his beloved Son' (Col. 1:13).

Jesus' ministry involved direct conflict with Satan and evil forces. It began with him facing Satan's temptations (Matt. 4:1–10 = Luke 4:1–12), and Jesus regularly cast out demons. Mark's Gospel devotes considerable attention to his battle against them. This conflict is part of the bigger picture that Christ came to bring victory over and liberation from Satan, who is the accuser holding the power of death. Jesus breaks this power by his cross and resurrection:

- Hebrews 2:14–15:

  He himself likewise partook of the same things, that through death he might destroy the one who has the power of death, that is, the devil, and deliver all those who through fear of death were subject to lifelong slavery.

- Colossians 2:15: God 'disarmed the rulers and authorities and put them to open shame, by triumphing over them in [Christ]'.

Satan's power is exercised through sin, law and death and Romans 6—8 shows how Christ has dealt with each of these in turn.

This model of the work of Christ was important in the Early Church, in a culture where there was a deep awareness of the power of evil spirits. *Athanasius in The

Incarnation of the Word, one of the best-known apologetic works from the fourth century, argues for Jesus' superiority on the grounds that demons are cast out in his name. Others in the Early Church elaborated on this model, explaining exactly how Christ gained the victory over Satan. The idea arose that God somehow tricked Satan into accepting Christ in our place. From this *Gregory of Nyssa expounded the 'fishhook theory', whereby Satan swallowed the bait of Christ's humanity, only to be caught on the hook of his deity. Satan thought it was worth accepting the innocent one in the place of the guilty, but did not realize that because of Christ's deity he would not be able to hold him. *Augustine in his popular preaching expounded the same idea in his mousetrap theory, where Satan is likened to a mouse attracted by the bait of Christ's blood. Others suggested that a ransom was paid *to* Satan, but this idea met with opposition from *Gregory of Nazianzus in the Early Church and in the Middle Ages from both *Anselm and *Abelard.

Since the Enlightenment with its rejection of the supernatural, this model of the work of Christ has been largely neglected in the West, where there is little awareness of evil spirits. It remains highly relevant, however, in large areas of Africa and Asia. Even in the West, with the rise of the occult it is more obviously relevant than it once was. It is this model of the work of Christ that underlies the imagery of C. S. Lewis's popular *The Lion, the Witch and the Wardrobe.*

CHRIST AS THE SECOND ADAM (CCC 518, 538, 460)

According to this model, the human race fell in Adam, who introduced sin and death, and rises again in Christ. The contrast between Adam and Christ was made by Paul in Romans 5:12–21, and is summarized in 1 Corinthians 15:22: 'For as in Adam all die, so also in Christ shall all be made alive.' This contrast was developed in the second century by *Irenaeus, who saw Christ as the Second Adam who 'recapitulates', or sums up (based on a word in Ephesians 1:10) the human race and introduces a new redeemed humanity. Irenaeus drew many parallels between Adam and Christ:

- Adam was born from virgin earth while Christ was born by a virgin birth. (This works better in English than in the original Greek!)
- Eve's sin introduced sin whereas Mary's act of obedience paved the way for salvation – 'And Mary said, "Behold, I am the servant of the Lord; let it be to me according to your word"' (Luke 1:38).
- Adam fell through contact with a tree while Christ saved us by dying on a tree.

Christ is the Second Adam who retraces Adam's steps, getting it right where Adam failed.

This model brings out the fact that Christ saves us not by the cross on its own but by all that he did: his Incarnation (becoming human), his life of obedience, his cross and resurrection, his Ascension and Second Coming all work together to bring our salvation.

Christ humbled himself in the Incarnation in order to raise us up. 'For you know the grace of our Lord Jesus Christ, that though he was rich, yet for your sake he became poor, so that you by his poverty might become rich' (2 Cor. 8:9). This idea was taken up by Irenaeus, and Athanasius took

it a stage further, arguing that Christ shares with us even his divinity.

> Our Lord Jesus Christ, the Word of God, of his boundless love, became what we are that he might make us what he himself is. (Irenaeus, *Against Heresies*, Book 5, preface)

> He became human that we might become divine. (Athanasius, *Incarnation of the Word* 54).

This idea of deification seems very foreign to us today, but it has its roots in the New Testament: God 'has granted to us his precious and very great promises, so that through them you may become partakers of the divine nature' (2 Pet. 1:4). There is an important point here. Christ came not just to bring us gifts but to share his very life with us. God does not merely 'sponsor' us; he actually adopts us into his own family.

The hope that human race will rise again is founded on the fact Christ rose from the dead as the firstfruits from the dead:

> For as by a man came death, by a man has come also the resurrection of the dead. For as in Adam all die, so also in Christ shall all be made alive. But each in his own order: Christ the firstfruits, then at his coming those who belong to Christ. (1 Cor. 15:21–23)

The resurrection lies at the heart of the Christian faith and Paul could state that 'if Christ has not been raised, your faith is futile and you are still in your sins' (1 Cor. 15:17). While the resurrection cannot be proved conclusively (how many historical 'facts' can be?) there is strong evidence for it. Paul lists a range of eyewitnesses to whom the risen Christ had appeared, including 'more than five hundred brothers' (1 Cor. 15:4–8). Many doubters have been won for the Christian faith by being persuaded by the evidence for the resurrection. Pinches Lapide was an Orthodox Jewish theologian who was persuaded that the bodily resurrection of Jesus was the only way to account for the historical evidence and concluded that Jesus was the Messiah *for the Gentiles* (not for Jews).[2]

It is because he ascended into heaven that Jesus is able to intercede for humanity: 'Consequently, he is able to save to the uttermost those who draw near to God through him, since he always lives to make intercession for them' (Heb. 7:25). Likewise, his Ascension is the basis for the gift of the Holy Spirit: 'Being therefore exalted at the right hand of God, and having received from the Father the promise of the Holy Spirit, he has poured out this that you yourselves are seeing and hearing' (Acts 2:33).

Worship

O loving wisdom of our God!
when all was sin and shame,
a second Adam to the fight
and to the rescue came.
(*John Henry Newman, 'Praise to the Holiest
in the height'

CHRIST AS AN ATONEMENT FOR SIN
(CCC 599–623)

This model responds to the fact that humanity is alienated from God by sin. Christ has come to reconcile us to God and put us right with him. Salvation is achieved by the whole course of Christ's life,

but is focused especially on the cross. Paul declared that when he arrived at Corinth, he 'decided to know nothing among you except Jesus Christ and him crucified' (1 Cor. 2:2). He also declared it 'as of first importance . . . that Christ died for our sins in accordance with the Scriptures' (1 Cor. 15:3). Neither statement should be seen as belittling the resurrection. Also 'of first importance' is the fact that 'he was raised on the third day' (15:4). In the rest of that chapter he explains at length why the resurrection is so important. Paul's point in 1 Corinthians 2:2 was that he preached only the Christ who was crucified, not that he preached only the crucifixion of Christ. The Western Church has always placed greater emphasis on the cross, while in the Greek East there has always been a greater emphasis upon the resurrection. Both are in danger of becoming one-sided.

About one third of Mark's Gospel is devoted to Jesus' death and resurrection. It is not normal, when writing about someone's life, to devote so much space to their end. Clearly the death and resurrection of Christ are at the heart of his significance and what he came to do for us. It is not for nothing that the cross has become the central symbol of the Christian faith. Our problem is not just ignorance and death, but also sin and guilt.

Christ died in our place, for our sins:

* 1 Peter 2:24: 'He himself bore our sins in his body on the tree, that we might die to sin and live to righteousness. By his wounds you have been healed.'
* 1 Peter 3:18: 'For Christ also suffered once for sins, the righteous for the unrighteous, that he might bring us to

God, being put to death in the flesh but made alive in the spirit.'

- 2 Corinthians 5:21: 'For our sake he made him to be sin who knew no sin, so that in him we might become the righteousness of God.'

On the cross Christ made our sin his own, and his righteousness became ours. This is known as the 'Great Exchange', an idea going back to the second century.

> Oh sweet exchange, oh unsearchable creation, oh unexpected benefits, that the wickedness of many should be hidden in a single righteous One, and that the righteousness of One should justify many transgressors! (*Epistle to Diognetus* 9)

Christ makes our sin his own and in return we receive his righteousness, which is not a bad deal! We are guilty but Christ bore our punishment in our place:

> He was wounded for our transgressions; he was crushed for our iniquities; upon him was the chastisement that brought us peace, and with his stripes we are healed. All we like sheep have gone astray; we have turned every one to his own way; and the LORD has laid on him the iniquity of us all. (Isa. 53:5–6)

Although the idea of Christ bearing our punishment is not stated in so many words in the New Testament, it is made clear that Jesus died a judicial death as a condemned criminal. Both the Old and the New Testament speak of death as the penalty for sin:

- Genesis 2:17: 'but of the tree of the knowledge of good and evil you shall not eat, for in the day that you eat of it you shall surely die'.

- Romans 6:23: 'The wages of sin is death, but the free gift of God is eternal life in Christ Jesus our Lord.'

So Christ died for our sins, bearing the judicial penalty of death in our place, thus freeing us from ultimate death.

We are condemned to death because, as Paul states, we were under the curse of the law, and we are freed from death because Christ took this curse upon himself:

- Galatians 3:13: 'Christ redeemed us from the curse of the law by becoming a curse for us'. This curse is not a purely abstract concept but refers to the specific curse of the law upon those who hang on a tree: 'his body shall not remain all night on the tree, but you shall bury him the same day, for a hanged man is cursed by God' (Deuteronomy 21:23).

The wrath of God is upon fallen humanity yet Christ drank from the cup of God's wrath taking the wrath upon himself instead of it falling on us. 'Father . . . Remove this cup from me. Yet not what I will, but what you will' (Mark 14:36). God's wrath is not explicitly mentioned here, but in the Old Testament there are two cups that God gives: the cup of blessing and the cup of wrath. There is no doubt which of these it was that Jesus had to bear. As a result, on the cross Jesus experienced our separation from God: 'My God, my God, why have you forsaken me?' (Mark 15:34, quoting Ps. 22:1). This is not to say Christ was actually separated from God or that God was actually angry with him. That would not be possible because Jesus is the second person of the Trinity and also because his work of salvation on the cross was the united work of Father, Son and Holy Spirit: 'how much more will the blood of *Christ*, who through the eternal *Spirit* offered himself without blemish to *God*, purify our conscience from dead works to serve the living God' (Heb. 9:14). The atonement was not one person of the Trinity working against another, but on the cross Christ experienced the sense of God's rejection, of separation from God, on our behalf.

This model of Christ as an atonement for sin is developed at length in Romans. Paul starts by arguing that all human beings are sinful and under God's wrath (1:18—3:20), then goes on to show how Christ dealt with this on the cross (3:21–26). The outcome of Christ bearing God's wrath is that we are reconciled to God: 'while we were enemies we were reconciled to God by the death of his Son' (5:10). The same point is made in 2 Corinthians 5:19: 'in Christ God was reconciling the world to himself.'

There are other images in Scripture which also describe Christ's work as an atonement for sin:

- Jesus gave his life as a ransom, paying the price that we owed: 'The Son of Man came not to be served but to serve, and to give his life as a ransom for many' (Mark 10:45).
- Humanity is in bondage but Christ has redeemed us, as someone might buy back a slave's freedom: 'In him we have redemption through his blood, the forgiveness of our trespasses, according to the riches of his grace' (Eph. 1:7); 'in whom [Christ] we have redemption, the forgiveness of sins' (Col. 1:14).
- We are impure as a result of sin and Christ offered himself as a sacrifice for our sins, a picture drawn from the Old Testament cultic system. This imagery is developed at length in Hebrews, especially in 9:11—10:25. Likewise, sin makes us unclean, but 'the blood of Jesus . . . cleanses us from all sin' (1 John 1:7).

It is important to see that these are different metaphors for the work of Christ and not to confuse them. So, for example, the cross as a sacrifice is clearly offered to God: 'Christ . . . offered himself without blemish to God' (Heb. 9:14). But it would be taking the metaphor too far to ask *from whom* God has redeemed us.

The Early Church held this model of the work of Christ alongside the other three models. In the eleventh century, however, Anselm made it the centre of his account of Christ's work. For him the central issue that Christ came to deal with is that our sin has dishonoured God, so Christ on the cross restores God's honour by offering satisfaction. (This is tied in both with the concept of honour and satisfaction in the feudal system and also with the medieval idea of offering satisfaction for sins through the sacrament of penance.) Others in the Middle Ages (such as *Bernard of Clairvaux) spoke rather of Christ bearing our punishment on the cross. It was this approach, known as Penal Substitution, that became central for the sixteenth-century Reformers.

What do you think? The question

Which of these models should we be preaching today?

Worship

Here is love vast as the ocean,
loving kindness as the flood,
when the Prince of life, our ransom,

124

shed for us his precious blood.
Who his love will not remember?
Who can cease to sing his praise?
He can never be forgotten
throughout heaven's eternal days.

On the mount of crucifixion
fountains opened deep and wide;
through the floodgates of God's mercy
flowed a vast and gracious tide.
Grace and love, like mighty rivers,
poured incessant from above,
and heaven's peace and perfect justice
kissed a guilty world in love.
(William Rees)

Sceptic's corner

Why can't God just forgive us, like the father of
the Prodigal Son?

Answer: First, the parable of the Prodigal Son
is not about the atonement. In fact it is one of
three parables which are told to explain why *Jesus*
(not the Father) associated with tax collectors and
'sinners' (Luke 15:1–2). Second, the objection
seems to assume that it is a greater thing simply to
forgive than also to deal with the consequences of
the evil deed. God does not merely forgive us, he
also takes upon himself the negative consequences
of our sin. He does not just shrug off our sin and
say that it does not matter.

PENAL SUBSTITUTION

The Protestant Reformers in the sixteenth
century regarded Penal Substitution as
central to the work of Christ, though they
did not fall into the mistake of imagining
that it was all that he came to do. The same
has been true of the Evangelical tradition,
for which Penal Substitution has remained
central. Some have overemphasized it to
the point where the other approaches are
practically ignored, but no Evangelical
theologian of any significance has ever
denied that other models are valid.

Penal Substitution is a doctrine that needs
to be stated very carefully as it is easily
caricatured, whether by supporters who state
it badly or by opponents who deliberately
misrepresent it. *Calvin, who states the
doctrine very carefully, taught that Christ
bore God's wrath and the punishment that
was due to us. Yet he was adamant that
there is no question of God being angry
with Christ and he was also careful to avoid
ever saying that God punished Christ. The
key point is that the atonement was the
united work of Father and Son, not the Son
persuading a reluctant Father or the Father
imposing something on a reluctant Son.

Historically Penal Substitution is a Catholic
doctrine in that it has been taught in a
wide range of the Christian tradition and
in all ages. Since the eighteenth-century
Enlightenment, however, it has come
increasingly under attack and today it is
not so widely held outside the Evangelical
tradition. Also, it has been attacked in recent
years by some within that tradition. A heated
debate was sparked by the publication in 2003
of Steve Chalke's book *The Lost Message of
Jesus*, which contains some very negative
comments on the doctrine, found on just
a handful of pages. It says nothing new but
it stirred up controversy because this was a
popular book by a well-known author, not
an academic tome for scholars. 'Chalkegate',
as the controversy is sometimes called, has
provoked a spate of books on the theme.
One good effect is that it has encouraged

people to examine the doctrine more carefully and to distinguish between what it actually says and what is a caricature of it, whether by its supporters or its detractors.

Errors to avoid

Penal Substitution is a valid part of the total picture, but we must not forget that it is only one aspect of one of the four models. There are two errors to be avoided. One is to reject Penal Substitution, which is a part of the biblical and historic Christian portrayal of the work of Christ. The other is to reduce the work of Christ to that one aspect, whether by denying the others or simply by ignoring or neglecting them. It has a legitimate place as one part of one of the models.

What do you think? My answer

These are the four different models, pictures, metaphors or maps of Christ's work. As we have seen, they are four angles on the one reality. They are *not* to be seen as alternatives – contrary to the impression given by Boyd and Eddy.[3] We have no right to pick and choose, whether by denying the truth of any of them or by adopting one model for ourselves to the exclusion of the others. All four are essential for an accurate picture of what Christ has done. All four should be preached today.

It is also worth noting that they merge into one another and that a full account of one will often require bringing in others. The model of Christ as Second Adam can be seen as the framework within which Christ functions as a teacher, puts us right with God and defeats Satan. Again, the way in which Christ defeats Satan is by dealing with our sin and guilt, which has alienated us from God.

Sceptic's corner

Isn't this divine child abuse?

Answer: This is a deliberately disingenuous charge. It relies for its force on the implication that Jesus was somehow an underage child. It leaves out of account the fact that the atonement is the united work of Father, Son and Holy Spirit. Also, it is an accusation not just against Penal Substitution but against *any* theory that ascribes saving value to the cross, including those which see it merely as a demonstration of God's love.

Credal statement

We confess Jesus Christ
    as Lord and God, the eternal Son of the Father;
    as truly human, born of the virgin Mary;
    as Servant, sinless, full of grace and truth;
    as the only Mediator and Saviour of the whole world, dying on the cross in our place, representing us to God, redeeming us from the grip, guilt and punishment of sin;
    as the Second Adam, the head of a new humanity, living a life of perfect obedience, overcoming death and decay, rising from the dead with a glorious body, being taken up to be with the Father, one day returning personally in glory and judgement to bring eternal life to the redeemed and eternal death to the lost to establish a new heaven and a new earth, the home of righteousness, where there will be no more evil, suffering or death;
    as Victor over Satan and all his forces, rescuing us from the dominion of darkness, and bringing us into his own kingdom;
    as the Word who makes God known.
(*London School of Theology Doctrinal Basis*)

PRAYER

Almighty God, you have given your only Son to be for us both a sacrifice for sin and also an example of godly life: give us grace that we may always most thankfully receive these his inestimable gifts, and also daily endeavour to follow the blessed steps of his most holy life; through Jesus Christ our Lord. (*Common Worship*: Post Communion Prayer for Ash Wednesday)

Question to answer

• What did Christ come to do for us?

NOTES

1 J. Denney *The Death of Christ*. London: Tyndale Press, 1951, 103.

2 P. Lapide *The Resurrection of Jesus*. London: SPCK, 1984.

3 ATS ch. 8/7.

RESOURCES

J. K. Beilby and P. R. Eddy (eds) *The Nature of the Atonement: Four Views*. Downers Grove: IVP, 2006.

S. R. Holmes *The Wondrous Cross: Atonement and Penal Substitution in the Bible and History*. Milton Keynes: Paternoster, 2007.

I. H. Marshall *Aspects of the Atonement: Cross and Resurrection in the Reconciling of God and Humanity*. Milton Keynes: Paternoster, 2007.

J. R. W. Stott *The Cross of Christ*. Leicester: IVP, 1986.

D. J. Tidball *The Message of the Cross*. Leicester: IVP, 2001.

D. J. Tidball et al. (eds) *The Atonement Debate*. Grand Rapids: Zondervan, 2008.

Chapter 13

THE PERSON OF CHRIST (CHRISTOLOGY)

Aims of this chapter

In this chapter we look at the person of Christ, asking:

- Who is Christ? (We will answer this by looking at the four major heresies condemned in the early centuries and the positive truths that they denied.)
- Where does the Virgin Birth fit in?
- What does it all mean for preaching Christ today?

The doctrine of the person of Christ (who he is) has always been intimately connected to the doctrine of the work of Christ (what he has done). This was true in the New Testament, it was true in the early centuries and it remains true today.

Errors to avoid

The bulk of this chapter is about avoiding the four errors from the Early Church.

WHO IS CHRIST? (CCC 461–83)

Answering this question is a huge task, and can be approached in many different ways. One way is to tackle it via the titles of Christ found in the New Testament such as 'Son of Man', 'Messiah', 'Son of God' or 'Lord'. Here, however, we will adopt a different approach. In the early centuries of the Church, among the various attempts to explain who Christ was there emerged four major errors or heresies that had to be opposed. In AD 451 the *Definition* of the *Council of Chalcedon condemned each of these,[1] but despite this all four are still around today. We shall look at each heresy in turn, noting the positive truths that they denied.

THE DEITY OF CHRIST – AGAINST ARIANISM

The first heresy to be looked at began with Arius, a teacher in the Alexandrian Church in the early fourth century. Arius denied the deity of Christ, arguing that there is only one God, the Father. Christ, he claimed, was neither divine nor human but rather a super-creature. Arius accepted, with the New Testament, that the universe was created through Christ, but believed that God had previously created Christ himself, out of nothing. So for Arius Christ was not a mere man – he is exalted above all the rest of creation, the highest of God's creatures, a super-angel. Yet Christ remains a creature created by God out of nothing, and is not himself God.

Arius's doctrine was condemned at the *Council of Nicea (in modern-day Turkey), which was convened by the Emperor Constantine in AD 325. This is the first of the 'General Councils' of the Church. It produced a creed called the Creed of Nicea. (This is not to be confused with a later revision produced by the *Council of Constantinople in AD 381, which is today known as the 'Nicene Creed'.) The Creed of Nicea affirmed positively that Christ is true God, fully God, and negatively that he was not created and that he had no beginning but is eternal. Arius himself recognized that these last two points went to the heart of the matter.

The Council of Nicea did not end the debates over the Trinity, and *Athanasius, who was Bishop of Alexandria for 45 years, defended the full deity of Christ against all attempts to deny or dilute it. By the end of the fourth century the issue was resolved and Arianism was finally excluded from the Church. That does not mean that the idea died out and today it is held by the Jehovah's Witnesses. Arianism is still alive and kicking – and knocking on our doors!

The New Testament, contrary to Arius's claim, proclaims the deity of Christ very clearly.

- **Christ is directly called God**. Arius held that only the Father is God, yet Scripture also explicitly refers to Christ as God:
  - John 1:1: 'In the beginning was the Word, and the Word was with God, and the Word was God.'
  - John 20:28: 'Thomas answered him, "My Lord and my God!"' – and Jesus did not object.
  - Hebrews 1:8: 'But of the Son he says, "Your throne, O God, is for ever and ever, the sceptre of uprightness is the sceptre of your kingdom."'

There are also other passages where the translation is disputed (Rom. 9:5; 2 Pet. 1:1) or where the text is uncertain (John 1:18).

- **Old Testament passages referring to 'Yahweh' are applied to Jesus**, thus identifying Jesus with God. If this happened just once or twice it might be unintentional but it happens repeatedly. The best examples are:
  - Joel 2:32: 'And it shall come to pass that everyone who calls on the name of the LORD shall be saved.' This is quoted of Jesus in Romans 10:13.
  - Isaiah 45:23: 'By myself I have sworn; from my mouth has gone out in righteousness a word that shall not return: "To me every knee shall bow, every tongue shall swear allegiance."' This is applied to Jesus in Philippians 2:10–11.
- **Jesus is worshipped**. For the early disciples, who were Jews, this would be idolatry unless Jesus was divine.
  - Matthew 28:17: 'When they saw him they worshipped him, but some doubted.'
  - Luke 24:52: 'They worshipped him and returned to Jerusalem with great joy.'
  - Revelation 5:13–14:

I heard every creature in heaven and on earth and under the earth and in the sea, and all that is in them, saying, 'To him who sits on the throne and to the Lamb be blessing and honour and glory and might for ever and ever!' And the four living creatures said, 'Amen!' and the elders fell down and worshipped.

The same book of Revelation later makes it clear that only God is to be worshipped:

I, John, am the one who heard and saw these things. And when I heard and saw them, I fell down to worship at the feet of the angel who showed them to me, but he said to me, 'You must not do that! I am a fellow servant with you and your brothers the prophets, and with those who keep the words of this book. Worship God.' (22:8–9)

This shows that the worship accorded to Jesus in chapter 5 is not honorific veneration of a super-angel but an acknowledgement of his deity.

The deity of Christ is not some irrelevant theological speculation but is vital for the work of Christ in a number of ways.

- Jesus came to reveal God to us. 'No one has ever seen God; the only God, who is at the Father's side, he has made him known' (John 1:18). A 'super-creature' would not suffice for this; it is important that Jesus is himself God. Arius claimed that because Christ was created by the Father he did not himself fully know God. This would undermine his ability to reveal God to us.
- If Jesus was not God it undermines the truth of Romans 8:32: 'He who did not spare his own Son but gave him up for us all, how will he not also with him graciously give us all things?' God did what Abraham was willing, but not required, to do (Gen. 22).

- If Arius is right, John 3:16 needs to be rewritten: 'God so loved the world, that he sent one of his creatures to do his dirty work.' If there is a bomb that needs to be defused it is one thing to risk an expensive robot, another to risk your own son. In the 1970s some Liberal theologians published a book denying the Incarnation, entitled *The Myth of God Incarnate*. If they are right the book could also have been called *The Myth of a God of Love*.
- How is it that the death of one man can suffice for the whole of humanity? How can the one counter-balance the many? If Jesus is the incarnate Word his deity gives unlimited value to his death, which is sufficient and more than sufficient to cover the sins of all humanity.

THE HUMANITY OF CHRIST – AGAINST DOCETISM

Arius denied the deity of Christ; others in the Early Church denied his humanity. This error arose at an early date and was already opposed in the New Testament:

Every spirit that confesses that Jesus Christ has come in the flesh is from God, and every spirit that does not confess Jesus is not from God. (1 John 4:2–3)

Many deceivers have gone out into the world, those who do not confess the coming of Jesus Christ in the flesh. Such a one is the deceiver and the antichrist. (2 John 7)

The undermining of the humanity of Christ often took the form of the statement that Jesus only *appeared* to be human and to suffer. This view is known as Docetism, from the Greek word *dokeo*, 'to appear'.

If Jesus is truly divine, the argument went, then surely as God he could not really have had a human body and suffered. Such an approach is found in some of the apocryphal gospels written after the first century and influenced by Gnosticism, one of which suggests that Jesus did not really suffer on the cross.[2] Orthodox Christians were not always free of Docetic tendencies. *Clement of Alexandria affirmed against Docetism that Jesus had a real body and that he ate and drank, but could not believe that Jesus actually *needed* the food. He ate not because his body required it but to protect his disciples from Docetism!

A more subtle way of undermining the humanity of Jesus was propounded by Apollinaris (d. 392), who was a leading opponent of Arius. Apollinaris held that just as we are a soul or mind living in a body, so Jesus is the divine Word in a body. In other words, the divine Word takes the place of the human soul or mind. The problem with such an approach is that the core of Jesus' being is not actually human – he is an alien being masquerading in a human body. He is, literally, 'not all there'. The idea that Jesus did not have a human mind or soul was condemned in AD 381 by the Council of Constantinople, the second of the General Councils.

As with his deity, the New Testament clearly proclaims the humanity of Christ, against any form of Docetism.

- **Jesus grew up as others do**. Jesus is depicted as growing in wisdom, needing to learn as children do:
  - Luke 2:40: 'And the child grew and became strong, filled with wisdom. And the favour of God was upon him.'
    - Luke 2:52: 'And Jesus increased in wisdom and in stature and in favour with God and man.'
- **Jesus was tempted as we are**. In the Gospels we see Jesus tempted by the devil (Matt. 4:1–10; Luke 4:1–12) on more than one occasion (Luke 4:13). He was made like us 'in every respect' so that he could be tempted (Heb. 2:14–18). Indeed, he is 'one who in every respect has been tempted as we are, yet without sin', which is why he is equipped to be our high priest to whom we can turn, being able to sympathize with our weakness (Heb. 4:15). This is possible only because of his full humanity. An Apollinarian Christ, with no human soul, could not be tempted as we are and would not be able to relate to us and our struggles.
- **Jesus was hungry and thirsty and experienced human emotions like anger and sorrow**.
  - Matthew 4:2: 'After fasting forty days and forty nights, he was hungry.'
  - John 19:28: 'After this, Jesus . . . said . . . "I thirst."'
  - Mark 1:41: 'Moved with pity, he stretched out his hand and touched him . . .' Some copies instead read that Jesus was 'moved with *anger*'. His behaviour in cleansing the temple (Mark 11:15–17) suggests the same.
  - John 11:35: 'Jesus wept.'
- **Jesus did not know everything**. Further evidence that he had a human mind is that he confessed to ignorance as to the timing of his return:
  - Mark 13:32: 'But concerning that day or that hour, no one knows, not even the angels in heaven, nor the Son, but only the Father.'
- **Jesus prayed to God as his Father and related to him as a human being**. Jesus

131

did not preach and perform miracles of himself but was dependent upon the Father both for his teaching and for his power. Interestingly, the following statements by Jesus come from John's Gospel, which is clearer than the other Gospels on his deity.

- John 5:19: 'Truly, truly, I say to you, the Son can do nothing of his own accord, but only what he sees the Father doing. For whatever the Father does, that the Son does likewise.'
- John 7:16: 'My teaching is not mine, but his who sent me.'
- John 8:26, 28: 'I have much to say about you and much to judge, but he who sent me is true, and I declare to the world what I have heard from him . . . I do nothing on my own authority, but speak just as the Father taught me.'

- **The Holy Spirit came upon Jesus at his baptism** (Matt. 3:16; Mark 1:10; Luke 3:22; John 1:32–33). It was by the Spirit of God that Jesus cast out demons (Matt. 12:28). Again, the picture is not of Christ exercising his own independent divine power but of him acting as a human being in obedience to his Father and in the power of the Spirit.

As with his deity, the humanity of Christ is vital for the work of Christ in a number of ways. If he was not fully human he would not be the Second Adam, he would not be our example and a pattern for us to follow, and he could not have died in our place. *Gregory of Nazianzus coined a slogan that expresses this well: 'That which he has not assumed he has not healed' (*Epistle* 101 to Cledonus). In other words, if he did not have a human soul or mind then our souls or minds are not healed. It is by becoming fully one with us that he saves us fully.

What do you think? The question

Is Mary 'Mother of God'?

THE UNITY OF CHRIST: THE INCARNATION – AGAINST ADOPTIONISM

In response to the first two heresies the Church affirmed the full deity and the full humanity of Christ. But how on earth can the same Jesus Christ be both human and divine? Our third heresy is an attempt to answer this question, known as Adoptionism. On this view, Jesus was a human being like us who was *adopted* by God the Father as his Son, either at his birth, his baptism or his resurrection.

This heresy is illustrated by the story of a conversation between a priest and a rabbi. The rabbi asked the priest what would happen if he was a very good priest. 'I might become a bishop,' was the answer. The rabbi then asked what would happen if he was a very good bishop. 'I might become a cardinal.' 'And suppose you were a very good cardinal?' 'I might become pope.' 'And suppose you were a very good pope?' the rabbi asked. 'What do you mean?' said the priest, 'Only God is above the pope.' 'Why not?' replied the rabbi, 'One of our boys made it.' That reflects an Adoptionist view of Jesus.

A more subtle form of Adoptionism regards the human Jesus and the divine Word as two separate beings, though outwardly they may appear to be one. Jesus is a human being who is indwelt from the beginning by the divine Word. This view of Christ has been compared to a pantomime horse, which outwardly appears (not always very convincingly!) to be one, but under the surface is composed of two actors. Nestorius, who became Bishop of Constantinople in AD 428, fell into a similar trap, despite his orthodox intentions. He struggled with the idea that Christ was divine from birth, famously stating, 'I could not call a two or three months old baby God.' Nestorius was opposed by *Cyril, the Bishop of Alexandria. Cyril obtained the support of Rome, and Nestorius was deposed in AD 431 by the *Council of Ephesus, the third of the General Councils.

The particular point of controversy was the use of the term *theotokos*, or 'Mother of God', to refer to Mary.[3] The issue at this stage was not the status of Mary, but rather the identity of Jesus. Was the baby born of Mary truly the eternal Word of God or was he a merely human baby who enjoyed a special relationship with God? Ultimately the controversy was about the very doctrine of the Incarnation. *Theotokos* affirms that the baby born of Mary was truly Emmanuel, God with us, something that at heart Nestorius did not believe.

At stake in this debate is the doctrine of the Incarnation, as stated in John 1:14: 'The Word became flesh and dwelt among us, and we have seen his glory, glory as of the only Son from the Father, full of grace and truth.' Nestorius (like a good number of modern theologians) reduced Jesus to a super-prophet. He was like us, only much better. This issue is no less important than the deity of Christ, and for the same reasons. In many ways the Nestorian way is diametrically opposed to the Arian way, yet ironically it also ends up by denying the deity of Jesus of Nazareth, though for very different reasons. The Arian Jesus is the incarnation of a super-human being, though one who was created by God. The Nestorian Jesus is purely human, though having a unique relationship with the eternal and divine Word. The doctrine of the Incarnation affirms that Jesus of Nazareth was none other than the eternal Word, made flesh.

The Nestorian Christ

© Miriam Kendrick 2013 www.miriamkendrick.co.uk

What do you think? My answer

The term *theotokos* is not found in the New Testament, but Luke 1:43 points to it: 'And why is this granted to me that the mother of my Lord should come to me?'

Worship

Christ, by highest Heav'n adored;
Christ the everlasting Lord;
Late in time, behold Him come,
Offspring of a virgin's womb.
Veiled in flesh the Godhead see;

Hail the incarnate Deity,
Pleased with us in flesh to dwell,
Jesus our Emmanuel.
(*Charles Wesley, 'Hark! the herald angels sing')

TWO NATURES OF CHRIST – AGAINST HYBRID

How can the same one person be both divine and human? The last of the four heresies, the most subtle of them all, attempts to answer this. This heresy argued that Jesus was a hybrid, a mongrel, a blend of deity and humanity. This can be compared to a mule, which is half-horse and half-donkey, but is itself neither. It is what the Early Fathers called a *tertium quid*, a 'third something' which is neither of the two original things. If you mix blue and yellow paint you end up with green paint, which is neither blue nor yellow. On this view, Jesus is human and divine by virtue of being a blend of the two, which makes him neither fully God nor fully man.

This view was attributed in AD 449 to the monk Eutyches at Constantinople, who was accused of confusing the humanity and deity of Christ, though many historians have concluded that what was confused was Eutyches's muddled theology! *Leo I (Bishop of Rome) wrote against this in his *Tome* (449). At the Council of Chalcedon (451), the fourth General Council, this heresy was condemned, alongside the previous three.

D. M. Baillie wittily commented that 'Eutyches . . . is dead, and he is not likely to be as fortunate as Eutychus [Acts 20:9–10] in finding an apostle to revive him!' But the rumours of Eutyches's death are greatly exaggerated. Many of those who imagine that they hold to an orthodox Chalcedonian view of the person of Christ in fact hold to a version of Eutychianism. Many seek to explain the unity of Christ by at some point postulating a blend of humanity and deity – e.g. the idea that he had a single divine–human will.

VIRGIN BIRTH

Matthew (1:18–25) and Luke (1:26–38) both teach that Jesus was conceived without a human father, as viewed from the perspective of Joseph and Mary, respectively. This is known as the Virgin Birth or, more accurately, the Virginal Conception. It is important not to confuse this with the idea of the Incarnation. It is not that Jesus is human on his mother's side and divine on his father's side – that would yield a Eutychian hybrid. Jesus is God because he is the eternal Word of the Father who has become a human being. After all, the paternal contribution to the conception of a child is just the three billion letters of code contained in the father's genome. That is a lot of information, but would hardly suffice to make Jesus divine.

Other major figures in the Bible had births which are in some way miraculous – Isaac, Samuel, John the Baptist. It is fitting that Jesus, who is so much greater than they, should also have a miraculous birth which points to his unique role.[4]

COUNCIL OF CHALCEDON

To answer the question 'who was Christ?', Chalcedon produced a *Definition*, which affirmed that Jesus Christ is one person (against Nestorius) fully God (against Arius) and fully man (against Apollinaris), made known in two natures which are not confused or blurred together (against Eutyches). This *Definition* was intended to unite the Church but had the opposite effect, never being accepted by the Egyptian or Ethiopian churches. The debate over the person of Christ rumbled on for a further 230 years, giving birth to two more General Councils (*Constantinople 553 and 680–81), the fifth and sixth of the General Councils. Despite these efforts the Eastern Church was never reunited.

Credal statement

Following the holy fathers, we confess with one voice that the one and only Son, our Lord Jesus Christ, is perfect in Godhead and perfect in manhood, truly God and truly man, that he has a rational soul and a body. He is of one substance with the Father as God, he is also of one substance with us as man. He is like us in all things except sin. He was begotten of his Father before the ages as God, but in these last days and for our salvation he was born of Mary the virgin, the *theotokos*, as man. This one and the same Christ, Son, Lord, Only-begotten is made known in two natures [which exist] without confusion, without change, without division, without separation. The distinction of the natures is in no way taken away by their union, but rather the distinctive properties of each nature are preserved. [Both natures] unite into one person and one hypostasis. They are not separated or divided into two persons but [they form] one and the same Son, Only-begotten, God, Word, Lord Jesus Christ, just as the prophets of old [have spoken] concerning him and as the Lord Jesus Christ himself has taught us and as the creed of the fathers has delivered to us. (*Chalcedonian Definition*)

The teaching of the *Definition* can be summarized in the phrase 'one person in two natures'. But what does this *mean*?

What is the difference between 'person' and 'nature'? The two terms can best be thought of as the answers to two different questions: *Who* was Jesus Christ? The one person of God the Word, made flesh. *What* was he? Truly divine and truly human – two natures. To put it differently, there was in Jesus Christ only one 'I', only one 'subject' of all that he experienced. This one subject or person is God the Word – there is not someone else (another 'person') who was the human Jesus. The Word remained God, with no lessening of his deity or divine nature, and yet he also took everything that belongs to humanity or human nature.

Sceptic's corner

Isn't this talk of persons and natures far removed from the dynamic picture of Christ that we see in the New Testament? Do you really expect people to preach this?

Answer: The *Chalcedonian Definition* sets limits, declaring that four different views are heresy. It could be said that the *Definition* is as much an exercise in negative as positive theology (see Chapter 3). Chalcedon is intended not itself to be preached but rather to inform and guide what is preached. It has a similar function to a corset, whose purpose is to maintain the shape of the body, but without itself being seen. Its purpose is to ensure that the sermon is not Arian, Apollinarian, Nestorian or Eutychian.

STATIC OR DYNAMIC?

Chalcedon is often criticized for presenting a static, analytic picture of Christ in terms of persons and natures, and to some extent that is true. Alongside this we also need the dynamic narrative of how the Word became flesh, which was brilliantly presented in the fifth century by Cyril of Alexandria, a much maligned figure.[5]

In all eternity God exists as Father, Son and Holy Spirit. A little over 2,000 years ago the Son 'became flesh': that is, he took human nature and became a human embryo. He did not thereby cease to be God or abandon his divine functions.[6] Rather, he embarked upon a new form of existence over and above his previous existence as God. In this human life he accepted human limitations. The Incarnation begins not just with the birth of Jesus but with his conception (Matt. 1:20; Luke 1:34–35) and during his first few weeks as an embryo, before he had a brain, he knew nothing. During his ministry in particular, while his teaching came from God the extent of what he knew was always within the capacity of his human brain. So, for example, the human Jesus did not know my name or the date of the Battle of Hastings. While he was in Galilee he was not also in Jerusalem. In the Garden of Gethsemane he referred not to his own limitless power but to the Father's readiness to rescue him: 'Do you think that I cannot appeal to my Father, and he will at once send me more than twelve legions of angels?' (Matt. 26:53).

At the Ascension Jesus was exalted to the right hand of God, appearing there now as one of us, as a human being (Heb. 9:24), representing us to God and interceding for us (Heb. 7:25). We do not need intermediaries but can turn directly to him:

We do not have a high priest who is unable to sympathize with our weaknesses, but one who in every respect has been tempted as we are, yet without sin. Let us then with confidence draw near to the throne of grace, that we may receive mercy and find grace to help in time of need. (Heb. 4:15–16)

PRAYER

Almighty God, you have given us your only-begotten Son to take our nature upon him and as at this time to be born of a pure virgin: grant that we, who have been born again and made your children by adoption and grace, may daily be renewed by your Holy Spirit, through Jesus Christ your Son our Lord. (*Common Worship*: Collect for Christmas Day)

Question to answer

- Who is Christ?

NOTES

1 For more on this, see A. N. S. Lane 'Christology Beyond Chalcedon' in H. H. Rowdon (ed.) *Christ the Lord*. Leicester: IVP, 1982, 257–81.
2 Gospel of Peter 4:10.
3 Cf. CCC 495, 509.
4 For more on this, see A. N. S. Lane 'The Rationale and Significance of the Virgin Birth' in D. F. Wright (ed.) *Chosen by God. Mary in Evangelical Perspective*. London: Marshall Pickering, 1989, 93–119.
5 For more on this, see A. N. S. Lane 'Cyril of Alexandria and the Incarnation' in I. H. Marshall, V. Rabens and C. Bennema (eds) *The Spirit and Christ in the New Testament and Christian Theology*. Grand Rapids: Eerdmans, 2012, 285–302.
6 ATS ch. 7/6.

RESOURCES

R. J. Bauckham *God Crucified: Monotheism and Christology in the New Testament*. Carlisle: Paternoster, 1998.

G. McFarlane *Why Do You Believe What You Believe About Jesus?*. Carlisle: Paternoster, 2000.

D. Macleod *The Person of Christ*. Leicester: IVP, 1998.

N. T. Wright *The Challenge of Jesus*. London: SPCK, 2000.

Chapter 14

THE UNIQUENESS OF CHRIST

Aims of this chapter

In this chapter we look at the uniqueness of Christ, asking:

- Is Christ the only way to God?
- What about modern pluralism?
- What about other religions?
- Why do people deny the uniqueness of Christ today?

IS CHRIST THE ONLY WAY TO GOD?
(CCC 65–67, 73)

Is Christ the only way to God? Until the nineteenth century the universal Christian response was 'Yes'. Jesus Christ holds a unique place as God's only Son, the only Saviour. The Christian faith is God's final revelation to be given in this age.

Error to avoid

Today there are many who deny the uniqueness of Christ and most of this chapter will be devoted to responding to that error. We first look at the teaching of the New Testament, then consider the alternative view and go on to consider the issues.

NEW TESTAMENT

The New Testament teaches in a variety of ways the uniqueness and finality of Jesus.

JESUS AS THE COMPLETE AND FINAL REVELATION OF GOD

Jesus Christ brings to fulfilment the incomplete revelation found in the Old Testament. This is the thrust of the whole of Hebrews and is clearly stated in 1:1–2:

> Long ago, at many times and in many ways, God spoke to our fathers by the prophets, but in these last days he has spoken to us by his Son, whom he appointed the heir of all things, through whom also he created the world.

JESUS AS GOD'S OWN AND ONLY SON

Christ is unique, not as the highest among many but as God's own and only Son:

- In the parable of the vineyard the owner sends various servants to the tenants, who mistreat them. Finally he sends his own son, whom they kill (Mark 12:1–11). There is a clear contrast between prophets, who are God's servants, and Jesus, who is God's Son.

- John 3:16: 'God so loved the world, that he gave his only Son, that whoever believes in him should not perish but have eternal life.'

JESUS AS THE DIVINE WORD INCARNATE

- John 1:1, 14: 'In the beginning was the Word, and the Word was with God, and the Word was God . . . And the Word became flesh and dwelt among us.'

Jesus is no mere prophet but God's Son, the Word of God himself. Because of this he will not be superseded by any future prophet or messiah.

And then if anyone says to you, 'Look, here is the Christ!' or 'Look, there he is!' do not believe it. False christs and false prophets will arise and perform signs and wonders, to lead astray, if possible, the elect. (Mark 13:21–22)

There is no way to upstage the Incarnation of God's own Son.

JESUS AS THE ONE SAVIOUR OF THE WHOLE WORLD

- John 4:42: 'They said to the woman, "It is no longer because of what you said that we believe, for we have heard for ourselves, and we know that this is indeed the Saviour of the world."'
- 1 John 2:2: 'He is the propitiation for our sins, and not for ours only but also for the sins of the whole world.'
- John 14:6: 'Jesus said to him, "I am the way, and the truth, and the life. No one comes to the Father except through me."'
- Acts 4:12: 'There is salvation in no one else, for there is no other name under heaven given among men by which we must be saved.'

Because of this, we will be judged by our relationship to him:

- John 3:18: 'Whoever believes in him is not condemned, but whoever does not believe is condemned already, because he has not believed in the name of the only Son of God.'
- John 3:36 'Whoever believes in the Son has eternal life; whoever does not obey the Son shall not see life, but the wrath of God remains on him.'

The Early Church (of the first three centuries) stood firm on the uniqueness of Christ, despite the fact that it made them unpopular and that they were persecuted and even martyred for it. In the great majority of cases, early Christians were martyred not for worshipping Christ, but for refusing to worship pagan gods. Those who were martyred were usually offered freedom in exchange for tossing some incense onto an altar, in worship of a pagan deity, but preferred death to this denial of Christ. It is because they remained firm that eventually the Roman Empire was won for Christ. As *Tertullian put it, 'the blood of the martyrs is the seed [of the church]'. Without their resolve it would have been easy for the Roman state to extinguish Christianity.

What do you think? The question (CCC 839–56)

Are all other religions false religions?

MODERN PLURALISM

The traditional view is rejected by many in the modern West. A leading exponent of the alternative view is *John Hick. In his

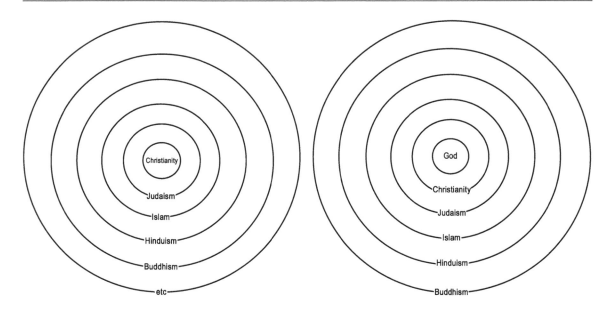

Christ at the Centre

God at the centre

God and the Universe of Faiths (1973). Hick compared the change from the traditional view to the 'Copernican Revolution' of the sixteenth century, which was discussed in Chapter 5. Previously people believed that the earth was at the centre of the universe and that the sun, moon, planets and stars all rotated round the earth. Copernicus proposed that the sun lay at the centre and that the earth was just one of the planets rotating round the sun. Hick calls for a similar revolution in theology. Christians traditionally have put Jesus and Christianity at the centre. Other religions have done the same, putting themselves as the centre. Now, says Hick, we need to put *God* at the centre and see all the religions as different planets rotating around this centre. There is no single valid prophet or religion; no prophet or religion is unique or final. The different religions should be viewed as different ways of salvation for different

cultures. Against Hick's illustration of the Copernican Revolution, though, it has been pointed out that there is life on only one of the planets!

Hick argues that the different world religions should view each other much as different Christian denominations currently view each other. They are all different paths to the same God. The religions each need to admit that they do not have the whole truth. We should acknowledge that other religions are valid and that we can learn some things from all of them. Hick views Jesus as God's agent within Christianity, but holds that the eternal Word is also at work in other religions. The exclusive claims made by and for Jesus, in John's Gospel especially, Hick sees as later accretions.

The problem with Hick's view is that not all religions have a concept of a monotheistic

God. To see different religions as different ways of salvation is a problem when some offer eternal life as the reward while others, like Buddhists, seek Nirvana or extinction as deliverance from an endless round of existence. How can the religions all be paths to the one God when not all believe in one God? How can they all be ways to salvation when they differ so widely as to the final destiny to be desired? Hick's approach, which claims to take an inclusive approach to all religions, looks more like an attempt to interpret other religions in line with a very Liberal Christianity!

Sceptic's corner

Hick uses several arguments to defend his view, to which we will respond in turn:

THE EUROPEAN MISSIONARY APPROACH HAS FAILED

Hick claims that the European missionary approach has failed and is over – so a new approach is now needed. It is true that the missionary movement has not yet succeeded in converting all of the world, but the achievements since the nineteenth century have been immense. For example, over half of Africans today call themselves Christian, where there were hardly any in the eighteenth century. It is claimed that by 2000 some two-thirds of Christians worldwide came from the countries evangelized by nineteenth-century Western missionaries. This success has been achieved precisely because missionaries believed firmly in the uniqueness and finality of Christ. At one stage the life expectancy of a European missionary in

parts of West Africa was a few months – yet they continued to come.

Nor is the missionary movement over, even though the likes of Hick have abandoned it. There are still large numbers of cross-cultural missionaries round the world. Some 20,000 of these come from South Korea, a country that has become strongly Christian in the last century or so owing to the missionary movement. According to some accounts this makes them second only to the United States as a sending country. The proportion of Christians in China continues to grow and the Chinese Church is itself sending out missionaries. Apart from cross-cultural missionaries, the task of preaching the gospel is being performed by local Christians all round the world.

THE TRADITIONAL VIEW ASSUMES THE SUPERIORITY OF EUROPEAN RACE AND CULTURE

Hick claims that the traditional view of the uniqueness of Christianity assumes the superiority of European race and culture. There may have been some truth in this where the nineteenth-century missionary movement is concerned, but it is true neither of the origins of the Christian faith nor of today. As regards the former, Christianity originated as a Jewish religion in the Middle East, not in Europe. It is true that for many centuries Christianity was predominantly European – but no longer. Christianity is now a genuinely worldwide faith, with a church in just about every country in the world. In fact in the last century or so Christianity has become the first truly worldwide religion in human history. Ironically, one of the few places in the world where it is declining is in its one-time heartland, Europe. So Hick's argument is somewhat out of date. The traditional gods of Europe are pagan gods – Zeus, Odin, etc. If the early Christians had followed Hick's approach, we would still be worshipping them, and probably practising human sacrifice. The assumption of European/Western cultural superiority manifests itself today not in Christian evangelism but in the attempt to export the current Western views of individualism, democracy, pluralism, egalitarianism and tolerance to the rest of the world.

ALL NON-CHRISTIANS ARE ETERNALLY LOST

Hick claims that the traditional view implies that all non-Christians are eternally lost. That does not necessarily follow. It is one thing to say that Christ is the only Saviour, that no one can be saved except through him; it is another thing to say that everyone who hasn't heard of him is lost. What about those dying in infancy or Jews in Old Testament times? Surely they are not all lost? Likewise, we cannot assume that those who never hear of him are all lost. Some Christians claim that they are, but many who hold to the uniqueness of Christ would deny this. The opposite of believing in Christ is not ignorance of him but rejecting him: 'Whoever believes in the Son has eternal life, but whoever *rejects* the Son will not see life' (John 3:36, TNIV). We will return to this issue in the final chapter.

BASIC ISSUES

1 **The person of Christ**. If Jesus is God incarnate, then he must be God's

---

What do you think? My answer

Hick claims that the traditional Christian view implies that all other religions are totally evil. That does not follow from the uniqueness of Christ. Judaism and Islam contain much truth, since both worship the God of Abraham and draw upon biblical revelation. Judaism is built on the Old Testament and Islam draws upon the data of both Old and New Testaments. For some centuries Christians saw the fledgling Islamic movement as a Christian heresy, rather than a new religion. This was the view taken by *John of Damascus in the eighth century, for example. There is no need to claim that the other religions are completely devoid of truth. The Christian claim is not that they lack all truth, but that they lack the supreme truth, Christ as God's unique and final revelation:

> The kingdom of heaven is like treasure hidden in a field, which a man found and covered up.

Then in his joy he goes and sells all that he has and buys that field. Again, the kingdom of heaven is like a merchant in search of fine pearls, who, on finding one pearl of great value, went and sold all that he had and bought it. (Matt. 13:44–46)

Whatever gain I had, I counted as loss for the sake of Christ. Indeed, I count everything as loss because of the surpassing worth of knowing Christ Jesus my Lord. For his sake I have suffered the loss of all things and count them as rubbish, in order that I may gain Christ. (Phil. 3:7–8)

Relative to Christ, other ways are mere rubbish. In fact Paul's language is rather more graphic than our sanitized modern translations and it might be more accurate to say that he considered them as so much bullshit – not language that I would use, but that is what Paul wrote!

unique and final revelation. John Hick understood the logic of this, so argued against the Incarnation in part on the ground that it would make Christ unique and the only Saviour.[1] Again, if Christ died for the sins of the world, then he must be unique, as no other religious leader claims to have done so. But for Liberal Christians Jesus is simply an inspired man (not God incarnate) who came to teach us the way (not to die for our sins). Such a Christ is not unique.

2 **Pluralism**. Hick's view is very popular in our society not because of its intellectual rigour so much as because it coheres well with modern views of religion. Different religions are tolerated, but they are viewed as aspects of culture and as expressions of people's private values. Religion is not favoured when it makes universal truth claims or claims absolute truth and uniqueness. The only ultimate truth allowed is pluralism itself, and this is jealously guarded. In school today children are taught that science and history are about facts, and religion is about personal and cultural values. Different cultural groups have different religions, just as they wear different clothes and eat different foods. School is to teach children to be tolerant and appreciative of different cultures' foods, customs and religions. Likewise, on the BBC different religions are each given their slot to say what they believe – so long as they do not claim uniqueness. Hick's views fit very well into this modern Western pluralism.

There is a clear conflict between biblical Christianity and modern Western pluralism. Christians today need to hold firm to the uniqueness of Christ, as did the early Christians in the pagan Roman Empire and the pioneer missionaries of the eighteenth and nineteenth centuries. They were ready to give their lives for this, and many were called upon to do so. In each case their firm and sacrificial stand resulted in the triumph of the gospel, in the Roman Empire and in many areas of the non-European world.

Credal statement

We affirm that there is only one Saviour and only one gospel, although there is a wide diversity of evangelistic approaches. We recognise that everyone has some knowledge of God through his general revelation in nature. But we deny that this can save, for people suppress the truth by their unrighteousness. We also reject as derogatory to Christ and the gospel every kind of syncretism and dialogue which implies that Christ speaks equally through all religions and ideologies. Jesus Christ, being himself the only God-man, who gave himself as the only ransom for sinners, is the only mediator between God and people. There is no other name by which we must be saved. All men and women are perishing because of sin, but God loves everyone, not wishing that any should perish but that all should repent. Yet those who reject Christ repudiate the joy of salvation and condemn themselves to eternal separation from God. To proclaim Jesus as 'the Saviour of the world' is not to affirm that all people are either automatically or ultimately saved, still less to affirm that all religions offer salvation in Christ. Rather it is to proclaim God's love for a world of sinners and to invite everyone to respond to him as Saviour and Lord in the wholehearted personal commitment of repentance and faith. Jesus Christ has been exalted above every other name; we long for the day when every knee shall bow to him and every tongue shall confess him Lord. (*Lausanne Covenant*, art. 3: The Uniqueness and Universality of Christ, from *Lausanne Congress (1974))

Worship

There's no greater Name than Jesus,
Name of Him who came to save us,
In that saving Name of Jesus
Every knee should bow.

Let everything that is 'neath the ground,
Let everything in the world around,
Let everything that's high o'er the sky
Bow at Jesus' Name.
(Michael Baughen)

PRAYER

My Lord Jesu, I confess and know that thou
only art the true, the beautiful, and the good.
Thou alone canst make me bright and
glorious, and canst lead me up after thee.
Thou art the way, the truth, and the life,
and none but thou . . . Thou art the way; thou
alone. (*John Henry Newman, *Meditations*)

Question to answer

- Is Christ the only way to God?

NOTE

1 J. Hick, 'Jesus and the World
Religions' in J. Hick (ed.) *The Myth
of God Incarnate*. London: SCM Press,
1977, 167–85.

RESOURCES

S. W. Chung *Christ the One and Only:
A Global Affirmation of the Uniqueness of
Jesus Christ*. Milton Keynes: Paternoster,
2005.

J. R. Edwards *Is Jesus the Only Savior?*.
Grand Rapids: Eerdmans, 2005.

M. Nazir-Ali *The Unique and Universal
Christ: Jesus in a Plural World*. Milton
Keynes: Paternoster, 2008.

J. G. Stackhouse (ed.) *No Other Gods
before Me? Evangelicals and the Challenge
of World Religions*. Grand Rapids: Baker,
2001.

C. J. H. Wright *Thinking Clearly about the
Uniqueness of Jesus*. Crowborough: Monarch,
1997.

Chapter 15

HOLY SPIRIT

Aims of this chapter

In this chapter we look at the Holy Spirit, asking:

- Who (or what) is the Holy Spirit?
- Is the Holy Spirit God?
- Is the Holy Spirit personal?
- What does the Holy Spirit do in us?
- What are the gifts of the Spirit?

PART 1: THE PERSON OF THE HOLY SPIRIT (CCC 687–747)

THE 'ANONYMITY' OF THE HOLY SPIRIT

The Holy Spirit is self-effacing – his function is to point to Jesus, not to himself:

- John 15:26: 'When the Helper comes, whom I will send to you from the Father, the Spirit of truth, who proceeds from the Father, he will bear witness about me.'
- John 16:13–15:

When the Spirit of truth comes, he will guide you into all the truth, for he will not speak on his own authority, but whatever he hears he will speak, and he will declare to you the things that are to come. He will glorify me, for he will take what is mine and declare it to you. All that the Father has is mine; therefore I said that he will take what is mine and declare it to you.

As a result of this anonymity and because the first priority was to resolve the status of Christ, the Holy Spirit was somewhat neglected in the theology of the second- and third-century Church. The creed produced at the *Council of Nicea in AD 325 simply concluded: 'And [we believe] in the Holy Spirit'. A measure of neglect has continued until recently, an honourable exception being *Calvin, who was described by *B. B. Warfield as 'the theologian of the Holy Spirit', because of the prominence he gave the Holy Spirit in his teaching. In the twentieth century there has been considerably more interest in the Spirit, thanks especially to Pentecostalism.

THE DEITY OF THE HOLY SPIRIT

The deity of Christ was resolved in the middle of the fourth century. That then posed the question of the status of the Spirit. There were some who affirmed the deity of the Son, but denied the deity of the Spirit. This is frankly a ridiculous position – a trinity within which two members are divine and the third not. It gives us the worst of both worlds – the problems associated with plurality in God and also the incoherence of a mixed trinity. After a brief controversy the *Council of Constantinople, in AD 381, resolved the issue, producing the so-called Nicene Creed, which affirms the deity of the Spirit, though without actually calling him 'God'.

Credal statement

And [we believe] in the Holy Spirit, the Lord and life-giver, who proceeds from the Father [and the Son]. Together with the Father and the Son he is worshipped and glorified. He spoke through the prophets. (Nicene Creed)

What is the biblical basis for the deity of the Spirit? The Old Testament contains many references to the Spirit of the Lord. There is no question of this being a creature, but is the Spirit of the Lord any more distinct from the Father than is, say, 'the arm of the Lord' or 'the eyes of the Lord'? There are various pointers to the deity of the Spirit in the New Testament:

- Paul affirms that 'the Lord is the Spirit' (2 Cor. 3:17).
- It is blasphemy against the Spirit in particular that will not be forgiven: 'Every sin and blasphemy will be forgiven people, but the blasphemy against the Spirit will not be forgiven. And whoever speaks a word against the Son of Man will be forgiven, but whoever speaks against the Holy Spirit will not be forgiven, either in this age or in the age to come' (Matt. 12:31–32). It would make no sense if blasphemy against the Spirit (who is not God) cannot be forgiven,

while blasphemy against the Father and Son (who are God) can be forgiven.
- John 14—16 is thoroughly Trinitarian, indicating the place of the Spirit within the Godhead.
- 'Binitarianism' (the belief that Father and Son are God, Holy Spirit is not) was so obviously incoherent that it very soon died out. Arianism, denial of the deity of Christ, is a perennial heresy and Arians still come knocking on our doors trying to sell us the *Watchtower* magazine. Some other heresies, by contrast, are very short-lived and Binitarianism is one of these.

THE PERSONALITY OF THE HOLY SPIRIT

The Spirit may be divine, but should we think of him (or 'it'?) as an impersonal force of God? No one suggests that the eyes of the Lord or the hand of the Lord should be understood as a person. The Old Testament references to the 'Spirit of God' *can* equally be read that way, but the New Testament clearly indicates that this is wrong. The Greek word for Spirit, *pneuma*, is neuter, which has encouraged some people to think of the Holy Spirit as just a force, as an 'it'. There are good reasons, though, for thinking that this is wrong:

- In John 16:13 the grammar very clearly affirms the personality of the Spirit: 'When the Spirit [neuter] of truth comes, he [masculine, not "it" neuter] will guide you into all the truth.' John defies the laws of grammar in order to affirm the personality of the Spirit.
- Ephesians 4:30: 'Do not grieve the Holy Spirit of God, by whom you were sealed for the day of redemption.' You can grieve a person, but not an impersonal force. You can misuse electricity but you cannot grieve it.

- Finally, the idea of an impersonal Spirit makes nonsense of the Trinity. It is incoherent to have a trinity composed to two persons and an impersonal force – Father, Son and Wind!

FILIOQUE

The Nicene Creed as originally drawn up at the Council of Constantinople (381) affirmed that the Spirit 'proceeds from the Father' – following John 15:26: 'When the Helper comes, whom I will send to you from the Father, the Spirit of truth, *who proceeds from the Father*, he will bear witness about me.' In the Western (Latin) Church the idea grew that the Spirit proceeds from the Father *and the Son* and this idea came to be incorporated into the Nicene Creed, the Latin word *filioque* ('and from the Son') being added. The Eastern (Greek) Church protested vehemently, denying that the Western Church had the authority to change the creed unilaterally. Rome itself was one of the last places in the West to accept the addition of the word – for good reason, as when it finally was accepted this soon led to a breach between the Roman Catholic and Eastern Orthodox Churches (1054), which has not been healed to this day.

PART 2: THE WORK OF THE HOLY SPIRIT

The following three headings are inspired by Brenton Brown's chorus 'Over All the Earth', which contains the repeated prayer that God would 'reign in me again'. These headings represent three major aspects of the work of the Spirit, but are not intended to be an exhaustive account.

REIN ME IN

The Holy Spirit works in us *before* we come to believe. God does not simply wait to see

who will believe in him but makes the first move in our hearts, drawing us to faith in Christ. He takes the initiative by working in people by his Spirit to lead them to faith. This is traditionally known as 'prevenient grace' – from the Latin word *praevenio*, which means 'come before'. This inner work of the Holy Spirit, drawing us to Christ, came to be called 'grace', following the usage of Luke: 'When [Paul] arrived, he greatly helped those who through grace had believed' (Acts 18:27). 'Prevent us' in this prayer from the sixteenth-century Book of Common Prayer becomes 'Go before us' in the contemporary *Common Worship* – see the first of the 'Prayers' at the end of this chapter.

> Prevent us, O Lord, in all our doings with thy most gracious favour, and further us with thy continual help; that in all our works, begun, continued, and ended in thee, we may glorify thy holy Name, and finally by thy mercy obtain everlasting life; through Jesus Christ our Lord. (Book of Common Prayer, Communion Service)

In what way does the Spirit work in us? One important way is to convict the world (i.e. non-Christians) of their sin, to show them their guilt and need of Christ:

> And when he comes, he will convict the world concerning sin and righteousness and judgement: concerning sin, because they do not believe in me; concerning righteousness, because I go to the Father, and you will see me no longer; concerning judgement, because the ruler of this world is judged. (John 16:8–11)

In 1 Thessalonians 1:5 Paul writes of his preaching that 'our gospel came to you not only in word, but also in power and in the

Holy Spirit and with full conviction'. Ulm 'Cathedral', in southern Germany, has two distinctive points. It has the highest church tower in the world, with 768 steps to the top, for which I can vouch as I have twice climbed it. It also has a distinctive baroque canopy above the pulpit. In this there is a miniature pulpit with a dove in it. The symbolism is clear. Unless the divine preacher is at work in the hearts of the congregation the words of the human preacher will be ineffective.

Worship

Breathe on me, Breath of God,
Fill me with life anew;
That I may love what thou dost love
And do what thou wouldst do.
(Edwin Hatch)

REIGN IN ME

The Holy Spirit is at work in Christians in a variety of ways.

Indwelling

The Holy Spirit works in unbelievers to bring them to faith. He then lives within us when we have come to faith: 'You know [the Spirit of truth], for he dwells with you and will be in you' (John 14:17). Indeed, this is the distinctive mark of being a Christian: 'You, however, are not in the flesh but in the Spirit, if in fact the Spirit of God dwells in you. Anyone who does not have the Spirit of Christ does not belong to him' (Rom. 8:9). The indwelling Spirit is immediately described as *Christ* in us: 'If Christ is in you, although the body is dead because of sin, the Spirit is life because of righteousness' (Rom. 8:10). Similarly, 'To them God chose to make known how great among the Gentiles are the riches of the glory of this mystery, which is Christ in you, the hope of

glory' (Col. 1:27). While the Spirit is *at work* in unbelievers to lead them to faith, when we believe he is not just at work in us (from time to time) but *dwells* within us.

The indwelling Holy Spirit witnesses to our adoption by bearing witness to our spirit that we are children of God:

- Romans 8:15: 'For you did not receive the spirit of slavery to fall back into fear, but you have received the Spirit of adoption as sons, by whom we cry, "Abba! Father!"'
- Galatians 4:6: 'And because you are sons, God has sent the Spirit of his Son into our hearts, crying, "Abba! Father!"'

Prompting

The Holy Spirit works within us, prompting us to do this or not to do that. There is a conflict between the Spirit and the flesh, our fallen sinful nature:

- Romans 8:13: 'If you live according to the flesh you will die, but if by the Spirit you put to death the deeds of the body, you will live.'
- Galatians 5:17, 25:

   The desires of the flesh are against the Spirit, and the desires of the Spirit are against the flesh, for these are opposed to each other, to keep you from doing the things you want to do . . . If we live by the Spirit, let us also walk by the Spirit.

The Christian life is a series of responses to this prompting, which we either follow or do not. *John Stott summarizes our response with five 'D's: the Spirit enables us to *discern* God's will, *distinguish* right from wrong, *desire* God's way, *determine* to follow it and *do* it.[1]

148

How we respond to the Spirit's prompting has consequences for now and for eternity:

> Do not be deceived: God is not mocked, for whatever one sows, that will he also reap. For the one who sows to his own flesh will from the flesh reap corruption, but the one who sows to the Spirit will from the Spirit reap eternal life. And let us not grow weary of doing good, for in due season we will reap, if we do not give up. (Gal. 6:7–9)

We sow the one sort of fruit or the other according to whether we follow the leading of the flesh or the Spirit.

Error to avoid

We must not grieve the Holy Spirit by resisting his inner leading, by failing to respond to him:

- Ephesians 4:30: 'And do not grieve the Holy Spirit of God, by whom you were sealed for the day of redemption.'

(This is a practical error, a mistake in how we live, and is included because theology is about more than just head knowledge.)

THE FRUIT OF THE SPIRIT

The fruit that the Holy Spirit bears in our lives is a Christ-like character. There are lists which describe the different aspects of this character:

- Galatians 5:22–23: 'The fruit of the Spirit is love, joy, peace, patience, kindness, goodness, faithfulness, gentleness, self-control; against such things there is no law.'
- 2 Peter 1:5–7: 'Make every effort to supplement your faith with virtue, and virtue with knowledge, and knowledge with self-control, and self-control with steadfastness, and steadfastness with godliness, and godliness with brotherly affection, and brotherly affection with love.'
- 1 Corinthians 13:4–7 also describes the fruit that the Spirit brings:

> Love is patient and kind; love does not envy or boast; it is not arrogant or rude. It does not insist on its own way; it is not irritable or resentful; it does not rejoice at wrongdoing, but rejoices with the truth. Love bears all things, believes all things, hopes all things, endures all things.

These are three different lists, but with significant overlap. Clearly, each is a representative list, not an exhaustive one. In all of these lists love is pre-eminent, since God is love. For more on the pre-eminence of love, see Chapter 11.

These things are described as fruit, but that does not mean that they come automatically. It is not like growing hair while one sleeps; it requires our choices and our effort: 'For this very reason, *make every effort* to supplement your faith with virtue' (2 Pet. 1:5). We need to walk by the Spirit (Gal. 5:16–25). It is the Holy Spirit who bears the fruit but we cannot just lie back and leave it to the Spirit – just as farmers and gardeners cannot leave all the work to the rain and sun.

Worship

Holy Spirit, right divine,
King within my conscience reign;
Be my Lord, and I shall be
Firmly bound, forever free.
(Samuel Longfellow, 'Holy Spirit, truth divine')

RAIN ON ME

Baptism in/with/of the Holy Spirit[2]

John the Baptist promised that, unlike him, Jesus would baptize with the Holy Spirit (Matt. 3:11; Mark 1:8; Luke 3:16; John 1:33). To what does this refer? Paul tells the Corinthians that 'in one Spirit we were all baptized into one body – Jews or Greeks, slaves or free – and all were made to drink of one Spirit' (1 Cor. 12:13). It is noteworthy that he states that *all* believers have received this baptism – not just some. We will see (Chapter 18) that receiving the Spirit is one of the features of Christian initiation (becoming a Christian) and it is to this that baptism in the Spirit refers.

In Acts we also read of people being *filled* with the Holy Spirit, when the Spirit comes upon them for a specific purpose. This is not a one-off experience but happens more than once to the same person:

- Acts 2:4: 'They were all filled with the Holy Spirit.'
- Acts 4:8: 'Then Peter, filled with the Holy Spirit, said to them . . .'
- Acts 4:31: 'And when they had prayed, the place in which they were gathered together was shaken, and they were all filled with the Holy Spirit.'
- Acts 13:9: 'Saul, who was also called Paul, filled with the Holy Spirit, looked intently at him.'
- Acts 13:52: 'The disciples were filled with joy and with the Holy Spirit.'

Over the centuries various minority groups have taught that baptism in, with or of the Holy Spirit refers to a 'second blessing' subsequent to conversion – something that not all Christians have but which all Christians should seek to attain. In four different centuries this approach was applied in four different ways:

- In the seventeenth century a few of the English Puritans taught that this was a separate, later, experience for *assurance*, to confirm that one is a Christian.
- In the eighteenth century the *Wesleys taught that there is a second blessing for *holiness*, bringing the gift of entire sanctification or Christian perfection, which we will consider further in Chapter 21.
- In the nineteenth century D. L. Moody and R. A. Torrey taught that there is a baptism of the Holy Spirit for *power* in ministry, linking this to Acts 1:8: 'You will receive power when the Holy Spirit has come upon you, and you will be my witnesses in Jerusalem and in all Judea and Samaria, and to the end of the earth.'
- In the twentieth century Pentecostals taught that there is a baptism of the Holy Spirit to bestow gifts such as praying in tongues.

These four views are not simply four different ways of describing the same event. For example, many of the early Pentecostals also held to the Wesleyan idea of 'entire sanctification'. They held that one should first receive the gift of entire sanctification, before receiving the baptism of the Spirit for the gift of tongues – first cleanse the dish, then fill it. Again, Torrey was very explicit that baptism of the Spirit as he saw it was for power and *not* for holiness. The four groups were not describing the same gift in different ways but were teaching about four *different* 'second blessings'.

What do you think? My answer

It is certainly true that many Christians have special experiences of the Holy Spirit after conversion and these can be immensely significant in the path of discipleship – though not all alleged experiences of the Spirit are positive or helpful. But there is no *one* experience that is intended for all Christians. Nor are such experiences what is meant in the New Testament by the baptism of the Spirit. That refers to the *initial* receiving of the Spirit at conversion, as we shall see in Chapter 18. In 1 Corinthians 12:13 we read that *all* are baptized by one Spirit into one body. Romans 8:9–11 teaches that without the indwelling of the Spirit one is not a Christian. In Acts we see people being filled with the Spirit not once for all but repeatedly.

THE GIFTS OF THE SPIRIT[3]

The fruit of the Spirit is for all Christians – love, joy, peace, patience, etc., are not optional. By contrast, different gifts of the Spirit are given to different Christians and no one has all of the gifts. In 1 Corinthians 12:14–26 Paul compares this to the diversity of the various members of a human body. All have some gift (1 Cor. 12:7). What are these gifts? There are lists in Romans 12:6–8; 1 Corinthians 12:8–10, 28–30; 13:1–3; Ephesians 4:11–13; and 1 Peter 4:11. In addition, Matthew 19:11–12 and 1 Corinthians 7:7 describe celibacy as a gift. Sometimes what is listed is the person (e.g. prophet) rather than the gift received (e.g. prophecy). For consistency the latter description is here followed throughout.[4]

- Apostleship (1 Cor. 12:28–29; Eph. 4:11)
- Prophecy (Rom. 12:6; 1 Cor. 12:10[†], 28–29, 13:2; Eph. 4:11)
- Speaking (1 Pet. 4:11)
- Service (Rom. 12:7; 1 Pet. 4:11) – the related word *diakonos* is sometimes translated 'deacon'
- Evangelism (Eph. 4:11)
- Wisdom (1 Cor. 12:8)
- Knowledge (1 Cor. 12:8, 13:2)
- Pastoring (Eph. 4:11)
- Teaching (Rom. 12:7; 1 Cor. 12:28–29; Eph. 4:11)
- Exhortation (Rom. 12:8)
- Faith (1 Cor. 12:9, 13:2)
- Healing (1 Cor. 12:9, 28, 30)
- Working miracles (1 Cor. 12:10, 28–29[†])
- Ability to distinguish spirits (1 Cor. 12:10)
- Contributing (Rom. 12:8) – probably personal giving, possibly managing the church's giving
- Leading (Rom. 12:8)
- Helping (1 Cor. 12:28)
- Showing mercy (Rom. 12:8) – probably care for the sick, poor and aged
- Administration (1 Cor. 12:28)
- Speaking in tongues (1 Cor. 12:10, 28, 30; 13:1[†])
- Interpretation of tongues (1 Cor. 12:10, 30)
- Celibacy (Matt. 19:11–12; 1 Cor. 7:7)
- Voluntary poverty (1 Cor. 13:3)
- Martyrdom (1 Cor. 13:3).

As with the fruit of the Spirit, this list of 24 is representative rather than exhaustive. For example:

- 1 Peter 4:9 mentions hospitality just before the reference to gifts (4:10–11). Certainly some people have a gift in this area.
- It makes sense to regard the gift of leading in worship as a spiritual gift, even though it is not mentioned in any of the lists.

- In the Old Testament the Holy Spirit gives the gift of craftsmanship to those building the Tabernacle:

The LORD said to Moses, 'See, I have called by name Bezalel the son of Uri, son of Hur, of the tribe of Judah, and I have filled him with the Spirit of God, with ability and intelligence, with knowledge and all craftsmanship, to devise artistic designs, to work in gold, silver and bronze, in cutting stones for setting, and in carving wood, to work in every craft.' (Exod. 31:1–5)

Similarly Exodus 35:30–35.

It should not be imagined that for all of these gifts one either has them or one does not. Some have a clear gift of evangelism, but that does not mean that no one else has any gifting in that area. Some have a particular gift of service, but that does not exempt the rest of us from seeking to serve.

Spiritual gifts are related to and involve natural gifts – e.g. in gifts of pastoring or administration. God is not likely to call someone autistic to be a pastor or someone who is hopelessly disorganized to be an administrator. God takes up and uses our natural gifts and empowers us to use them. Also, these gifts are not peculiar to Christianity. Speaking in tongues, prophecy and healing are all found in other religions. As a student I was told, 'If you speak in tongues you *know* that you're a Christian' – but that is not true. In general, there are three potential sources of all such activity. It can be a natural gift; it can be given directly by God; it can be inspired by Satan. We cannot always tell which one or more of these is/are involved in any specific instance.

Worship

Come Holy Ghost, our souls inspire
And lighten with celestial fire;
Thou the anointing Spirit art,
Who dost thy sevenfold gifts impart.
(Ninth century, tr. John Cosin)

Credal statement

We believe in the Holy Spirit
    who with the Father and the Son is worthy of our worship,
    who convicts the world of guilt in regard to sin, righteousness and judgement,
    who makes the death of Christ effective to sinners,
    enabling them to turn to God in repentance
    and directing their trust towards the Lord Jesus Christ;
    who through the new birth unites us with Christ, who is present within all believers;
    and makes us partake in Christ's risen life, pointing us to Jesus, freeing us from slavery to sin,
    producing in us his fruit, granting to us his gifts, and empowering us for service in the world.
    (*London School of Theology Doctrinal Basis*)

Sceptic's corner

Weren't these gifts for a time only? 'As for prophecies, they will pass away; as for tongues, they will cease; as for knowledge, it will pass away' (1 Cor. 13:8). And aren't most alleged prophecies or healings simply the product of fraud or gullibility?

Answer: The time when the gifts come to an end is when Christ returns, as is clear from 1 Corinthians 13:8–12. 'The perfect comes' when we see 'face to face' (13:10, 12). But that does not mean that we have to accept all that claims to be a manifestation of the Spirit. I am sure that God can and does heal today, but many allegedly miraculous healings have a natural explanation and, sadly, some so-called healers are fraudulent. As regards prophecy, Paul himself tells us to 'weigh what is said' (1 Cor. 14:29). Sadly, some leaders have confidently prophesied future events, such as the coming of revival to Britain by the end of the twentieth century, leaving people confused and disillusioned when this does not take place.

PRAYERS

Go before us, Lord, in all we do with your most gracious favour, and guide us with your continual help, that in all our works begun, continued and ended in you, we may glorify your holy name, and finally by your mercy receive everlasting life; through Jesus Christ our Lord. (*Common Worship*: Post Communion Prayer for Fourth Sunday before Lent)

Almighty God, who through thine only-begotten Son Jesus Christ hast overcome death and opened unto us the gate of everlasting life: we humbly beseech thee that, as by thy grace preceding us thou dost put into our minds good desires, so by thy continual help we may bring the same to good effect; through Jesus Christ thy Son our Lord. (*Common Worship*: Collect for Fifth Sunday of Easter, traditional language)

Questions to answer

- Who (or what) is the Holy Spirit?
- What does the Holy Spirit do in us?

NOTES

1 J. Stott, *Evangelical Truth*. Leicester: IVP, 1999, 117.
2 ATS Appendix 8 (second edn).
3 ATS ch. 15/14; CCC 2004.
4 The list draws on J. M. Boice, *Foundations of the Christian Faith*. IVP, 1986, 610. The order followed means that every gift appears in the same order as in all six lists except on three occasions, marked with a †.

RESOURCES

C. O. Brand (ed.) *Perspectives on Spirit Baptism: Five Views*. Nashville: B&H, 2004.

D. Bridge and D. Phypers *Spiritual Gifts and the Church*. Leicester: IVP, 1973.

S. B. Ferguson *The Holy Spirit*. Leicester: IVP, 1996.

J. Goldingay *Signs, Wonders and Healing*. Leicester: IVP, 1989.

W. Grudem (ed.) *Are Miraculous Gifts for Today? Four Views*. Grand Rapids: Zondervan, 1996.

G. McFarlane *Why Do You Believe What You Believe About the Holy Spirit?*. Carlisle: Paternoster, 1998.

T. Smail *The Giving Gift: The Holy Spirit in Person*. London: Hodder & Stoughton, 1988.

Chapter 16

THE TRINITY

Aims of this chapter

In this chapter we look at the doctrine of the Trinity, asking:

- Is there a doctrine of the Trinity in the Old Testament?
- Is there a doctrine of the Trinity in the New Testament?
- What is the doctrine of the Trinity? (We will answer this by looking at the three major heresies condemned in the early centuries and the positive truths that they denied.)
- How is the doctrine of the Trinity being (mis)used today?

INTRODUCTION

The doctrine of the Trinity has in the past often been neglected. In many churches there is very little preaching on it, making members vulnerable to the blandishments of Jehovah's Witnesses and such like. Liturgical churches have an advantage here, as the doctrine of the Trinity is embedded into most liturgies. With non-liturgical churches it depends much more on the person leading and that person may or may not have a clearly Trinitarian theology.

While the doctrine has been neglected in the past, today it has become very fashionable in some theological circles to the point where it is conscripted as the justification for all sorts of ideas, on which more later.

The Christian doctrine of the Trinity is complex and mysterious, by contrast with the simple doctrine of God held by Judaism, Islam and Unitarians. Christians hold that God *is* love, in a way that is not possible for these others. In eternity, apart from creation, Father, Son and Holy Spirit love one another. Without the Trinity, God is unable to exercise love until he creates something separate from himself, so God's love is not an eternal part of his character, any more than his role in upholding the universe. For Christians, by contrast, creation arises from the overflow of the love between the members of the Trinity. As *Moltmann put it, 'creation is a part of the eternal love affair between the Father and the Son' (*The Trinity and the Kingdom of God*, 59).

Originally and fundamentally the Greek word 'trinity' (*trias*) simply means a group of three, a trio. Later it has come to have the connotation of 'three in one' and some have tried to liken the word to 'triunity', but the essential meaning refers to threeness.

THE TRINITY IN THE OLD TESTAMENT

There is a heavy emphasis in the Old Testament on the unity of God. That there is one God is declared in the *Shema*: 'Hear, O Israel: The LORD our God, the LORD is one' (Deut. 6:4 – see also 4:35). There is a similar emphasis in Isaiah: 'I am the LORD; that is my name; my glory I give to no other, nor my praise to carved idols' (42:8); 'Thus says the LORD, the King of Israel and his Redeemer, the LORD of hosts: "I am the first and I am the last; besides me there is no god"' (44:6). The Israelites constantly had to be weaned off their addiction to other 'gods'. They finally learned this lesson as a result of the Exile and since then the Jews have been strictly monotheistic.

There is a strong emphasis in the Old Testament on the unity of God, but this God also had his attributes:

- **His word**: 'By the word of the LORD the heavens were made, and by the breath of his mouth all their host' (Ps. 33:6).
- **His wisdom**: 'The LORD possessed [or fathered] me at the beginning of his work, the first of his acts of old. Ages ago I was set up, at the first, before the beginning of the earth' (Prov. 8:22–23).
- **His Spirit**: 'Where shall I go from your Spirit? Or where shall I flee from your presence?' (Ps. 139:7).

These are not to be seen as distinct beings but more as God's attributes personalized. Also in the Old Testament the angel of the Lord was equated with God himself, e.g. by Samson's parents:

The angel of the LORD appeared no more to Manoah and to his wife. Then Manoah knew that he was the angel of the LORD. And Manoah said to his wife, 'We shall surely die, for we have seen God.' (Judg. 13:21–22)

In Genesis 18 three men appeared to Abraham and one of them is described as the LORD:

And the LORD appeared to him by the oaks of Mamre, as he sat at the door of his tent in the heat of the day. He lifted up his eyes and looked, and behold, three men were standing in front of him . . . The LORD said to Abraham, 'Why did Sarah laugh and say, "Shall I indeed bear a child, now that I am old?"' (18:1–2, 13).

The Old Testament material on God's word and Spirit is taken up in the New Testament and leads to the view of God as a trinity, but it would be wrong to suppose that there was already a doctrine of the Trinity in the Old Testament. The references to the Angel of the Lord have often been understood, with hindsight, as appearances of the pre-incarnate Christ. The plural in Genesis 1:26 ('Let us make man in our image') is probably the 'royal we' rather than a reference to the doctrine of the Trinity. The traditional Jewish teaching is that 'us' refers to God and the angels, but that would mean that we are made in the image of both God and angels!

What do you think? The question

Where in the New Testament do we find the Trinity?

What do you think? My answer

The answer to the above question is that it is found nowhere . . . and everywhere. It is found nowhere in the sense that the word 'trinity' is not mentioned, in the sense that there is no developed, worked-out doctrine of the Trinity. Yet at the same time it is found everywhere. The New Testament is throughout about Father, Son and Holy Spirit. For example, all three are found in the first chapter:

> Now the birth of *Jesus Christ* took place in this way. When his mother Mary had been betrothed to Joseph, before they came together she was found to be with child from *the Holy Spirit* . . . But as he considered these things, behold, an angel of *the Lord* appeared to him in a dream, saying, 'Joseph, son of David, do not fear to take Mary as your wife, for that which is conceived in her is from *the Holy Spirit*' . . . 'They shall call his name Immanuel' (which means, *God with us*) (Matt. 1:18, 20, 23)

All three are also found in the last chapter: 'Then the angel showed me the river of the water of life, bright as crystal, flowing from the throne of *God* and of *the Lamb* . . . *The Spirit* and the Bride say "Come!"' (Rev. 22:1, 17). (In the New Testament and in normal speech, 'God' often means 'God the Father' in particular.) The Trinity also appears more explicitly in a number of specific places, as we are about to see.

THE TRINITY IN THE NEW TESTAMENT

One way to approach the New Testament teaching on the Trinity is to look for Trinitarian formulas:

- Matthew 28:19: 'Go therefore and make disciples of all nations, baptizing them in the name of the Father and of the Son and of the Holy Spirit.' This is highly significant as it means that the early Christians were baptized into a Trinitarian faith.
- 2 Corinthians 13:14: 'The grace of the Lord Jesus Christ and the love of God and the fellowship of the Holy Spirit be with you all' – 'the grace'.
- Ephesians 2:18: 'For through him [Christ] we both have access in one Spirit to the Father' – the Christian pattern of prayer is Trinitarian: to the Father, through the Son, in the Spirit.

There are also many passages where Father, Son and Holy Spirit appear together, such as Ephesians 3:14–17:

> For this reason I bow my knees before *the Father* . . . that according to the riches of his glory he may grant you to be strengthened with power through *his Spirit* in your inner being, so that *Christ* may dwell in your hearts through faith.

This is especially true of John 14—16, three thoroughly Trinitarian chapters. For example: 'If you love *me*, you will keep my commandments. And I will ask *the Father*, and he will give you another Helper, to be with you for ever, even *the Spirit of truth*' (John 14:15–17).

This evidence is all significant, but even more compelling is the way in which the Trinity are all involved in the history of Christ.

THE HISTORY OF CHRIST

The history of Christ is a story of the interplay between Father, Son and Holy Spirit.

- Father and Son together in eternity:
  - John 17:5: 'And now, Father, glorify me in your own presence with the glory that I had with you before the world existed.'
  - Colossians 1:17: Christ 'is before all things, and in him all things hold together.'
- The sending of the Son:
  - John 3:16: 'God so loved the world, that he gave his only Son.'
  - Romans 8:3: 'By sending his own Son in the likeness of sinful flesh and for sin, he condemned sin in the flesh.'
- The birth of Christ:
  - Luke 1:35: 'And the angel answered her, "The Holy Spirit will come upon you, and the power of the Most High will overshadow you; therefore the child to be born will be called holy – the Son of God."'
- The baptism of Christ:
  - Mark 1:10–11: 'And when he came up out of the water, immediately he saw the heavens opening and the Spirit descending on him like a dove. And a voice came from heaven, "You are my beloved Son; with you I am well pleased."' (Similarly in the other Gospels.)
- The ministry of Jesus: he exercised his ministry as the Son, in an intimate relationship to God as his Father:
  - Matthew 11:27 'All things have been handed over to me by my Father, and no one knows the Son except the Father, and no one knows the Father except the Son and anyone to whom the Son chooses to reveal him.'
  - John 5:19: 'Jesus said to them, "Truly, truly, I say to you, the Son can do nothing of his own accord, but only what he sees the Father doing. For whatever the Father does, that the Son does likewise."'

- John 7:16: 'Jesus answered them, "My teaching is not mine, but his who sent me."'
- John 8:28: 'Jesus said to them, "When you have lifted up the Son of Man, then you will know that I am he, and that I do nothing on my own authority, but speak just as the Father taught me."'

The Holy Spirit descended on Jesus at his baptism and it is through the power of the Spirit that Jesus works:

- Matthew 12:28: 'If it is by the Spirit of God that I cast out demons, then the kingdom of God has come upon you.'
- The cross: a dramatic event between Father and Son. Jesus submits to the Father's will in Gethsemane:
  - Mark 14:36: 'Abba, Father, all things are possible for you. Remove this cup from me. Yet not what I will, but what you will.' This leads to 15:34 where he experiences being forsaken by God: 'At the ninth hour Jesus cried with a loud voice, "Eloi, Eloi, lema sabachthani?" which means, "My God, my God, why have you forsaken me?"' The Father did not spare his own Son: 'He who did not spare his own Son but gave him up for us all, how will he not also with him graciously give us all things?' (Rom. 8:32), clearly looking back at Abraham in Genesis 22.

There is just one passage in the New Testament where the Spirit is mentioned in relation to the cross: 'how much more will the blood of Christ, who through the eternal Spirit offered himself without blemish to God, purify our conscience from dead works to serve the living God' (Heb. 9:14).

- The resurrection:
  - 1 Corinthians 6:14: 'God raised the Lord and will also raise us up by his power.'

- 1 Peter 3:18, 'Christ also suffered once for sins, the righteous for the unrighteous, that he might bring us to God, being put to death in the flesh but made alive in the spirit [or, some translations, by the Spirit].'
- The Ascension: Jesus ascended to the Father, and so is able to give the gift of the Holy Spirit:
  - Acts 2:33: 'Being therefore exalted at the right hand of God, and having received from the Father the promise of the Holy Spirit, he has poured out this that you yourselves are seeing and hearing.'
  - John 16:7: 'It is to your advantage that I go away, for if I do not go away, the Helper will not come to you. But if I go, I will send him to you.'
  - Ephesians 4:8: 'Therefore it says, "When he ascended on high he led a host of captives, and he gave gifts to men."'

So we see that every stage of Jesus' life and ministry, from his sending by the Father to his return in the Ascension, involved the combined work of Father, Son and Holy Spirit. The 'history of Christ' cannot properly be understood other than in Trinitarian terms.

THE DOCTRINE OF THE TRINITY
(CCC 232–67)

The New Testament is all about Father, Son and Holy Spirit in action. It is irreducibly Trinitarian. But what is the *doctrine* of the Trinity? How do we understand the relationship between Father, Son and Holy Spirit? This was worked out by the Church in the following three centuries and reached a conclusion in the latter part of the fourth century. The doctrine developed especially by the process of excluding wrong views

about the Trinity – just as we have seen that the doctrine of the person of Christ was developed in response to four heresies. With the Trinity there are three basic errors and there are three positive points in response to these errors. Each of these seeks to explain the doctrine, but does so by leaving out an essential element. As someone once said, 'If you've explained it, you are a heretic.' There remains an irreducible element of paradox and mystery. We cannot fully understand the Trinity, and should not seek to define the indefinable or to unscrew the inscrutable.

Sceptic's corner

Surely, this appeal to mystery is just an excuse to cover up an incoherent doctrine?

Answer: When it comes to mystery there is an important balance to maintain. To suggest that there is no mystery, that we know and understand God fully, is highly implausible. After all, there is still so much about the physical creation that we do not yet fully understand. If we could fully understand God then we might suspect that we had made him in our own image. It is not at all unreasonable to hold that God transcends our understanding. This does not, however, mean that we know *nothing* about God, that God is a total mystery. We do know something; God is not totally hidden from us, but our knowledge is partial and incomplete: 'Now we see in a mirror dimly, but then face to face. Now I know in part; then I shall know fully, even as I have been fully known' (1 Cor. 13:12). (For more on this, see Chapter 3.) We do not see nothing, but we do not see everything – perhaps like looking at the garden from a frosted bathroom window.

Errors to avoid

This section is about avoiding the three errors from the Early Church. These are represented in the diagram below, with the name of the heresy outside the triangle and the truth being denied written within the triangle. The boundaries of the triangle can be compared to an electric fence round a field, blocking the way to danger. Orthodoxy itself is to be compared not to a single spot but to a field within which there is room to move around. Everyone does not have to understand everything in exactly the same way, but there are limits beyond which one moves into heresy. The aim of creeds and definitions is to exclude wrong views, dead-end paths, just as signs might warn of a cliff edge or a minefield.

ARIANISM

FATHER, SON, HOLY SPIRIT EACH GOD

ONE GOD

FATHER ≠ SON ≠ HOLY SPIRIT

TRITHEISM   **MODALISM**

1 **The first error is Tritheism**, the belief that there are three Gods. Against this the Bible (especially the Old Testament) is clear that there is only one God. The apostles were all Jews and held firmly to monotheism. It was wrong, therefore, for *Justin Martyr in the second century and *Origen in the third to speak of Christ as a 'second God'. If the Father is God and Christ is a 'second God' that makes two Gods. No Christians have ever openly taught that there are three Gods, but some have leaned too far in the direction of the threeness to the extent of imperilling the unity of God. Today many refer to the 'social Trinity', portraying Father, Son and Holy Spirit as like three people in perfect harmony. While this may be true so far as it goes, *on its own* it does not provide an adequate basis for the claim that there is only one God but leaves us with three Gods in a perfect relationship with one another.

2 **The second error is Arianism**, the denial of the deity of Christ, on which see Chapter 13. Others denied the deity of the Spirit, on which see Chapter 15. Against this we must affirm that Father, Son and Holy Spirit are each God. The *Council of Nicea (325) rejected Arius and affirmed the full deity of Christ; the *Council of Constantinople (381) affirmed the full deity of the Holy Spirit.

3 **The final error is Modalism**, also known as 'Monarchianism', or 'Sabellianism' (from Sabellius, an early advocate). This view claims that the Father *is* the Son *is* the Holy Spirit. Father, Son and Holy Spirit are just three aspects or manifestations of the one divine personality – just as I function as a father, a son and a husband. It is like the situation where one actor plays several different roles in a film – like Peter Sellers in *Doctor Strangelove* or Alec Guinness in *Kind Hearts and Coronets*. As one early writer put it, 'the Father became his own Son'. This teaching was popular at the end of the second century and even received some support from the Bishop of Rome.

It is by no means dead today and is the teaching of what is called 'Oneness

Pentecostalism', which makes up about 10 per cent of contemporary worldwide Pentecostalism. Against this teaching we must affirm that the Father is not the Son, who is not the Holy Spirit. Modalism teaches about a God in three guises who is essentially one, not three. If Father, Son and Holy Spirit are really just the same one solitary person acting out different roles then it undermines the truth of God's revelation, since the way he reveals himself is not the way he actually is.

Evangelicals have always formally professed belief in the Trinity, but their prayers have often betrayed a confused understanding of it. Part of the problem is that not all who engage in extempore prayer are good at thinking on their feet and people sometimes forget who they are praying to – thanking the Father that he died on the cross, for example. More serious is the widespread practice of praying to the Father 'in your name'. To whom does the 'you' refer? If it is the Father, I cannot see any sense in the idea of praying to the Father in the name of the Father. It has no biblical warrant but is an empty formula that means nothing. If the 'you' refers to Jesus then the formula is Modalist.

The orthodox doctrine of the Trinity was spelt out simply and clearly in the so-called *Athanasian Creed. (It has been said of this that it is neither by Athanasius, having been composed around the year 500 in France, nor strictly a creed.) This covers both the Trinity and the person of Christ and on the former states:

Credal statement

Now this is the Catholic faith: that we worship one God in trinity and trinity in unity – neither confusing the persons, nor dividing the substance. For the Father's person is one, the Son's another and the Holy Spirit's another. But the deity of Father, Son and Holy Spirit is one. Their glory is equal and their majesty coeternal.

Whatever the Father is, such is the Son and such also the Holy Spirit. The Father is uncreated, the Son uncreated and the Holy Spirit uncreated. The Father is infinite, the Son infinite and the Holy Spirit infinite. The Father is eternal, the Son eternal and the Holy Spirit eternal. Yet there are not three eternals but only one eternal – just as there are not three uncreateds nor three infinites but only one uncreated and only one infinite. Likewise, the Father is almighty, the Son almighty and the Holy Spirit almighty – yet there are not three almighties but only one almighty.

Thus the Father is God, the Son is God and the Holy Spirit is God – yet there are not three Gods but only one God. Thus the Father is Lord, the Son Lord and the Holy Spirit Lord – yet there are not three Lords but only one Lord. For just as Christian truth compels us to acknowledge each person by himself to be God and Lord, so the Catholic religion forbids us to speak of three Gods or Lords.

The Father is neither made nor created nor begotten from anything. The Son is from the Father alone – not made nor created but begotten. The Holy Spirit is from the Father and the Son – not made nor created nor begotten but proceeding. So there is one Father, not three Fathers; one Son, not three Sons; one Holy Spirit, not three Holy Spirits. And in this trinity no one is before or after another; no one is greater or less than another, but all three persons are coeternal and coequal with each other. Thus in all things, as has been said, both trinity in unity and unity in trinity are to be worshipped. This is how to think of the Trinity if you want to be saved.

SOCIAL DOCTRINE OF THE TRINITY

Today the doctrine of the Trinity has moved from being largely neglected to becoming somewhat overworked, at least in some quarters. It has become fashionable to think of the Trinity as being like three human persons in an intimate fellowship. There is a famous icon painted by Andrei Rublev from the fifteenth century, found on the front cover of this book, which portrays the Trinity as three men seated round a table, based on the account of Genesis 18. Such thinking can lead in a tritheist direction if one is not careful – just as comparing God to one person can lead to Modalism. (*Augustine produced a series of analogies comparing God to the memory, understanding and will of a single person.) It is important not to rely solely on one analogy.[1]

There are many today who seek to argue from their social doctrine of the Trinity to the organization of human society, especially using it as the basis for an 'anti-hierarchical egalitarianism'. A good example of this is Jürgen Moltmann in his *The Trinity and the Kingdom of God*. Without going into the details of this, two fundamental problems can be mentioned.

1 **It is highly speculative**. How do such people know so much about the inner life of the Trinity and how the three persons relate to one another? It is a basic principle to start from what is known and move from there to what is unknown. This approach, by contrast, argues from what we know very little about (the inner workings of the Trinity) to what we know much more about (human society). As *Calvin put it in response to whose who sought to pry into God's inmost being, 'Let us then willingly leave to God the

knowledge of himself' (*Institutes* 1:13:22). Also, as Lesslie Newbigin wryly commented, 'the doctrine of the Trinity was not developed in response to the human need for participatory democracy!'[2]

2 **The pattern of Christ's life is one of obedient submission to the Father**, and hardly provides a warrant for anti-hierarchical egalitarianism. What we do know of the Trinity is that it embodies a loving, trusting relationship, not an egalitarian one. Can one really imagine that the Son might have sent the Father to die for our sins? Jesus' life models voluntary obedient submission, not democracy. The weakness of this approach is that it draws controversial conclusions from a highly speculative account of the inner life of God and uses this to subvert the explicit social structures taught in the New Testament.

Worship

Holy, holy, holy, Lord God Almighty!
Early in the morning our song shall rise to Thee;
Holy, holy, holy, merciful and mighty!
God in three Persons, blessèd Trinity!
(Reginald Heber)

PRAYER

Almighty and everlasting God, you have given us your servants grace, by the confession of a true faith, to acknowledge the glory of the eternal Trinity and in the power of the divine majesty to worship the Unity: keep us steadfast in this faith, that we may evermore be defended from all adversities; through Jesus Christ your Son our Lord, who is alive and reigns with you, in the unity of the Holy Spirit, one God, now and for ever. (*Common Worship*: Collect for Trinity Sunday)

Question to answer

- What three truths does the doctrine of the Trinity affirm against heresies?

NOTES

1 ATS Appendix 2 (second edn).
2 L. Newbigin 'The Trinity as Public Truth' in K. J. Vanhoozer (ed.) *The Trinity in a Pluralistic Age*. Grand Rapids: Eerdmans, 1997, 7.

RESOURCES

T. George (ed.) *God the Holy Trinity: Reflections on Christian Faith and Practice*. Grand Rapids: Baker, 2006.

S. J. Grenz *Rediscovering the Triune God: The Trinity in Contemporary Theology*. Minneapolis: Augsburg Fortress, 2004.

S. R. Holmes *The Holy Trinity*. Milton Keynes: Paternoster, 2012.

R. Letham *The Holy Trinity: In Scripture, History, Theology, and Worship*. Phillipsburg, New Jersey: P&R, 2004.

A. McGrath *Understanding the Trinity*. Eastbourne: Kingsway, 1987.

Chapter 17

GOD

Aims of this chapter

So far we have looked at God as Trinity, based on the biblical revelation of God as Father, Son and Holy Spirit. There are also questions about God that are raised by philosophers and that are less directly answered in Scripture. In this chapter we will look at some of these questions, such as:

- How does God relate to time?
- Does God change?
- Does God suffer?
- Does God know the future?
- Can God do everything?
- How does God relate to us?

INTRODUCTION

It is not only theologians who study God. Philosophers have also written about God, from *Greek philosophers before the time of Christ to philosophical theologians, whether Christian or not. So how should the Christian doctrine of God relate to the teaching of the philosophers?

Systematic theologies in the past often used to have a section on God, which considered philosophical questions such as God's relation to time, and would only after that move on to consider Christ and the Trinity. Such an approach has rightly been criticized, by *Barth and *Moltmann among others, on the grounds that the doctrine of God was determined by philosophy before any specific Christian content had been introduced. Greek Platonist philosophy presented a picture of a remote and impersonal God who is more accurately called 'it' than 'he' and who is not capable of entering into relationship with us. In this book, by contrast, we have considered first Christ and the Holy Spirit (Chapters 13–15), then the doctrine of the Trinity (Chapter 16) and turn only now to these philosophical questions.

The French mathematician and philosopher *Blaise Pascal wrote the following words at the time of his conversion: 'God of Abraham, God of Isaac, God of Jacob, not of the philosophers and scholars. Certitude, certitude, feeling, joy, peace. God of Jesus Christ.' In recent years many have sought to make a sharp contrast between the God of philosophy and the God of revelation. The former lies outside of time and is immutable, impassible, omniscient and omnipotent. The latter is a God of love who is thoroughly involved with his creation in time, who makes himself vulnerable, who grieves and suffers and who changes his plans in the light of his interaction with us. Some have rejected the former, philosophical, view of God (often called Classical Theism) in favour of what they would see as a more biblical view. This is the approach taken by *Process Theology, which is based upon twentieth-century Process Philosophy rather than ancient Greek philosophy. It is also, to a lesser extent, the approach taken by some American Evangelicals known as Open Theists.

We will discuss each of these issues in turn, taking into account the points raised in Chapter 3.

Credal statement

There is but one only, living, and true God, who is infinite in being and perfection, a most pure spirit, invisible, without body, parts, or passions; immutable, immense, eternal, incomprehensible, almighty, most wise, most holy, most free, most absolute; working all things according to the counsel of His own immutable and most righteous will.

(*Westminster Confession of Faith* (1647), 2:1)

THE ETERNITY OF GOD: IS GOD IN TIME? (CCC 338)

What was God doing before the creation of the universe? One ancient answer is that God was preparing hell for the curious! *Augustine, by contrast, took the question seriously. God created the universe 'not in time but with time' (*City of God* 11:6). What does that mean? Augustine argued that the question of what God was doing before creation is based on a fallacy, namely that

time already existed and that at some point within this time God created the universe. In fact, though, time is part of the created universe and was created with it. Such was the teaching of Plato, who taught that time was related to the movement of the stars; it is also the teaching of modern physics, which since Einstein refers to the 'space–time continuum'. To ask what happened before the creation is, therefore, like asking what lies to the north of the North Pole.

Since God transcends his creation it follows that he must be outside of time. This should (in terms explained in Chapter 3) be seen as a negative rather than a positive statement. It is not a positive statement about the nature of God's eternity and whether that might be timeless or whether God has his own time. (It is questionable whether created temporal beings are capable of grasping what God's eternity is like.) It is the negative statement that God is the transcendent Creator who is not limited by *our* time but transcends it. As Isaiah put it, God is 'the One who is high and lifted up, who inhabits eternity' (57:15). A 'god' who was restricted to our time would in fact be part of creation and therefore an idol. God does not move with us from 2012 to 2013 for the same reason that he does not travel from London to New York, because he transcends both space and time.

What about our destiny in the Age to Come? Is it to exist in a timeless eternity? This idea was encouraged by the translation of Revelation 10:6 in the King James Version: an angel swore 'that there should be time no longer'. Modern versions more accurately, if rather more prosaically, translate this as 'that there would be no more delay'!

THE IMMUTABILITY OF GOD: DOES GOD CHANGE?

Does God change? Scripture twice states that he does not:

- Malachi 3:6: 'I the LORD do not change.'
- James 1:17: 'Every good gift and every perfect gift is from above, coming down from the Father of lights with whom there is no variation or shadow due to change.'

We need to ask, though, what sort of change is in mind. In fact there are five different types of change to consider:

1 **Ontological change**. God cannot cease to be God. In the Incarnation 'the Word became flesh' (John 1:14) but, as we saw in Chapter 13, he did not thereby cease to be God or abandon his divine functions.
2 **Ethical change**. God is consistently good and loving. There is no danger of him changing and becoming evil.
3 **Emotional change**. The Bible presents a passionate and compassionate God, as we shall see, but this need not imply change. God does not undergo mood swings but is consistently loving and compassionate.
4 **Changing purposes**. God chose us in Christ 'before the foundation of the world' and we have been 'predestined according to the purpose of him who works all things according to the counsel of his will' (Eph. 1:4, 11). Yet at the same time Scripture shows God apparently changing his mind. He commanded the people of Israel to take possession of the promised land, but when they proved disobedient he changed his mind and required them to spend forty years in the wilderness (Deut. 1:19–40). God chose Saul to be king over Israel

(1 Sam. 9:15–17), but when Saul proved disobedient God changed his mind and stated, 'I regret that I have made Saul king' (1 Sam. 15:11). On the other hand, when Saul begs for forgiveness he is told that 'the Glory of Israel will not lie or have regret, for he is not a man, that he should have regret' (1 Sam. 15:29). How should we hold these things together? We will return to that at the end of the chapter.

5 **Temporal change**. Does God experience sequence? We have argued that God transcends our time. His relation to it may be compared to that of an author to a book.

If God is immutable in these ways, how can he meaningfully relate to us? We will conclude this chapter by considering that question.

Worship

O God, our help in ages past,
Our hope for years to come,
Our shelter from the stormy blast,
And our eternal home.

Before the hills in order stood,
Or earth received her frame,
From everlasting Thou art God,
To endless years the same.
(Isaac Watts)

What do you think? The question

Does God suffer?

THE IMPASSIBILITY OF GOD: DOES GOD SUFFER?

Classical Theism portrays God as timeless, immutable and impassible. He is not affected by us and has no emotions. Such a belief underlies this prayer of *Anselm:

> How are you at once both merciful and impassible? For if you are impassible you do not have any compassion; and if you have no compassion your heart is not sorrowful from compassion with the sorrowful, which is what being merciful is. But if you are not merciful, whence comes so much consolation for the sorrowful?
>
> How then are you merciful and not merciful, O Lord, unless it be that you are merciful in relation to us and not in relation to yourself? In fact, you are merciful according to our way of looking at things and not according to your way. For when you look upon us in our misery it is we who feel the effect of your mercy, but you do not experience the feeling. Therefore you are both merciful because you save the sorrowful and pardon sinners against you; and you are not merciful because you do not experience any feeling of compassion for misery.
> (*Proslogion* 8)

The *Thirty-Nine Articles* (art. 1) and the *Westminster Confession of Faith* 2:1 both state that God is 'without body, parts or passions'. This has been the official belief for the great majority of Christian history, though it has not always been reflected in popular preaching. It would, however, appear to be contrary to the biblical portrayal of a passionate God, who experiences:

- **Grief**, as in Genesis 6:6: 'the LORD regretted that he had made man on the earth, and it grieved him to his heart.'
- **Pity**, as in Judges 2:18: 'the LORD was moved to pity by their groaning because of those who afflicted and oppressed them.'

- **Anger**, as in Jeremiah 21:5: 'I myself will fight against you with outstretched hand and strong arm, in anger and in fury and in great wrath.'
- **Yearning**, as in Jeremiah 31:20: 'Is Ephraim my dear son? Is he my darling child? For as often as I speak against him, I do remember him still. Therefore my heart yearns for him; I will surely have mercy on him, declares the LORD.'
- **Compassion**, as in Hosea 11:8: 'How can I give you up, O Ephraim? How can I hand you over, O Israel? How can I make you like Admah? How can I treat you like Zeboiim? My heart recoils within me; my compassion grows warm and tender.'

During the twentieth century the consensus view changed from an impassible to a passible God. The suffering of the First World War led some to make this change in the interests of theodicy. At the same time the influence of Greek philosophy, especially Platonism, was waning and some philosophers were arguing that reality should be seen as changing and developing. A. N. Whitehead, the founder of Process Philosophy, described God as 'the fellow sufferer who understands'. *Dietrich Bonhoeffer observed that 'only the suffering God can help'. *Jürgen Moltmann did much to popularize the idea of a passible God, especially in his *The Crucified God* (1972), where he speaks not just of God the Son suffering for us on the cross, but also of God the Father suffering the loss of his Son.

The Early Church Fathers affirmed the impassibility of God, an idea derived from Platonism. This should be seen not as a positive statement of what God is but rather as a negative statement of what he is *not*. He is not fickle and sensuous like sinful human beings nor like the pagan gods that they had invented. Because God transcends the universe and is outside time he is not subject to impermanence and to human passions as we are. But what about the biblical portrayal of God, what about the Passion of Christ? They did not lose sight of this; they believed that this impassible God is passionate. *Cyril of Alexandria brought out this paradox in his statement that the incarnate Word 'suffered impassibly'. The fathers did not portray God as cold and aloof but spoke, as does the Bible, of God's anger, grief, compassion and pity. Were they not simply contradicting themselves? No. They portrayed a God who is passionate and loving, but not subject to emotional mood swings. His compassion, pity, etc., are the outworkings in time of his eternal and consistent love.

How should we understand the scriptural statements quoted above about God's passions? These are anthropomorphic, referring to God in human terms that we can understand. They are not to be understood univocally, as if God's grief (for example) was no different from ours. But equally they should not be understood equivocally, as if God's grief had nothing in common with ours. They are to be understood analogically, as described in Chapter 3.

Someone who contributed significantly to the emphasis on God's passion is the Jewish scholar A. J. Heschel, in his 1962 *The Prophets*. He also emphasized the transcendence of God's passion, as in this echoing of Isaiah 55:8–9:

> My pathos is not your pathos . . . For as the heavens are higher than the earth, so are my ways higher than your ways and my pathos than your pathos. (*Prophets*, 276)

God has compassion on us and grieves over us. Unlike our suffering, this is not forced upon him because he is weak but is freely and voluntarily embraced. God's attitude towards us may change from compassion, to grieving, to anger, to pity, but these changes are because we have changed, not because God is fickle or changeable. They are the different outworkings in different situations of his consistent and unchanging love.

In the Incarnation, God the Son enters our human existence and shares in human suffering. We are saved not by his divine suffering but by the human suffering that Christ endured when he went to the cross. God in Christ voluntarily placed himself in a position where he would endure this suffering.

What do you think? My answer

God is a passionate and compassionate God, but in a changelessly consistent fashion, not subject to mood swings. Some, like *Jonathan Edwards, would say that God has settled affections, not changing passions.

THE OMNISCIENCE OF GOD: DOES HE KNOW THE FUTURE? (CCC 2115)[1]

Until recently it was accepted by almost all Christians that God knows the future:

> To confess that God exists and at the same time to deny that he has foreknowledge of future things is the most manifest folly . . . For one who is not prescient of all future things is not God. (Augustine, *City of God* 5:9)

> Everyone who believes in God at all believes that He knows what you and I are going to do tomorrow. (C. S. Lewis)[2]

This is closely connected with the question of God and time. If God transcends time then he manifestly knows the future. Conversely, to claim that God is ignorant of the future requires the belief that God is confined to our time.

Open Theists, Evangelicals who deny God's knowledge of the future, would still claim that God is omniscient in that he knows all that there is to know. He does not know the future, they would say, for the same reason that he does not know the name of Henry VIII's seventh wife – because neither exists. Of course the future, unlike Henry VIII's seventh wife, *will* come to exist – and then God will know it. There is, however, an important difference between the future and Henry VIII's seventh wife. It is logically impossible to know the latter since it never exists. It is *not* logically impossible to know the future and Open Theists believe that God sometimes prophesies the future, including matters of detail.

It is important to be aware of the implications of the Open Theists' claims:

- Since they have a strong emphasis on unpredictable human free will, the logic of their case is that God did not know whether or not humanity would fall until after the event.
- Chaos theory teaches that minute events like the fluttering of a butterfly in Brazil can bring about a major event like a tornado in Texas. Given the number of such minute events every day and granted an element of autonomy on the part of God's creatures, even God could not predict next year's events reliably.
- Several assassination attempts on Hitler failed because of random actions by bystanders, none of which could have been predicted if they were acting from genuine libertarian free will.
- Every one of us exists as we do only because one specific sperm among hundreds of millions won a gruelling race. Given the free action of the parents during intercourse, even God could not predict the identity of the child to be conceived.

In the light of the above, what sense would it have to say that God chose us before the foundation of the world (Eph. 1:4)?

What about the teaching of Scripture? There are general statements about God's knowledge of the future, such as:

> I am the Lord; that is my name; my glory I give to no other, nor my praise to carved idols. Behold, the former things have come to pass, and new things I now declare; before they spring forth I tell you of them. (Isa. 42:8–9)

> I am God, and there is no other; I am God, and there is none like me, declaring the end from the beginning and from ancient times things not yet done, saying, 'My counsel shall stand, and I will accomplish all my purpose,' calling a bird of prey from the east, the man of my counsel from a far country. I have spoken, and I will bring it to pass; I have purposed, and I will do it. (Isa. 46:9–11)

There are also specific prophecies, such as:

> Behold, a man of God came out of Judah by the word of the Lord to Bethel. Jeroboam was standing by the altar to make offerings. And the man cried against the altar by the word of the Lord and said, 'O altar, altar, thus says the Lord: "Behold, a son shall be born to the house of David, Josiah

by name, and he shall sacrifice on you the priests of the high places who make offerings on you, and human bones shall be burned on you."' (1 Kings 13:1–2)

(Sceptics can, of course, always claim that such a prophecy was written after the event, but Open Theists claim to hold to the truthfulness of Scripture.)

On the other side, Open Theists point to passages which imply God's ignorance of the future:

- **God expresses surprise** at people's behaviour, as in Jeremiah 3:7: 'I thought, "After she has done all this she will return to me," but she did not return, and her treacherous sister Judah saw it.' Similarly, in Jeremiah 19:5 God refers to human sacrifice, 'which I did not command or decree, nor did it come into my mind'.
- **God expresses ignorance** of the future, as in Jeremiah 36:3: 'It may be that the house of Judah will hear all the disaster that I intend to do to them, so that every one may turn from his evil way, and that I may forgive their iniquity and their sin.'
- **God learns from experience**, as in Genesis 22:12: 'now I know that you fear God, seeing you have not withheld your son, your only son, from me.'

Open Theists take these passages literally, but by the same token we would have to conclude that God is not even fully aware of the *present*:

- Genesis 3:9: 'The LORD God called to the man and said to him, "Where are you?"'
- Genesis 18:21: 'I will go down [to Sodom] to see whether they have done altogether according to the outcry that has come to me.'

Also, there are vastly more passages ascribing bodily parts to God than those ascribing lack of knowledge and fewer passages qualifying these, yet Open Theists do not claim that God has a physical body. Three principles need to be borne in mind:

1 Scripture teaches us about God in positive anthropomorphic language and this needs to be qualified by negative statements affirming God's transcendence. The Lord hears our prayers but that does not mean that he has ears and auditory equipment as we do.
2 Scripture is accommodated to our capacity and presented from our perspective. Those who are accustomed to communicate with tiny children have some small inkling of what it might involve for God to communicate with us.
3 Finally, Scripture teaches us about God primarily through narrative, rather than abstract theology.

Open Theists hold to a strong view of libertarian free will (on which see Chapter 8) and argue that this would be undermined by God's foreknowledge of the future. If God transcends time, however, this is not strictly *fore*knowledge since all of time is present to him in eternity. Also, God's knowledge of the future need not conflict with free will if what God knows is that tomorrow I will *freely* do this or that. If Open Theists hold that God foreknew that Adam would sin, does that prove that Adam had no free will? If, on the other hand, they hold that God did *not* foresee the Fall, that manifestly clashes with the biblical account. To give but one example, the names of the elect have been 'written before the foundation of the world in the book of life of the Lamb who was slain' (Rev. 13:8).

THE OMNIPOTENCE OF GOD: CAN HE DO EVERYTHING? (CCC 268–78)

One of the names of God in the Bible is 'the Almighty':

- Genesis 17:1: 'When Abram was ninety-nine years old the LORD appeared to Abram and said to him, "I am God Almighty."'
- Psalm 91:1: 'He who dwells in the shelter of the Most High will abide in the shadow of the Almighty.'
- Revelation 15:3: 'Great and amazing are your deeds, O Lord God the Almighty! Just and true are your ways, O King of the nations!'

Also, the angel Gabriel tells Mary, 'Nothing will be impossible with God' (Luke 1:37). With reference to the difficulty of salvation, Jesus responds: 'With man it is impossible, but not with God. For all things are possible with God' (Mark 10:27).

There are some qualifications that need to be made. First, God cannot do things that are logically impossible. So, for example, he cannot make a circular square, nor can he create a weight so heavy that he cannot lift it. Second, he cannot act contrary to his nature. So, for example, 'it is impossible for God to lie' (Heb. 6:18). Finally, although God is omnipotent he voluntarily chooses to make himself vulnerable for us, supremely in the Incarnation of his Son.

Sceptic's corner

If God is as portrayed in this chapter, how can he meaningfully relate to us? How can temporal beings relate to a God who is outside time? How can a God who already knows the future genuinely interact with us? How can a God who is impassible relate to us?

Answer: See the next section.

HOW DOES GOD RELATE TO US?

Those who regard God as the All-matey rather than the Almighty may find the picture of God presented in this chapter hard to grasp, but such over-familiarity with God is far removed both from the religion

Errors to avoid

There are two opposite errors to avoid in relating to God. On the one hand is the error of over-familiarity with God, of failing to take into account the fact that we are dealing with the eternal, sovereign Creator of the universe. This is an error to which Evangelicals are especially prone. On the other hand is the error of failing to take advantage of the access won for us by Christ. This is seen especially with those who think that they cannot approach God directly but must come to him via the mediation of Mary or of one of the saints.

- Hebrews 10:19–22: 'Therefore, brothers, since we have confidence to enter the holy places by the blood of Jesus, by the new and living way that he opened for us through the curtain, that is, through his flesh, and since we have a great priest over the house of God, let us draw near with a true heart in full assurance of faith, with our hearts sprinkled clean from an evil conscience and our bodies washed with pure water.'

of the Bible and from historic Christianity. In both Old and New Testaments the effect of coming face to face with God was awe and reverence:

- Isaiah 6:1, 5: 'In the year that King Uzziah died I saw the LORD sitting upon a throne, high and lifted up . . . And I said: "Woe is me! For I am lost; for I am a man of unclean lips, and I dwell in the midst of a people of unclean lips; for my eyes have seen the King, the LORD of hosts!"'
- Revelation 1:17: 'When I saw him [the ascended Christ], I fell at his feet as though dead.'

The Bible portrays God as interacting with us. As we have seen, it presents God as working 'all things according to the counsel of his will' (Eph. 1:11) and also as changing his mind. He tells Hezekiah that he will die and then changes his mind in response to Hezekiah's prayer (2 Kings 20:1–7). How can that be? We need to distinguish between two different things. God's eternal purposes are fixed and unchanging and are worked out in history, on which see Chapter 9. But God also acts, reacts and interacts in history. So, for example, he knew that Saul would rebel and lose his kingship. This did not take him by surprise when it happened. But does he not then change his mind about Saul? His attitude towards Saul does change, but because Saul has changed, not because God has changed. *Thomas Aquinas aptly noted that for God to will a change (in his attitude towards us) is not the same as God changing his will.

To change your will is one matter, and to will a change in something is another. While remaining constant, a person can will this to happen now and the contrary to happen afterwards. (*Sum of Theology* 1a:19:7)

Classical Theism can lead to the position that God is unchanged by his interaction with us, that his relation to us can be compared to that of the sun, which profoundly affects life on earth, but is not in the least affected by what happens to us. That is not the biblical picture of God. The supreme example of God interacting with us is, of course the Incarnation of Christ. Does this mean that God changes? If not, can we meaningfully claim that God shares in our condition? It is possible to argue that the Incarnation does indeed affect God, but that this does not mean that he is imprisoned in our time. As *Moltmann puts it:

The pain of the cross determines the inner life of the triune God from eternity to eternity. (*The Trinity and the Kingdom of God*, 160–61)

PRAYER

'O my God,' I say, 'take me not away in the midst of my days – you whose years endure throughout all generations!' Of old you laid the foundation of the earth, and the heavens are the work of your hands. They will perish, but you will remain; they will all wear out like a garment. You will change them like a robe, and they will pass away, but you are the same, and your years have no end. The children of your servants shall dwell secure; their offspring shall be established before you. (Ps. 102:24–28)

Questions to answer

- Does God change?
- Does God know the future?

171

NOTES

1 ATS ch. 3.
2 C. S. Lewis *Mere Christianity*. London: Fontana, 1955, 144.

RESOURCES

J. K. Beilby and P. R. Eddy (eds) *Divine Foreknowledge: Four Views*. Downers Grove: IVP, 2001.

M. J. Erickson *What Does God Know and When Does He Know It? The Current Controversy over Divine Foreknowledge*. Grand Rapids: Zondervan, 2003.

G. E. Gannsle (ed.) *God and Time: Four Views*. Downers Grove: IVP, 2001.

T. Tiessen *Providence and Prayer: How Does God Work in the World?* Downers Grove: IVP, 2000.

B. Ware (ed.) *Perspectives on the Doctrine of God: Four Views*. Nashville: B&H, 2008.

REDEMPTION: PERSONAL

Chapter 18

CHRISTIAN INITIATION

Aims of this chapter

In this chapter we look at Christian initiation, asking:

- How does one become a Christian according the New Testament?
- How does that compare with practice today?
- What are repentance and faith?
- Is baptism part of the gospel message?
- How do we receive the Spirit?

FOUR SPIRITUAL DOORS[1]

There are 14 passages in Acts where we have an account of people becoming Christians (see Table 18.1). From these passages we see a clear pattern of four recurring steps to becoming a Christian:[2]

- Repentance (mentioned nine times – twice being indirect mentions)
- Faith in Jesus (mentioned 12 times – once in a variant reading)
- Baptism (mentioned ten times)
- Receiving the Spirit (mentioned seven times).

Not all four are mentioned every time, but this does not mean that any of them are optional, for three reasons:

1 Constantly bringing up all four would be tedious, and Luke is too good a writer for that.

2 Also, where the same event is described more than once we sometimes find different items mentioned. So Acts 15:7–9 mentions only faith and the Holy Spirit, but this refers back to 10:34–35, 43–48 and 11:15–18, where all four are mentioned. Acts 9:17–18 mentions only baptism and the Spirit while 22:10, 14–16 mentions only baptism, with repentance implied.

3 Finally, it is clear that omission of any of the steps was considered unacceptable. In Acts 8:14–17 the Samaritans' failure to receive the Spirit is rectified,[3] and in 8:18–23 Simon's lack of repentance is castigated: 'Repent, therefore, of this wickedness of yours, and pray to the Lord that, if possible, the intent of your heart may be forgiven you' (v. 22). Again, the Ephesian disciples had not received the Spirit and this needed to be rectified (Acts 19:1–7). So it is clear from Acts that all four are required, even if they are not all mentioned every time.

Becoming a Christian can involve a variety of issues and throughout history different

TABLE 18.1 THE FOUR SPIRITUAL DOORS

	Acts	Repentance	Faith	Baptism	Spirit
1	2:37–41, 44	✓	✓	✓	✓
2	3:17–20; 4:3–4	✓	✓	INTERRUPTED (4:1–3)	INTERRUPTED (4:1–3)
3	8:12–24	✓	✓	✓	✓
4	8:36–38	—	[v. 37]	✓	—
5	9:17–18	—	—	✓	✓
6	10:34–35, 43–48	(v. 22)	✓	✓	✓
7	11:15–18	✓	✓	✓	✓
8	15:7–9	—	✓	—	✓
9	16:14–15	—	✓	✓	—
10	16:30–34	—	✓	✓	—
11	17:30–34	✓	✓	—	—
12	19:1–7	✓	✓	✓	✓
13	20:20–21	✓	✓	—	—
14	22:10, 14–16	(v. 10)	—	✓	—
TOTALS		7 + 2	11 + 1	10	7

Christians have described their conversion in many different ways. For *Justin Martyr it was about finding the true philosophy; for *Cyprian it was moral renewal; for *Luther it was a gracious God; for *Calvin it was true religion; for *John Wesley it was assurance of salvation. For C. S. Lewis a key point was the acceptance of the existence of God, a point that was not in question for the other named figures. The 'presenting issue' in the human biography of conversion will vary according to historical situation, culture and individual history, but the biblical pattern of fourfold initiation stands as a theological norm or criterion by which to test the genuineness of conversion.

The conversions described in Acts are all instantaneous, with the converts being able to name the day and hour of their conversion. Evangelicals have traditionally emphasized the need for conversion and many would echo the words of Charles Wesley's hymn:

> Long my imprisoned spirit lay,
> fast bound in sin and nature's night;
> thine eye diffused a quickening ray;
> I woke, the dungeon flamed with light;
> my chains fell off, my heart was free,
> I rose, went forth, and followed thee.
> (*Charles Wesley, 'And can it be')

But is conversion always instantaneous? Theologically there is no such concept as a 'half-Christian' but in practice the process of conversion can be long drawn out. In tropical regions it is usually very clear when the sun rises; in regions nearer the poles a sunrise can take longer and it can be hard to say exactly when it happens. The important thing is that the sun has risen, not that we can time it precisely. Similarly, when crossing some borders one knows exactly when one changes country; with other borders there may be a long period when it is not clear which country one is in, even though at every point one is actually in one country or the other.

Credal statement

Question. What is required of persons to be baptized?

Answer. Repentance, whereby they forsake sin; and Faith, whereby they steadfastly believe the promises of God, made to them in that Sacrament.
(Book of Common Prayer, Catechism)

How does this compare with evangelism today? If they are lucky, enquirers may be told to repent and believe – but they may simply be told to invite Jesus into their hearts or some such unbiblical phrase. Today baptism and receiving the Spirit are unlikely to be mentioned, and consequently we are in danger of producing converts who, like the disciples at Ephesus, can say 'we have not even heard that there is a Holy Spirit' (Acts 19:2). Sadly most evangelism today offers something less than the full fourfold New Testament initiation and as a result we are in danger of producing stunted and defective births. Evangelical tradition has prevailed over the pattern set out in Scripture.

REPENTANCE (CCC 1422–98)

Repentance is more than just acknowledging that one is a sinner, and it is more than just being sorry or regretful. The Greek word *metanoia* means a change of mind and heart, a turning from sin to God. It involves repentance for specific sins as well as a general state of sinfulness. The Old Testament prophets taught this,

as did John the Baptist, who issued specific instructions to tax collectors and soldiers (Luke 3:12–14). Where necessary, repentance involves making restitution: 'Zacchaeus stood and said to the Lord, "Behold, Lord, the half of my goods I give to the poor. And if I have defrauded anyone of anything, I restore it fourfold"' (Luke 19:8). At times this can be very costly. A couple who became Christians confessed to the Inland Revenue that they had previously failed to declare income, and it cost them their house. Repentance also involves accepting the lordship of Christ over the whole of our life. There are no no-go areas, contrary to the approach of one king in the Dark Ages. He decided to become a Christian and arranged for his whole army to be baptized by marching through a river – but with their sword arms raised because he did not wish their baptism to affect that area of their lives.

Repentance involves total commitment *in principle*, but at conversion this is still only theoretical. The Christian life is a lifetime of putting this commitment into practice. This can be compared to marriage, where huge promises are made at the wedding which need to be honoured throughout the marriage that follows. There is a tension here between two points.

- On the one hand, one cannot be a Christian without following Christ; we cannot have Christ as Saviour without having him as Lord. There is no forgiveness of sins without repentance. At a wedding the bridegroom does not promise his bride Sundays to Fridays but reserve Saturdays for his mistress.
- Yet on the other hand, we are not required to sort our lives out before God accepts us. We do not come to Christ because we

have been sorted out; we come in order to be sorted out. We are all a work in progress. If you bring in a builder to sort out the dry rot this means being committed to the task. You do not ask him to do every room but to leave the rot in the kitchen.

Credal statement

Men ought not to content themselves with a general repentance, but it is every man's duty to endeavour to repent of his particular sins, particularly. (*Westminster Confession of Faith* (1647), 15:5)

FAITH (CCC 142–84)

In Acts we see that people believe both in the Lord Jesus and in the gospel. For example, John wrote his Gospel 'so that you may believe that Jesus is the Christ, the Son of God, and that by believing you may have life in his name' (20:31). In other words, the object of faith in the New Testament is Christ, Christ as presented in the gospel – who he is and what he has done.

Saving faith is not just accepting facts in our head:

- **Faith needs to move from the head to the heart** in the form of trust. There is a well-known story about the tightrope walker Charles Blondin, who many times crossed the Niagara Gorge. On one occasion he asked a spectator if he believed that Blondin could safely carry him across in a wheelbarrow. The man said that he did believe – but declined to put it to the test. That was probably a wise decision, since Blondin was a fallible human, though a better illustration would be deciding to trust Blondin in order to escape a fierce

Bet you're pleased you opted out.

© Miriam Kendrick 2013 www.miriamkendrick.co.uk

lion.[4] Either way, Christian faith is about being prepared to put it to the test, about getting into the wheelbarrow.

We shall possess a right definition of faith if we call it a firm and certain knowledge of God's benevolence toward us, founded upon the truth of the freely given promise in Christ, both revealed to our minds and sealed upon our hearts through the Holy Spirit. (*Calvin, *Institutes* 3:2:7)

As this quotation shows, faith involves believing certain things in our minds (against an anti-intellectualism) but it is more than mere head knowledge.

- **It also needs to move from the heart to the lips**; faith must be confessed openly. This takes place initially in baptism: 'If you confess with your mouth that Jesus is Lord and believe in your heart that God raised him from the dead, you will be saved. For with the heart one believes and is justified, and with the mouth one confesses and is saved' (Rom. 10:9–10).

- **Faith must also move from words to actions**, as James repeatedly affirms: 'So also faith by itself, if it does not have works, is dead' (2:17); 'As the body apart from the spirit is dead, so also faith apart from works is dead' (2:26). The Reformers taught that we are justified by faith alone, and not by works, as we shall see in Chapter 20, but they agreed that it is not possible to be saved *without* works. Justification is not *by* works, but nor is it *without* works.

Credal statement

Question 21. What is true faith?

Answer: True faith is not only a certain knowledge, whereby I hold for truth all that God has revealed to us in his word, but also an assured confidence, which the Holy Ghost works by the gospel in my heart; that not only to others, but to me also, remission of sin, everlasting righteousness and salvation, are freely given by God, merely of grace, only for the sake of Christ's merits. (*Heidelberg Catechism* (1563))

Sceptic's corner

The fundamentalist atheists like to draw a contrast between atheistic scientists, who accept nothing without proof, and religious people, who believe things without evidence.

Answer: There are three fallacies in this argument:

1. It ignores the fact that most of the founders of modern science and many of its practitioners today, at the highest level, are believers.
2. It confuses the practice of science with other areas of life. The scientist (atheist or Christian alike) follows the scientific method in professional life, testing theories and seeking verification. The same scientist (atheist or Christian alike) needs to exercise faith in other areas of life. If she trusts her spouse or her friends, this trust is not scientifically proved. If he holds that altruistic love is a desirable thing, that is not scientifically provable.
3. Christian faith is not scientifically provable, but it is not **without** evidence. The resurrection of Jesus cannot be proved, but there is good evidence for it. Faith is based on evidence but goes beyond what can be proved. It is not a leap into the dark with no rational justification at all.

What do you think? The question

Is baptism part of the gospel message?

BAPTISM (CCC 1212–84)

In the New Testament all Christians were baptized. Baptism is a vital part of the initiation process described in Acts, being mentioned in 10 of the 14 passages. Paul could assume that all of his readers had been baptized:

- Ephesians 4:4–6: 'There is one body and one Spirit – just as you were called to the one hope that belongs to your call – one Lord, one faith, one baptism, one God and Father of all, who is over all and through all and in all.'

After the Day of Pentecost (Acts 2) there is not a single example of an unbaptized Christian in the New Testament.

In Acts we see that baptism was immediate. It always took place on the same day as conversion, with one exception. The Philippian jailer was baptized the same hour of the *night*! 'And he took them the same hour of the night and washed their wounds; and he was baptized at once, he and all his family' (16:33). Paul did not suggest that they should get some sleep and have the baptism in the morning. It was so much part of the initiation process that it happened on the spot. It was not an optional extra. The apostles did not ask their converts, 'Will that be with or without baptism, sir?' It was not delayed until new converts requested it, nor until their genuineness was proved. It was part of the gospel message. This is very clear in Acts.

Baptism is also part of the so-called 'Great Commission', which commands baptism but makes no mention of faith: 'Go therefore and make disciples of all nations, baptizing them in the name of the Father and of the Son and of the Holy Spirit, teaching them to observe all that I have commanded you' (Matt. 28:19–20). Between Acts and the third century, however, there was a significant shift from immediate baptism to a three-year period of preparation for baptism.

According to the New Testament, one becomes a Christian at least in part by baptism, as will be seen in the next chapter. This is something that many find it hard to accept, for two main reasons. First, there has been a polarization between Protestants, who teach that we become Christians by faith, and Catholics, who teach that we become Christians by baptism. The New Testament knows no such dichotomy. Second, the legacy of Christendom means

that in Europe we are faced with hoards of baptized unbelievers, people who were baptized as babies but in many cases have had no other exposure to the Christian faith. Needless to say, that was not an issue for the New Testament writers. When they wrote of faith they meant the faith that expressed itself in baptism (as in Acts) and when they wrote of baptism they meant the baptism that was an expression of faith. Faith and baptism are the proverbial two sides of the coin.

The story of Naaman the Syrian, who came to Elisha to be healed of leprosy (2 Kings 5:10–14), illustrates the relation between faith and baptism. Naaman had to believe the word of Elisha, but he wasn't actually healed until he submitted to washing himself in the River Jordan, as commanded. It was only then that 'his flesh was restored like the flesh of a little child, and he was clean' (v. 14). This story was seen as a picture of baptism in the Early Church, e.g. by *Irenaeus. The intimate link between conversion and baptism can be compared to the way in which some evangelists invite those responding to their message to come forward – in fact such a practice has been seen as a surrogate baptism, an attempt to fill the void that comes from ignoring baptism. It is helpful to have an outward visible response to the gospel, not as a substitute for an inner invisible response but as confirmation of it.

What do you think? My answer

Yes, baptism is part of the gospel message as we see it in the New Testament. It is not an optional extra or something to be considered at a later stage of discipleship.

RECEIVING THE SPIRIT
(CCC 1285–1321)

Receiving the Spirit is mentioned in just 7 of our 14 passages, but that does not mean that it was an optional extra. It was expected to happen and when it did not, steps were taken to rectify the situation. This happens twice in Acts:

> Now when the apostles at Jerusalem heard that Samaria had received the word of God, they sent to them Peter and John, who came down and prayed for them that they might receive the Holy Spirit, for he had not yet fallen on any of them, but they had only been baptized in the name of the Lord Jesus. Then they laid their hands on them and they received the Holy Spirit. (Acts 8:14–17)

This can be seen as an extended initiation process, which takes place over a few days.

In Acts 19:1–7, Paul meets some 'disciples' of John the Baptist at Ephesus who had never heard of the Holy Spirit and had received only John's baptism. One wonders whether they had even heard of Jesus. Paul preached to them and, 'on hearing this, they were baptized in the name of the Lord Jesus. And when Paul had laid his hands on them, the Holy Spirit came on them, and they began speaking in tongues and prophesying' (vv. 5–6).

In Acts receiving the Spirit is expected to come at the time of baptism/conversion, not as a second blessing but as part of Christian initiation.[5] Indeed, according to Paul no one is a Christian who has not received the Spirit: 'You, however, are not in the flesh but in the Spirit, if in fact the Spirit of God dwells in you. Anyone who does not have the Spirit of Christ does not belong to him' (Rom. 8:9).

The Spirit came upon Jesus at his baptism and in line with that we see people receiving the Spirit in Acts when they believe and are baptized. Sometimes this happens after baptism, as at Pentecost: 'And Peter said to them, "Repent and be baptized every one of you in the name of Jesus Christ for the forgiveness of your sins, and you will receive the gift of the Holy Spirit"' (2:38), and sometimes beforehand, as with Cornelius: 'While Peter was still saying these things, the Holy Spirit fell on all who heard the word' (10:44); 'As I began to speak, the Holy Spirit fell on them just as on us at the beginning' (11:15).

In Acts, as well as this initial reception of the Spirit, which is what is meant by baptism in the Spirit, there are times when people are filled with the Spirit specifically for a particular task, and this can happen to the same person more than once. See Chapter 15 for more on this.

Three times in Acts there is reference to the laying on of hands to receive the Spirit:

- Acts 8:17: 'Then they laid their hands on them and they received the Holy Spirit.'
- Acts 9:17: 'So Ananias departed and entered the house. And laying his hands on him he said, "Brother Saul, the Lord Jesus who appeared to you on the road by which you came has sent me so that you may regain your sight and be filled with the Holy Spirit."'
- Acts 19:6: 'And when Paul had laid his hands on them, the Holy Spirit came on them, and they began speaking in tongues and prophesying.'

There is not enough evidence to be dogmatic, but it is likely that this was the regular practice as part of Christian baptism, despite Luke only mentioning it occasionally. Support for this can be found in Hebrews 6:1–2 where the author mentions as foundational: repentance, faith, baptisms (plural) and the laying on of hands. In this context the last of these most likely means the laying on of hands to receive the Spirit. Certainly this was part of the regular practice by the second century. In due course this laying on of hands (together with anointing) was called 'confirmation' and came to be seen as a separate sacrament.

There is a lot of sense in making the laying on of hands to receive the Spirit part of the ceremony of baptism, especially where it is a new convert that is being baptized. Otherwise there is always the danger that no one remembers to mention the Holy Spirit and then the new convert will be able to say, like the disciples at Ephesus, 'we have not even heard that there is a Holy Spirit' (Acts 19:2). One of the functions of ritual and ceremonies is precisely to ensure that what is important does not get forgotten, rather than just 'trusting to luck' that it will happen. When I leave home in the morning I have a routine procedure to ensure that I am not leaving anything behind.

Worship

Baptized in water,
sealed by the Spirit,
cleansed by the blood of Christ our king;
heirs of salvation,
trusting his promise –
faithfully now God's praise we sing.
(Michael Saward)

Error to avoid

Does receiving the Spirit always lead to some spectacular event, such as praying in tongues or prophesying? David Pawson maintains that it always does.[6] Certainly this often happened in Acts, but there is no theological reason why it should always happen. Indeed, to the contrary, Paul rejects the idea that all should have any particular gift: 'Are all apostles? Are all prophets? Are all teachers? Do all work miracles? Do all possess gifts of healing? Do all speak with tongues? Do all interpret?' (1 Cor. 12:29–30). Also, if no one can receive the Spirit without such a manifestation then the devastating conclusion follows that the overwhelming majority of Christians throughout history never received the Spirit – and so were not even Christians according to Romans 8:9! This would include many leading evangelists and missionaries. We need rather more evidence to unchurch such a multitude than the fact that such manifestations took place in *some* of the incidents recorded by Luke.

PRAYER

Almighty and everlasting God, you hate nothing that you have made and forgive the sins of all those who are penitent: create and make in us new and contrite hearts that we, worthily lamenting our sins and acknowledging our wretchedness, may receive from you, the God of all mercy, perfect remission and forgiveness; through Jesus Christ your Son our Lord. (*Common Worship*, Collect for Ash Wednesday)

Question to answer

- How does one become a Christian according to the New Testament?

NOTES

1 See D. Pawson *The Normal Christian Birth*. London: Hodder & Stoughton, 1989. His title is a deliberate play on Watchman Nee's *The Normal Christian Life*.

2 J. D. G. Dunn *Baptism in the Holy Spirit*. London: SCM Press, 1970, 91 speaks of three elements, but this is because he counts faith and repentance as one, 'being the opposite sides of the same coin'.

3 Since the expansion of the Church outside the Jewish community was such a momentous step, it was appropriate that this should involve the whole Church, including the Jerusalem apostles.

4 For the historical event underlying this story, involving the Prince of Wales in 1860, see K. Wilson *Everybody's Heard of Blondin*. Sevenoaks: Hawthorns Publications, 1990, 62–64.

5 On this, cf. M. Turner *Baptism in the Holy Spirit*. Cambridge: Grove Books (Renewal Series 2), 2000.

6 Pawson, *The Normal Christian Birth*, 71–77. See ATS Appendix 9 (second edn).

RESOURCES

J. D. G. Dunn *Baptism in the Holy Spirit*. London: SCM Press, 1970.

P. Helm *The Beginnings: Word and Spirit in Conversion*. Edinburgh: Banner of Truth, 1986.

H. T. Kerr and J. M. Mulder *Conversions: The Christian Experience*. Grand Rapids: Eerdmans, 1983.

D. Pawson *The Normal Christian Birth*. London: Hodder & Stoughton, 1989.

G. T. Smith *Beginning Well: Christian Conversion & Authentic Transformation*. Downers Grove: IVP, 2001.

M. Turner *Baptism in the Holy Spirit*. Cambridge: Grove Books (Renewal Series 2), 2000.

Chapter 19

BAPTISM

Aims of this chapter

In this chapter we look at baptism, asking:

- What does baptism do?
- What is the relationship between faith and baptism?
- What is necessary for salvation?
- Should we baptize babies?
- Can we be rebaptized?

WHAT DOES BAPTISM DO?[1]
(CCC 1213–84)

For many the answer is very simple: 'Nothing whatsoever!' Baptism is just a sign, just a way in which we profess our faith. It is true that we confess our faith in baptism, but it is mistaken to see this as all that baptism does.

CONFESSION OF FAITH
Baptism was an occasion for the confession of faith:

- Acts 22:16: 'Rise and be baptized and wash away your sins, calling on his name.'
- Romans 10:9–10 mentions confessing 'with your mouth that Jesus is Lord'.

This does not explicitly mention baptism but it was at baptism that such faith and outward confession took place and these verses are widely and rightly seen as referring to baptism.

This confession took place because faith is a condition of baptism:

> And as they were going along the road they came to some water, and the eunuch said, 'See, here is water! What prevents me from being baptized?' And Philip said, 'If you believe with all your heart, you may." And he replied, "I believe that Jesus Christ is the Son of God. (Acts 8:36–37)[2]

What is never found in the New Testament is the idea of baptism as testimony to unbelievers – indeed there is no recorded example of an unbeliever being present at a baptism. So, for example, the Philippian jailer and his family were baptized at night (Acts 16:33) and there was no thought of waiting till morning and inviting the neighbours to witness it.

Today in many churches baptism is seen as a way of testifying to one's faith before unbelieving friends and family. There is nothing wrong with this and it can be a powerful form of witness. What it is wrong to pretend, however, is that this is the meaning or purpose of baptism in the New Testament, since it is neither.

SALVATION

- 1 Peter 3:21 is very blunt: 'baptism . . . now saves you.'
- Mark 16:16: 'Whoever believes and is baptized will be saved.'[3]
- Romans 10:9–10:

If you confess with your mouth that Jesus is Lord and believe in your heart that God raised him from the dead, you will be saved. For with the heart one believes and is justified, and with the mouth one confesses and is saved.

As already noted, this probably refers to baptism.

UNION WITH CHRIST (IN HIS DEATH, BURIAL AND RESURRECTION)

- Romans 6:3–4:

Do you not know that all of us who have been baptized into Christ Jesus were baptized into his death? We were buried therefore with him by baptism into death, in order that, just as Christ was raised from the dead by the glory of the Father, we too might walk in newness of life.

- Galatians 3:27: 'As many of you as were baptized into Christ have put on Christ.'
- Colossians 2:11–12:

In him also you were circumcised with a circumcision made without hands, by putting off the body of the flesh, by the circumcision of Christ, having been buried with him in baptism, in which you were also raised with him through faith in the powerful working of God, who raised him from the dead.

FORGIVENESS OF SIN AND WASHING

- Acts 2:38: 'Repent and be baptized every one of you in the name of Jesus Christ for the forgiveness of your sins, and you will receive the gift of the Holy Spirit.'
- Acts 22:16: 'And now why do you wait? Rise and be baptized and wash away your sins, calling on his name.'

There are other references to washing in the New Testament which probably refer to baptism:

- 1 Corinthians 6:11: 'And such were some of you. But you were washed, you were sanctified, you were justified in the name of the Lord Jesus Christ and by the Spirit of our God.'
- Ephesians 5:26: '. . . that he might sanctify her, having cleansed her by the washing of water with the word'.
- Titus 3:5: 'he saved us, not because of works done by us in righteousness, but according to his own mercy, by the washing of regeneration and renewal of the Holy Spirit.'
- Hebrews 10:22: 'let us draw near with a true heart in full assurance of faith, with our hearts sprinkled clean from an evil conscience and our bodies washed with pure water.'

REGENERATION/NEW BIRTH

- John 3:3, 5: 'Jesus answered him, "Truly, truly, I say to you, unless one is born again he cannot see the kingdom of God . . . Unless one is born of water and the Spirit, he cannot enter the kingdom of God."'

- Titus 3:5: 'he saved us, not because of works done by us in righteousness, but according to his own mercy, by the washing of regeneration and renewal of the Holy Spirit.'

Neither of these passages mentions baptism explicitly, but there are good reasons for thinking that it is intended. There is a clear parallel between 'water and the Spirit' and what we see happening in Acts, where people are baptized in water and receive the Spirit. The Early Church from the second century understood John 3:5 to refer to water baptism. Elsewhere the New Testament talks of regeneration as happening through the word of truth (Jas. 1:18) and the word of God (1 Pet. 1:23).

RECEIVING THE HOLY SPIRIT

- Acts 2:38: 'Repent and be baptized . . . and you will receive the gift of the Holy Spirit.'
- Acts 19:5–6: 'On hearing this, they were baptized in the name of the Lord Jesus. And when Paul had laid his hands on them, the Holy Spirit came on them.'

On the other hand, receiving the Spirit sometimes preceded baptism, as with Cornelius and his family (Acts 10:44, 11:15).

ENTRY INTO THE CHURCH

Baptism is not just a private matter between God and the individual. It is performed by someone else on behalf of the Church. Almost all denominations understand baptism to bring a person into the universal Church. On the Day of Pentecost those who were baptized were 'added' to the Church (Acts 2:41). 'In one Spirit we were all baptized into one body' (1 Cor. 12:13).

In almost all churches, while anyone may attend one cannot belong to the local church without having been baptized. In other words, baptism does make a difference, so we should be careful to whom it is given. Baptism without real faith does not bring salvation, but it does bring entry into the visible Church. (For more on the 'visible Church', see Chapter 25.) This can be compared to the way in which matriculation makes one a member of a university, or to the bestowal of nationality.

Can the *benefit* of baptism be lost if people later deny their faith? First, receiving baptism is no guarantee of receiving the benefits of baptism – baptism without faith is not effective. Second, there is the vexed question of whether those who fall away were or were not true Christians in the first place, an issue that will be discussed in Chapter 22.

Worship

The servants of God are baptized,
with Jesus made visibly one;
come, Spirit, and clothe them with power,
the world and its pleasures to shun.

The servants of Christ are baptized,
united with Christ in his death;
come, Spirit, descend on their souls
and fill with your life-giving breath.
(Nick Needham)

Sceptic's corner

How can an outward act like baptism have any spiritual significance? To say that baptism saves is to teach that we are saved by our works.

Answer: Some Christians try to be more 'spiritual' than the New Testament. Outward observances without the inner attitude of the heart are condemned throughout the Bible. But the opposite extreme, inner change that is not expressed outwardly and physically, is not commended. We are physical as well as spiritual beings and the gospel addresses us at the physical as well as the spiritual level.

The idea that baptism is a 'work' is wide of the mark. Baptism is not something that we do but something that is done to us, something that we receive. It speaks not of our performance but of our coming with empty hands to receive God's grace.

Credal statement

What gifts or benefits does Baptism bestow?

Answer: It effects forgiveness of sins, delivers from death and the devil, and grants eternal salvation to all who believe, as the Word and promise of God declare. (*Luther, *Small Catechism*)

What is the origin of the rite of baptism? Christian baptism follows on from the baptism of John the Baptist, but where did he get the idea? We cannot be certain, but there are two possible antecedents. The Qumran community practised baptism for ritual purity and John the Baptist did baptize in the desert (Mark 1:4), in the geographical proximity of Qumran. Like John, the Qumran community also practised asceticism and looked for the coming of the Messiah. Another possible antecedent is proselyte baptism, given to those who convert to Judaism.

THE RELATIONSHIP BETWEEN FAITH AND BAPTISM

The New Testament writers viewed faith and baptism as a unity, as can be seen from the way in which they glide naturally from one to the other:

- Galatians 3:25–27: 'Now that faith has come, we are no longer under a

Error to avoid

The New Testament teaching on baptism (pages 184–6) makes no sense while we think of faith and baptism as separate, as alternative ways to salvation. From that starting point we are forced to choose between salvation by faith or salvation by baptism – it must be one or the other. In the New Testament, however, faith was expressed in baptism and baptism was the outward expression of faith. This is what we see in Acts. From this perspective it does make sense to talk of salvation by faith and baptism, as in Mark 16:16: 'Whoever believes and is baptized will be saved, but whoever does not believe will be condemned.'[4] That is why Paul can talk both about salvation through faith and about salvation through baptism. For New Testament Christians, baptism was the decisive turning point. This is still true today for converts from Islam and Judaism, who often when asked for the date of their conversion will point to their baptism. It is when one of their number is baptized that Jews and Muslims regard that person as having become a Christian, not when they merely talk about believing in Jesus. At that point Orthodox Jews hold a funeral service for the convert, with an empty coffin. Muslims are liable to do the same – with a full coffin. Many modern Western Christians find it hard to conceive of baptism this way, but they are the ones who have departed from the New Testament.

guardian, for in Christ Jesus you are all sons of God, through faith. For as many of you were baptized into Christ have put on Christ.'

- In Romans Paul expounds justification by faith in chapters 3—5, then turns to baptism in chapter 6. This isn't a change of topic. The faith described in chapters 3—5 is a faith that expressed itself in baptism; the baptism described in chapter 6 is the baptism that came at the point of conversion.
- Colossians 2:11–12: 'In him also you were circumcised with a circumcision made without hands, by putting off the body of the flesh, by the circumcision of Christ, having been buried with him in baptism, in which you were also raised with him through faith in the powerful working of God, who raised him from the dead.'

Paul can glide naturally from faith to baptism because the two go together and are not separate.

Today, we need to recover the New Testament concept of the unity of faith and baptism. We can do this in three stages:

1 We need to *think* of faith and baptism as a unity, not as two separate things.

2 We need to *teach* this, whether from the pulpit or when talking to a non-Christian friend. Baptism is part of the gospel message: 'Go therefore and make disciples of all nations, baptizing them in the name of the Father and of the Son and of the Holy Spirit' (Matt. 28:19). In Acts, as we have seen, it is part of Christian initiation. It is something to be discussed with those interested in becoming Christians, not something to be deferred to a later date.

3 We should seek to *practise* this unity, to recover the largely extinct practice of

converts' baptism. We will not be able to do this in all cases in the modern West, for a variety of reasons:

(a) A high proportion of Christians today were brought up in a Christian home and the majority of these grow into faith gradually rather than in one crisis event, making it hard for their baptism to coincide with their conversion. One could, of course, take great care to insulate one's children from any contact with the Christian faith and then, when they reach a suitable age, fill the bath with water in anticipation, sit them down and preach to them with the hope that they will repent, believe, be baptized and receive the Spirit all at once!

(b) In addition, many of those raised in a Christian home will already have been baptized as babies.

(c) Apart from those raised in a committed Christian home, many millions of people in Britain (and other European countries) have been baptized or 'christened' but have had little or no other contact with the Church.

Given all of these factors, there is no way that all baptisms today will be converts' baptisms, as in Acts. But if as many as 10 per cent of baptisms were like those in Acts, we would then be better able to understand the New Testament approach to baptism because, even if we ourselves had not experienced it, we would know many Christians who have and it would no longer just be something that we read about in a book.

Another reason why converts' baptism is rare today is that many churches feel the need to delay the baptism of new converts in order to check the genuineness of their conversion. Experience shows that such a delay is no guarantee that the baptized convert will continue walking in the faith.

In Acts the four steps of initiation normally occur at the same time and they are seen as a unity. We should think of this as a *fourfold* initiation. It is a single event with four aspects, not four separate events or four stages. It is not like passing three successive years of study in order to gain a degree. But while the four steps should be seen as a single event ideally or theoretically, in practice they are often drawn out over a period of time. When this happens, we should think of one extended event rather than four separate events. To give a crude analogy, the four steps are not like four separate chocolates in a box, which can each be eaten when one chooses, but more like a single stick of chewing gum that can be stretched over a considerable distance.

What do you think? The question

Is baptism necessary?

WHAT IS NECESSARY FOR SALVATION?

Are all the four elements of initiation (repentance, faith, baptism, receiving the Spirit) necessary for salvation? There are examples in Scripture of those who were saved without one or other of these, most notoriously the thief on the cross. 'And he said, "Jesus, remember me when you come into your kingdom." And he said to him, "Truly, I say to you, today you will be with me in Paradise"' (Luke 23:42–43). This man was presumably not baptized – though a colleague of mine was taught as a

youngster that Jesus baptized him by spitting at him! Also, to be pedantic, the pattern of fourfold initiation begins with the Day of Pentecost, which was yet to come. But there certainly are believers who die before they are able to receive baptism. Second, Old Testament believers did not actually believe in *Jesus*. Third, if it is possible for those who die in infancy to be saved, then they are saved without repenting or believing. So do we conclude that it is not necessary to be baptized, nor to believe, nor to repent, in order to be saved? No. There is a fundamental difference between those who are *unable* to do these things and those who *refuse* to, between can't and won't.

It is important to distinguish between the norm and exceptions. The lawyers have a well-known saying: 'Hard cases make bad law.' Laws should be made for normal situations and then allowances made for the exceptions. For example, Sikhs cannot wear motorcycle helmets because of their turbans. The response to this is not to make helmets optional for all but to make special provision for Sikhs. Again, some countries require a yellow-fever vaccination of visitors, but people who are allergic to eggs cannot have this vaccination. The response is not to dispense with the requirement, but to allow those with this allergy to enter the country at their own risk. Likewise, our practice here should be based on the New Testament norm, which is fourfold initiation, not on the exceptions or problem cases. We can leave the problem cases for God to handle!

Mark 16:16 is relevant: 'Whoever believes and is baptized will be saved, but whoever does not believe will be condemned.' Salvation comes through faith and baptism, but it is those who do not believe, not those who are not baptized, who are said to be condemned. Faith is more crucial than baptism. John 3:5 links entering God's kingdom with being born of water and the Spirit, which in my view is rightly seen as referring to baptism, but verse 8 goes on to talk of the sovereignty of the Spirit in a way that does not encourage us to restrict his working: 'The wind blows where it wishes, and you hear its sound, but you do not know where it comes from or where it goes. So it is with everyone who is born of the Spirit.' We cannot limit the working of the Spirit, as stated in these two documents:

> We can set no limits to the power of Christ: he is leading men to salvation in his own way. Yet this does not at all entitle us to hold baptism in contempt. It is not that Christ is bound to baptism as a means of grace, but we in our faith are. (*Baptists and Reformed in Dialogue* (1977))

> God has bound salvation to the sacrament of Baptism, but he himself is not bound by his sacraments. (*CCC 1257)

Hmm... I think he needs to go in again.

© Miriam Kendrick 2013 www.miriamkendrick.co.uk

What do you think? My answer

Is baptism necessary? Necessary for what? It is necessary in that the Church has no right not to practise it and to require it of converts. It is necessary in that it is not optional for those becoming Christians. It is not necessary in that believers who for some reason (such as premature death) fail to be baptized do not miss salvation.

INFANT BAPTISM?[5]

Paedobaptists believe in the baptism of babies. Some will baptize the children of committed Christians only; others are willing to offer baptism more widely. By contrast, Baptists ('Credobaptists') will baptize believers only. There are important differences among Baptists concerning the age at which they will baptize. Many Southern Baptists in the USA will baptize 4- or 5-year-olds. Most British Baptists normally require a child to be 11 or 12 years old before considering baptism – comparable to the age at which Jewish children have their Bar Mitzvah. Others prefer to wait until they have reached adulthood and can genuinely decide for themselves.

When did infant baptism begin? There is little hard evidence before the third century, though the New Testament does mention household baptisms:

- Acts 16:15: 'After she [Lydia] was baptized, and her household as well . . .'
- Acts 16:33: The Philippian jailer 'took them the same hour of the night and washed their wounds; and he was baptized at once, he and all his family'.
- 1 Corinthians 1:16: 'I did baptize also the household of Stephanas.'

190

This shows that Luke and Paul thought in terms of households, not just isolated individuals. There is no proof that these households contained babies. Also Acts 18:8 states that 'Crispus, the ruler of the synagogue, believed in the Lord, together with his entire household.' Does this prove that there were no small children – or rather that as part of the family they were counted as believers? On third-century tombstones some who died as babies are called 'believers' on the basis of having been baptized.

In the third and fourth centuries there was huge variety, with people being baptized at every conceivable age – at birth, at 3 years old, at 18, after getting married, on their deathbed, etc. It is significant that during these centuries no one objected in principle to anyone else's practice. This suggests that the variety goes back to apostolic times. If there had been one single practice in the first century that would have been known and people who departed from it would have been accused of departing from the practice of the apostles.[6]

When did the Baptist view begin? While there is plenty of evidence in the third and fourth centuries for children of Christian homes not being baptized at an early age, for significant opposition *in principle* to infant baptism we have to wait for the Anabaptist movement in the sixteenth century.

There are two basic approaches to this issue, each with variations. The first approach is to baptize babies, to give them a Christian upbringing and to work towards their affirming their own personal faith in confirmation or some other ceremony. The second approach is to have a service of dedication, to give them a Christian upbringing and to work towards their affirming their own personal faith in believers' baptism. Neither of these approaches is the converts' baptism that we see in Acts. Both are adaptations of that pattern to the changed situation of a child growing up in a Christian home. Both involve an initial ceremony, followed by a period of Christian upbringing followed (one hopes) by a ceremony involving personal commitment. In fact the two approaches have a great deal in common, other than the timing of the water. For both there is a *process*, of initiation (unlike the sudden conversions in Acts) and initiation is not complete until all four elements have taken place. Infant baptism does not on its own make someone a Christian.

Many suggest today that these two approaches should be seen as 'equivalent alternatives'.[7] There are an increasing number of churches that adopt the 'dual practice' approach, allowing parents to choose which approach to follow. This is to return to the situation as we see it in the third and fourth centuries, the earliest period for which we have clear evidence. The Bunyan Meeting Free Church, *John Bunyan's church in Bedford, has operated this way since the seventeenth century. Today many paedobaptist churches allow Christian parents to opt for the dedication rather than baptism of their offspring, thus adopting a *de facto* dual practice approach.

Credal statement

In some churches which unite both infant-baptist and believer-baptist traditions, it has been possible to regard as equivalent alternatives for entry into the Church both a pattern whereby baptism in infancy is followed by later profession of faith and a pattern whereby believer baptism follows upon a presentation and blessing in infancy. (*Baptism, Eucharist and Ministry* (1982), 'Baptism' 12 commentary)

REBAPTISM?

Baptism is irreversible, in that once baptized you cannot become unbaptized; nor can you be properly baptized more than once, e.g. on returning from wandering from the faith. Baptism refers to the beginning of the Christian life, not to further stages that might follow. After all, it is not possible to be circumcised more than once or to become uncircumcised! What about someone who decides that he was not genuinely a Christian at the time of his baptism? That is not a ground for rebaptism any more than deciding that one did not truly love one's spouse at the time of the wedding would be a ground for remarriage.

What about those who were baptized as babies and feel the need for (re)baptism as adult believers? The key point is the validity of the first baptism. If infant baptism is indeed baptism, then it should not be repeated. Those who do not believe that infant baptism is baptism at all will seek baptism as believers – not *re*baptism but their first baptism.

PRAYER

Lord God our Father, through our Saviour Jesus Christ you have assured your children of eternal life and in baptism have made us one with him: deliver us from the death of sin and raise us to new life in your love, in the fellowship of the Holy Spirit, by the grace of our Lord Jesus Christ. (*Common Worship*: Post Communion Prayer for Second Sunday of Easter)

Grant, Lord, that we who are baptized into the death of your Son our Saviour Jesus Christ may continually put to death our evil desires and be buried with him; and that through the grave and gate of death we may pass to our joyful resurrection; through his merits, who died and was buried and rose again for us, your Son Jesus Christ our Lord. (*Common Worship*: Collect for Easter Eve)

Question to answer

● What does baptism do?

NOTES

1 Baptism and its effects can be described by a long series of Bs: Bath, (new) Birth, Belonging, Believing, (changed) Behaviour, (new) Beginning, Burial (with Christ), Badge (of ownership), Blessing, Bestowal (of salvation) and (cheating) o-Bedience.
2 Verse 37 is a variant reading but at the very least expresses an early Christian viewpoint.
3 This is part of the longer ending of Mark that may not be part of the original Gospel, but at the very least expresses an early Christian viewpoint. See D. A. Black (ed.) *Perspectives on the Ending of Mark: Four Views*. Nashville: B&H Academic, 2008.
4 See the previous note.
5 ATS ch. 14/12.
6 I have argued this in 'Did the Apostolic Church Baptise Babies? A Seismological

Approach', *Tyndale Bulletin* 55:1 (May 2004), 109–30.

7 I have argued for this approach in D. F. Wright (ed.) *Baptism: Three Views*. Downers Grove: IVP, 2009.

RESOURCES

J. H. Armstrong (ed.) *Understanding Four Views on Baptism*. Grand Rapids: Zondervan, 2007.

G. R. Beasley-Murray *Baptism in the New Testament*. London: Macmillan, 1962.

G. R. Beasley-Murray *Baptism Today and Tomorrow*. London: Macmillan, 1966.

D. Bridge and D. Phypers *The Water that Divides*. Leicester: IVP, 1977; reprinted by Christian Focus, 2008.

B. Witherington *Troubled Waters: Rethinking the Theology of Baptism*. Waco: Baylor University Press, 2007.

D. F. Wright *What has Infant Baptism Done to Baptism?* Milton Keynes: Paternoster, 2005.

D. F. Wright (ed.) *Baptism: Three Views*. Downers Grove: IVP, 2009.

Chapter 20

JUSTIFICATION AND ASSURANCE

Aims of this chapter

In this chapter we look at justification and assurance, asking:

- What are justification and sanctification?
- On what basis does God accept us?
- By what will we be tested at the Last Judgement?
- Can we be sure of our salvation?
- Is assurance of salvation integral to saving faith or is it merely a subsequent possibility?
- Where should we look for assurance?
- Can we have assurance of *final* salvation or only of our present condition?

PART 1: JUSTIFICATION

JUSTIFICATION BY FAITH (CCC 1987–2005, 2017–24)

Arguably the best-known doctrine of the Reformation is justification by faith alone. It has been a bone of contention between Protestants and Catholics throughout the centuries, but the gulf is not as wide as with some other doctrines. In 1999, following a couple of decades of dialogue, the Roman Catholic Church and the Lutheran World Federation signed a common declaration, the **Joint Declaration on the Doctrine of Justification*. This was signed on 31 October, a significant choice of day, being Reformation Day, the anniversary of the day in 1517 when *Martin Luther nailed his Ninety-Five Theses to the church door in Wittenberg.[1]

Credal statement

By grace alone, in faith in Christ's saving work and not because of any merit on our part, we are accepted by God and receive the Holy Spirit, who renews our hearts while equipping and calling us to good works. (*Joint Declaration on the Doctrine of Justification* 3:15)

JUSTIFICATION AND SANCTIFICATION

In Reformation theology, following the apostle Paul, justification is seen as a term from the law court. It means acquittal, receiving a not-guilty verdict, being pronounced innocent. Our sins are not counted or reckoned against us and we are declared righteous. Justification is God looking on us 'just-as-if' we had never sinned. Christ's righteousness is reckoned or 'imputed' to us. Justification is a legal picture or model. This is not the only way to describe our relationship to God, but it is one way of viewing it, and an important one.

Sanctification, by contrast, is the process of being transformed into the image of Christ, as will be seen in the next chapter. The distinction between justification and sanctification is fundamental to the Reformation doctrine. It can be stated in a number of different ways:

Justification	Sanctification
God accepting me	God changing me
how God looks on me	what God does in me
my status	my state
my relationship to God	my actual condition
Christ for me on the cross	Christ in me by the Spirit.

Justification and sanctification can be distinguished (they are different from one another), but not separated. (The *Definition of *Chalcedon* makes the same point about the two natures of Christ.) We cannot have one without the other because they both flow from our union with Christ. It is in Christ that we are accepted by God: '*in him* we have redemption through his blood, the forgiveness of our trespasses, according to the riches of his grace' (Eph. 1:7); and it is in Christ that we are made new: 'if anyone is *in Christ*, he is a new creation. The old has passed away; behold, the new has come' (2 Cor. 5:17). We have neither justification nor sanctification independently of or outside of Christ. This is why justification is not a 'legal fiction'.

They are distinct but inseparable, like the heat and light of the sun. The sun provides us with both heat and light. These are distinct in that we are warmed by the heat, not by the light, and we see by the light, not by the heat. They are also inseparable in that the sun never gives us one without the other. This analogy was used frequently in the Reformation. Justification and sanctification can also be compared to the two legs of a pair of trousers, which cannot be separated, unlike a pair of socks, which can all too easily become separated. When you open the washing machine, finding one leg of a pair of trousers is a guarantee of finding the other; finding one sock provides no such guarantee. The two legs are inseparable because they both emerge from the top of the trousers, just as justification and sanctification flow from Christ.

THE BASIS FOR JUSTIFICATION OR ACCEPTANCE BY GOD

The true basis for acceptance is the work of Christ on the cross, the 'Great Exchange' described in Chapter 12, whereby Christ took our sin upon himself and made his righteousness ours: 'For our sake he made him to be sin who knew no sin, so that in him we might become the righteousness of God' (2 Cor. 5:21). This becomes effective for us when by faith we are united to Christ.

> As long as Christ remains outside of us, and we are separated from him, all that he has suffered and done for the salvation of the human race remains useless and of no value for us. (*Calvin, *Institutes* 3:1:1)

JUSTIFICATION BY FAITH ALONE

Justification is received by 'faith alone' (*sola fide*) – the Reformation slogan. But why by faith rather than by love, say? It is not because faith is superior to love because it is not: 'faith, hope, and love abide, these three; but the greatest of these is love' (1 Cor. 13:13). Nor is it because our faith has value in itself, but rather because faith unites us with *Christ*, in whom we are justified. Faith has been described as the empty hands by which we receive Christ. Faith appropriates justification not as a worker earns wages but as one accepts a free gift. Faith does not achieve salvation but receives it.

Justification is received 'by faith alone', but this is not a *naked* faith. As Calvin put it, 'it is therefore faith alone which justifies, and yet the faith which justifies is not alone'. We are justified by faith alone, but not without repentance or baptism. We are justified not by faith without the Holy Spirit but by faith which receives the Holy Spirit. We are not justified by a faith which is devoid of love: 'No other faith justifies but faith working through love [Gal. 5:6]' (Calvin, *Institutes* 3:11:20). Justification is not *by* works, but neither is it *without* works, a point on which all the Reformers agreed.

How can one say that we are justified not *by* works, but not *without* works? It is like the distinction between cause and symptoms. You cannot have chickenpox *without* spots (it is the unavoidable evidence of having it), but you do not get chickenpox *by* having spots! The gospel is unconditional in that anyone can come to Christ; it is not unconditional in the sense that we can continue to live how we like. To quote the bumper sticker, it may be true that 'Christians aren't perfect' but is it true that they are 'just forgiven'? That is not how Paul saw it. He wrote to the Corinthians:

> Do you not know that the unrighteous will not inherit the kingdom of God? Do not be deceived: neither the sexually immoral, nor idolaters, nor adulterers, nor men who practice homosexuality, nor thieves, nor the greedy, nor drunkards, nor revilers, nor swindlers will inherit the kingdom of God. And such *were* some of you. But you were washed, you were sanctified, you were justified in the name of the Lord Jesus Christ and by the Spirit of our God. (1 Cor. 6:9–11)

Christians are not perfect, but they are transformed, not 'just forgiven'.

JUSTIFICATION BY FAITH IN THE NEW TESTAMENT

Justification by faith alone is taught especially by Paul:

- Romans 3:21—4:25: We are justified, reckoned righteous, not by works of the law but by the cross of Christ, through faith. E.g. 3:28: 'We hold that one is justified by faith apart from works of the law;' and 4:4–5: 'Now to the one who works, his wages are not counted as a gift but as his due. And to the one who does not work but trusts in him who justifies the ungodly, his faith is counted as righteousness.'
- Romans 10:1–13, where there is a contrast between the righteousness of works of the law and the righteousness of God, through faith: 'Being ignorant of the righteousness that comes from God, and seeking to establish their own, they did not submit to God's righteousness' (10:3).
- Justification by faith is the theme of Galatians, especially 2:15—3:25: 'a person is not justified by works of the law but through faith in Jesus Christ' (2:16).
- In Philippians 3:4–11 Paul contrasts his Jewish heritage with his desire to 'gain Christ and be found in him, not having a righteousness of my own that comes from the law, but that which comes through faith in Christ, the righteousness from God that depends on faith' (3:8–9).
- The most down-to-earth account is in Jesus' parable of the Pharisee and the tax collector (Luke 18:9–14), which in today's terms might be a parable of the church leader and the bailiff. The former trusts in his own works, for which he thanks God; the latter casts himself on God's mercy, recognizing the inadequacy of his own works: 'I tell you, this man [the tax collector] went down to his house justified, rather than the other. For everyone who exalts himself will be humbled, but the one who humbles himself will be exalted' (18:14).

What do you think? The question

By what will we be tested at the Last Judgement?

Sceptic's corner

Is there not a total contradiction between Paul's teaching that we are justified by faith apart from works and James's teaching that we are not justified by faith alone but by works (Jas. 2:14–26): 'You see that a person is justified by works and not by faith alone' (2:24)?

Answer: There is certainly a verbal contradiction, but we need to note the meaning of the words. Theology is not like maths and words do not have one meaning only. The Bible contains almost no 'technical language' – that came later as theology became an academic discipline, for which precise definitions become important.

For Paul to be 'justified' means to be 'reckoned righteous by God', as in Genesis 15:6: Abraham 'believed the LORD, and he counted it to him as righteousness'. James likewise teaches that we are reckoned righteous by faith, and also cites Genesis 15:6 in support: 'the Scripture was fulfilled that says, "Abraham believed God, and it was counted to him as righteousness" – and he was called a friend of God' (2:23) – but this is not what James calls justification. For Paul, justification refers to what happened to Abraham in Genesis 15; for James it refers to what happened to him in Genesis 22, when he was willing to sacrifice

Isaac (Jas. 2:21). Also, Paul and James both use the word 'faith' differently. For Paul it refers to a living trust in Christ which leads to good works, while James writes of a dead faith without works (2:14–17), that is in the head alone and which even the demons have (2:19). 'Faith apart from works is dead' (2:26). Neither Paul nor James thought that *such* a 'faith' could save. So they were using the same words but with different meanings; their teachings are not in contradiction to each other but should be seen as complementary.

© Miriam Kendrick 2013 www.miriamkendrick.co.uk

Credal statement

Question 61: Why do you say that you are righteous by faith alone?

Answer: Not because I please God by virtue of the worthiness of my faith, but because the satisfaction, righteousness, and holiness of Christ alone are my righteousness before God, and because I can accept it and make it mine in no other way than by faith alone. (*Heidelberg Catechism* (1563))

Worship

O perfect redemption, the purchase of blood,
to every believer the promise of God;
the vilest offender who truly believes,
that moment from Jesus a pardon receives.
(Frances J. van Alstyne, 'To God be the glory!')

Nothing in my hand I bring,
simply to the cross I cling;
naked, come to thee for dress;
helpless, look to thee for grace;
foul, I to the fountain fly;
wash me, Saviour, or I die.
(Augustus M. Toplady, 'Rock of Ages')

What do you think? My answer

Many Christians would say that the final judgement is on the basis of faith. In fact the New Testament consistently teaches that we will be judged by our *works*:

THE BASIS FOR THE LAST JUDGEMENT
- Matthew 7:21–23:

  Not everyone who says to me, 'Lord, Lord', will enter the kingdom of heaven, but the one who does the will of my Father who is in heaven. On that day many will say to me, 'Lord, Lord, did we not prophesy in your name, and cast out demons in your name, and do many mighty works in your name?' And then will I declare to them, 'I never knew you; depart from me, you workers of lawlessness.'

- Matthew 16:27: 'The Son of Man is going to come with his angels in the glory of his Father, and then he will repay each person according to what he has done.'

- Matthew 19:29: 'Everyone who has left houses or brothers or sisters or father or mother or children or lands, for my name's sake, will receive a hundredfold and will inherit eternal life.'
- Matthew 25:31–46, the parable of the sheep and the goats, is very clear, the judgement being according to how we have treated 'one of the least of these my brothers' (25:40).
- John 5:28–29: 'An hour is coming when all who are in the tombs will hear his voice and come out, those who have done good to the resurrection of life, and those who have done evil to the resurrection of judgement.'
- Romans 2:6–8:

He will render to each one according to his works: to those who by patience in well-doing seek for glory and honour and immortality, he will give eternal life; but for those who are self-seeking and do not obey the truth, but obey unrighteousness, there will be wrath and fury.

- 2 Corinthians 5:10: 'We must all appear before the judgement seat of Christ, so that each one may receive what is due for what he has done in the body, whether good or evil.'
- Revelation 20:11–13:

Then I saw a great white throne and him who was seated on it. From his presence earth and sky fled away, and no place was found for them. And I saw the dead, great and small, standing before the throne, and books were opened. Then another book was opened, which is the book of life. And the dead were judged by what was written in the books, according to what they had done.

And the sea gave up the dead who were in it, Death and Hades gave up the dead who were in them, and they were judged, each one of them, according to what they had done.

So, according to the New Testament we are justified by faith, but the final judgement is on the basis of works. There is no contradiction here. The cause of our acceptance by God is justification by faith; the symptom or evidence of this is good works. The way we live shows what we really believe. There was a time when I would have said that I liked porridge. It was after I lived somewhere that served porridge for breakfast and I went some weeks without ever opting for it that I realized I did not really like porridge. In the final episode of the TV series *Lark Rise to Candleford*, one of the characters (Queenie) states that 'what a person truly believes isn't what they think, isn't what they say, it's what they do'.

NEW PERSPECTIVES ON PAUL[2]

So far we have been considering the traditional Protestant understanding of justification, but this has been questioned recently by a number of New Testament scholars, of whom we will mention two. J. D. G. Dunn argues that the 'works of the law' that cannot justify us according to Paul relate to specific Jewish 'social boundary markers', such as circumcision and the food laws. So Paul's message of justification by faith is primarily about breaking down barriers between Jews and Gentiles. Tom Wright also claims that Paul's doctrine is not primarily about how we find peace with God, but rather about what defines the people of God. Justification by faith is the declaration that those who believe in Jesus are members of the true covenant family; it is about *who* belongs to the people of God, rather than *how* to join. While the views of these two scholars have much in common they are not identical, which is why we should speak of 'new perspectives', in the plural.

It is too early to start revising the traditional doctrine of justification, for several reasons. First, these new perspectives have by no means won universal acceptance among New Testament scholars and there remains considerable opposition to them. The jury is still out. Second, Tom Wright himself has said on a number of occasions that if his view of Paul is correct it would not mean that the Reformation doctrine of justification is mistaken. Rather, we should see that doctrine not as itself Paul's doctrine of justification but as an implication of Paul's doctrine. So even if Wright is right it does not mean that the Reformers were wrong.

PART 2: ASSURANCE OF SALVATION
(CCC 1821, 2005)

The sixteenth-century Reformers taught that it is possible to have assurance of salvation, to be certain that one's sins are forgiven and that one is right with God. That has also been the consistent position of the Evangelical tradition. Such confidence before God is a great strength of that tradition, but it is always in danger of lapsing into self-confidence or arrogance, both of which are deeply unattractive. 'Let anyone who thinks that he stands take heed lest he fall' (1 Cor. 10:12). The final verse of Toplady's hymn 'A debtor to mercy alone' seems to have lost sight of this warning:

> Yes, I to the end shall endure,
> As sure as the earnest is given;
> More happy, but not more secure,
> The glorified spirits in heaven.

Among those who believe in the possibility of assurance there remain significant differences, as can be seen by considering three questions:

1 Is assurance of salvation integral to saving faith or is it merely a subsequent possibility? Is it part of the basic package, as it were, or an optional extra? The first view was the majority position at the Reformation, being held by Luther, *Melanchthon and Calvin.[3] Trusting in the promises of God implies trusting that we have received what is promised. There was, however, an alternative Reformed tradition according to which assurance is something separate from saving faith, which may well come later, like two different courses of a meal. This position was taught by *Bullinger, who greatly influenced the English Reformation, and is also found in the *Westminster Confession of Faith* (1647) ch. 18, which became the doctrinal basis for English-speaking Presbyterianism. In some groups, such as the Scottish Free Presbyterians (not to be confused with the Free Church of Scotland, the 'Wee Frees') this has led to assurance becoming a rare phenomenon. They point out that sheep (who outnumber people in the Scottish Highlands and Islands) bear a mark of ownership on their ears, which can be seen by all but the sheep themselves. The implication of this analogy is that it will be clear to others that people are true Christians, but they themselves may have great difficulty realizing it.

2 Where should we look for assurance? This is related to the previous question. Those who teach that assurance comes later usually teach that it is to be sought by looking for evidence of salvation in our good works, in the fruit of the Spirit,

in our experience, etc. – i.e. by self-examination, by looking within. The danger of this is that the more one looks within, the more introverted one can become and it is possible to become enmeshed in a morass of introspection. The more we become aware of our shortcomings, the less assurance we have. Those who teach that assurance is integral to saving faith base it upon the work of Christ as declared in the gospel. Tightrope walkers look ahead to their goal and if they look down at their feet they are in danger of falling off the rope. Likewise, we should look away to Christ for assurance, not look within.

3 Can we have assurance of *final* salvation or only of our present condition? In other words, does salvation come with a lifetime guarantee? The answer to this question hangs on the question of perseverance, an issue that will be discussed in Chapter 22.

Sceptic's corner

If we hold that assurance is integral to saving faith, does that mean that those who are unsure of their salvation are thereby proved not to be real Christians?

Answer: This is an important question as such a conclusion would be pastorally disastrous. It is true that saving faith implies assurance, but there are various reasons why a genuine believer might lack assurance. First, all believers to some extent wrestle with doubt and, as Calvin put it, in this life our faith is always such that we need to pray, 'Lord, I believe; help my unbelief!' (Mark 9:24). The fact that saving faith implies assurance does not mean that the believer always grasps that implication. Second, believers may lack assurance

because they have been taught to search for it in the wrong place, by looking within rather than looking to Christ and the gospel.

Worship

Bold shall I stand in thy great day,
For who aught to my charge shall lay?
While through thy blood absolved I am,
From sin and fear, from guilt and shame.
(Nicolaus von Zinzendorf, tr. *John Wesley,
'Jesus, thy blood and righteousness')

PRAYER

God, be merciful to me, a sinner!
(Luke 18:13)

Questions to answer

- On what basis does God accept us?
- Can we be sure of our salvation?

NOTES

1 For more on this, see A. N. S. Lane *Justification by Faith in Catholic–Protestant Dialogue: An Evangelical Assessment*. London and New York: T. & T. Clark (Continuum), 2002; A. N. S. Lane, 'Justification' in *Oxford Handbook of Ecumenical Studies*. Oxford: OUP, forthcoming.

2 For more on this, see M. B. Thompson *The New Perspective on Paul*. Cambridge: Grove Books, 2002.

3 For more on this, see A. N. S. Lane, 'Calvin's Doctrine of Assurance Revisited' in D. W. Hall (ed.) *Tributes to John Calvin: A Celebration of his Quincentenary*.

Phillipsburg, New Jersey: P&R, 2010, 270–313.

RESOURCES

J. K. Beilby and S. E. Enderlein (eds) *Justification: Five Views*. Downers Grove: IVP, 2011.

J. and A. McGrath *The Dilemma of Self-Esteem*. Wheaton, Illinois: Crossway, 1992.

J. Piper *Counted Righteous in Christ*. Wheaton, Illinois: Crossway, 2002.

M. A. Seifrid *Christ, Our Righteousness: Paul's Theology of Justification*. Leicester: IVP, 2000.

Chapter 21

SANCTIFICATION

Aims of this chapter

In this chapter we look at sanctification, starting with a fundamental tension found in the New Testament. We will then ask:

- What is sanctification?
- Is sanctification God's work or ours?
- How do past, present and future relate in sanctification?
- Is it possible for Christians to avoid all sin?

Sceptic's corner

Talk of sanctification is just a cover for petty legalism and rule-keeping.

Answer: Undoubtedly Christians sometimes fall into that trap, but that is to misunderstand the true nature of sanctification, as we shall see:

WHAT IS SANCTIFICATION?
(CCC 2012–16, 2028–29)

We can do no more here than consider a few specific points relating to sanctification.

The heart of sanctification is being transformed into the likeness of Christ, becoming more like him: 'We all, with unveiled face, beholding the glory of the Lord, are being transformed into the same image from one degree of glory to another. For this comes from the Lord who is the Spirit' (2 Cor. 3:18). This is a thoroughly positive goal and is vastly more than a list of 'dos and don'ts'. Yet it is also a hugely ambitious goal and the more comfortable target of becoming more respectable fades into insignificance by comparison. Being transformed into Christ's likeness will involve us in pain and hardship and at times we may well wish that God would settle for second best. As C. S. Lewis put it:

> It is a serious thing to live in a society of possible gods and goddesses, to remember that the dullest and most uninteresting person you talk to may one day be a creature which, if you saw it now, you would be strongly tempted to worship, or else a horror and a corruption such as you now meet, if at all, only in a nightmare.[1]

The extent of transformation is shown by Paul in his command to 'present your bodies as a living sacrifice . . . Do not be

Tension to hold[2]

In the New Testament we see a tension. In the parable of the Pharisee and the tax collector (Luke 18:9–14) the Pharisee thanked God for all his good works and that he was better than others. The tax collector by contrast beat his breast and said, 'God be merciful to me, a sinner.' It was the tax collector, not the Pharisee, who was accepted by God. The grace of God is shown to the worst of sinners and this is the only ground on which we can approach God. But that is only half of the story. A few chapters earlier in the same Gospel (Luke 14:25–33) Jesus speaks uncompromisingly of the demands of discipleship and warns that 'any one of you who does not renounce all that he has cannot be my disciple' (14:33). The promise of acceptance to the worst sinner does not rule out the demand for total commitment from all believers.

The same tension is found in Paul. He teaches justification by faith alone, that we are accepted by God not on the ground of our good works or merits but solely on the basis of Christ's death for us on the cross. But alongside this comforting message of grace, the same Paul also warns the Corinthian Christians that those indulging in a variety of activities, such as adultery, theft or drunkenness, will not inherit the kingdom of God. 'And such,' he says, '*were* some of you' – before they came to Christ (1 Cor. 6:9–11). The good news of free acceptance does not rule out the need for obedience. Likewise, 1 John 1:9 teaches that, 'If we confess our sins, he is faithful and just to forgive us our sins and to cleanse us from all unrighteousness.' A few verses previously, though, we read, 'If we say we have fellowship with him while we walk in darkness, we lie and do not practise the truth' (1:6).

Being faithful to this tension is a challenge for Christian theology, but not just for theologians. The tension is something that needs to be lived out by *all* Christians in their day-to-day discipleship. There are two opposite dangers to avoid in tackling this tension. One danger is antinomianism, which says that it does not matter how we live.[3] The other danger is legalism, which says that we need to earn God's acceptance by our works. We need to live in tension between these two. Tension is not the same as balance. When I stand upright I am balanced; if two people are pulling my arms in opposite directions I am in tension. Living the New Testament tension means feeling both the pressure towards antinomianism and the pressure towards legalism. Martyn Lloyd-Jones once argued that a preacher who is never misunderstood to be teaching antinomianism is probably not preaching justification by faith alone. By the same token, a preacher who is never misunderstood to be teaching legalism is probably not preaching the radical demands of discipleship.

A similar point was made by *Dietrich Bonhoeffer, the German theologian who joined the resistance against Hitler and was hanged by the Nazis in the closing days of the war. In his *Cost of Discipleship* he talks of the distinction between cheap and costly grace. Cheap grace breaks our tension by offering forgiveness without repentance, grace without discipleship. Cheap grace proclaims the forgiveness of sins without the resolve to forsake sin. Cheap grace interprets 'grace alone' to mean that we can remain as we are without changing. Costly grace, however, calls us to follow Christ. It is costly because it cost God the life of his Son and because it costs us our life.

> The only man who has the right to say that he is justified by grace alone is the man who has left all to follow Christ . . . Those who try to use this grace as a dispensation from following Christ are simply deceiving themselves.[4]

It is important to maintain this tension in the overall thrust of a preaching ministry. One of my students once told me that at church he expects to hear the basic message: 'You're OK. God has accepted you in Christ.' That is certainly an important part of the gospel and in a Western world that is obsessed with the need for self-esteem it is the only message heard in many churches. But there is an equal need for another message: 'You're not OK. Your life falls short of what is expected of a Christian. Don't just relax and enjoy justification but repent and get on with sanctification.' Indeed, without this second message the first ceases to be the biblical doctrine of justification by faith and becomes instead a secular message of self-esteem. As *Luther pointed out, if we take away the law we lose the gospel as well. We *are* OK in that God has accepted us freely in Christ, but we are *not* OK in that our lives still fall very short of God's goal for us and he will not let up on us until he has reached that goal.

The same tension also works itself out in the doctrine of the Church. On the one hand, the Church is the community of forgiveness. Moral achievement is not a precondition for entry. The Church is the school for forgiven sinners, the hospital for those who are being healed from sin. When the Church becomes a moralistic club for the respectable it has lost touch with its calling. Yet, at the same time, the Church is meant to witness not just to human impotence but to renewal by God's grace. We are rightly scandalized by those episodes of church history where the Church has exemplified the basest of moral behaviour. The Church has to maintain the difficult balance of welcoming sinners without sanctioning and approving their continuation in sin. We can come to God just as we are, but we are not meant to stay that way.

It is vital to maintain this tension between the good news of free grace and the call to discipleship not as an optional extra for the zealous but as part of the basic package. As is often stated, the entrance fee for the Christian faith is nothing, but the annual subscription is everything. When we are in Christ we receive the free gift of justification but we also need to press on with the arduous task of sanctification. At different times one or other side of this tension has been lost. At times the Church has lapsed into preaching cheap grace, as Bonhoeffer put it, and Christians have been shamefully indistinct from the ungodly. At other times the stress has been on the moral demands of Christian faith and the radical message of forgiveness has faded into the background. The New Testament gospel offers us forgiveness and encouragement, but does not allow us to think that we are fine as we are.

conformed to this world, but be transformed by the renewal of your mind' (Rom. 12:1–2). J. B. Phillips famously translated this as 'Do not let the world squeeze you into its mould.' This points to conformity to God's will in mind and action. The extent of transformation is also shown by the two great commandments, to love God and neighbour (Matt. 22:37–40), as expounded in Chapter 11.

To be transformed into the likeness of Christ involves discipleship. Three important aspects of discipleship are seen in Luke 9:23: 'If anyone would come after me, let him deny himself and take up his cross daily and follow me.' So discipleship is:

- **Following Christ** – to be Christ's disciples, learning from him.
- **Denying oneself**. What does this mean? Giving up chocolates for Lent? It is much more than that. It means saying 'No' to ourselves, to our own desires, and saying 'Yes' to God's will. This applies in two ways: Negatively it means not doing that which is wrong, such as lying or stealing, yet it also means more than this. Positively it means seeking God's will for our lives and being willing to follow wherever he leads. This might, for example, involve a call to remain single – not because celibacy is superior in its own right but in order to devote oneself to God's service. *John Stott renounced marriage, an academic career and the offer of a bishopric, all because he sensed a primary calling to a particular pastoral ministry.[5] It involves responding to the promptings of the Holy Spirit and being malleable; it involves saying 'No' to self-will.
- **Taking up one's cross daily** – Luke's Gospel is the only one to include the word 'daily'. This is not a once-for-all call

but one for each and every day. Taking up or bearing one's cross does not mean putting up patiently with the hardships of life, be this a pain in the back (sports injury) or a pain in the backside (awkward relatives). It means voluntary acceptance of and submission to the will of God.

The process of sanctification can be compared to the two different strategies for dealing with excess weight. Corsets don't cure it but they hold it in and conceal it. Their effect is immediate. By contrast, taking exercise and eating a sensible diet take time to work, but do actually deal with the problem and cure it. When it comes to sanctification we are faced with two similar strategies. We can restrain our sinful nature so that its worst effects are avoided – we can hold back our anger and not come to blows with others, and we can contain our lust and not go to the point of committing adultery. Restraining sin in this way is important, but it is not enough. We need also to seek a cure. We need to work on our anger and lust, not just contain them. While those battling excess weight may opt to go for one strategy without the other, with sanctification both are important.

SANCTIFICATION: PAST, PRESENT AND FUTURE

Another major aspect of sanctification is that we should 'become what we are'. Christians are united with Christ and share in his history:

- We are crucified with Christ and 'united with him in a death like his' (Rom. 6:5–8).
- We are raised with him: 'If then you have been raised with Christ, seek the things that are above, where Christ is, seated at the right hand of God' (Col. 3:1).

- And we are also seated with him in the heavenlies: God 'raised us up with him and seated us with him in the heavenly places in Christ Jesus' (Eph. 2:6).

When did this happen? We were crucified with Christ in AD 33 or thereabouts and we enter into this at our baptism/conversion. When we are baptized into Christ we are baptized into his death:

> Do you not know that all of us who have been baptized into Christ Jesus were baptized into his death? We were buried therefore with him by baptism into death, in order that, just as Christ was raised from the dead by the glory of the Father, we too might walk in newness of life. (Rom. 6:3–4)

There is the story of the Frenchman who took British nationality. After the naturalization ceremony he was asked what difference it made. 'Put it like this,' he answered, 'This morning the Battle of Waterloo was a defeat; now it is a victory.' The outcome of the battle had not changed, but his relationship to it had. Likewise at conversion we move from being in Adam to being in Christ. We need by faith to reckon this to be true: 'You also must consider yourselves dead to sin and alive to God in Christ Jesus' (Rom. 6:11). We also need to work it out in our lives: 'You have died, and your life is hidden with Christ in God' (Col. 3:3) leads on to 'Put to death therefore what is earthly in you: sexual immorality, impurity, passion, evil desire, and covetousness . . . Put on then, as God's chosen ones, holy and beloved, compassion, kindness, humility, meekness, and patience . . .' (3:5–14). We *have died* with Christ, but we also need to *put to death* all that is sinful. We enjoy the new life in Christ

'already, but not yet', a formula popularized by G. E. Ladd.

We are living in the period between the First and Second Comings of Christ, when we enjoy the benefits of salvation already in part, but not yet fully – 'already, but not yet'. We are in the Last Days: 'Long ago, at many times and in many ways, God spoke to our fathers by the prophets, but in these last days he has spoken to us by his Son' (Heb. 1:1–2). This did not necessarily mean that the End was about to happen. The Last Days were introduced by the First Coming of Christ, but they won't come to fruition until the Second Coming. This situation can be compared to that of engagement, where two people are already committed to each other but have not yet reached the commitment of marriage. In Ephesians 1:14 the Holy Spirit is called 'the guarantee of our inheritance until we acquire possession of it', and the word for 'guarantee' or 'down payment' (*arrabon*) is the word that is used in modern Greek for an engagement ring. Our present experience of salvation is also described as the firstfruits of a harvest: 'We ourselves, who have the firstfruits of the Spirit, groan inwardly as we wait eagerly for adoption as sons' (Rom. 8:23).

IS SANCTIFICATION GOD'S WORK OR OURS?

Is sanctification something we receive passively by faith, or something that we acquire by our own effort, actively working for it? This is a silly polarization as both are true.

The New Testament describes sanctification as the work of God and calls upon us to rest passively in it. For example:

- John 15:4: 'Abide in me, and I in you. As the branch cannot bear fruit by itself, unless it abides in the vine, neither can you, unless you abide in me.'
- Romans 6:11: 'So you also must consider yourselves dead to sin and alive to God in Christ Jesus.'
- Galatians 2:20:

  I have been crucified with Christ. It is no longer I who live, but Christ who lives in me. And the life I now live in the flesh I live by faith in the Son of God, who loved me and gave himself for me.

- 1 Thessalonians 5:23: 'Now may the God of peace himself sanctify you completely, and may your whole spirit and soul and body be kept blameless at the coming of our Lord Jesus Christ.'

But we are also told to strive for sanctification:

- Colossians 3:2, 5: 'Set your minds on things that are above, not on things that are on earth . . . Put to death therefore what is earthly in you: sexual immorality, impurity, passion, evil desire, and covetousness, which is idolatry.'
- Romans 8:12–13:

  So then, brothers, we are debtors, not to the flesh, to live according to the flesh. For if you live according to the flesh you will die, but if by the Spirit you put to death the deeds of the body, you will live.

- Romans 12:1–2: 'I appeal to you therefore, brothers, by the mercies of God, to present your bodies as a living sacrifice, holy and acceptable to God, which is your spiritual worship.'

Both sides are held together in Philippians 2:12–13: 'Work out your own salvation with fear and trembling, for it is God who works in you, both to will and to work for his good pleasure.' God does it but we have to work it out in our lives by our own efforts. In 2 Peter 1:3–7 Peter begins with the statement that God's 'divine power *has granted to us* all things that pertain to life and godliness, through the knowledge of him who called us to his own glory and excellence'. He continues by urging his readers to '*make every effort* to supplement your faith with virtue, and virtue with knowledge, and knowledge with self-control, and self-control with steadfastness, and steadfastness with godliness, and godliness with brotherly affection, and brotherly affection with love'.

There is a slogan that used to be used by those advocating the one side only: 'Don't wrestle, nestle.' In fact we are called to do both: wrestle *and* nestle! Another such slogan is 'Let go and let God.' This similarly presents one side only of the picture. Some preachers have pointed to Exodus 14:13–14 where Moses tells the people of Israel, facing the threat of an Egyptian army, to 'Fear not, stand firm, and see the salvation of the LORD, which he will work for you today . . . The LORD will fight for you, and you have only to be silent.' In the very next verse, however, the Lord tells Moses to get on and do something: 'Why do you cry to me? Tell the people of Israel to go forward.'

Credal statement

They, who are once effectually called, and regenerated, having a new heart, and a new spirit created in them, are further sanctified, really and personally, through the virtue of Christ's death and resurrection, by His Word and Spirit dwelling in them: the dominion of the whole body of sin is destroyed, and the several lusts thereof are more and more weakened and mortified; and they more and more quickened and strengthened in all saving graces, to the practice of true holiness, without which no man shall see the Lord. (*Westminster Confession of Faith* (1647), 13:1)

Sceptic's corner

Why are some non-Christians better people than so many Christians?

Answer: This is a serious question. The key issue is not whether a particular Christian is better or worse than a particular non-Christian (something that it is hard to measure anyway) but whether a particular person becomes better on becoming a Christian. If not, we have grounds for questioning (not denying) whether that person is indeed a true Christian. But here and now we are all a 'work in progress'. The person with a foul temper who is converted may still have a volatile temper and compare badly with others who are not Christians, but the more significant question is whether that individual is becoming *less* foul-tempered on growing in grace.[6]

CORPORATE SANCTIFICATION

Just as sin is not purely individual but has a corporate dimension (see Chapter 7), so also there is a corporate dimension to sanctification. As we engage in the task of sanctification we are greatly influenced both by society at large and by the Church as a community when it comes to what is and is not acceptable. A few examples will illustrate this:

- Divorce was rare in Western societies until the 1950s, but with the progressive liberalization of divorce laws since the 1960s it has now reached epidemic proportions. What was once stigmatized by society is now completely acceptable and very easily obtained. 'Till death do us part' has become 'till one of us changes our mind.' The Church has not remained immune from this and the majority of Western churches now accept divorce.[7] The result is that a Christian couple going through difficult times in their marriage are now far more likely to resort to divorce than to persevere with the marriage. They make their individual decisions, but these are hugely influenced by social pressures.[8]

- Many Christians today, including pastors, struggle with pornography. The ready acceptance of this in society at large – its legalization and availability on the internet – makes it much more likely that a Western Christian today will have this problem, compared with one living in the 1950s.

Lest it be thought that I am a grumpy old man looking back at a past golden age, let me point to two areas where the movement has been in the other direction.

- In the 1950s racism was socially acceptable. At that time a famous hotel in Nairobi had a sign that said, 'No blacks or dogs beyond this point'. In the 1970s I heard Christian students make racial comments that would be totally unacceptable today, when the social pressure is strongly against racism.
- In the eighteenth century it was acceptable to own and trade in slaves. It is well known that the hymn writer John Newton, of 'Amazing grace' fame, was a former slave trader. What is less well known is that he continued in this occupation for a time *after* his conversion. The achievement of reformers like William Wilberforce was not just to change the law but eventually to change social attitudes. I have not heard of any Christians today tempted to engage in people-trafficking.

Christians do not engage in sanctification as hermetically sealed individuals. We are all greatly influenced by what is deemed by the Church to be acceptable or unacceptable. This is why church discipline is very important, whether exercised informally (peer pressure) or formally. In turn, the Church is not hermetically sealed from society at large. Changes in social attitudes often lead to changed attitudes within the church community. This can be a good thing as, for example, the Church no longer accepts racism or the marginalization of the disabled. It can also be a bad thing as the Church is influenced by social attitudes towards, for example, cohabitation or materialism. As Western society increasingly rejects the Christian values that it has

inherited from the past this is likely to become a growing problem, as it was for the Church living in a pagan society in the early centuries.

> ### What do you think? The question
>
> Is it possible for Christians to avoid all sin?

PERFECTION?[9]

The Christian life involves struggle. Conversion brings a real change within us. We now love God and desire to serve him. Sin no longer *reigns* within us, but it still *remains* within us. We are plagued by sinful desires and lust which lead us to sin. So the Christian life is a daily struggle against sin. Conversion is the beginning, not the end, of the struggle against sin. *John Wesley observed that many Christians imagine at conversion that the battle is over, only to discover that it has just begun.

> How naturally do those who experience such a change [conversion] imagine that all sin is gone; that it is utterly rooted out of their heart, and has no more any place therein. How easily do they draw that inference, 'I *feel* no sin, therefore I *have* none; it does not *stir*, therefore it does not *exist*; it has no *motion*, therefore it has no *being*. But it is seldom long before they are undeceived, finding sin was only suspended, not destroyed. Temptations return and sin revives; showing it was but stunned before, not dead. They now feel two principles in themselves, plainly contrary to each other: 'the flesh lusting against the Spirit' [Gal. 5:17, KJV]; nature opposing the grace of God. (*The Scripture Way of Salvation* 5–6)

We should look for a slow but steady progress towards the goal of perfection. Unfortunately there are no short cuts, no quick fixes. We should expect to sin less and less, but not expect to be sinless.

Some Christians, however, have taught that perfection is possible in this life. There are three main types of such teaching.

1 Some have taught that Christians can reach a stage of perfection where they cannot sin *whatever* they do. This can soon lead to gross immorality. J. H. Noyes was a big noise on the American revivalist scene, based in upstate New York. He pronounced himself sinless in 1834 and declared that the perfect cannot sin. The outcome was sexual licence. Noyes advocated 'spiritual marriage', to be sealed by a 'new physical sacrament'. As has been wryly observed, it may have been physical but there was nothing particularly new about it!

2 The Wesleys taught a very different version of Christian perfection. They believed in 'entire sanctification', a second blessing to be received by faith. This involves perfect love ruling in the heart and expelling all sin – all self-love, all pride, etc. The perfect Christian is free of all sins of the heart. They did not believe that this is something that we can achieve – it is a free gift, offered to all believers, which must be received by faith. Also, entirely sanctified Christians are not *unable* to sin. It is possible to fall from this state by sinning again. John Wesley expounded this doctrine in his classic work *A Plain Account of Christian Perfection*.

3 A third version of perfection claims no more than that Christians can avoid all *wilful* sin. This may be true, but it is misleading to describe this as perfection.

Certainly, if all that is needed to be perfect is to avoid wilful sin, then I am perfect for about a third of the time – while I am asleep! There is a lot more to sin than wilful sin. Someone who is selfish and proud may manage to avoid wilful sin for a time, but they are certainly not perfect.

What do you think? My answer

In the Age to Come all Christians will reach perfection in Christ's kingdom, where there will be no more sin. In this life, while we 'already' make progress towards that goal, we do 'not yet' reach it. Wesley liked to quote 1 Thessalonians 5:23–24:

> Now may the God of peace himself sanctify you completely, and may your whole spirit and soul and body be kept blameless at the coming of our Lord Jesus Christ. He who calls you is faithful; he will surely do it.

> Perfection is indeed promised – 'at the coming of our Lord Jesus Christ'. The disagreement with Wesley concerns the *timing* of the gift, not the desire for it, which is why those who do not expect it in this life can nevertheless enjoy singing Wesleyan hymns which pray for it:

Worship

O for a heart to praise my God,
A heart from sin set free,
A heart that always feels thy blood
So freely shed for me.

A heart in every thought renewed
And full of love divine,
Perfect and right and pure and good,
A copy, Lord, of thine.

Thy nature, gracious Lord, impart;
Come quickly from above;
Write thy new name upon my heart,
Thy new, best name of Love.
(Charles Wesley)

PRAYER

Almighty God, who alone can bring order to the unruly wills and passions of sinful humanity: give your people grace so to love what you command and to desire what you promise, that, among the many changes of this world, our hearts may surely there be fixed where true joys are to be found; through Jesus Christ your Son our Lord. (*Common Worship*, Collect for Third Sunday before Lent)

Question to answer

- What is sanctification?

NOTES

1 C. S. Lewis, 'The Weight of Glory' in *The Weight of Glory and Other Addresses*. Grand Rapids: Eerdmans, 1965.

2 For more on this, see <http://klice.co.uk/uploads/whitfield/Vol%206.4%20Lane.pdf>.

3 The term 'antinomianism' is also used to refer to the view that Christians can rely on the Spirit to guide them and do not need the written law.

4 D. Bonhoeffer *The Cost of Discipleship*. London: SCM Press, 1959, 35–47.

5 <http://howardsnyder.seedbed.com/2013/04/19/john-stotts-celibacy>.

6 For more helpful comments on this question, see C. S. Lewis, *Mere Christianity*. London: Fontana, 1955, 172–80.

7 H. W. House *Divorce and Remarriage: Four Christian Views*. Downers Grove: IVP, 1990; M. L. Strauss *Remarriage after Divorce in Today's Church: Three Views*. Grand Rapids: Zondervan, 2006.

8 For a study that supports the peer effects of divorce, see <http://douthat.blogs.nytimes.com/2010/06/24/how-divorce-spreads>.

9 ATS ch. 10/9.

RESOURCES

D. L. Alexander (ed.) *Christian Spirituality: Five Views of Sanctification*. Downers Grove: IVP, 1988.

M. E. Dieter (ed.) *Five Views on Sanctification*. Grand Rapids: Zondervan, 1987.

S. Neill *Christian Holiness*. London: Lutterworth, 1960.

J. Webster *Holiness*. London: SCM Press, 2003.

Chapter 22

PERSEVERANCE AND REWARD

Aims of this chapter

In this chapter we look at perseverance and reward, asking:

- Can converted Christians lose their salvation?
- Should we be motivated by desire for reward?
- Will all Christians receive equal reward in the Age to Come?
- Do our good works merit reward?

PART I: PERSEVERANCE[1]
(CCC 162, 1274, 1821, 2016)

Can converted Christians lose their salvation? This is a controversial topic with various views being held. We will examine these by asking three questions of the New Testament:

IS PERSEVERANCE TO THE END NECESSARY FOR SALVATION?
The consensus throughout the New Testament is that it is. Final salvation is not unconditional but requires holiness and perseverance to the end:

- Hebrews 12:14: 'Strive for peace with everyone, and for the holiness without which no one will see the Lord.'

- Mark 13:13: 'You will be hated by all for my name's sake. But the one who endures to the end will be saved.'
- Colossians 1:21–23:

  He has now reconciled [you] in his body of flesh by his death, in order to present you holy and blameless and above reproach before him, if indeed you continue in the faith, stable and steadfast, not shifting from the hope of the gospel that you heard.

- Hebrews 10:39: 'We are not of those who shrink back and are destroyed, but of those who have faith and preserve their souls.'
- Mark 8:38: 'Whoever is ashamed of me and of my words in this adulterous and sinful generation, of him will the Son of Man also be ashamed when he comes in the glory of his Father with the holy angels.'

We need holiness and perseverance, but that does not mean that we need to be perfect or that we may not fall seriously along the way. After all, David was guilty of adultery and murder and Peter denied Christ. We remain forgiven sinners – but sinners who are in the process of sanctification. As we saw in Chapter 20, judgement is by works, which means that some proof of sanctification is required to pass the test.

IS IT POSSIBLE TO LOSE SALVATION?
Again the New Testament says 'Yes':

• John 15:2, 6:

Every branch of mine that does not bear fruit he takes away, and every branch that does bear fruit he prunes, that it may bear more fruit . . . If anyone does not abide in me he is thrown away like a branch and withers; and the branches are gathered, thrown into the fire, and burned. (John 15:2, 6)

• Hebrews 6:4–8:

It is impossible to restore again to repentance those who have once been enlightened, who have tasted the heavenly gift, and have shared in the Holy Spirit, and have tasted the goodness of the word of God and the powers of the age to come, if they then fall away, since they are crucifying once again the Son of God to their own harm and holding him up to contempt. (6:4–6)

• Hebrews 10:26–31:

If we go on sinning deliberately after receiving the knowledge of the truth, there no longer remains a sacrifice for sins, but a fearful expectation of judgement, and a fury of fire that will consume the adversaries. (10:26–27)

• 2 Peter 2:20–22:

If, after they have escaped the defilements of the world through the knowledge of our Lord and Saviour Jesus Christ, they are again entangled in them and overcome, the last state has become worse for them than the first. For it would have been better for them never to have known the way of righteousness than after knowing it to turn back from the holy commandment delivered to them. (2:20–21)

This is not just a theoretical possibility. The parable of the sower (Mark 4:1–20) implies that many will fall away and that preachers should expect this:

These are the ones sown on rocky ground: the ones who, when they hear the word, immediately receive it with joy. And they have no root in themselves, but endure for a while; then, when tribulation or persecution arises on account of the word, immediately they fall away. (4:16–17)

If one of the 12 apostles, chosen by Jesus, could fall away and be lost, who is exempt? Paul did not see himself as exempt, but feared disqualification: 'I discipline my body and keep it under control, lest after preaching to others I myself should be disqualified' (1 Cor. 9:27).

WILL GOD KEEP CHRISTIANS FROM COMPLETELY FALLING AWAY?
Again the New Testament seems to say 'Yes':

• John 10:27–29:

My sheep hear my voice, and I know them, and they follow me. I give them eternal life, and they will never perish, and no one will snatch them out of my hand. My Father, who has given them to me, is greater than all, and no one is able to snatch them out of the Father's hand.

- Romans 8:33–39:

  I am sure that neither death nor life, nor angels nor rulers, nor things present nor things to come, nor powers, nor height nor depth, nor anything else in all creation, will be able to separate us from the love of God in Christ Jesus our Lord. (8:38–39)

- Philippians 1:6: 'I am sure of this, that he who began a good work in you will bring it to completion at the day of Jesus Christ.'

How can we hold these three points together? There are different views on this, each of which involves denying or playing down one of the above three points. Two of these views are well established and have been around for centuries.

According to the traditional *Arminian* view (named after *Jakob Arminius), *Christians can and do fall away and lose their salvation.*[2] God will keep us and no one can snatch us from his hand but we retain the option of rejecting him. This can be compared to the situation of a shipwrecked sailor who has been rescued by a lifeboat. The sailor is now out of danger from the elements, but retains the freedom to jump back into the water should he so wish. Put like that the analogy is reassuring, but the reality is less so. No rescued sailors in their right mind would jump back into the water, but the incentives to abandon the Christian walk are far more persuasive. There is the lure of sin, there is the pressure to conform to society around, and there can be intellectual doubts and questioning. A better analogy would be someone who is very sick and has been accepted onto a gruelling and painful course of medical treatment. She will not be expelled from the programme, but there is no guarantee that she will not herself give up on it.

In favour of the Arminian view is the fact that it coheres with experience (those who abandon the Christian walk) and that it is in line with at least part of what is taught in Scripture.

According to the traditional *Calvinist* view, salvation requires perseverance to the end, but *God keeps true Christians from finally falling away.* This is sometimes called 'the perseverance (or "preservation") of the saints' because it teaches that Christians will persevere to the end and be saved. But what about the warning passages? These are there to keep us from falling away, by showing us the consequence of apostasy.

And what about those who *do* fall away? There are two possible explanations. They may be true believers who have fallen away for a time, but in due course will repent and return. Alternatively it may be that they were never true believers and that they will not repent or return: 'They went out from us, but they were not of us; for if they had been of us, they would have continued with us. But they went out, that it might become plain that they all are not of us' (1 John 2:19). In Acts, Simon Magus 'believed' and was baptized, but soon proved himself not to be genuine (8:13, 18–23). We should be cautious about ever stating that this is true of any specific individual as we are not to know what may have happened at the end of someone's life.

We should not despair of the eternal salvation of persons who have taken their own lives. By ways known to him alone, God can provide the opportunity for salutary repentance. The Church prays for persons who have taken their own lives. (*CCC 2283)

Error to avoid

The two historic views discussed so far are agreed that salvation requires perseverance. More recently, however, a third view has emerged, according to which *all who are converted will be saved regardless of how they then live*. They will be saved even if they immediately renounce their faith and lead a life of debauched atheism. Many people today find this view attractive, but it is blatantly unbiblical. There is much in the New Testament that makes it clear that discipleship is not an optional extra and that remaining faithful is a condition of salvation. The whole letter to the Hebrews focuses on warning Jewish believers not to forsake Christ *and so lose their salvation*. Also, much of the teaching of Jesus warns against thinking that a profession of faith is of use if it is not backed up by our lives.

Apart from being unbiblical, this approach is dangerous, for a number of reasons. It encourages a false complacency, the idea that there can be salvation without discipleship, on the error of which see the previous two chapters. Also it encourages a 'tip and run' approach to evangelism which is concerned only to lead people to make a 'decision', with scant concern about how these 'converts' will subsequently live. This is in marked contrast to the attitude of the apostle Paul, who was deeply concerned about his converts' lifestyle and discipleship. One only needs to read Galatians or 1 Corinthians to see that he did not hold to this recent view. The author of Hebrews was desperately concerned that his readers might lose their salvation by abandoning Christ and reverting to Judaism. These three letters make no sense if salvation is guaranteed by one single 'decision for Christ'. This view is pastorally disastrous.

© Miriam Kendrick 2013 www.miriamkendrick.co.uk

CONCLUSION

The New Testament seems to both affirm and deny the possibility of losing one's salvation and the temptation is to heed one side only and explain away the other. Is there a way of resolving this tension? To some extent, yes. It should be possible for all to agree that those who *profess* to be Christians are able to fall away and be lost. This is confirmed by biblical teaching, by biblical examples (like Judas) and by common experience. This is the reality for pastors looking out over their flock – there is no guarantee that the people that they see before them will not fall away and be lost. In fact one might say that statistically it is almost certain that some will do so. The Arminian would say that such people had lost their salvation while the Calvinist would say that they never really had it. The practical reality remains much (but not entirely) the same whatever one's theology. Also, on both views there will be genuine Christians who will stray for a time before returning to the path of discipleship.

216

It is important to remember that we cannot read other people's hearts – indeed, it is hard enough to read our own hearts much of the time. All that we see of others is their outward behaviour. We should give the benefit of doubt to those who credibly profess to be Christians, but that does not mean that we *know* that they are. When people turn away we must not presume to judge whether they are genuine Christians who are straying or pseudo-Christians who are declaring their true state.

Where the two positions clearly diverge is when we consider the question of our own salvation. Does assurance of present salvation guarantee final salvation? In the cold light of logic it would appear that we cannot believe both in the certainty of final salvation and in the real possibility of losing it. But this is a matter of practical living, not just theory. There is a tension here similar to that described in the last chapter. Pastorally the warnings are given to keep us from straying when we are tempted; the promises are given to encourage us when we doubt our strength to persevere. Arminians and Calvinists can agree on that much, even though they differ on the theory.

See Chapter 23 for more on Arminianism and Calvinism.

PART 2: REWARD (CCC 2006–2011, 2025–27)

What do you think? The question

Should we be motivated by desire for reward?

BIBLICAL TEACHING

The Old Testament has much to teach about rewards and punishment in this life.

These are promised and threatened in the law (e.g. Lev. 26) and their outworking can be seen in the history of Israel, especially the Exile. But such judgement can be a blunt instrument. Often in this life the righteous suffer and the wicked prosper. The book of Job is a protest against those who think to the contrary, as is Ecclesiastes. The teaching on reward and punishment and the protest of Job and Ecclesiastes cannot be reconciled in this life. What brings the two into harmony is the idea of reward and punishment beyond death, added in the New Testament.

The strongest teaching about reward in the New Testament comes in the teaching of Jesus, especially as found in Matthew, much of which is paralleled in other Gospels:

- Beatitudes (5:3–12), e.g. 'Blessed are the poor in spirit, for theirs is the kingdom of heaven' (5:3).
- 'If you love those who love you, what reward do you have?' (5:46) – i.e. there is reward for loving those who do not love us.
- God will see and reward giving to the needy in private (6:1–4): 'When you give to the needy, do not let your left hand know what your right hand is doing, so that your giving may be in secret. And your Father who sees in secret will reward you' (6:3–4).
- Similarly with prayer: 'When you pray, go into your room and shut the door and pray to your Father who is in secret. And your Father who sees in secret will reward you' (6:6).
- Giving is an investment for eternity: 'Lay up for yourselves treasures in heaven, where neither moth nor rust destroys and where thieves do not break in and steal' (6:20). In heaven there is no inflation and the banks do not go bust.

- 'The one who receives a prophet because he is a prophet will receive a prophet's reward, and the one who receives a righteous person because he is a righteous person will receive a righteous person's reward. And whoever gives one of these little ones even a cup of cold water because he is a disciple, truly, I say to you, he will by no means lose his reward' (10:41–42).
- We will be repaid according to what we have done (16:27).
- 'Everyone who has left houses or brothers or sisters or father or mother or children or lands, for my name's sake, will receive a hundredfold and will inherit eternal life' (19:29).
- Our faithfulness now will affect our status at the end, as seen in the parable of the talents, where the servants are rewarded according to what they have done in this life (25:14–30).

There is also plenty about rewards in the rest of the New Testament:

- Ephesians 6:8: 'Whatever good anyone does, this he will receive back from the Lord, whether he is a slave or free.'
- At the end of his life Paul looks forward to the reward that awaits him at the End; 2 Timothy 4:7–8: 'Henceforth there is laid up for me the crown of righteousness, which the Lord, the righteous judge, will award to me on that Day' (4:8).
- 2 John 8: 'Watch yourselves, so that you may not lose what we have worked for, but may win a full reward.'
- In Revelation 2—3 particular rewards are promised to each of the seven churches.
- Revelation 11:18:

The nations raged, but your wrath came, and the time for the dead to be judged, and for rewarding your servants, the prophets and saints, and those who fear your name, both small and great, and for destroying the destroyers of the earth.

WILL ALL CHRISTIANS RECEIVE EQUAL REWARD IN THE AGE TO COME?

Today many think 'Yes', probably influenced by the egalitarian spirit of the age. But this is not what we see in the New Testament:

- In Matthew 19:28, the apostles are promised a special reward: 'When the Son of Man will sit on his glorious throne, you who have followed me will also sit on twelve thrones, judging the twelve tribes of Israel.'
- It is those whose work is of quality that receive a reward: 'The fire will test what sort of work each one has done. If the work that anyone has built on the foundation survives, he will receive a reward' (1 Cor. 3:13–14).
- Martyrs will receive a special recognition: 'Then they were each given a white robe and told to rest a little longer, until the number of their fellow servants and their brothers should be complete, who were to be killed as they themselves had been' (Rev. 6:11).

If a reward is promised to a particular group or to people who do particular things, it implies that others do not receive it. To teach that all will receive the identical rewards would be highly demotivating, making a life of discipleship ultimately irrelevant. If the laziest Christian received the same reward as the apostle Paul, who poured out his life for his ministry and died as a martyr, that would suggest that God does not put a high value on our work.

Against this teaching many cite Matthew 20:1–16, the parable of the vineyard workers. Those who work only for one hour receive the same reward as those who have worked all day. If this parable were all that the New Testament taught about reward we could reasonably conclude that all receive the same reward – but as we have seen, this is not all that the New Testament teaches and a large number of passages teach the opposite. We must ask what is the point of the parable, since parables often teach one main point. The punch line of this parable is the generosity of God and the fact that Gentiles (late-comers) will be accepted alongside Jews: 'Am I not allowed to do what I choose with what belongs to me? Or do you begrudge my generosity?' (20:15).

Sceptic's corner

Is hoping for reward not an unworthy motive? Should we not be serving God out of love and gratitude, rather than desire for reward?

Answer: This is undoubtedly true as regards our primary motive. Someone who gave *merely* as an investment programme with an eye to future reward would not be acting virtuously. Cynical calculation for reward is not the right spirit. But if we stop there we are being more 'spiritual' than Jesus and the apostles, especially Jesus who taught so much about reward. We need to distinguish between our primary motivation and what may serve as an encouragement. Many parents use bribes to induce their children to do things like learn the piano, but the child will not get far if the bribe is the *only* motive. I found the promise of reward a powerful motive in persuading my children to work hard for key exams – but it only worked because they also desired to do well.

The way in which we have become 'more spiritual' than Jesus was well illustrated by H. J. Cadbury.[3] He points out that today we seek to encourage giving by appealing to people's altruism, focusing on the need, e.g. showing pictures of starving children. Jesus, by contrast, spoke of our reward. More strongly still, he emphasized that we should give because *we* need it. To put it very crudely, stingy people are going to hell. 'God said to him, "Fool! This night your soul is required of you, and the things you have prepared, whose will they be?" So is the one who lays up treasure for himself and is not rich towards God' (Luke 12:20–21).

Cadbury is certainly right about today. I have spoken on this subject a number of times and always invite my audience to tell me reasons why we should give. Normally no one mentions the fact that we should give because *we* need it. I suspect that Cadbury sees this as an example of how Jesus' teaching falls short of what we now know to be right – but I may be doing him an injustice. On reflection, however, I am more and more persuaded that Jesus was right. If we give because of the needs of others *only*, it puts us in a position of superiority and can very easily become patronizing. If, however, we give at least in part because our spiritual health depends on it and because of the promised reward, then we are not so superior. We are spiritually poor and giving to those in need is one way to remedy our plight. Also, Jesus was aware that the motive of reward can be effective. Secular fundraisers recognize the same principle when they speak of the importance of 'donor satisfaction'.

There is a difference between 'extrinsic' and 'intrinsic' rewards. A child might be offered a bribe for learning the piano (an extrinsic reward) but the real (intrinsic) reward is being able to play the piano. The ultimate reward for being generous is becoming a generous person. As adults we are better able to appreciate intrinsic rewards, which is not to say that there is no place for extrinsic rewards. A colleague used to motivate himself to mark exam scripts by rewards of chocolate, a practice I have happily adopted.

What do you think? My answer

Our primary motivation should be love for God and neighbour, as we saw in Chapter 11, and without this nothing that we do has value before God. Like children, however, we can be greatly encouraged by the incentive of reward and God offers us this as a secondary motivation.

GOD'S GENEROSITY

God promises to reward us and we are judged by works. But this does not mean that we *earn* the reward. Judged strictly, all our works and all our righteousness fall short. 'Enter not into judgement with your servant, for no one living is righteous before you' (Ps. 143:2). 'You also, when you have done all that you were commanded, say, "We are unworthy servants; we have only done what was our duty"' (Luke 17:10). The good news is that God relates to believers not as a strict judge but as a loving parent. When a child comes back from school with her first feeble attempt at writing, the parents are delighted at this great leap forward and do not immediately point out all its imperfections. Similarly God, our loving Father, accepts and rewards our feeble and imperfect efforts. As George McDonald put it, 'God is easy to please, but hard to satisfy.'[4] Both halves of this

statement are important. God is pleased with and rewards the least progress, but he will not rest until he has brought us to perfection, until he has transformed us into the image of Christ.

Underlying this is a sound pastoral and psychological principle. We need encouragement, and receiving nothing but criticism can be highly demotivating. Some children suffer from such an environment at home and I heard a woman recall such an experience on the radio. She returned home from school to report to her mother that she had gained 98 per cent in a maths test. 'And what happened to the other 2 per cent, dear?' was the only encouragement that she received. Some, inaccurately, perceive God to be like this. Encouragement is very important, but if all we give is encouragement people can soon become proud and complacent. In America, which has been heavily influenced by the emphasis on self-esteem, students' perception of their competence in maths has steadily risen, while their actual achievement has declined. In a 1989 study of eight nations, the American students had the highest estimate of their mathematical competence, the Korean students the lowest. In terms of actual competence, the Koreans scored the highest and the Americans the lowest.[5] We need to be told of the need to improve as well as to be encouraged for the progress that we have made.

Worship

And although we be unworthy, through our manifold sins, to offer unto thee any sacrifice, yet we beseech thee to accept this our bounden duty and service; not weighing our merits, but pardoning our offences, through Jesus Christ our Lord. (Book of Common Prayer, Communion Service)

220

Credal statement

The persons of believers being accepted through Christ, their good works also are accepted in him, not as though they were in this life wholly unblameable and unreproveable in God's sight; but that he, looking upon them in his Son, is pleased to accept and reward that which is sincere, although accompanied with many weaknesses and imperfections. (*Westminster Confession of Faith* (1647), 16:6)

PRAYERS

O God, you declare your almighty power most chiefly in showing mercy and pity: mercifully grant to us such a measure of your grace, that we, running the way of your commandments, may receive your gracious promises, and be made partakers of your heavenly treasure; through Jesus Christ your Son our Lord. (*Common Worship*: Collect for Eleventh Sunday after Trinity)

Stir up, O Lord, the wills of your faithful people; that they, plenteously bringing forth the fruit of good works, may by you be plenteously rewarded; through Jesus Christ our Lord. (*Common Worship*: Post Communion Prayer for Sunday next before Advent)[6]

Questions to answer

- Can converted Christians lose their salvation?
- What role is there for reward in the Christian life?

NOTES

1 ATS ch. 11/10.
2 Not all Arminians take this view and the initial Arminian statement of faith, the *Remonstrance* of 1610, declared uncertainty on the issue.
3 H. J. Cadbury *The Peril of Modernizing Jesus*. London: SPCK, 1962, ch. 5.
4 As cited by C. S. Lewis in *Mere Christianity*. London: Fontana, 1955 168–69.
5 See, for example, <http://www.latimes.com/news/opinion/la-op-selfhelp1jan01,1,4617597.story>.
6 In the Book of Common Prayer this is the Collect for the last Sunday before Advent. Because of its opening words, this date was known as 'Stir up Sunday' and is the traditional date for starting to prepare Christmas puddings.

RESOURCES

H. W. Bateman (ed.) *Four Views on the Warning Passages in Hebrews*. Grand Rapids: Kregel, 2007.

I. H. Marshall *Kept by the Power of God: A Study of Perseverance & Falling Away*. Carlisle: Paternoster, 1995, revised edn.

J. M. Pinson (ed.) *Four Views on Eternal Security*. Grand Rapids: Zondervan, 2002.

T. R. Schreiner and A. B. Caneday *The Race Set before Us: A Biblical Theology of Perseverance & Assurance*. Leicester: IVP, 2001.

S. H. Travis '"Your Reward is Great in Heaven"', in J. Colwell (ed.) *Called to One Hope*. Carlisle: Paternoster, 2000, 3–16.

REDEMPTION: CORPORATE

Chapter 23

GRACE AND ELECTION

Aims of this chapter

In this chapter we look at grace and election, asking:

- Does God choose who will be saved, or do we?
- Can we serve God through our unaided free will?
- Can we take the initiative in seeking God's grace?
- Does God's grace make conversion possible (for *all*) or inevitable (for *some*)?
- Does God want all to be saved?
- Does God select who will be saved?

DOES GOD CHOOSE WHO WILL BE SAVED, OR DO WE?[1]

Scripture clearly teaches that we are called upon to choose God, as for example in Deuteronomy 30:19: 'I call heaven and earth to witness against you today, that I have set before you life and death, blessing and curse. Therefore choose life, that you and your offspring may live.' Yet Scripture also teaches that God has chosen us, as for example in Ephesians 1:4: '[God] chose us in [Christ] before the foundation of the world, that we should be holy and blameless before him.' The question therefore is: which causes the other, which is ultimate?

There are two main answers to this question, often called Calvinism and Arminianism. These names are somewhat misleading in that the two views go back to the Early Church, over 1,000 years before the time of either *Calvin or *Arminius.

Error to avoid

The Calvinist view (see overleaf) has been very popular in the past but is less popular today. It is now perceived as offending against many of the principles of modern Western culture, a culture which favours a democratic inclusive egalitarianism and stresses the rights of the individual. Arminianism sits more happily with these principles. This in itself does not prove it right or wrong, but it is worth noting why ideas become more or less popular at different times. Anthony Kenny, a Roman Catholic theologian who left the Roman Church, described his theological training in Rome. He recalls how disgusted many of his American fellow students were to discover how unegalitarian was Roman Catholic teaching on grace, based on the *Council of Trent (1545–63).[2] We must not allow our cultural prejudices to decide the issue for us, but should examine the teaching of Scripture and see how we can hold the various strands together.

- **The Calvinist answer** is that it is *God's choice* or election that is ultimate. Yes, we do choose God, but we do so because he first chose us.
- **The Arminian answer** is that it is *our choice* that is ultimate. Yes, in some sense God chooses us, but the reason why I am a Christian and my next-door neighbour is not is because I have chosen God.

PART 1: GRACE

CAN WE SERVE GOD THROUGH OUR UNAIDED FREE WILL? (CCC 1999–2000)

Can we serve God, obey him and do his will, by our unaided free will without God's grace – i.e. without the help of the Holy Spirit within? Scripture and Christian tradition concur in saying 'No'.

- John 15:1–6: 'I am the vine; you are the branches. Whoever abides in me and I in him, he it is that bears much fruit, for apart from me you can do nothing' (15:5).
- Romans 8:1–8: 'Those who are in the flesh cannot please God' (8:8).

By contrast, early in the fifth century Pelagius taught that we can serve God through our unaided free will, for which he was vigorously opposed by *Augustine, who devoted the last 20 years of his life to this. Pelagius taught that there are three stages to a good work: the ability, the will and the deed. God has given us free will and the rest is up to us. So, for example, God has given me the ability to get up and face the day, so all that is needed is for me to exercise my will and to get out of bed. If God has commanded something, it must be possible. Pelagianism has been called the national heresy of the English (especially

of 'public-school religion'), though Pelagius himself was either Scottish or Irish.

It is true that God commands nothing contrary to human nature in itself – such as telling us to jump 20 feet high. But some of God's good commands are beyond the reach of *fallen* human nature, on which see Chapters 7 and 8. In the Age to Come there will be no more sin and we will perfectly fulfil God's law, on which see Chapter 29.

CAN WE TAKE THE INITIATIVE IN SEEKING GOD'S GRACE? (CCC 2001, 2021–22)

If we are unable to serve God without his grace, without the Holy Spirit empowering us within, are we at least able to take the initiative in seeking this help? No. Scripture teaches that it is God who makes the first move, not us:

- John 6:44: 'No one can come to me unless the Father who sent me draws him.'
- John 6:65: 'No one can come to me unless it is granted him by the Father.'
- John 16:8–11: 'When [the Spirit] comes, he will convict the world concerning sin and righteousness and judgement' (16:8).

Rather than us taking the initiative, it is the Holy Spirit who convicts us of our need. Why is this necessary? Because without his intervention we are:

- **Blind**: 2 Corinthians 4:3–6: 'In their case the god of this world has blinded the minds of the unbelievers, to keep them from seeing the light of the gospel of the glory of Christ, who is the image of God' (4:4).
- **Dead**: Ephesians 2:1–2: 'You were dead in the trespasses and sins in which you once walked, following the course of this world, following the prince of the power of the air, the spirit that is now at work in the sons of disobedience.'

Western theology since the time of Augustine has generally accepted that we need God to make the first move – which is called 'prevenient grace' (for more on which, see Chapter 15). (The situation has been less clear in the Eastern Orthodox Church.) In the sixth century the *Second Council of Orange rejected the idea that we can make the first move, known as 'Semi-Pelagianism'.

Credal statement

If anyone maintains that God awaits our will to be cleansed from sin, but does not confess that even our wish to be cleansed comes to us through the infusion and working of the Holy Spirit, he resists the Holy Spirit himself who says through Solomon, 'The will is prepared by the Lord' [Prov. 8:35 LXX] and the salutary word of the Apostle, 'It is God who works in you both to will and to accomplish' [Phil. 2:13]. (Council of Orange (529), canon 4)

DOES GOD'S GRACE MAKE CONVERSION POSSIBLE (FOR *ALL*) OR INEVITABLE (FOR *SOME*)? (CCC 2002)

If we are unable to turn to God without him making the first move, does he give this prevenient grace to all, leaving us to decide whether to respond or not, or is this grace given to some only in such a way that our response is guaranteed? This is the point at which Calvinists and Arminians diverge.

Calvinists and 'efficacious grace'

Calvinists believe in 'efficacious grace', which does not just make our conversion possible but effects it, brings it about. This grace infallibly achieves its goal – which is that *we* should repent, believe and respond gladly and willingly to the gospel. There are passages of Scripture to which they point. Faith and repentance are both described as gifts of God:

- Acts 11:18: 'When they heard these things they fell silent. And they glorified God, saying, "Then to the Gentiles also God has granted repentance that leads to life."'
- Acts 16:14: 'One who heard us was a woman named Lydia, from the city of Thyatira, a seller of purple goods, who was a worshipper of God. The Lord opened her heart to pay attention to what was said by Paul.'
- Acts 18:27: 'When he wished to cross to Achaia, the brothers encouraged him and wrote to the disciples to welcome him. When he arrived, he greatly helped those who through grace had believed.'

- Ephesians 2:8: 'For by grace you have been saved through faith. And this is not your own doing; it is the gift of God.'

More significantly, they are given specifically to those whom God has *chosen*:

- Matthew 11:25–27: 'I thank you, Father, Lord of heaven and earth, that you have hidden these things from the wise and understanding and revealed them to little children' (11:25).
- Matthew 13:11–17: 'To you it has been given to know the secrets of the kingdom of heaven, but to them it has not been given' (13:11).
- John 6:37: 'All that the Father gives me will come to me, and whoever comes to me I will never cast out.'
- John 10:26–29:

  You do not believe because you are not part of my flock. My sheep hear my voice, and I know them, and they follow me. I give them eternal life, and they will never perish, and no one will snatch them out of my hand. My Father, who has given them to me, is greater than all, and no one is able to snatch them out of the Father's hand.

Some Calvinists use the term 'effectual calling' to describe this efficacious grace.

Credal statement

Question: What is effectual calling?

Answer: Effectual calling is the work of God's Spirit, whereby, convincing us of our sin and misery, enlightening our minds in the knowledge of Christ, and renewing our wills, he doth persuade and enable us to embrace Jesus Christ, freely offered to us in the gospel. (*Westminster Shorter Catechism* (1647), q. 31)

Others have sometimes used the term 'irresistible grace',[3] but this is unhelpfully ambiguous. The statement 'I couldn't resist him' might appear either in an account of rape or in an account of falling in love. If we are to use it of God's grace it is only in the second of these senses. There is the story of the man who was walking by the sea shore and picked up a bottle with a note in it, granting him three wishes. He immediately wished that he should have a villa beside a beautiful Swiss lake – and this was granted. After a while the bills started coming in and so he wished that he might have a well-endowed Swiss bank account – which was also granted. A short time later he started to feel lonely so wished that he might become irresistible to women – and promptly turned into a box of chocolates![4] If God's grace is irresistible it is in that sense only.

Arminians and prevenient grace

By contrast, Arminians believe that prevenient grace is 'sufficient' – that it works in people in such a way as to leave them the ultimate choice as to whether or not to accept it. It is sufficient to enable us to turn to God, should we so choose. In other words, prevenient grace makes our conversion possible, but not inevitable. Arminians point to passages of Scripture that speak of people resisting the Spirit, implying that grace is not always efficacious:

- Acts 7:51: 'You stiff-necked people, uncircumcised in heart and ears, you always resist the Holy Spirit. As your fathers did, so do you.'
- Ephesians 4:30: 'Do not grieve the Holy Spirit of God, by whom you were sealed for the day of redemption.'
- 1 Thessalonians 5:19: 'Do not quench the Spirit.'

For Arminians this proves that grace is not efficacious, it does not always infallibly achieve its goal. The Holy Spirit seeks to 'rein us in' but leaves us the choice of accepting or rejecting his prompting. This is argued in the initial Arminian statement of faith, the *Remonstrance* of 1610.

Credal statement

The grace of God is the beginning, progress and end of all good, so that even the regenerate can neither think, will nor effect any good, nor withstand any temptation to evil, without grace precedent (or prevenient), awakening, following and cooperating. So all good deeds and all movements towards good that can be conceived in thought must be ascribed to the grace of God in Christ. But with respect to the mode of operation, grace is not irresistible, for it is written of many that they resisted the Holy Spirit (Acts 7). (*Remonstrance* (1610), art. 4)

In response Calvinists would concede that there are times when God's grace is resisted, but also claim that God works efficaciously to ensure that the elect will eventually respond to him and be saved.

*John Wesley held that all people without exception receive God's prevenient grace (especially through conscience) and that we are saved or otherwise according to our response to it. This can be called a consistently Arminian position since if some people received no opportunity at all they could be seen as predestined to damnation without any choice of their own. This topic will be considered further in Chapter 29.

It is worth noting that this question cannot be settled by analysing our own experience, let alone other people's, since both Calvinists and Arminians agree that God makes the first move and that conversion occurs when *we* respond. For example, C. S. Lewis describes his own conversion in Calvinist-sounding terms,[5] but was nonetheless an Arminian. Conversely, someone might have had no conscious sensation of God's grace at work in her before her conversion and yet for theological reasons reach a Calvinist position. Augustine began by ascribing his conversion to his own free will but eventually ascribed it to God's grace and wrote his *Confessions* to express this conviction.

Classical Arminianism is clear that we can make no move towards God without his prevenient grace; some Arminians today would hold to a Semi-Pelagian position, claiming that we can turn to God without any prior move on his part.

PART 2: ELECTION

This leads us to the issue of election, which is the reverse side of the question of whether grace makes conversion possible for all or inevitable for some. We will start by asking two questions of the Scripture.

DOES GOD WANT ALL TO BE SAVED?
(CCC 1037, 1058)
The Bible says 'Yes'. God does not want people to perish and be lost:

- Ezekiel 18:23, 32:

  Have I any pleasure in the death of the wicked, declares the Lord GOD, and not rather that he should turn from his way and live? . . . I have no pleasure in the death of anyone, declares the Lord GOD; so turn, and live.

- 2 Peter 3:9: 'The Lord is not slow to fulfil his promise as some count slowness, but is patient towards you, not wishing that any should perish, but that all should reach repentance.'
- Jesus wept over the disobedience of Jerusalem: Matthew 23:37: 'O Jerusalem, Jerusalem, the city that kills the prophets and stones those who are sent to it! How often would I have gathered your children together as a hen gathers her brood under her wings, and you would not!'
- Indeed, God desires that all will be saved: God 'desires all people to be saved and to come to the knowledge of the truth' (1 Tim. 2:4).

Given the earlier passages, this should be understood as referring to all individual people, not just all sorts of people. If this was all that the New Testament had to say, the position would be very clear, but there are also many passages that point in a different direction.

DOES GOD SELECT WHO WILL BE SAVED?

Here, again, the New Testament appears to say 'Yes' – and in a wider range of passages. To give some examples:

- Acts 13:48: 'When the Gentiles heard this, they began rejoicing and glorifying the word of the Lord, and as many as were appointed to eternal life believed.'
- Romans 9:6–18: 'So then it depends not on human will or exertion, but on God, who has mercy' (9:16).
- Ephesians 1:3–12: 'even as [God] chose us in [Christ] before the foundation of the world, that we should be holy and blameless before him. In love he predestined us for adoption through Jesus Christ, according to the purpose of his will' (1:4–5).

- 2 Thessalonians 2:13: 'But we ought always to give thanks to God for you, brothers beloved by the Lord, because God chose you as the firstfruits to be saved, through sanctification by the Spirit and belief in the truth.'

The belief in election arises not from philosophical speculation but from a concern to be faithful to the teaching of Scripture in passages like this.

What do you think? The question

Does God choose who will be saved, or do we?

DOES GOD CHOOSE WHO WILL BE SAVED, OR DO WE?

We return to the question with which we began. As we noted then, there are two basic answers to the question.

Calvinism: God chooses

The doctrine of election was set out clearly by Augustine in the late fourth and early fifth centuries. In the years after his conversion (386) he held to the power of free will but after about ten years of experience and after studying Paul he changed his mind and argued that God selects who will be saved. God's selection is not based on his foreknowledge of any merit in us (whether of faith or of works), though Augustine also maintained that God's choice was not arbitrary. Those whom he has elected (i.e. chosen) God infallibly saves by his efficacious grace; those whom he has not chosen he simply allows to go their own way.

The Augustinian view was widely held in the Middle Ages. All of the sixteenth-century Reformers held to it, though Luther's colleague *Melanchthon later changed his mind. It was also held by many of the leaders of the eighteenth-century Evangelical Revival, such as George Whitefield. It has proved no obstacle to evangelism, as can be seen from Calvinist evangelists such as Whitefield and, in the nineteenth century, C. H. Spurgeon.

It is important to realize that the Augustinian doctrine is not that the elect will be saved regardless of whether they believe or not, but rather that God saves them by bringing them to faith – as in 1 Thessalonians 1:4–5: 'For we know, brothers loved by God, that he has chosen you, because our gospel came to you not only in word, but also in power and in the Holy Spirit and with full conviction.' Again, it is not that God would reject the non-elect (= reprobate) if they believed but rather that no one comes to faith except through God's grace. Election does not mean that there is no need for evangelism or for pastoral care, for it is *through* such means that God saves his elect. Augustine argued this in a book called *Rebuke and Grace*.

Arminianism: we choose

The view that ultimately it is our choice was widely held before Augustine and remains the view of the Eastern Orthodox Church. It was held by many in the Middle Ages. Luther's colleague Melanchthon broke ranks with the other Reformers on this issue and in the seventeenth century the Dutchman Arminius (died 1609) rejected the views of the Reformed Church. In the eighteenth-century Evangelical Revival the Wesleys followed Arminius and pioneered Evangelical Arminianism. Ever since then, Evangelicals have been divided between Calvinism and Arminianism. Many have taken a belligerent stance for one side or the other, while many

others have regarded it as a secondary issue or have claimed to hold a middle position.

For Arminius, election means that God chooses to save *whoever* will repent, believe and persevere to the end – it is like a blank cheque where the name is still to be added in. He also understood election to refer to God's choice of specific individuals based on God foreseeing what they will freely choose. God chose Paul because he foresaw his faith.

Credal statements

God by an eternal and unchangeable purpose in Jesus Christ his Son, before the foundations of the world were laid, determined to save, out of the human race which had fallen into sin, in Christ, for Christ's sake and through Christ, those who through the grace of the Holy Spirit shall believe on the same his Son and shall through the same grace persevere in this same faith and obedience of faith even to the end – and on the other hand to leave under sin and wrath the contumacious and unbelieving and to condemn them as aliens from Christ, according to the word of the Gospel in John 3:36 and other passages of Scripture. (*Remonstrance* (1610), art. 1)

To this the Calvinist *Synod of Dort (1618–19) responded:

Election is the unchangeable purpose of God, whereby before the foundation of the world he has out of mere grace, according to the sovereign good pleasure of his own will, chosen from the whole human race (which had fallen through their own fault from their primitive state of rectitude into sin and destruction) a certain number of persons to redemption in Christ. From eternity he appointed Christ to be the mediator and head of the elect and the foundation of salvation. (Canon 1:7)

What do you think? My answer

Calvinists stress the efficacy of God's saving purposes and point to many passages of Scripture which speak of election and predestination. Arminians, by contrast, stress God's love for *all*, as shown by the passages quoted above about God's desire that none should perish. Some object that the doctrine of election is unfair in that God does not give the same opportunity to everyone. It should be remembered that as sinners we are in the same situation as the elderly lady who objected to an artist's portrayal of her. 'You haven't done me justice,' she complained. 'Madam, what you need is not justice but mercy,' was the response!

Worship

Church of God, elect and glorious,
holy nation, chosen race;
called as God's own special people,
royal priests and heirs of grace:
know the purpose of your calling,
show to all his mighty deeds;
tell of love which knows no limits,
grace which meets all human needs.
(James Seddon)

PRAYERS

Almighty God, who alone can bring order to the unruly wills and passions of sinful humanity: give your people grace so to love what you command and to desire what you promise, that, among the many changes of this world, our hearts may surely there be fixed where true joys are to be found; through Jesus Christ your Son our Lord. (*Common Worship*: Collect for Third Sunday before Lent)

Almighty God, who through your only-begotten Son Jesus Christ have overcome death and opened to us the gate of everlasting life: grant that, as by your grace going before us you put into our minds good desires, so by your continual help we may bring them to good effect; through Jesus Christ our risen Lord. (*Common Worship*: Collect for Fifth Sunday of Easter)

Question to answer

- Does God choose who will be saved, or do we?

NOTES

1 ATS ch. 9/8.
2 A. Kenny *A Path from Rome*. Oxford: OUP, 1985, 78.
3 This was not a term used by either Augustine or Calvin.
4 Those who wish to indulge in the knee-jerk reaction of 'sexism' or 'stereotyping' might care to consult <http://alcoholism.about.com/cs/basics/l/aa001109a.htm or http://psychcentral.com/lib/2006/does-chocolate-addiction-exist>.
5 *Surprised by Joy*. London: Collins, 1959, 182–83.

RESOURCES

C. O. Brand *Perspectives on Election: Five Views*. Nashville: B&H, 2006.

D. A. Carson *Divine Sovereignty & Human Responsibility: Biblical Perspectives in Tension*. London: Marshall Pickering, 1994, second edn.

J. I. Packer *Evangelism and the Sovereignty of God*. London: IVP, 1961.

R. A. Peterson and M. D. Williams *Why I Am Not an Arminian*. Downers Grove: IVP, 2004.

C. H. Pinnock (ed.) *The Grace of God, the Will of Man*. Grand Rapids: Zondervan, 1989.

J. L. Walls and J. R. Dongwell *Why I Am Not a Calvinist*. Downers Grove: IVP, 2004.

Chapter 24

THE CHURCH I (ECCLESIOLOGY)

Aims of this chapter

In this chapter we look at the doctrine of the Church, asking:

- What is the Church?
- Can you be a Christian without belonging to a local church?
- What are the four traditional marks of the Church?
- What does it mean to call the Church apostolic?

WHAT IS THE CHURCH? (CCC 751–57)

We will answer this question by looking at some New Testament images of the Church:

PEOPLE OF GOD

The Church is the people of God (as was Israel in the Old Testament):

> You are a chosen race, a royal priesthood, a holy nation, a people for his own possession, that you may proclaim the excellencies of him who called you out of darkness into his marvellous light. Once you were not a people, but now you are God's people; once you had not received mercy, but now you have received mercy. (1 Pet. 2:9–10)

The continuing status of the Jewish people is a highly controversial issue. It is addressed in Romans 9—11, but need not detain us here.

'Church' refers to the whole people of God, not just to the clergy. To refer to someone being ordained as 'going into the Church' is an unfortunate manner of speaking. Roman Catholics used to be inclined to think of the Church as the clergy but one of the reforming ideas of the *Second Vatican Council (1962–65) was that the Church is the whole people of God.

Second, 'Church' refers primarily to the people and not to a building. This does not mean that it is wrong to call the building a 'church'. I recently read a statement that such and such a building is not a church but that the church owns the building and meets in it. How would we react to a statement at the entrance to a bank that this building is not a bank but the bank owns the building and functions in it? Of course a church is a body of people and a bank is a financial institution, but there is nothing improper in also referring to the buildings where they respectively function as churches and banks. It is also true that the architecture of a church building can tell us a lot about the theology of the church held by those who designed it.

Third, in popular usage the 'Church' is an institution. It is an organization and to 'go into the Church' is to enter the employment of that organization. Against this view Christians often insist that the Church is a community rather than an organization. But although the Church is much *more* than a mere institution or organization, it is not *less* than these. While the Church may be the people of God, it is also a very human group of people living within history. Like any such grouping (be it a family, a darts club, a hospital or whatever) it cannot avoid having structures and allocating power. Church politics are an inevitable consequence of the human historical character of the Church, even if they have often also served to illustrate its fallen, sinful nature.

BODY OF CHRIST
This is an awesome image, though we have been dulled to its impact by familiarity. It is an intimate image which implies the *unity* between Christ and his people. This image is used in two different ways. Sometimes the Church is seen as the whole body, including the head:

- Romans 12:4–5: 'As in one body we have many members, and the members do not all have the same function, so we, though many, are one body in Christ, and individually members one of another.'
- In 1 Corinthians 12:12–27 Paul compares Christians with parts of the head, such as an eye or ear.

Other times we are the body and Christ is the head:

- Ephesians 4:15: 'Speaking the truth in love, we are to grow up in every way into him who is the head, into Christ.'
- Ephesians 5:23: 'The husband is the head of the wife even as Christ is the head of the church, his body, and is himself its Saviour.'

There is no problem here, just different applications of the same analogy. The intimate link between the body and the head is shown by Jesus' words to Paul on the Damascus road when he was persecuting the Christians: 'Falling to the ground he heard a voice saying to him, "Saul, Saul, why are you persecuting me?" And he said, "Who are you, Lord?" And he said, "I am Jesus, whom you are persecuting"' (Acts 9:4–5).

BRIDE OF CHRIST
In the Old Testament, Israel was 'married' to Yahweh, but was often guilty of committing adultery with other gods. This is graphically portrayed by Hosea's relationship with his unfaithful wife. In the New Testament, the Church is the bride of Christ, 'engaged' to him:

- Ephesians 5:25–27:

  Husbands, love your wives, as Christ loved the church and gave himself up for her, that he might sanctify her, having cleansed her by the washing of water with the word, so that he might present the church to himself in splendour, without spot or wrinkle or any such thing, that she might be holy and without blemish.

- Hence the marriage supper of the Lamb: 'Let us rejoice and exult and give him

Over the centuries it has been notable that significantly more women than men have become Christians. Could this image give a clue as to why? At a superficial level, the thought of becoming someone's bride may not immediately excite most men. At a deeper level, if our relationship with Christ is one that is aptly compared to that of a bride with her bridegroom, maybe that relationship comes more easily and naturally to women than to men. Nuns, unlike monks, wear a ring to signify marriage to Christ.

the glory, for the marriage of the Lamb has come, and his Bride has made herself ready' (Rev. 19:7); 'I saw the holy city, new Jerusalem, coming down out of heaven from God, prepared as a bride adorned for her husband' (Rev. 21:2). Like the image of the body, this portrays the intimate unity between Christ and his people, but this time with a clearer distinction between them, in that bride and groom are two separate people.

GOD'S TEMPLE OR HOUSE
We are corporately, as a body, described as God's temple: 'Do you [plural] not know that you are God's temple and that God's Spirit dwells in you?' (1 Cor. 3:16). The same image is also used of us as individual Christians, with implications for our behaviour: 'Or do you [singular] not know that your body is a temple of the Holy Spirit within you, whom you have from God?' (1 Cor. 6:19). The Church is also portrayed as a building, being built 'in Christ': 'In [Christ] you also are being built together into a dwelling place for

God by the Spirit' (Eph. 2:22). Individual believers are incorporated into it as living stones: 'As you come to him, a living stone rejected by men but in the sight of God chosen and precious, you yourselves like living stones are being built up as a spiritual house' (1 Pet. 2:4–5). This is the ultimate builder's nightmare – working not with uniform lifeless bricks which stay where they are put but with disparate living stones with a mind of their own, obstinate and disobedient! No wonder church leadership is such a difficult task. An analogy here would be a group of gymnasts together forming a pyramid. They need to compensate for one another's small movements, which could easily destroy the balance. Success requires the cooperation and vigilance of each and every member.

NEW COMMUNITY/HUMANITY BRINGING TOGETHER JEWS AND GENTILES
Paul expounds this in Ephesians 2:11–22:

> [Christ] himself is our peace, who has made us both one and has broken down in his flesh the dividing wall of hostility by abolishing the law of commandments and ordinances, that he might create in himself one new man in place of the two, so making peace. (2:14–15)

This was very important to Paul and in Ephesians 3:1–6 he presents it as a 'mystery' that was given to him by revelation: 'This mystery is that the Gentiles are fellow heirs, members of the same body, and partakers of the promise in Christ Jesus through the gospel' (3:6). In the second century Aristides, one of the early Apologists, spoke of the Church as the 'third race', alongside Jews and Gentiles (*Apology* 2).

FELLOWSHIP

This was an important part of church life in the first century, starting with the Day of Pentecost (Acts 2:42–47): 'They devoted themselves to the apostles' teaching and fellowship, to the breaking of bread and the prayers' (2:42). The early Christians met for a 'love feast' or *agape*, referred to in Jude 12. Just such a meal is described in 1 Corinthians 11:17–34, here called the Lord's Supper (1 Cor. 11:20), for more on which see Chapter 26. This aspect of the Church was rather neglected under Christendom, when for example an entire village might meet in the church for worship and in the pub for relaxation. As we move into the era of Post-Christendom, Christians are again a minority in society. This has led to a rediscovery of the dimension of fellowship especially by Evangelicals, who have always been inclined to think of genuine Christians as a minority.

What do you think? The question

Can you be a Christian without belonging to a local church?

DO THE WALLS MAKE CHRISTIANS?

This question is taken from an incident described by Augustine (*Confessions* 8:2:3–5). Victorinus, a pagan, was one of the greatest philosophers in the West. One day he confided to Simplician, one of the clergy at Milan, that he had become a Christian. Simplician replied that he would believe this when he saw him in church, to which Victorinus mockingly responded, 'Do the walls make Christians?' But he went away and reflected on the matter and in due course returned and asked for baptism. As a VIP he was offered a private baptism but he declined and decided to bear witness publicly to his faith. This little incident poses the question: is it possible to be a Christian without belonging to a local, visible congregation?

C. K. Barrett made the perceptive comment that 'in the New Testament the Church is at the same time central and peripheral'.[1] It is peripheral because the heart of New Testament Christianity is Christ, the gospel and faith in him; at the same time it is central in that there is no such thing as a Christian faith which refuses baptism and there is no such thing as a conversion which does not lead to belonging to the Church. Evangelicals have always tended to be weak on ecclesiology. Most (but not all) Evangelical bases of faith make no reference to the Church beyond maybe referring to the idea of the mystical body of Christ. The visible Church and its local manifestation is usually absent. Indeed, some are now suggesting that belonging to a local church is an optional extra, that it is not part of the essence of being a Christian. This is the product of modern individualism and anti-institutionalism, attitudes that have affected not just the Church but also political parties, and other voluntary organizations.

Such an approach is foreign both to the New Testament and to historic Christianity.

The images of the Church in the New Testament, discussed above, all imply that being a Christian is a corporate matter and not purely individual. We are baptized into Christ: 'As many of you as were baptized into Christ have put on Christ' (Gal. 3:27). We are also baptized into his body: 'In one Spirit we were all baptized into one body – Jews or Greeks, slaves or free – and all were made to drink of one Spirit' (1 Cor. 12:13). God's aim is not to save us as isolated individuals but to bring us into his family: 'Those whom he foreknew he also predestined to be conformed to the image of his Son, in order that he might be the firstborn among many brothers' (Rom. 8:29). To become a child of God inevitably implies that the other children of God become one's brothers and sisters, that one has become part of God's family. This family is composed of those who love one another, not like a dysfunctional family that never meets.

Billy was a unique child and would often, while playing football alone, give himself a red card

© Miriam Kendrick 2013 www.miriamkendrick.co.uk

THE TRADITIONAL MARKS OF THE CHURCH (CCC 811–12, 870)

The Nicene Creed affirms faith 'in one holy catholic and apostolic Church'. These four adjectives are the four traditional marks

What do you think? My answer

You cannot be a member of a family as an isolated individual any more than you can play football on your own. Imagine the following conversation: 'What do you do for sport?' 'I play football.' 'Who with?' 'No one – I play on my own.' That is not possible, any more than one could play football on the Internet. Tom Wright warns that while it is dangerous to think that church membership suffices without individual faith and conduct, it is equally dangerous to regard church membership as insignificant.[2]

Furthermore, the Church is part of the gospel, as we have seen from Paul (Eph. 3:6). Some imagine that the good news is about individual salvation, which is then followed by the bad news – the Church! In fact an important part of the good news is that we become part of God's family. For many people what attracts them to Christian faith is belonging to a caring and believing community. This can be true for a wide range of people: lonely old folk, teenagers in need of a caring peer group, single people, single parents, stay-at-home mums, families whose extended family are distant, etc. The fellowship of the Church is an important part of the Christian message – it is in families that we learn so many of the lessons of life. There is nothing wrong with people being drawn to Christian faith by this, though they need to see that becoming a Christian involves more than just joining a group of people.

of the Church, which we will consider in a different order, one in this chapter, the other three in the next.

APOSTOLIC (CCC 857–65, 869)

The Church was *founded* on the apostles:

- Ephesians 2:19–20: 'So then you are no longer strangers and aliens, but you are fellow citizens with the saints and members of the household of God, built on the foundation of the apostles and prophets, Christ Jesus himself being the cornerstone.'
- Revelation 21:14: 'The wall of the city had twelve foundations, and on them were the twelve names of the twelve apostles of the Lamb.'

From the Day of Pentecost it is built upon their *teaching*. The new disciples 'devoted themselves to the apostles' teaching and fellowship' (Acts 2:42). In particular, the apostles were witnesses to the resurrection of Jesus, as Paul describes in 1 Corinthians 15:3–8. 'Am I not an apostle? Have I not seen Jesus our Lord?' (1 Cor. 9:1).

The apostles' teaching is to be handed down in the Church, as Paul urges in 2 Timothy 2:2: 'What you have heard from me in the presence of many witnesses entrust to faithful men who will be able to teach others also.' This process of handing on is what is called tradition, for more on which see Chapter 1. This teaching is also written down for us in the apostolic Scriptures, i.e. the New Testament. It is for this faith that the Church is to contend: 'Beloved, although I was very eager to write to you about our common salvation, I found it necessary to write appealing to you to contend for the faith that was once for all delivered to the saints' (Jude 3).

In the second century the Church faced the serious threat of Gnosticism, a radically different religion that did not even believe that the world was created by the Supreme God. There were different Gnostic sects, each presenting a totally different picture of Christianity and each claiming their own separate scriptures and traditions. In response to this the mainstream Catholic Church emphasized the teaching of the apostles. But many different Gnostic groups claimed that they had received some secret teaching from this or that apostle.

At the end of the century *Irenaeus responded by appealing to apostolic teaching as found in the apostolic Scriptures (the New Testament) and in the apostolic tradition handed down in the churches founded by the apostles and taught there by their successors. (This apostolic tradition was a succinct summary of the gospel, which developed into creeds like the so-called *Apostles' Creed.) After all, he argued, to whom would the apostles have entrusted their teaching if not to the churches that they themselves had founded? These churches all agree as to the nature of the Christian faith. By contrast the Gnostic groups all disagree with one another.

All who wish to see the truth can clearly contemplate, in every church, the tradition of the apostles manifested throughout the whole world. We can list those who were by the apostles appointed bishops in the churches and their successors down to our own time. They neither taught nor knew anything like what these heretics rave about. Suppose the apostles had known hidden mysteries which they were in the habit of imparting to 'the perfect' privately and in secret. Surely they would have handed them down especially to those to whom they were also entrusting the churches themselves. For they wanted their successors to be perfect and blameless in everything. (Irenaeus, *Against Heresies* 3:3:1)

This was a very powerful argument then, at a time when Irenaeus had known Polycarp who had heard the apostle John and in a situation where the issues dividing Catholic Christianity from Gnosticism make the issues dividing Protestants and Roman Catholics (for example) appear trivial in the extreme by comparison. Indeed, Irenaeus's argument is the only one that works in this situation, as I discovered one day when I was hitchhiking and was given a lift by two self-confessed 'Gnostics'. I first tried to answer them from the New Testament but this did not work. They, like their second-century forebears, did not accept what they called '*your* Scriptures'. As Irenaeus himself put it, 'when they are refuted from the Scriptures, they turn round and accuse these same Scriptures, as if they were not correct or authoritative'. Orthodox Christianity and Gnosticism are two religions, with two different sets of Scriptures. The question is: which religion and which set of Scriptures goes back to Christ and the apostles? It is this question which is answered by Irenaeus's argument – and it is hard to see how it can be answered otherwise.

At its heart the sixteenth-century Reformation was a conflict over what it means for the Church to be apostolic. Which is the true apostolic Church: the Roman Catholic Church or the Protestant churches? The former claimed to be apostolic because the pope is the successor of Peter and the bishops are the successors of the apostles, a claim to *institutional* continuity with the apostles. It follows that they are the true Church and therefore that what they teach is true and apostolic Christianity. The Reformers, by contrast, claimed *doctrinal* continuity with the apostles. They appealed to the apostolic teaching found in the New Testament against the teaching of the Roman Catholic Church. The Roman Church had departed from the apostolic gospel and so was no true church. The issue is whether the Church defines the gospel or the gospel defines the Church, the latter being what is meant by the slogan *sola scriptura*, on which see Chapter 1.

*Calvin stated that a true church exists wherever the word of God is purely preached (and heard) and the sacraments are rightly administered:

> Wherever we see the Word of God purely preached and heard, and the sacraments administered according to Christ's institution, there, it is not to be doubted, a church of God exists. (*Institutes* 4:1:9)

Essentially the one mark of the Church is the word, the sacraments being 'visible Words', on which see Chapter 26. If a 'church' does not meet these criteria, as the Reformers felt was the case with the Roman Catholic Church, it must be reformed, even if that involves division. This teaching is expressed in a number of confessions of faith, including the *Thirty-Nine Articles* of the Church of England:

Credal statement

The visible Church of Christ is a congregation of faithful men, in the which the pure Word of

God is preached, and the Sacraments be duly ministered according to Christ's ordinance in all those things that of necessity are requisite to the same. (*Thirty-Nine Articles*, art. 19)

Sceptic's corner

How pure need the preaching be and who decides?

Answer: The Reformation soon and inevitably led to divisions in the Church. Protestant churches have tended to move in one of two directions. Some churches, like most state churches these days, retain unity by becoming broad and comprehensive, at the cost of sound doctrine. Other churches maintain 'pure doctrine' but at the cost of unity, fragmenting into small groups. The Protestant dilemma is that there is no infallible pope or council to decide what is in fact pure doctrine.

Calvin helpfully drew a distinction between essential doctrines, which should be accepted by all (such as the deity of Christ) and secondary issues where disagreement need not impair unity (such as precisely where the soul goes at death). The distinction between essential and secondary is very widely accepted; where to draw the line between the two is far more controversial. Calvin's examples are equivalent to saying that an American lives 'somewhere between New York and Los Angeles'. *John Stott offers a helpful list of doctrines that should be regarded as secondary by Evangelicals.[3] A slogan was coined in the seventeenth century: *ecclesia reformata semper reformanda*: the reformed Church is always in need of reform. In other words, we cannot expect perfection in the Church here and now, and this applies also to the area of doctrine. Interestingly, *Joseph Ratzinger (later Pope

Benedict XVI), commenting on the texts of the Second Vatican Council, affirmed the idea of the *ecclesia semper reformanda* (the Church always in need of reform).

Worship

One holy apostolic church,
the body of the Lord:
our task, to witness to his name
in full and glad accord;
one Lord confessed, one faith believed,
one baptism its sign;
one God and Father over all,
one fellowship divine.
(James Seddon)

PRAYERS

Almighty God, who built your Church upon the foundation of the apostles and prophets, with Jesus Christ himself as the chief cornerstone: so join us together in unity of spirit by their doctrine, that we may be made a holy temple acceptable to you; through Jesus Christ your Son our Lord. (*Common Worship*: Collect for Simon and Jude)

Lord God, the source of truth and love, keep us faithful to the apostles' teaching and fellowship, united in prayer and the breaking of bread, and one in joy and simplicity of heart, in Jesus Christ our Lord. (*Common Worship*, Post Communion for Conversion of Paul)

Question to answer

- What is the Church?

NOTES

1 C. K. Barrett *Church, Ministry and Sacraments in the New Testament*. Exeter: Paternoster, 1985, 9.
2 N. T. Wright *The Epistles of Paul to the Colossians and to Philemon.*, Leicester: IVP, 1986, 129–30.
3 J. Stott *Evangelical Truth*. Leicester: IVP, 1999, 142–43.

RESOURCES FOR CHAPTERS 24 AND 25

E. Clowney *The Church*. Leicester: IVP, 1995.

V.-M. Kärkkäinen *An Introduction to Ecclesiology: Ecumenical, Historical and Global Perspectives*. Downers Grove: IVP, 2002.

J. G. Stackhouse (ed.) *Evangelical Ecclesiology: Reality or Illusion?*. Grand Rapids: Baker, 2003.

RESOURCE FOR CHAPTER 24

C. E. Braaten and R. W. Jenson (eds) *Marks of the Body of Christ*. Grand Rapids: Eerdmans, 1999.

THE CHURCH 2

In this chapter we will continue to look at the doctrine of the Church, asking:

- What does it means to call the Church holy?
- If the Church is mixed, where is the 'true Church'?
- What does it means to call the Church one?
- What does it means to call the Church catholic?
- How should we seek to recover the unity of the Church today?

HOLY (CCC 823–29, 867)

The Church is holy. What does this mean? Not that she is perfect. As has been said, if you find a perfect church, do not join it – otherwise it will not remain perfect for long. The New Testament meaning of holiness is that we are set aside for God, which leads on to the idea of purity, of becoming more like Christ. 'Husbands, love your wives, as Christ loved the church and gave himself up for her, that he might sanctify her, having cleansed her by the washing of water with the word' (Eph. 5:25–26). Similarly, all Christians are called 'saints' (the same Greek word as 'holy') which means that we are set apart for God and are becoming holy. Paul addressed the Christians at Corinth (even them!), many of whom were far from perfect, as 'those sanctified in Christ Jesus, called to be saints together with all those who in every place call upon the name of our Lord Jesus Christ' (1 Cor. 1:2). The Church and Christians are holy because of the forgiveness of sins, because of the indwelling of the Holy Spirit and because they are becoming holy like Christ.

But what about believers who commit serious sins? How to handle this was a major cause of controversy and division in the Early Church. They had a (by our standards) very strict discipline with long periods of 'penance' (up to 20 years) for major sins. During this time the penitent was unable to take communion and might be required to display penitence by exercises like wearing sack-cloth. Many councils decreed what penalties should follow what sin, as with this 'canon' or legal pronouncement from the *Council of Nicea (325), which lists different stages on the way to being restored to full communion:

Concerning those who have fallen without compulsion, without the spoiling of their property, without danger or the like, as happened during the tyranny of Licinius, the Synod declares that, though they have deserved no clemency, they shall be dealt with mercifully. As many as were communicants, if they heartily repent, shall pass three years among the hearers; for seven years they shall be prostrators; and for two years they shall communicate with the people in prayers, but without oblation. (Canon 11)

Three sins were regarded as especially serious and at times some questioned whether these could *ever* be forgiven in this life:

- **Murder**: not too many Christians were guilty of this and it was not a source of controversy.
- **Adultery**: this was more controversial and was obviously rather more common. In the early third century there were moves to relax the discipline and make it easier for offenders eventually to be reconciled to the Church. *Tertullian was biting in his sarcasm about this:

Christian modesty is being shaken to its foundations . . . The 'high priest', the 'bishop of bishops' [Bishop of Carthage] issues an edict: 'I remit to all who have discharged the requirements of repentance, the sins both of adultery and of fornication.' O edict, on which cannot be inscribed 'Good deed'! And where will this liberality be posted up? On the very spot, I suppose, on the very gates of lust, under the very titles of lust [i.e. on the doors of the brothels]. That is the place to publish such a repentance – where the sin itself happens. That is the place to announce such a pardon – where people will enter in the hope of it. (*Modesty* 1)

As always, Tertullian's rhetoric is brilliant, but his harsh approach is out of keeping with the message of the New Testament.

- **Apostasy** was a burning issue at times because remaining loyal to Christ could cost you your life in the Roman Empire. Many were faced with the choice of either offering a sacrifice to a pagan god or being put to death. Understandably some found this too high a price to pay and renounced Christ or else offered worship to pagan gods. The Church's response was not sympathy at the ordeal but exclusion because of the sin of apostasy. In AD 249–251, after two centuries of local persecution, there was the first empire-wide persecution, under the Emperor Decius. This caught the Church by surprise, coming after a period of relative peace, and many Christians lapsed, renouncing Christ, but afterwards wanted to return. The decision was made that they could do so after a period of penance.

At Rome Novatian objected to this laxity and set himself up as a rival bishop. The Novatianists were 'rigorists', arguing that the holiness and purity of the Church would be destroyed by readmitting the lapsed. They referred to the mainstream Catholic Church as 'the church of the apostates'. The latter disagreed. They pointed to the forgiveness of King David (after adultery and murder) and of the apostle Peter (who had denied Christ). The Church is a school for sinners, not a club for the perfect. Christians are convalescents, being cured of sin, not those whose cure is already complete. We need to pray daily 'Forgive us our trespasses.' Rigorism is in danger of becoming a new Pharisaism.

It should not, however, be imagined that discipline was lax in the Catholic Church. People who were cohabiting without being married were not even allowed to become catechumens and *start* preparation for baptism, whereas recently the Church of Scotland was debating whether to allow such folk to train for the ministry. Despite this strict discipline (or because of it?) this same Church won over the whole Roman Empire.

These issues resurfaced at the time of the Reformation. The Anabaptists were rigorists who, unlike the mainstream Reformers, rejected the Catholic view of the holiness of the Church. Their approach is expressed in the *Schleitheim Confession* of 1527. For them the Church was for committed disciples only and it was a nonsense to envisage the Church embracing the whole of society. The holiness of the Church was to be maintained by discipline, by excluding those who were unholy and would not repent of their sin. The Anabaptists were suspicious of the Reformers' emphasis on justification by faith. They sought gathered churches of voluntarily committed disciples, separated from the world, and pointed out that the New Testament knows of no other form of church. Their Catholic and Protestant opponents retorted that the Old Testament Church was clearly a national Church. (On the relevance or otherwise of the Old Testament here, see Chapter 11.) *Calvin held that the holiness of the Church consists in our aspiration for holiness and in the forgiveness of sins. He showed no lack of zeal for church discipline, but while it was important for the *well*-being of the Church, he did not see it as necessary for the existence of the Church, as a test of the true Church. So it is right to strive for the purity of the Church, but lack of purity (as at Corinth) is no ground for leaving the Church.

THE INVISIBLE CHURCH (CCC 827)

What about 'sinners', what about nominal Christians, what about those who falsely claim to be converted? Where is the true Church, the pure Church, the body of genuine Christians? For the rigorists, like Novatian, the 'true Church' is the visible Church, kept pure by a strict application of discipline. The mainstream Catholic Church saw this as impossible. We cannot read people's hearts. Not all who profess to be Christians are genuine, but it is only God who knows for sure who is and is not genuine:

- Acts 8:13: 'Even Simon himself believed, and after being baptized he continued with Philip.' Yet he soon proved himself not to be genuine (8:18–23).
- 2 Timothy 2:19 'God's firm foundation stands, bearing this seal: "The Lord knows those who are his," and, "Let everyone who names the name of the Lord depart from iniquity."'
- 1 John 2:19: 'They went out from us, but they were not of us; for if they had been of us, they would have continued with us. But they went out, that it might become plain that they all are not of us.'

*Augustine in the fourth century developed the concept of the 'invisible Church', which is already implicit in the New Testament. He distinguished between the 'visible Church', the mixed body that we see, and the 'invisible Church', the body of true Christians. The visible Church consists of professing Christians – those who are baptized and in good standing. Among these are both genuine Christians and nominal Christians, those without true faith or true love. The invisible Church is invisible only in the sense that its boundaries are known to God alone. There was no

245

suggestion that one might belong to the invisible Church *instead of* the visible Church. The idea, rather, was that the boundaries of the true Church are invisible to us, but known to God who reads people's hearts. No membership list is infallible because we cannot see people's hearts, only their outward actions.

The parable of the wheat and the tares (or weeds) shows that it is not possible here and now to distinguish between those who are genuine disciples of Christ and those who are simply pretending:

> The kingdom of heaven may be compared to a man who sowed good seed in his field, but while his men were sleeping, his enemy came and sowed weeds among the wheat and went away. So when the plants came up and bore grain, then the weeds appeared also. And the servants of the master of the house came and said to him, 'Master, did you not sow good seed in your field? How then does it have weeds?' He said to them, 'An enemy has done this.' So the servants said to him, 'Then do you want us to go and gather them?' But he said, 'No, lest in gathering the weeds you root up the wheat along with them. Let both grow together until the harvest, and at harvest time I will tell the reapers, Gather the weeds first and bind them in bundles to be burned, but gather the wheat into my barn.' (Matt. 13:24–30)

Jesus explains (13:36–43) that the field is the world and the harvest is the close of the age. Wheat and tares are indistinguishable in the early stages so they are left to grow side by side and are separated at the End.

The doctrine of the invisible Church does not mean that there should be no discipline, only that discipline cannot guarantee a totally pure Church. Essentially the doctrine states that the visible Church will always be mixed, containing the righteous and the unrighteous, the pure and the wicked, genuine Christians and 'hypocrites'. We should give the benefit of doubt to those who credibly profess to be Christians, taking their claim at face value, but that does not mean that we *know* that they are.

The concept of a mixed visible Church, containing both true and nominal Christians, was originally developed in opposition to rigorist attempts to exclude the unworthy. But it laid the basis for the eventual concept of the Church as embracing the whole of society – a situation where all belonged to the Church and received its spiritual ministrations, much as all citizens may be covered by a National Health Service. The cure for sin is available to all, but of course the success rate is not perfect, just as with a health service. This concept prevailed for over 1,000 years of Christendom. The Anabaptists opposed it with their concept of 'gathered churches' of committed disciples. The collapse of Christendom has led to the triumph of the Anabaptist view of the Church, in a dilute form. These days all churches are, to a greater or lesser extent, gathered churches of voluntary members. It is increasingly true that people belong to a church because they have chosen to do so, not just because everyone in their family or society does so. This change has come about not because the Anabaptists succeeded in persuading everyone but because circumstances have changed and the doctrine of the Church is one that cannot evade harsh reality. The 'voluntarist' view of the Church is an inevitable concomitant of the rise of modern liberal society with its stress on individual choice. The idea of the 'gathered Church' may have begun as a principled appeal to the New Testament against the norms of contemporary society; it has now become a comfortable way of accommodating to the norms of liberal society.

ONE (CCC 813–22, 846–48, 866)

In the New Testament the unity of the Church is fundamental. Christ has only *one* body: 'There is one body and one Spirit – just as you were called to the one hope that belongs to your call' (Eph. 4:4). Christ has only one bride – he is no bigamist! It is a nonsense in New Testament terms to have more than one Church. But surely it is all right to have rival denominations which have an underlying spiritual unity? Not if we are to be faithful to the New Testament. The big issue in New Testament days was how to accommodate Jews and Gentiles. Paul was totally against allowing them to form separate congregations. He opposes this in Galatians 2:11–13 where the issue was Jewish food laws – table fellowship with Gentiles who ate bacon sandwiches:

> But when Cephas came to Antioch, I opposed him to his face, because he stood condemned. For before certain men came from James, he was eating with the Gentiles; but when they came he drew back and separated himself, fearing the circumcision party. And the rest of the Jews acted hypocritically along with him, so that even Barnabas was led astray by their hypocrisy.

Such a separation is contrary to the mission of Christ, which was to bring the two groups together into one (Eph. 2:11–22). Indeed, Paul portrays this as part of his gospel in

Ephesians 3:1–6, as we saw in the previous chapter.

In 1 Corinthians 1:10–17, we see that Paul was against schisms:

> I appeal to you, brothers, by the name of our Lord Jesus Christ, that all of you agree and that there be no divisions among you, but that you be united in the same mind and the same judgement . . . Is Christ divided? Was Paul crucified for you? Or were you baptized in the name of Paul?' (1:10, 13)

In John 17 Jesus prays that his Church should be united; for example: 'Holy Father, keep them in your name, which you have given me, that they may be one, even as we are one' (17:11). It is true that Paul and Barnabas parted company following a disagreement (Acts 15:36–41), but this involved them pursuing their missionary work in different directions, not founding rival churches.

In the Early Church rigorists like Novatian went to the point of deserting the existing Church and setting up another, creating a schism. These were breakaway groups that were doctrinally orthodox, not heretical groups. Schism was viewed very seriously by the mainstream Catholic Church. As far as they were concerned, people like Novatian did not divide the Church, they simply left it. There cannot be two churches. *Cyprian, who was Bishop of Carthage at the time, argued against Novatian that there is no salvation outside the Church – meaning the one visible Catholic Church:

> If a branch is broken from a tree, it cannot bud; if a stream is cut off from

247

its source, it dries up . . . Nor can he who forsakes the church of Christ attain to the rewards of Christ. He is a stranger, he is an enemy. Without the church for your mother, you cannot have God for your Father. If it was possible to escape outside the ark of Noah, then it may be possible to escape outside of the church . . . There is only one baptism, but they [these schismatics] think that they can baptize. Although they forsake the fountain of life, they promise the grace of living and saving water. Men are not washed there, they are made foul; sins are not purged, they are piled up. That birth makes sons not for God but for the devil. (*The Unity of the Church* 5–6, 11)

The rigorists held to the same view, but with the difference that they saw *their* church as the true Church.

The Reformers still strongly affirmed the unity of the Church. It was sinful and spiritual suicide to depart from a true Church. They saw themselves not as leaving the Catholic Church but as reforming it. Their aim was to maintain national, state churches embracing the entire population, which they saw as the Catholic Church in their territory. Initially they maintained a united front, but before long controversy over the presence of Christ in Holy Communion (see Chapter 26) caused them to divide into two rival groups, Lutheran and Reformed. Once the principle of separation over doctrine had been conceded, further division was inevitable and not slow to appear. Protestants soon learned to live with division between different national churches (e.g. between the Lutheran Church in Denmark and the Reformed Church in Holland). It took them longer to come to terms with the idea of separate churches in a single locality (e.g. rival Lutheran and Reformed churches in the same state).

Far from being able to heal these splits Protestantism managed only to fragment yet further, a process which has not slowed down with time. If purity of doctrine is the mark of the true Church and if the Church can go astray, the door is opened to repeated division. Protestantism has had to face the question of *how* impure doctrine must be to justify a split, an issue considered in the previous chapter.

Worship

Elect from every nation,
yet one o'er all the earth;
her charter of salvation
one Lord, one faith, one birth;
one holy name she blesses,
partakes one holy food,
and to one hope she presses
with every grace endued.
(Samuel John Stone, 'The Church's one
  foundation')

One is the body and one is the Head,
one is the Spirit by whom we are led;
one God and Father,
one faith and one call for all.
(John L. Bell)

Sceptic's corner

How can we talk of 'one Church' when the Church is so divided?

Answer: Initially the Reformers followed the same line as Cyprian, that there was just one Church. But before long splits took place. At first there was division between the Lutheran and Reformed churches in different countries. Then the two churches began to coexist in the same place. Eventually the traditional line became untenable and there was an acceptance of the plurality of churches – not as something desirable but as a fact of life. It is now generally accepted on all sides that true Christians are found in many different churches. Even the Roman Catholic Church has come to accept that other churches have *some* validity, though it claims a unique status for itself.

Such a realistic approach has become inevitable and in some ways is a great gain. Christians in different denominations are able to accept one another and to work together. Rival churches no longer regard one another as anti-Christian. But there has been a heavy price to be paid in that this approach makes nonsense of the New Testament doctrine of the unity of the Church. For something like half of its existence the Church managed to maintain the New Testament belief in the visible unity of the Church as the unique bride of Christ. This unity has now been fragmented into a free market of competing denominations. Market competition may well serve to foster greater efficiency, and in some ways favours the 'customer', but at the cost of Paul's vision of the uniting of humanity in Christ and in defiance of Christ's prayer for unity. Some are comfortable with today's situation, but somehow I doubt that hundreds of rival denominations competing with one another is what Jesus and Paul had in mind when they spoke of the unity of the Church! We shall return to this issue at the end of the chapter.

What do you think? The question

How should we seek to recover the unity of the Church today?

CATHOLIC (CCC 830–38, 868)

The Church is also Catholic. What does that mean? 'Catholic' is simply the Greek word for 'universal' or 'worldwide'. It was first used of the Church at the beginning of the second century by Ignatius, Bishop of Antioch (*Smyrneans* 8). As there is only one Church and since the gospel is for all of humanity, the Church is worldwide, not confined to one region. Augustine contrasted the worldwide Catholic Church with the schismatic Donatists, confined to North Africa, who were 'frogs in the marshes croaking "we are the only Christians"'. Today the Church has for the first time become genuinely 'catholic' in that every country (even Saudi Arabia) has at least some Christians, which was not previously true. By the end of the second century the term 'Catholic' was used to refer to the one true mainstream Church, as opposed to heresies or schismatic groups (like Novatianists) that had broken away.

The Protestant Reformers saw themselves not as *leaving* the Catholic Church but as reforming it. So, for example, the Church of England saw itself as the Catholic Church in England, now Reformed. The Reformers referred to Roman Catholics as Romanists or papists not as terms of abuse but because they did not concede that the Roman Church was the true Catholic Church. On the other hand, in his catechisms Luther changed the reference in the Apostles' Creed to 'the holy *Christian* church'. Calvin used the term 'Catholic' in a positive way, but less frequently over the years. As the Roman claim to Catholicity became more strident, Protestant claims became more muted, but did not cease.

Credal statement

The Christian Church is the community of brethren in which, in Word and Sacrament, through the Holy Spirit, Jesus Christ acts in the present as Lord. With both its faith and its obedience, with both its message and its order, it has to testify in the midst of the sinful world, as the Church of pardoned sinners, that it belongs to him alone and lives and may live by his comfort and under his direction alone, in expectation of his appearing. (*Barmen Declaration* (1934), art. 3)

THE UNITY OF THE CHURCH TODAY

There are three major ways in which Christians today respond to the visible disunity of the Church:

1 Some see the unity of the Church purely as an invisible, spiritual unity, claiming that visible organizational unity is irrelevant. It is true that the New Testament concept of the unity of the Church is far more than merely organizational, but it would be a mistake to suggest that it is also less than this. It stretches credulity to believe that a situation where churches of many rival denominations compete for members within the same locality is really what the New Testament meant by unity, however friendly and cooperative may be the relations between the different churches. Paul's responses to divisions in Galatia and Corinth, quoted above, indicate that for him a merely mystical, spiritual unity was not enough. He was concerned for a unity that is concrete and visible. An alleged 'unity' that coexists with hostility is not very convincing to unbelievers.

I do not ask for these only, but also for those who will believe in me through their word, that they may all be one, just as you, Father, are in me, and I in you, that they also may be in us, so that the world may believe that you have sent me. The glory that you have given me I have given to them, that they may be one even as we are one, I in them and you in me, that they may become perfectly one, so that the world may know that you sent me and loved them even as you loved me. (John 17:20–23)

It is because of Christians' unity that the world will believe – and this clearly means a visible unity. Simply appealing to an underlying invisible, spiritual unity has in practice often been an excuse to justify the fact that rival groups of Christians cannot get on with one another, especially where there are no significant doctrinal issues at stake.

2 The twentieth century has seen the pursuit of visible organizational unity by bringing denominations together. A huge amount of effort has been expended on this, with very little success. There have been a few mergers of different denominations, but the result has sometimes been three denominations where previously there were two. Also, the most visible manifestation of the ecumenical movement, the *World Council of Churches, has often acted in ways that are not calculated to increase enthusiasm for such an approach to unity. There has, however, been considerable success in increasing cooperation between churches and in lowering the barriers between them. In many cases doctrinal discussions have led to lessening of conflicts and healing of old wounds. Noteworthy examples of this are the 1982 document *Baptism, Eucharist and Ministry* and the 1999 document *Joint

Declaration on the Doctrine of Justification.
Also, there is often a grass-roots unity at
a local level between churches of various
denominations, who may join together to
evangelize, celebrate, worship and pray.

3 There is a third way, which is a distinctively
Evangelical way. Evangelicals cooperate
with one another and enjoy considerable
unity through para-church bodies, in which
denominational differences are transcended.
These include Bible societies, missionary
organizations and theological colleges –
like the London School of Theology.
In particular, many young Evangelicals
have the experience in their student days
of involvement with a Christian Union
or some other student Christian group,
where they are all united in the cause
of the gospel despite denominational
differences. Such an experience is
likely to colour their approach to other
Christians for the rest of their lives.
This provides a real, though only partial,

answer to the phenomenon of disunity.
The active unity enjoyed serves to lower
barriers between different denominations.

Error to avoid

It is right and proper to seek greater unity between
Christians from different churches, but focusing on
that can distract our attention from the key issue.
The biggest scandal today is not the fact that there
are rival denominations but the fact that within too
many congregations there is bickering and disunity.
It is true that Jesus' prayer of John 17:20–23 does
not apply *only* at the local congregational level, but
unity, like charity, begins at home.

Question to answer

- Describe the four traditional marks of the
  Church.

What do you think? My answer

It is true that there is an underlying spiritual
unity between all Christians by virtue of their
union with Christ, even when they hate one
another! It is also right to avoid unnecessary
division between churches and it is good by
dialogue to reach greater understanding between
rival theological traditions. It does no service to
pretend that differences do not exist where they
do, but too often in the past differences have
been magnified by polemics and exacerbated by
linguistic confusion. There is also great value in
the inter-denominational cooperation fostered
by para-church bodies.

PRAYER

Almighty and everlasting God, by whose
Spirit the whole body of the Church is
governed and sanctified: hear our prayer
which we offer for all your faithful people,
that in their vocation and ministry they
may serve you in holiness and truth to
the glory of your name; through our
Lord and Saviour Jesus Christ. (*Common
Worship*: Collect for the Fifth Sunday
after Trinity)

RESOURCE FOR CHAPTER 25

A. F. Gibson (ed.) *The Church and Its Unity*.
Leicester: IVP, 1992.

Chapter 26

HOLY COMMUNION

Aims of this chapter

In this chapter we look at Holy Communion, asking:

- What should it be called?
- What is its meaning and purpose?
- Is the bread Christ's body?
- What is a sacrament?

We will start by looking at the different names that are used for this service and then go on to consider different aspects of it found in the New Testament. (CCC 1322–1419)

NAMES (CCC 1328–32)

Holy Communion has gone by a variety of different names:

- **Breaking of Bread**. This term appears in Acts:
  - Acts 2:42: 'They devoted themselves to the apostles' teaching and fellowship, to the breaking of bread and the prayers.'
  - Acts 20:7: 'On the first day of the week, when we were gathered together to break bread, Paul talked with them . . .'

- **Lord's Supper**. This term comes just once in the New Testament:
  - 1 Corinthians 11:20: 'When you come together, it is not the Lord's supper that you eat.'
  We shall ask below exactly what that term refers to.
- **Holy Communion**. This exact phrase does not come in the New Testament, but the idea of communion is found in 1 Corinthians 10:16: 'The cup of blessing that we bless, is it not a participation in the blood of Christ? The bread that we break, is it not a participation in the body of Christ?' Participation can also be translated 'communion'.
- **Eucharist**. This is the Greek word for thanksgiving. At the Last Supper Jesus gave thanks for both the bread and the wine (Matt. 26:27; Mark 14:23; Luke 22:19; 1 Cor. 11:24). At Holy Communion *we* 'bless' or give thanks for the cup (1 Cor. 10:16).
- **Mass**. Roman Catholics use the word 'mass'. Originally the word had no theological significance, probably being derived from the closing words of the Latin liturgy: '*Ite, missa est.*' The *Today's English Version* translation of that phrase might be 'That's it, folks.'

REMEMBRANCE (CCC 1356–64)

Communion is a service of remembrance looking back to Christ and the cross. It will come as a surprise to some to learn that there are only two passages in the New Testament that refer to it as a remembrance.

- Luke 22:19: 'And he took bread, and when he had given thanks, he broke it and gave it to them, saying, "This is my body, which is given for you. Do this *in remembrance of* me."'
- 1 Corinthians 11:23–25:

  The Lord Jesus on the night when he was betrayed took bread, and when he had given thanks, he broke it, and said, 'This is my body which is for you. Do this *in remembrance of* me.' In the same way also he took the cup, after supper, saying, 'This cup is the new covenant in my blood. Do this, as often as you drink it, *in remembrance of* me.'

The reason why it will come as a surprise to some that these are the only two passages is that in some churches one would gain the impression that this was the *only* thing that the New Testament teaches about communion, that this was its sole purpose. In fact it is just one of a number of things and is only mentioned in these two passages.

The Last Supper of Jesus with his disciples was a Passover meal, to which Jesus gave a new significance. The Passover meal looks back to the Exodus and the original event of the Passover; communion looks back to the cross: 'as often as you eat this bread and drink the cup, you proclaim the Lord's death until he comes' (1 Cor. 11:26). *John

Wesley referred to it as a 'converting ordinance', a means of leading people to saving faith.

Jesus is our Passover/Paschal lamb. This is stated explicitly in 1 Corinthians 5:7: 'Christ, our Passover lamb, has been sacrificed.' In John 19:33–36 we read that Jesus' legs were not broken and that this happened 'that the Scripture might be fulfilled: "Not one of his bones will be broken,"' quoting Exodus 12:46, which refers to the Passover lamb. There are other places where Jesus is referred to as 'the Lamb':

- John 1:29: 'Behold, the Lamb of God, who takes away the sin of the world!'
- 1 Peter 1:19: '. . . the precious blood of Christ, like that of a lamb without blemish or spot.'

These references should be seen as referring to the Passover lamb, as should the many passages referring to the Lamb in the book of Revelation.

ANTICIPATION (CCC 1344, 1402–05)

The Passover meal looked back to the Exodus but in later Judaism the idea came that it also looks forward to the Messiah. Since the Middle Ages Jews have concluded the meal with the words, 'Next year in Jerusalem.' Similarly, communion looks back to the cross and also forward. Jesus stated at the Last Supper that he would not again eat the Passover or drink wine until its fulfilment in the coming of the kingdom of God (Mark 14:25; Matt 26:29; Luke 22:16, 18). Communion looks forward in anticipation to the 'Messianic banquet'. This is also described as the 'marriage supper' of Jesus and his bride, the Church: 'Blessed are those who are invited to the marriage supper of the Lamb' (Rev. 19:9). This idea goes back to Old Testament passages like Isaiah 25:6: 'On this mountain the LORD of hosts will make for all peoples a feast of rich food, a feast of well-aged wine, of rich food full of marrow, of aged wine well refined.' So the communion service is a fellowship meal now in anticipation of the coming kingdom – 'until he comes' (1 Cor. 11:26). These words have the connotation of expectation, of looking forward, and do not just give a terminal date for the celebration of the ceremony.

NEW COVENANT

In Mark (14:24) and Matthew (26:28) Jesus calls the wine his blood of the covenant, while in Luke (22:20) and 1 Corinthians (11:25) the cup is called the New Covenant in his blood. This can be compared with Exodus 24, where the Mosaic Covenant is confirmed. Sacrifice is offered (v. 5) and then the people are sprinkled with blood from the sacrifice and told, 'Behold the blood of the covenant that the LORD has made with you in accordance with all these words' (v. 8). Through his sacrifice on the cross Christ has introduced the New Covenant promised in Jeremiah 31:31–34:

> Behold, the days are coming, declares the LORD, when I will make a new covenant with the house of Israel and the house of Judah . . . I will put my law within them, and I will write it on their hearts. And I will be their God, and they shall be my people. And no longer shall each one teach his neighbour and each his brother, saying, 'Know the LORD,' for they shall all know me, from the least of them to the greatest, declares the LORD. For I will forgive their iniquity, and I will remember their sin no more.

Communion is a covenant meal at which we reaffirm our membership of the New Covenant, looking back to the cross that makes it possible. This concept is unfamiliar to modern Western culture, though not completely without parallel. In Oxford and Cambridge colleges, the fellows are expected to eat dinner regularly together in the college hall, this helping to make them a community, not just a collection of individual academics. For Americans sharing a meal together at Thanksgiving is a highly significant part of family life.

UNITY (CCC 1396–1400)

Communion is a fellowship meal with Christ and also with one another. Much of Paul's criticism of the Corinthians in 1 Corinthians 11 is concerned with their failure in this area. He charges them with neglecting the poor – they eat to excess and get drunk; the poor go hungry (11:20–22, 33–34). He also rebukes them for their divisions (11:18–19), as he had already done in chapter 1.

Eating together is a way of expressing unity but also a way of building it. 'Because there is one bread, we who are many are one body, for we all partake of the one bread' (1 Cor. 10:17). Paul does not say that they partake of the one loaf because they are one body (true though that is) but the other way round. Communion does more than merely express an existing unity. Similarly, a kiss is an expression of love, but also serves to stimulate love. Families eat together because they are a family, but the eating together is also a way of cementing their unity. A survey conducted by Oxford University and Birds Eye confirmed this, concluding that 'Mealtimes are not just an everyday necessity. They are focal points to celebrate key moments or life events – daily rituals which keep us connected and reflect our ever adapting way of life.'[1] This is especially true in Eastern cultures where eating together implies a bond of friendship and entails mutual responsibilities.

The theme of unity is expressed in this Eucharistic prayer from the *Didache*, probably the earliest Christian writing outside the New Testament:

> As this broken bread was scattered on the mountains [when it was wheat] and being gathered together became one [loaf], so may your church be gathered from the ends of the earth into your kingdom. (*Didache* 9)

MEAL

The Last Supper was of course a meal that the disciples shared together. We read about a meal together in 1 Corinthians called (in 11:20) the Lord's Supper, during the course of which there is a 'communion service' in which token amounts of bread and wine are consumed (11:23–26), as at Passover. This meal is elsewhere called an *agape* or 'love feast' (Jude 12). Early in the second century the meal and the communion became separated. Christians met early in the morning, before work, for communion and again after work in the evening for the meal. The term 'Lord's Supper' is not found again in the writings that have survived to today until the early third-century *Apostolic Tradition*. There it refers not to communion but to the fellowship meal. It is likely, therefore, that in Early Church usage (including 1 Corinthians) 'Lord's Supper' refers to the fellowship meal or supper together, although in today's usage it refers to communion. This is an instance where it is usage that determines meaning and we should accept the contemporary use of the term.

The term 'breaking of bread' comes four times in Acts. It *need* refer to no more than a meal, as in 27:35 where, in front of a largely pagan audience, Paul 'took bread, and giving thanks to God in the presence of all . . . broke it and began to eat'. It is not very likely that in anticipation of their imminent shipwreck Paul decided to celebrate communion before a pagan congregation! In 20:7–11, by contrast, it refers to a meal together, a 'Lord's Supper' as in 1 Corinthians 11:20–22, during which Paul preached a rather long sermon: 'On the first day of the week, when we were gathered together to break bread, Paul talked with them, intending to depart on the next day, and he prolonged his speech until midnight' (20:7). In 2:42 it probably refers to communion: 'They devoted themselves to the apostles' teaching and fellowship, to the breaking of bread and the prayers.' In verse 46, however, it probably refers simply to table fellowship together: 'Day by day, attending the temple together and breaking bread in their homes, they received their food with glad and generous hearts.' So the term can refer to anything from an ordinary meal to a Christian fellowship meal to communion.

Eating together is a significant stage in any developing relationship. It is not a coincidence that visiting politicians and heads of state are not just plied with sandwiches but entertained at state banquets. This is true in Western culture; it is much truer in Eastern cultures.

From the early second century and in the great majority of churches today, communion consists of eating and drinking a token amount in the context of a church service. It has become divorced from the context of a real meal. This is not necessarily a bad thing, but it can be helpful occasionally at least to return it to its original context, to celebrate it in the setting of a proper meal, whether for a whole congregation or for a house group. This would also serve to accentuate the aspect of fellowship together. In many churches it is possible to go to communion without knowing or interacting with any of the other worshippers. The recently reintroduced ceremony of offering the 'peace' during the service goes a small way towards counteracting that. Less stilted and far more effective is the practice of serving coffee and other refreshments after the service. A fellowship lunch after church can be even more effective.

FEEDING ON CHRIST (CCC 1384, 1391)

In 1 Corinthians Paul refers to communion as a participation in the body and blood of Christ: 'The cup of blessing that we bless, is it not a participation in the blood of Christ? The bread that we break, is it not a participation in the body of Christ?' (10:16). The Greek word can be translated 'participation' or 'communion' or 'fellowship'. Earlier he says that the people of Israel under Moses 'all ate the same spiritual food, and all drank the same spiritual drink. For they drank from the spiritual Rock that followed them, and the Rock was Christ' (10:3–4).

A similar idea comes in John 6, especially verses 48–58, which talk of eating Christ's flesh and drinking his blood. For example: 'I am the living bread that came down from heaven. If anyone eats of this bread, he will live for ever. And the bread that I will give for the life of the world is my flesh' (6:51). The immediate context is the feeding of the 5,000, not the Last Supper, but given that there is reference to flesh (body), blood and bread (though not wine) it is hard to deny that it has *some* relevance to communion, especially given the parallel with 1 Corinthians 10:16.

Sceptic's corner

How can we possibly eat Christ's flesh?

Answer: The idea of eating Christ's flesh caused people problems then: 'When many of his disciples heard it, they said, "This is a hard saying; who can listen to it?"' (John 6:60). It also causes problems for many people today. It should not be interpreted as cannibalism, but that does not mean that we should swing to the opposite extreme and treat it as purely symbolic. Our relationship with Christ is so intimate that it is described in terms of our eating him. Sometimes lovers express their love for each other by saying that they would like to eat each other – and very occasionally one of them does! Christ feeds us with himself, not merely with external teaching. He gave his flesh and blood for us on the cross and he also feeds us with them.

What do you think? The question

Is the bread Christ's body?

'THIS IS MY BODY'[2]

All four accounts of the institution of the communion service record Jesus as saying 'This is my body' (Matt. 26:26; Mark 14:22; Luke 22:19; 1 Cor. 11:24). There is also a fifth passage which is similar: 'The bread that I will give for the life of the world is my flesh' (John 6:51b). Jesus did not say, 'This *symbolizes* my body', although there is a Greek word that would mean that. So how should we understand Jesus' words? We must avoid suggesting that there are only two alternatives – mere symbolism and total literalism.

In the twentieth century a rather Liberal bishop of Birmingham sent a consecrated wafer to a laboratory to be analysed and announced that it was still only bread, there was no physical or chemical change. It may come as a surprise to hear that there is no church whose teaching would imply otherwise, and that includes the Roman Catholic Church. The consecrated bread is still physically bread, but that does not prove that it is no more than a symbol.

What do you think? My answer

Is the bread Christ's body? Clearly it is, because Jesus said so – but what does that *mean*? It is not true in a crudely literal way – Jesus does not ask us to engage in cannibalism. But many statements are deeply true without being literally true. Jesus' statement has been taken in a variety of ways during the course of church history:

Error to avoid

A paperback is composed of no more than paper and ink. A sceptic could send it to a laboratory and announce that the scientists had discovered no words there, that it was 'nothing but' paper and ink. A sceptic could read Paul's letters and say that there was no word of God there, just the words of Paul. Christians accept that all the words are Paul's – but also claim that it *is* (not symbolizes) God's word. We all accept that paperbacks are just paper and ink – but also recognize that they contain words. A credit card is 'nothing but' plastic and metal – and yet it is a lot more. A banknote is 'nothing but' paper and metal, but it also has a value because of the promise written on it. We must not fall into the trap of what Donald McKay called 'Nothing buttery'. Paper and metal are not what a banknote *is*, but what it is made of.

Monopoly money, by contrast, *is* purely symbolic. There is the amusing story of how a boy in New Zealand took a 10,000 yen Monopoly note to his local bank – and they cashed it. The newspaper report was appropriately entitled 'Boy passes Go!'[3] We should not regard the bread and wine as being like Monopoly money.

Now you see, a materialist would say that this meal is nothing but matter, a view which can be called 'nothing buttery.'

It's utterly butterly dear.

© Miriam Kendrick 2013 www.miriamkendrick.co.uk

FOUR VIEWS

Since New Testament times the Church has developed various different doctrines on this matter, of which we will briefly mention four:

1 The Roman Catholic Church teaches that the bread *becomes* Christ's body (CCC 1373–81). There is a change in substance ('transubstantiation') but that is not necessarily the same as a *physical* change. The physical properties (called 'accidents') are unaltered and there is no change that could be detected by a physicist or a chemist. Popular Roman Catholic piety has often suggested a physical change, but the official theology steers clear of that. The change has been compared to the way in which a tree can be turned (by a carpenter) into a table – it is still the same physical 'stuff' (wood) but its 'substance' (ultimate reality) has changed (from tree to table).

2 While *Luther rejected the Roman Catholic doctrine of transubstantiation he continued all of his life to believe in the real presence of the body and blood of Christ in communion. He believed that the bread remained bread but that the body of Christ was present 'in, with and under' the bread. A crude analogy would be the way in which water fills a sponge in the bath – and if someone throws it at you, the water hits you as well as the sponge! Luther's fundamental concern was to avoid the reduction of communion to a subjective experience. There is a sacramental union between the bread and Christ's body so what happens to the one happens to the other. In particular, if we eat the bread we eat Christ's body. This means that Christ's body is received orally, through the mouth, and that *all* who receive the bread (including unbelievers and the unworthy) receive Christ's body – but to *benefit* from it one needs faith.

3 *Zwingli, who was bringing the Reformation to Zurich while Luther was reforming Saxony, taught that the bread is merely a symbol of Christ's body. He rejected the doctrine of the 'real presence'. Christ's body and blood are present only by faith in the mind of the believer, not in any material or bodily manner. Jesus has ascended into heaven and his body is now contained there. Being a human body, it cannot at the same time also be on earth. The bread and the wine are materially unchanged, though in the context of the service the bread becomes sacred bread and acquires a dignity – not because it has been changed but because of what it signifies (Christ's body). Essentially the bread and wine are just symbols, superb visual aids. Christ is of course present at communion – through his Holy Spirit, just as he is present wherever two or three gather in his name. But his body and blood are not present, except in our memories. This has been described as 'the doctrine of the real absence'.

4 *Calvin also taught that the bread is a symbol, but an effective symbol through which we can by faith feed on Christ's body. He agreed with Zwingli that Christ's body is located in heaven and is not to be found in, with or under the bread. Against Zwingli, however, he saw the essence of communion not as what we do (remember) but as God's gift to us. In particular, through communion we eat Christ's flesh and drink his blood. This happens not by him descending to earth nor by us ascending to heaven but by the Holy Spirit bridging the gap between us.

The sun's rays bring us a real communion with the sun and those who stay too long in the sun feel the effects. So also the Holy Spirit brings us a real communion with Christ's humanity in heaven. Calvin's teaching is well summarized by an exhortation from the Anglican Book of Common Prayer which in the contemporary *Common Worship* reads: 'Feed on him in your hearts by faith with thanksgiving' – in your heart, not your mouth; by faith, not with the teeth.[4]

SACRIFICE? (CCC 1359–72, 1410, 1414)

The Roman Catholic Church teaches that the Eucharist is a sacrifice that we offer to God – indeed, the self-same sacrifice that Christ offered on the cross. 'The sacrifice of Christ and the sacrifice of the Eucharist are *one single sacrifice*' (*CCC 1367). The Reformers were united in rejecting this, affirming that Christ's sacrifice for sin was once made and once offered, drawing on Hebrews especially:

- Hebrews 7:27: '[Christ] has no need, like those high priests, to offer sacrifices daily, first for his own sins and then for those of the people, since he did this once for all when he offered up himself.'
- Hebrews 9:12 '[Christ] entered once for all into the holy places, not by means of the blood of goats and calves but by means of his own blood, thus securing an eternal redemption.'
- Hebrews 10:14: 'By a single offering he has perfected for all time those who are being sanctified.'

The teaching of the Reformers is well expressed in this prayer from the Communion Service in the Book of Common Prayer:

Almighty God, our heavenly Father, who of thy tender mercy didst give thine only Son Jesus Christ to suffer death upon the Cross for our redemption; who made there (by his one oblation of himself once offered) a full, perfect, and sufficient sacrifice, oblation, and satisfaction, for the sins of the whole world; and did institute, and in his holy Gospel command us to continue, a perpetual memory of that his precious death, until his coming again: . . .

Although communion should not be seen as a sacrifice *for sin*, this is not the only kind of sacrifice. The same letter to the Hebrews which emphasizes the once-for-all completeness of Christ's sacrifice for sin urges us to offer to God our own sacrifice of praise and sharing:

Through him then let us continually offer up a sacrifice of praise to God, that is, the fruit of lips that acknowledge his name. Do not neglect to do good and to share what you have, for such sacrifices are pleasing to God. (13:15–16)

Communion can be seen as a sacrifice of praise and worship, but not as a sacrifice for sin.

MEETING WITH CHRIST

The two disciples who walked with Jesus to Emmaus (Luke 24:13–35) did not at first recognize him. It was when he broke the bread that they perceived who he was: 'When he was at table with them, he took the bread and blessed and broke it and gave it to them. And their eyes were opened, and they recognized him. And he vanished from their sight' (24:30–31). When they returned to Jerusalem they told the others that Jesus was made known to them in the breaking of bread. This can all be read at a superficial level as a purely historical account, but Luke is also implying that it is as we gather today to break bread that Christ is made known to us and we meet with him.

It is also noteworthy that Jesus was very cheeky in taking upon himself the role of the host in their house by breaking the bread. This points to the fact that at communion it is Jesus who is host and we are the guests. Some people refer to Jesus as the 'unseen guest' at every event, but at communion by contrast he is the 'unseen host'.

In Revelation 3:20 Jesus promises, 'Behold, I stand at the door and knock. If anyone hears my voice and opens the door, I will come in to him and eat with him, and he with me.' This promise of a fellowship meal with Christ points to a feature of communion.

THE SACRAMENTS (CCC 1210–11)

Baptism and Holy Communion are often described as 'sacraments'. Some theologians (like Calvin) have expounded a doctrine of the sacraments and then gone on to apply this doctrine to baptism and communion. The problem with that approach is that the New Testament does not itself link baptism and communion together and there is no biblical conception of a 'sacrament'. This does not prevent us from talking of sacraments, but we should start not with a doctrine of the sacraments but with what the New Testament actually teaches about baptism and of communion, as we have sought to do. Having done that, we can *then* proceed to ask what they have in common and thus develop the concept of a sacrament. *Augustine coined the definition of a sacrament as a 'visible word',

God's word expressed visibly. Given that the sacraments are intended not just to be looked at, it might be better to see them as 'tangible words'.[5] In the light of what we have seen about baptism and communion we can also say that they are effective words through which God acts for our salvation.

Credal statements

The Supper of the Lord is not only a sign of the love that Christians ought to have among themselves one to another; but rather is a Sacrament of our Redemption by Christ's death: insomuch that to such as rightly, worthily, and with faith, receive the same, the Bread which we break is a partaking of the Body of Christ; and likewise the Cup of Blessing is a partaking of the Blood of Christ . . . The Body of Christ is given, taken, and eaten, in the Supper, only after an heavenly and spiritual manner. And the mean whereby the Body of Christ is received and eaten in the Supper is Faith. (*Thirty-Nine Articles*, art. 28)

Worthy receivers, outwardly partaking of the visible elements, in this sacrament, do then also, inwardly by faith, really and indeed, yet not carnally and corporally but spiritually, receive and feed upon, Christ crucified, and all benefits of his death: the body and blood of Christ being then, not corporally or carnally, in, with, or under the bread and wine; yet, as really, but spiritually, present to the faith of believers in that ordinance, as the elements themselves are to their outward senses. (*Westminster Confession of Faith* (1647), 29:7)

Worship

Bread of Heaven, on you we feed,
for your flesh is food indeed;
always may our souls be fed
with this true and living bread;

day by day our strength supplied
through your life, O Christ, who died.

Vine of heaven, your precious blood
seals today our peace with God;
Lord, your wounds our healing give,
to your cross we look and live:
grafted, rooted, built in you,
Jesus, here our souls renew.
(Josiah Conder: modernized)

Broken for me, broken for you,
the body of Jesus broken for you.

He offered His body, He poured out His soul,
Jesus was broken that we might be whole:
Broken for me . . ..

Come to My table and with Me dine,
eat of My bread and drink of My wine:
Broken for me . . .

This is My body given for you,
eat it remembering I died for you:
Broken for me . . .

This is My blood I shed for you,
for your forgiveness, making you new:
Broken for me . . .
(Janet Lunt)

PRAYER

Lord Jesus Christ, we thank you that in
this wonderful sacrament you have given
us the memorial of your passion: grant us
so to reverence the sacred mysteries of
your body and blood that we may know
within ourselves and show forth in our
lives the fruit of your redemption, for
you are alive and reign, now and for
ever. (*Common Worship*: Post Communion
Prayer for Maundy Thursday)

Question to answer

- What is the meaning and purpose of Holy
  Communion?

NOTES

1 <http://www.birdseye.co.uk/~/media/
UK/PDF/Changing_Plates.pdf>.
2 ATS ch. 13.
3 <http://www.independent.co.uk/news/
world/boy-passes-go-1497127.html>.
4 For more on Calvin's teaching, see
A. N. S. Lane 'Was Calvin a Crypto-
Zwinglian?' in M. Holt (ed.) *Adaptations
of Calvinism in Reformation Europe:
Essays in Honour of Brian G. Armstrong*.
Aldershot, Hants: Ashgate, 2007,
21–41.
5 I am planning to publish a book on
the sacraments with the title *Tangible
Words*.

RESOURCES

J. H. Armstrong (ed.) *Understanding Four
Views on the Lord's Supper*. Grand Rapids:
Zondervan, 2007.

D. Bridge and D. Phypers *The Meal that
Unites?* London: Hodder & Stoughton,
1981.

J. E. Colwell *Promise and Presence: An
Exploration of Sacramental Theology*. Milton
Keynes: Paternoster, 2005.

E. Kreider *Given for You: A Fresh Look at
Communion*. Leicester: IVP, 1998.

I. H. Marshall *Last Supper and Lord's Supper*.
Carlisle: Paternoster, 1980.

G. T. Smith (ed.) *The Lord's Supper: Five
Views*. Downers Grove: IVP, 2008.

FUTURE GLORY (ESCHATOLOGY)

Chapter 27

THE END TIMES

Aims of this chapter

In this chapter we look at the End Times, focusing on the Millennium and the Parousia, asking:

- How will this age end?
- Will there be a literal Millennium?
- What is the Parousia?
- When will it happen?
- What will happen when Christ has returned?

What do you think? The question

Should we be expecting a literal Millennium?

PART I: THE MILLENNIUM[1] (CCC 676)

The Millennium is the 1,000-year rule of Christ on earth with some of his people, as described in Revelation 20:1–7:

Then I saw an angel coming down from heaven, holding in his hand the key to the bottomless pit and a great chain. And he seized the dragon, that ancient serpent, who is the devil and Satan, and bound him for a *thousand years*, and threw him into the pit, and shut it and sealed it over him, so that he might not deceive the nations any longer, until the *thousand years* were ended. After that he must be released for a little while.

Then I saw thrones, and seated on them were those to whom the authority to judge was committed. Also I saw the souls of those who had been beheaded for the testimony of Jesus and for the word of God, and those who had not worshipped the beast or its image and had not received its mark on their foreheads or their hands. They came to life and reigned with Christ for a *thousand years*. The rest of the dead did not come to life until the *thousand years* were ended. This is the first resurrection. Blessed and holy is the one who shares in the first resurrection! Over such the second death has no power, but they will be priests of God and of Christ, and they will reign with him for a *thousand years*.

And when the *thousand years* are ended, Satan will be released from his prison.

The Millennium is mentioned nowhere else in the Bible apart from this one passage. So how should we understand it? Three main views have been held: Pre-, Post- and

Amillennialism. There are two types of Premillennialism, which will be considered separately: Historic Premillennialism and Dispensational Premillennialism.

How we interpret Revelation 20 will largely be decided by our approach to the book of Revelation as a whole, on which see below. Also, our view of the Millennium will be influenced by other beliefs, such as our views of the physical creation and of our final destiny (on which, see Chapter 29) and whether all Old Testament prophecies need to have a literal fulfilment.

HISTORIC PREMILLENNIALISM

Historic Premillennialism is the belief that Christ will return before (pre) the Millennium. The Millennium will be a time of material and spiritual prosperity, and Christ will literally reign on earth. Many Old Testament prophecies will be literally fulfilled at this time. This view was held widely in the second century, especially in Asia Minor (modern-day Turkey), where Revelation was written. It was used to affirm the goodness of the physical creation, in particular against the heresy of Gnosticism.

Its leading second-century advocate was *Irenaeus, who quoted an alleged saying of Jesus:

> The days are coming when vines shall grow, each with 10,000 branches, each branch with 10,000 twigs, each true twig with 10,000 shoots, each shoot with 10,000 clusters and each cluster with 10,000 grapes. Each grape will yield twenty-five measures of wine. When any of the saints takes hold of one cluster, another will cry out, 'I am a better cluster, take me; bless the Lord through me.'
> (*Against Heresies* 5:33:3)

Taken literally, this works out at about 150,000 billion billion bottles of wine per vine and gives a fresh meaning to the promise that 'they shall sit every man under his vine and under his fig tree' (Mic. 4:4)! It should be noted, though, that the statement makes no mention of a Millennium and could equally be taken as a prophecy of the Age to Come – 1,000 years might be a little too short to consume all of that wine!

DISPENSATIONAL PREMILLENNIALISM

Premillennialism is also held today by Dispensationalists, who add to it a complex system of beliefs about God's different dealings with us in different dispensations (Adamic, Abrahamic, Mosaic, etc.). One of their foundational beliefs is that *all* Old Testament prophecy must be fulfilled *literally* – including, for example, Ezekiel's new Temple with animal sacrifices (40—48). Many Old Testament prophecies have yet to be fulfilled literally and the Millennium provides the setting in which that can take place. But why after Christ's death would there be any further need for animal sacrifice? This approach is a triumph of biblical literalism over theology!

Dispensationalists have also engaged in speculation about a rapture *prior* to Christ's return,[2] to be followed by a seven-year period of tribulation and persecution, with the reign of Antichrist. After the seven years Christ will return (for the second time) and will reign on earth for 1,000 years. This teaching has been popularized by the well-known *Left Behind* series of novels. Dispensationalism originated in nineteenth-century Britain but has almost entirely died out in its country of origin. Today it is found mainly in the USA (where there are tens of millions of Dispensationalists) and in parts of the world where American influence is strong.

POSTMILLENNIALISM

Postmillennialism is the belief that Christ will return after (post) the Millennium. There will be a future golden age of the Church, where things will be similar to now but much better. Most people will become Christians, the Jews will be converted and there will be little sin or crime. It will be a good time for lazy people to join the police. At the end of this time, Christ will return.

Premillennialism goes with a pessimistic view of church history – there will be decline until Christ returns and introduces the Millennium. Postmillennialism, by contrast, implies an optimistic view of church history and has been popular in times like the Victorian age, in which there was economic growth, the British Empire was spreading, the gospel was being preached round the world and a spirit of optimism was abroad. On the Postmillennial view the Millennium will be quantitatively rather than qualitatively different from today and not everyone who is then alive would acknowledge that it was happening. Postmillennialists commonly see the 1,000 years as referring a long period of time, not as an exact measurement. They do not interpret Revelation as literally as do the Premillennialists. Postmillennialism is the least popular of the four views. If one is going to see Revelation 20 as teaching a literal Millennium it does seem to imply that Christ will be on earth.

AMILLENNIALISM

Amillennialism is the belief that there will be no literal Millennium. Revelation 20 refers not to a literal 1,000 years but to the whole 'church age' between Christ's First and Second Coming. This was argued in the fifth century by *Augustine. He saw the 'first resurrection' of Revelation 20:4 as referring to the conversion of Christians and the reign of Christ with his saints as referring to the Church's mission on earth. The Millennium is the period between the First and Second Comings of Christ and is the sixth period of history, corresponding to the sixth day of creation. It will end with the return of Christ, who will introduce the eternal Sabbath.

A sense of proportion is needed in discussing the doctrine of the Millennium. It is mentioned just once in the Bible explicitly, and that in a book that is full of symbolism and notoriously difficult to understand – though, to be fair, other biblical teaching has been brought into developing doctrines of the Millennium. To elevate a particular interpretation of Revelation 20 as a test of orthodoxy, as happens in some circles, is bizarre in the extreme.

THE BOOK OF REVELATION[3]

The issue of the Millennium is closely tied in with the question of the interpretation of the book of Revelation. Amillennialists take the symbolism of the book least literally, Postmillennialists a little more, Premillennialists a lot more and Dispensationalist Premillennialists most of all. Also important is one's view of the structure of the book and whether the various visions are to be interpreted as referring to successive stages of church history. There are five main approaches to the book:

1 **The Preterist View** holds that the whole book refers to the original context in which it was given, until halfway through chapter 20 (or later), where attention turns to the End.

2 **The Historicist View** holds that the book covers the period from the first century to the End in chronological sequence. Those taking this view usually believe

that they are living just before the End! *Luther and many of the other Reformers took this approach, identifying the pope with the Antichrist.

3 **The Futurist View** holds that most of the book refers to the End Times. Dispensationalists see this as beginning with chapter 4, and some see the seven letters of chapters 2–3 as referring to seven periods of church history. Other Premillennialists hold that the reference to the End Times begins with chapter 7 or 8.

4 **The Idealist View** interprets the book poetically. Chapters 4 to 19/20 refer to the period between the First and Second Comings of Christ, but not in sequence and as symbolic imaginative descriptions of God's triumph over evil, not referring to specific events.

5 **The Cyclical View** holds that chapters 4 to 19/20 tell the story of the period between the First and Second Comings of Christ six times, repeating the pattern of suffering leading to judgement and the End. This view has been called 'progressive parallelism'. This was the approach of the oldest surviving

commentary on Revelation, by Victorinus of Pettau who was martyred around 304.

PART 2: THE PAROUSIA (CCC 668–82)

Parousia is a Greek word which was used for the 'presence' or 'arrival' of an important visiting figure, like the emperor. In the New Testament it refers to the Second Coming of Christ. This is a major New Testament theme, mentioned in over 300 verses – in striking contrast with the Millennium, which is mentioned in just one brief passage. It is affirmed in all the major creeds of the Church, and is held by orthodox Christians of all denominations and traditions.

To what does the Parousia refer? Various wrong ideas have been put forward:

What do you think? My answer

On the basis of the Cyclical View of the book of Revelation I am inclined to Amillennialism. The doctrine of the Millennium was popular in the second century because it affirms the goodness of the physical creation, in opposition to the Gnostic heresy. But if we take seriously the fact that the new creation includes a 'new earth' (see chapter 29) we do not need a literal Millennium in order to affirm the goodness of the physical realm. Above all we need humility in speculating about the End. When it happens we will probably all get a surprise.

Errors to avoid

Some have suggested that it refers to Christ's coming in the Holy Spirit at Pentecost. Others, similarly, have proposed his return 'in the gospel'. Another popular idea is that we each have an individual Parousia when we die, that death is the equivalent of the Second Coming. These three views all leave out an important element of the biblical narrative: the cosmic dimension. God's purposes include the renewal of the cosmos, of all creation, not just individual salvation. 'Then I saw a new heaven and a new earth, for the first heaven and the first earth had passed away, and the sea was no more' (Rev. 21:1).

The return of Christ will not go unnoticed. Jehovah's Witnesses have prophesied that the End would come on a variety of different dates and for some time maintained that he returned 'invisibly' in 1874, and then that he had done so in 1914. The Unification Church ('Moonies') claim that Sun Myung Moon was the Second Coming of Christ.

According to the New Testament Christ's coming will be manifest and will lead to the end of history:

- Mark 13:26: 'They will see the Son of Man coming in clouds with great power and glory.'
- 1 Corinthians 15:24: 'Then comes the end, when he delivers the kingdom to God the Father after destroying every rule and every authority and power.'
- Revelation 1:7: 'Behold, he is coming with the clouds, and every eye will see him.'

In the light of this, Jesus warned his disciples not to be taken in by false claims:

- Mark 13:5–6: 'See that no one leads you astray. Many will come in my name, saying, "I am he!" and they will lead many astray.'
- Mark 13:21–22: 'And then if anyone says to you, "Look, here is the Christ!" or "Look, there he is!" do not believe it. False christs and false prophets will arise and perform signs and wonders, to lead astray, if possible, the elect.'

Sceptic's corner

Didn't Jesus say that he would be returning within a few years?

Answer: Some of Jesus' references to the coming of the kingdom can be taken to imply this:

- Mark 9:1: 'Truly, I say to you, there are some standing here who will not taste death until they see the kingdom of God after it has come with power.'
- Mark 13:30: 'Truly, I say to you, this generation will not pass away until all these things take place.'

All such passages can, however, be understood differently. There is some indication that people asked questions about the fact that the Parousia did not happen as soon as expected:

- John 21:23: 'Jesus did not say to [the beloved disciple] that he was not to die, but, "If it is my will that he remain until I come, what is that to you?"'
- 2 Peter 3:9: 'The Lord is not slow to fulfil his promise as some count slowness, but is patient towards you, not wishing that any should perish, but that all should reach repentance.'

But there is no evidence of a widespread crisis of faith when the Parousia was delayed.

THE DATE OF THE PAROUSIA

Jesus taught that his return was 'at hand' and imminent. He also taught that it would be sudden and unexpected, e.g. in Matthew 24:37–44: 'Therefore you also must be ready, for the Son of Man is coming at an hour you do not expect' (24:44). But at the same time not even Jesus knew the day of his return: 'But concerning that day or that hour, no one knows, not even the angels in heaven, nor the Son, but only the Father' (Mark 13:32). This is certainly not a statement that the early Christians would have made up. Mark 13 mentions a number of signs, but these are rather vague and there is also uncertainty about how much of this chapter refers to the Parousia and how much to the Fall of Jerusalem in AD 70. Some since the nineteenth century have maintained that it refers only to the latter and this view is defended today by Tom Wright. Most agree, however, that in Mark 13 Jesus speaks both of the destruction of Jerusalem and of his own return. At the time when he spoke, both events lay in the future. When you view two mountain tops in the distance it is not always clear which feature belongs to which mountain; once you are between the two mountains there no longer remains any uncertainty. Nowadays we are living between those two 'mountain tops' – the one event has happened; the other has not.

The New Testament Church expected Jesus' return to be imminent, sudden and unexpected. The Thessalonians thought that he would be coming so soon that they stopped work, for which Paul had to rebuke them: 'We hear that some among you walk in idleness, not busy at work, but busybodies. Now such persons we command and encourage in the Lord Jesus Christ to do their work quietly and to earn their own living' (2 Thess. 3:11–12). In second-century Syria a bishop led his flock out into the desert to await the coming Christ. After a few days the local authorities rounded them up and brought them back. Since then there have been repeated attempts to predict the day of Christ's return. A recent example is Harold Camping, who confidently taught that this would take place on 21 May 2011 and then, when this date had passed, that it would be on 21 October 2011. The following year he confessed that he had sinned in making these attempts.

Camping's is just the most recent in a long succession of such attempts. They all have one thing in common – they have all been wrong. The success rate to date has not even been 0.1 per cent or 0.00001 per cent; it has been 0 per cent. This should teach us to view all such claims with a healthy scepticism. Jesus expects us to stay faithful and to keep working until he comes. As Luther allegedly stated, 'If I knew that the world would perish tomorrow, I would

© Miriam Kendrick 2013 www.miriamkendrick.co.uk

still plant an apple tree today.' The false prophecies provide us with entertainment, but they are dangerous for those who believe them. As a student in 1972 I was confidently told that if I trained for a profession I would be wasting my time since the End was about to come. Taking such teaching seriously could cause people to waste the potential of their life. On the other hand, we need to 'be ready, for the Son of Man is coming at an hour you do not expect' (Matt. 24:44).

Credal statement

As Christ would have us to be certainly persuaded that there shall be a day of judgement, both to deter all men from sin; and for the greater consolation of the godly in their adversity: so will He have that day unknown to men, that they may shake off all carnal security, and be always watchful, because they know not at what hour the Lord will come; and may be ever prepared to say, Come Lord Jesus, come quickly, Amen. (*Westminster Confession of Faith* (1647), 33:3)

270

FIRST VERSUS SECOND COMING OF CHRIST

The Old Testament points to the coming Day of the Lord and (without using the word) to the coming of the Messiah. The First Coming of Christ only partly fulfils these prophecies. In his sermon at Nazareth, when Jesus read from Isaiah 61 he stopped part way through, omitting the reference in 61:2 to 'the day of vengeance of our God':

> The Spirit of the Lord is upon me, because he has anointed me to proclaim good news to the poor. He has sent me to proclaim liberty to the captives and recovering of sight to the blind, to set at liberty those who are oppressed, to proclaim the year of the Lord's favour. (Luke 4:18–19)

Christ has inaugurated the New Age – but in part only. It has arrived 'already, but not yet'; there is more to come. The D-Day landings in Normandy marked the *beginning* of the end of the war in Europe, but the end itself came the following year on VE Day. Similarly victory has been won by Christ's cross, resurrection and Ascension, but will not be complete until his return. 'Christ, having been offered once to bear the sins of many, will appear a second time, not to deal with sin but to save those who are eagerly waiting for him' (Heb. 9:28). The present situation can also be compared to an engagement when two people are *already* committed to one another but have *not yet* made the commitment of marriage.

This point needs to be remembered when speaking with Jews about the coming of the Messiah. They look to the Messiah to bring a universal kingdom of peace and rightly point out that the coming of Jesus has not produced that. In response we need to make clear that while Christ has come once we, like them, are awaiting the coming (again) of the Messiah to destroy all evil.

THE RESURRECTION OF THE BODY
(CCC 988–1004, 1038, 1052)

When Christ returns the dead will rise:

- 1 Thessalonians 4:13–17: 'For the Lord himself will descend from heaven with a cry of command, with the voice of an archangel, and with the sound of the trumpet of God. And the dead in Christ will rise first' (4:16).
- This is the theme of the whole of 1 Corinthians 15, especially 15:20–22, 50–55. The final resurrection is, of course, based upon the resurrection of Christ. Jesus rose from the dead not as an isolated miracle but as the firstfruit of the resurrection of humanity:

> If Christ has not been raised, then our preaching is in vain and your faith is in vain . . . But in fact Christ has been raised from the dead, the firstfruits of those who have fallen asleep. For as by a man came death, by a man has come also the resurrection of the dead. For as in Adam all die, so also in Christ shall all be made alive. But each in his own order: Christ the firstfruits, then at his coming those who belong to Christ' (15:14, 20–23).

Most of the biblical references to the final resurrection, like those quoted above, refer just to the righteous, but there are three passages that refer also to the resurrection of the wicked:

- John 5:28–29: 'An hour is coming when all who are in the tombs will hear his voice and come out, those who have done good to the resurrection of life, and those who have done evil to the resurrection of judgement.'

- Acts 24:15: Paul has 'a hope in God, which these men themselves accept, that there will be a resurrection of both the just and the unjust.' 'These men' refers to the Pharisees, who held to the same belief on the basis of the Old Testament:
- Daniel 12:2: 'Many of those who sleep in the dust of the earth shall awake, some to everlasting life, and some to shame and everlasting contempt.'

LAST JUDGEMENT (CCC 678–79, 681–82, 1021–22, 1038–41, 1051, 1059)

After resurrection comes the Last Judgement, which we have already considered in Chapter 20.

- Revelation 20:11–15:

  And I saw the dead, great and small, standing before the throne, and books were opened. Then another book was opened, which is the book of life. And the dead were judged by what was written in the books, according to what they had done' (20:12).

The Last Judgement is for believers as well as unbelievers and is based upon what we have done. Christian believers also will be judged:

- 2 Corinthians 5:10: 'We must all appear before the judgement seat of Christ, so that each one may receive what is due for what he has done in the body, whether good or evil.'

God's judgement differs from human judgement in that he looks beyond outward deeds to the inner motivation:

Therefore do not pronounce judgement before the time, before the Lord comes, who will bring to light the things now hidden in darkness and will disclose the purposes of the heart. Then each once will receive his commendation from God' (1 Cor. 4:5)

As Archbishop James Ussher noted, we judge people's hearts by their deeds; God judges people's deeds by their hearts.

Worship

Lo! He comes with clouds descending,
Once for favoured sinners slain;
Thousand thousand saints attending,
Swell the triumph of His train:
Hallelujah! Hallelujah! Hallelujah!
God appears on earth to reign.

Every eye shall now behold Him
Robed in dreadful majesty;
Those who set at naught and sold Him,
Pierced and nailed Him to the tree,
Deeply wailing, deeply wailing, deeply wailing,
Shall the true Messiah see.
(*Charles Wesley)

PRAYERS

Our Lord, come. (1 Cor. 16:22)[4]

Now may the God of peace himself sanctify you completely, and may your whole spirit and soul and body be kept blameless at the coming of our Lord Jesus Christ. He who calls you is faithful; he will surely do it. (1 Thess. 5:23–24)

Question to answer

- How will this age end?

NOTES

1 ATS ch. 17/16.
2 ATS Appendix 13 (second edn).
3 ATS Appendix 11 (second edn).
4 Paul uses the Aramaic word *Maranatha*, indicating that this prayer probably goes back to the very earliest days of the Church.

RESOURCES FOR CHAPTERS 27–29

H. Schwarz *Eschatology*. Grand Rapids: Eerdmans, 2000.

T. Wright *Surprised by Hope*. London: SPCK, 2007.

RESOURCES FOR CHAPTER 27

C. L. Blomberg and S. W. Chung (eds) *A Case for Historic Premillennialism: An Alternative to 'Left Behind' Eschatology*. Grand Rapids: Baker, 2009.

D. L. Bock (ed.) *Three Views on the Millennium and Beyond*. Grand Rapids: Zondervan, 1999.

R. G. Clouse (ed.) *The Meaning of the Millennium*. Downers Grove: IVP, 1977.

S. J. Grenz *The Millennial Maze: Sorting Out Evangelical Options*. Downers Grove: IVP, 1992.

C. M. Pate (ed.) *Four Views on the Book of Revelation*. Grand Rapids: Zondervan, 1998.

Chapter 28

HELL

Aims of this chapter

In this chapter we look at the doctrine of Hell, asking:

- Will all be saved?
- What is Hell?
- Will the lost suffer for ever?

PART 1: UNIVERSALISM

Universalism, the doctrine that all will be saved regardless of how they have lived, is popular today. There were a few who taught it in the early centuries, most notably *Origen. His teaching was condemned in a number of 'anathemas' produced by the Emperor Justinian and probably endorsed by the *Council of Constantinople (553):

> If anyone says or thinks that the punishment of demons and of impious men is only temporary and will one day have an end, and that a restoration will take place of demons and impious men, let him be anathema. (Justinian, *Anathemas against Origen* 9)

*Augustine had earlier rejected the idea. After a long interval it began to re-emerge in the seventeenth century and it has become much more popular since the rise of Liberalism in the nineteenth century.

There are different types of universalist. Some teach universalism as a doctrinal truth; others regard it as a piece of speculation or offer it as 'wider hope' rather than a confident affirmation. *Karl Barth is one whose teaching has appeared to many to imply universalism, though he refused to affirm or to deny it.

THE NEW TESTAMENT

There are many passages in the Gospels that show that Jesus taught a 'dual outcome' – i.e. that some would be saved; others would not be. To give a few examples:

- Matthew 7:13–14: 'Enter by the narrow gate. For the gate is wide and the way is easy that leads to destruction, and those who enter by it are many. For the gate is narrow and the way is hard that leads to life, and those who find it are few.'
- Matthew 12:32: 'Whoever speaks a word against the Son of Man will be forgiven, but whoever speaks against the Holy

Spirit will not be forgiven, either in this age or in the age to come.'

- Matthew 25:46: 'These will go away into eternal punishment, but the righteous into eternal life.'
- John 3:36: 'Whoever believes in the Son has eternal life; whoever does not obey the Son shall not see life, but the wrath of God remains on him.'

There are six passages in Paul which, taken out of context, could imply universalism but which come in the context of his clear teaching about a dual outcome:

- Romans 5:18–19: 'As one trespass led to condemnation for all men, so one act of righteousness leads to justification and life for all men.' The previous verse specifies who it is that actually enjoys this benefit, namely 'those who receive the abundance of grace and the free gift of righteousness'.
- Romans 11:32: 'God has consigned all to disobedience, that he may have mercy on all.' The issue in this passage is the salvation of both Jews and Gentiles, not of every numerical individual. Shortly before, he writes of the dual outcome of 'vessels of wrath' and 'vessels of mercy' (9:22–23).
- 1 Corinthians 15:22: 'As in Adam all die, so also in Christ shall all be made alive.' This means that 'all who are in Christ will be made alive'. Earlier Paul writes clearly of a dual outcome: 'Do you not know that the unrighteous will not inherit the kingdom of God? Do not be deceived: neither the sexually immoral, nor idolaters . . . nor swindlers will inherit the kingdom of God' (6:9–10).
- Ephesians 1:10: God's plan is 'to unite all things in [Christ], things in heaven and things on earth.' Paul did not understand this to imply universalism as shortly after he wrote, 'You may be sure of this, that everyone who is sexually immoral or impure, or who is covetous (that is, an idolater), has no inheritance in the kingdom of Christ and God' (5:5).
- Philippians 2:10–11: God's plan is that 'at the name of Jesus every knee should bow, in heaven and on earth and under the earth, and every tongue confess that Jesus Christ is Lord, to the glory of God the Father.' Whatever that means it does not alter the fact that for some people, 'their end is destruction, their god is their belly, and they glory in their shame, with minds set on earthly things' (3:19).
- Colossians 1:19–20: God's aim was through Christ to 'reconcile to himself all things, whether on earth or in heaven, making peace by the blood of his cross'. This can be compared with 2:15: '[God] disarmed the rulers and authorities and put them to open shame, by triumphing over them in [Christ].' The picture in both passages is of the *Pax Romana*, the peace that ensues when the Roman army has defeated and executed its enemies. Having listed various sins, Paul warns that 'on account of these the wrath of God is coming' (3:5–6).

While there are these six passages in Paul which (out of context) can be read in a universalist way, the rest of his teaching shows that he believed in a dual outcome, as is the clear and unambiguous teaching of Jesus.

Credal statement

Question 20. Will all men, then, be saved through Christ as they became lost through Adam?

Answer: No. Only those who, by true faith, are incorporated into him and accept all his benefits. (*Heidelberg Catechism* (1563))

PART 2: HELL (CCC 1033–37)[1]

There is much in the New Testament on the danger and reality of Hell – especially from the lips of Jesus. The New Testament emphasis is not on rescuing other people from Hell, but on making sure we ourselves do not go there. If we see the threat of Hell as applying to others only we can easily become arrogant and complacent and other people will be very quick to detect that. If, on the other hand, we see it as a danger that faces us as much as our hearers it will instil a more humble attitude and discourage an attitude of complacent superiority. C. S. Lewis put it well:

> In all our discussions of Hell we should keep steadily before our eyes the possible damnation, not of our enemies nor our friends (since both these disturb the reason) but of ourselves. This chapter is not about your wife or son, nor about Nero or Judas Iscariot; it is about you and me.[2]

The stakes are high:

- Matthew 10:28: 'Do not fear those who kill the body but cannot kill the soul. Rather fear him who can destroy both soul and body in hell.'
- Matthew 5:29: 'If your right eye causes you to sin, tear it out and throw it away. For it is better that you lose one of your members than that your whole body be thrown into hell.' This is a deadly serious issue, even though we should not literally tear out our eye. 'What does it profit a man to gain the whole world and forfeit his soul?' (Mark 8:36).

What do you think? The question

How should we preach about Hell today?

NEW TESTAMENT IMAGERY

The New Testament uses a variety of imagery to describe Hell:

- **Death** is the most common image. The fate of the lost is referred to simply as death, or as loss of life, or as perishing. This is contrasted with eternal life: 'God so loved the world, that he gave his only Son, that whoever believes in him should not perish but have eternal life' (John 3:16). Hell is also repeatedly described in Revelation as the 'second death' (by contrast to the 'first death' that we experience at the end of this earthly life):

> Blessed and holy is the one who shares in the first resurrection! Over such the second death has no power, but they will be priests of God and of Christ, and they will reign with him for a thousand years . . . Then Death and Hades were thrown into the lake of fire. This is the second death, the lake of fire. (Rev. 20:6, 14)

- **Destruction** is another common image, using two different Greek words: 'The gate is wide and the way is easy that leads to destruction' (Matt. 7:13). This image is closely related to that of death. The destruction is eternal:
  - 2 Thessalonians 1:9: 'They will suffer the punishment of eternal destruction, away from the presence of the Lord and from the glory of his might.'
- **Fire** is the most common image after death and destruction: 'The angels will

come out and separate the evil from the righteous and throw them into the fiery furnace' (Matt. 13:49–50). The fire is several times referred to as eternal:
- Jude 7: 'Sodom and Gomorrah and the surrounding cities, which likewise indulged in sexual immorality and pursued unnatural desire, serve as an example by undergoing a punishment of eternal fire.'
- The fire is also described as unquenchable:
  - Mark 9:43, 47–48:

And if your hand causes you to sin, cut it off. It is better for you to enter life crippled than with two hands to go to hell, to the unquenchable fire . . . And if your eye causes you to sin, tear it out. It is better for you to enter the kingdom of God with one eye than with two eyes to be thrown into hell, where the worm does not die and the fire is not quenched.

- The imagery of undying worms and unquenched fire is drawn from Isaiah 66:24, where the reference is not to the torture of the living but to *dead* bodies:

And they shall go out and look on the dead bodies of the men who have rebelled against me. For their worm shall not die, their fire shall not be quenched, and they shall be an abhorrence to all flesh.

- **Separation from God** for eternity is mentioned just a few times:
  - Matthew 7:23: 'And then I will declare to them, "I never knew you; depart from me, you workers of lawlessness."'
  - Matthew 25:41: 'Then he will say to those on his left, "Depart from me, you cursed, into the eternal fire prepared for the devil and his angels."'

- 2 Thessalonians 1:9: 'They will suffer the punishment of eternal destruction, away from the presence of the Lord and from the glory of his might.'
- **Eternal punishment** and **eternal judgement** are both phrases which appear once only:
  - Matthew 25:46: 'And these will go away into eternal punishment, but the righteous into eternal life.'
  - Hebrews 6:2: '. . . and of instruction about washings, the laying on of hands, the resurrection of the dead, and eternal judgement'.

Sceptic's corner

Why does God ask us to forgive our enemies when he does not forgive his own enemies?

Answer: God does forgive his enemies and at great cost: 'While we were enemies we were reconciled to God by the death of his Son' (Rom. 5:10). But forgiveness and reconciliation is a two-way process. Forgiveness is offered to all but it needs to be accepted by us.

ETERNAL CONSCIOUS SUFFERING?
The teaching on Hell in the New Testament clearly implies a final loss and an irreversible condition. Judgement leads to a dual outcome which involves an eternal separation of the ways. But does Hell involve eternal consciousness and suffering? Does 'eternal punishment' mean a death which is final and not reversed throughout eternity or a death that continues to happen for all eternity?

The view of Hell as eternal conscious suffering has been the mainstream view for much of the Church's history. Augustine argued for it, in opposition to six alternative views (*City of God* 21:17–27). Significantly, all six views presupposed the immortality of the human soul, a doctrine inherited from Greek philosophy and long believed to be biblical. In the nineteenth century, however, the difference between the Greek and biblical views of the soul became clearer and this opened up a new option – that Hell involves eternal extinction.

There are three basic views that are held on this issue:

1 **Traditionalism**: Hell is eternal conscious suffering. There are different ways in which this suffering has been understood. In the Middle Ages the references to fire and worms were often taken very literally. Today there is more emphasis on Hell as separation from God and on psychological suffering. In *The Great Divorce* C. S. Lewis pictured Hell as the state of drifting further and further away from God and from other people. The atheist philosopher Jean-Paul Sartre wrote a play, *No Exit*, in which three people find that their Hell is to be locked into a room together for eternity. It is in this context that the famous quotation comes: 'Hell is other people' – meaning these specific 'other people', not social intercourse in general.

2 **Universalism**, the belief that all will eventually be saved, has already been discussed.

3 **Annihilationism**: the ultimate destiny of the lost is annihilation, extinction. This is not the same as the belief that bodily death is the end. The lost are raised from the dead to face God's judgement and the sentence is, as it were, the death penalty rather than life imprisonment.

© Miriam Kendrick 2013 www.miriamkendrick.co.uk

This view became a serious option in the nineteenth century, when it was realized that the New Testament does not teach the immortality of the soul. In recent years there has been renewed controversy over this issue, which was sparked in 1988 when *John Stott came out in support of the belief that the ultimate fate of the lost is annihilation.[3] His declaration led many other Evangelicals to admit to holding the same belief. After some years of controversy the Evangelical Alliance commissioned a report which concluded that both views were acceptable within Evangelicalism.[4]

Which view is supported by the New Testament? The dominant imagery used of Hell (death, destruction, fire) more naturally favours the idea of extinction. But how would this language have been understood at the time? In inter-testamental Judaism (from the time between the Old Testament and the coming of Christ) the language generally favours the idea of annihilation. One exception is the book of Judith (150–125 BC), which contains the statement:

Woe to the nations that rise up against my race; the Lord Almighty will take vengeance of them in the day of judgement, to put fire and worms in their flesh; And they shall weep and feel pain for ever. (16:17)

As the idea of the immortality of the soul prevailed in Judaism, so Judith's teaching became more common. So, in its context, the language of the New Testament could be taken either way.

The New Testament doctrine of Hell clearly implies suffering, as can be seen from the references to wailing and gnashing of teeth, such as Luke 13:28: 'In that place there will be weeping and gnashing of teeth.' But does this suffering continue for ever? The doctrine of eternal suffering gains some support from two passages in Revelation. In interpreting these passages we must bear in mind that this is a book that is full of imagery and that taking it too literally can mislead.

- Revelation 20:10: 'The devil who had deceived them was thrown into the lake of fire and sulphur where the beast and the false prophet were, and they will be tormented day and night for ever and ever.' This mentions Satan and the false prophet, not anyone else.
- Revelation 14:9–11 does refer to the torment of people:

If anyone worships the beast and its image and receives a mark on his forehead or on his hand, he also will drink the wine of God's wrath, poured full strength into the cup of his anger, and he will be tormented with fire and sulphur in the presence of the holy angels and in the presence of the Lamb. And the smoke of their torment goes up for ever and ever, and they have no rest, day or night, these worshippers of the beast and its image, and whoever receives the mark of its name.

That the smoke rises for ever is not the same as saying that the torment endures for ever. This imagery is derived from Isaiah 34:9–10:

The streams of Edom shall be turned into pitch, and her soil into sulphur; her land shall become burning pitch. Night and day it shall not be quenched; its smoke shall go up for ever. From generation to generation it shall lie waste; none shall pass through it for ever and ever.

Revelation 19:3 says of the destruction of Babylon that 'The smoke from her goes up for ever and ever.'

One of the Dead Sea Scrolls intriguingly appears to teach both the traditional view and annihilationism in the same sentence: The judgement on the wicked will be 'everlasting damnation by the avenging fury of the wrath of God, eternal torment and endless disgrace together with shameful extinction in the fire of the dark regions'.[5] This is perhaps a warning against taking apocalyptic language too literally.

Error to avoid

We must beware of overconfidence in our own theories. The sixteenth-century theologian *Erasmus warned against excessive dogmatism about Hell: '[The theologians] are happy too while they're depicting everything in Hell down to the last detail, as if they'd spent several years there!' (*Praise of Folly*).

THEOLOGICAL ARGUMENTS

In my judgement the exegesis is inconclusive and it is possible with integrity to argue either the traditional view or annihilationism. It is important, therefore, to consider the theological arguments.

IMMORTALITY OF THE SOUL

From the third to eighteenth centuries it was generally accepted, thanks to the influence of *Greek philosophy, that the human soul is immortal and *cannot* cease to exist. Such a belief makes sense if with the Greeks we believe that the soul is a divine spark that has always existed. By contrast, the biblical view, as we saw in Chapter 4, is that we are created by God and previously did not exist. The New Testament teaches that only God is immortal – he is 'the blessed and only Sovereign, the King of kings and Lord of lords, who alone has immortality' (1 Tim. 6:15–16). Human beings are not inherently immortal, but the gospel offers us the gift of eternal life and immortality: Jesus Christ has 'abolished death and brought life and immortality to light through the gospel' (2 Tim. 1:10).

The fact that we are not inherently immortal does not *prove* that God does not give everlasting existence to those suffering in Hell. It does, however, remove the strongest argument in favour of such a belief, namely that it would be impossible for the lost to cease to exist.

JUSTICE

Today many question the justice of Hell. Some speak of a God who is loving and affirming but never condemns anyone, but this is not the God of the Bible. Others question the idea that punishment involves *retribution*. Penal theory today recognizes a variety of aims of punishment: rehabilitation, deterrence, prevention – and retribution. It is the element of retribution that makes it punishment rather than social engineering. Retribution means that the punishment is deserved. We could effectively reduce speeding by executing offenders, but such a procedure would not be *just*.

Many object to Hell on the ground that a finite amount of sin cannot deserve an infinite punishment, though this objection does not apply to annihilationism. The traditional answer has been that sin is infinitely serious because it is against an infinite God.

DUALISM

The final goal is that 'God may be all in all' (1 Cor. 15:28). Will this be true if the lost remain in Hell? Augustine's answer was to compare Hell to the dark shadows that form part of a pleasing landscape. Similarly, it is asked whether the redeemed can be happy knowing that some of their loved ones are suffering in Hell. Revelation refers to the righteous rejoicing at the judgement of the wicked (18:20). This makes sense in the heat of the moment of judgement but it is harder to see this happening for all eternity. C. S. Lewis, in *The Great Divorce*, states that the redeemed are untouched by the misery of the lost, on the ground that otherwise one dissenter could eternally veto the joys of heaven. Annihilationism offers a simpler solution.

Worship

Unsurprisingly, Hell has not proved a popular theme for hymn writers. The following comes from the nineteenth-century hymn 'Great God, what do I see and hear!'

The ungodly, filled with guilty fears,
Behold his wrath prevailing.
For they shall rise, and find their tears
And sighs are unavailing.
The day of grace is past and gone;
Trembling they stand before his throne,
All unprepared to meet him.
(William B. Collyer, Thomas Cotterill et al.).

What do you think? My answer

Since the nineteenth century many people have rejected the Christian faith because of its doctrine of Hell. Most churches today have adopted a conspiracy of silence. They do not deny the doctrine, they affirm it in theory but they do not preach about it. Silence is no less betrayal than is denial. The doctrine of Hell is important because it brings home the urgency and seriousness of the gospel. As has been stated, without Hell the Christian faith can degenerate into a message about personal psychological fulfilment.

What is needed is a doctrine of Hell that is scriptural (unlike universalism) and preachable. This is by no means an impossible task. A recent survey of post-religious Britain showed that 32 per cent of the population retain some belief in Hell, including 15 per cent of those who claim to have no religion![6] It is possible to present the doctrine in a sensitive but forthright manner.[7]

PRAYER

From all evil and mischief; from sin, from the crafts and assaults of the devil; from thy wrath, and from everlasting damnation, Good Lord, deliver us.
(Book of Common Prayer, Litany)

Question to answer

- What is Hell?

NOTES

1 ATS ch. 18/17.
2 C. S. Lewis *The Problem of Pain*. London: Collins Signature Classics, 2012, 116.
3 D. L. Edwards and J. Stott *Essentials: A Liberal–Evangelical Dialogue*. London: Hodder & Stoughton, 1988, 312–20.
4 Evangelical Alliance Commission on Unity and Truth Among Evangelicals, *The Nature of Hell*. Carlisle: Paternoster & ACUTE, 2000.
5 1QS 4:12–13 (G. Vermes, *The Complete Dead Sea Scrolls in English*. London: Penguin, 1998, 102).
6 N. Spencer and H. Weldin *Post-religious Britain? The Faith of the Faithless*. London: Theos, 2012, 29–30.
7 A good example of this, from a student mission address that I heard live, is 'Hell: and a God of love?' in D. Watson *My God is Real*. London: Falcon, 1970, ch. 3.

RESOURCES FOR CHAPTER 28

ACUTE *The Nature of Hell*. Carlisle: Paternoster, 2000.

W. Crockett (ed.) *Four Views on Hell*. Grand Rapids: Zondervan, 1992.

E. W. Fudge and R. A. Peterson, *Two Views of Hell*. Downers Grove: IVP, 2000.

C. S. Lewis *The Great Divorce*. London: Fontana, 1972.

Chapter 29

FUTURE HOPE

Aims of this chapter

In this chapter we look at the Christian hope for the future, asking:

- What is the Christian hope for those who have died in Christ?
- How much can we know about the Age to Come?
- What happens between death and resurrection?
- Who will be saved?
- What of those who never hear?

What do you think? The question

What is the Christian hope for those who have died in Christ? (I.e. what is our *ultimate* hope?)

FUTURE HOPE (CCC 1023–29, 1042–50, 1052–53, 1060)

The most common answer to the above question is that we go to heaven when we die. Death brings the private salvation of the individual soul, which then goes to heaven. A few of the more theologically inclined will add a mention of the resurrection of the body; most Christians barely give it a thought. Funeral sermons often refer to the body in the coffin as if it was no more significant than a set of clothes. As one preacher delightfully put it, 'What is in the coffin is but the shell; the nut has gone!' This identification of salvation with going to heaven when we die is genuinely ecumenical, being held across all denominations. The problem is that this is not the Christian hope taught by the New Testament.

Future hope in the New Testament focuses on the Parousia, when Christ will return and the dead will rise. At that point we all will attain salvation together – it is a corporate event, not private and individual. Peter refers to 'an inheritance that is imperishable, undefiled, and unfading, kept in heaven for you, who by God's power are being guarded through faith for a salvation ready to be revealed in the last time' (1 Pet. 1:4–5). Peter does not say that we *go* to heaven to receive our inheritance. The idea that salvation is going to heaven is a Gnostic idea that has crept in through the back door. The Gnostics believed that we are essentially souls, divine sparks that are destined to return to their heavenly home. The material and bodily realm is bad and salvation means escaping it. The Early

Church effectively resisted Gnosticism, but at this point was influenced by it.

For Paul the survival of the soul without the resurrection of the body (salvation as 'going to heaven') was no gospel:

Now if Christ is proclaimed as raised from the dead, how can some of you say that there is no resurrection of the dead? But if there is no resurrection of the dead, then not even Christ has been raised. And if Christ has not been raised, then our preaching is in vain and your faith is in vain.' (1 Cor. 15:12–14)

Imagine a future with no brain.

Tom Wright summarizes the New Testament hope as not 'life after death' (going to heaven when we die) but 'life after life after death' – i.e. resurrection after an intervening period. This is not some modern invention. The three ancient creeds all refer to the Parousia and resurrection of the dead without any reference to the idea that we 'go to heaven when we die', as shown below.

Credal statements

[Christ] will come again with glory to judge the living and the dead . . . We look forward to the resurrection of the dead and the life of the age to come. (*Nicene Creed)

From [heaven] [Christ] will come to judge the living and the dead . . . I believe in . . . the resurrection of the flesh and eternal life. (*Apostles' Creed)

[Christ] will come from [heaven] to judge the living and the dead. When he comes, all men will rise again with their bodies and will render account for their own deeds. (*Athanasian Creed)

By contrast, our hymns and worship songs are all about going to heaven when we die and generally make no reference at all to the resurrection of the body. This is even true of that glorious hymn 'Thine be the glory, risen conquering Son', which focuses on the resurrection of *Christ*, but ends with the prayer, 'bring us safe through Jordan [death] to thy home above [heaven]'.

Worship

I scoured the hymn books for a hymn which referred to the resurrection of the body and discovered that traditional hymns place all the focus upon 'going to heaven when we die'. I did come across a hymn on the resurrection body but, significantly, this was dated as recently as 1987.[1]

In resurrection bodies
like Jesus' very own,
we'll rise to meet our Saviour
with joy around his throne:
we'll marvel at the mercy
that bids poor sinners come,
be welcomed at his table,
and share his heavenly home!
(Margaret Clarkson)

NEW HEAVEN(S) AND NEW EARTH

Rather than a future in heaven, the New Testament offers the hope of a new heaven and a new earth. This draws upon the prophecies of Isaiah:

- Isaiah 65:17: 'For behold, I create new heavens and a new earth, and the former things shall not be remembered or come into mind.'
- Isaiah 66:22: 'For as the new heavens and the new earth that I make shall remain before me, says the LORD, so shall your offspring and your name remain.'

- 2 Peter 3:13: 'According to his promise we are waiting for new heavens and a new earth in which righteousness dwells.'
- Revelation 21:1–3:

Then I saw a new heaven and a new earth, for the first heaven and the first earth had passed away, and the sea was no more. And I saw the holy city, new Jerusalem, coming down out of heaven from God, prepared as a bride adorned for her husband. And I heard a loud voice from the throne saying, 'Behold, the dwelling place of God is with man. He will dwell with them, and they will be his people, and God himself will be with them as their God.'

It might be objected that these are just a few, mostly apocalyptic, passages. They are reinforced, however, by the far more frequent affirmations of the resurrection of the body. Our future resurrection points to our destiny on the new earth, as opposed to the new heaven. By contrast, M. J. Erickson, in his widely used doctrine textbook, states that 'As God's abode, heaven is obviously[!] where believers will be for all eternity.'[2] Yet if Erickson is correct, why is the new Jerusalem to descend from heaven to earth? Is it so we can wave to it as we ascend to heaven? The new Jerusalem suggests our future destiny actually lies on the new earth.

Does it really matter whether we think of salvation as souls going to heaven or as being raised from the dead on a new earth? Yes it does, for a variety of reasons:

- The idea of salvation as going to heaven when we die trivializes death. An elderly couple died in a car crash and were being shown round the heavenly mansions together. As they went round the husband looked more and more glum. 'What's the matter?' asked his wife, 'Don't you like it here?' 'Oh yes,' he replied, 'I was just thinking that if you hadn't been so keen on healthy eating we might have got here ten years earlier!' For Paul death is 'the last enemy' (1 Cor. 15:26), and what gives us the victory over it is not going to heaven when we die but the resurrection of the body thanks to the death and resurrection of Christ (1 Cor. 15:50–57).
- The idea of salvation as souls going to heaven belittles the body and leads to neglect of the physical creation. It coheres with the idea that the soul is divine but the body and the material world are unimportant, on which see Chapter 4. By contrast, the resurrection of the body on the new earth affirms the goodness and significance of the physical creation.
- The idea of salvation as a private individual experience when we die is contrary to biblical hope, which is corporate rather than individual, cosmic rather than just focussed on human beings. 'God had provided something better for us, that apart from us [Christians] they [Old Testament believers] should not be made perfect' (Heb. 11:40).
- If salvation is going to heaven, the Parousia shifts from being at the heart of Christian hope to being just one item on a prophetic timetable. It is too important to abandon to the prophecy nutters!

Credal statement

The visible universe, then, is itself destined to be transformed, 'so that the world itself, restored to its original state, facing no further obstacles, should be at the service of the just', sharing their glorification in the risen Jesus Christ. (*CCC 1047, quoting from *Irenaeus)

Worship

Then I saw a new heaven and earth
for the first had passed away,
and the holy city, come down from God,
like a bride on her wedding day.
And I know how he loves his own
for I heard his great voice tell
they would be his people, and he their God,
and among them he came to dwell.

He will wipe away every tear,
even death shall die at last;
there'll be no more crying, or grief, or pain,
they belong to a world that's past.
And the One on the throne said, 'Look!
I am making all things new';
he is A and Z, he is first and last,
and his words are exact and true.
(Christopher Idle)

LIFE IN THE NEW AGE

What will our future destiny be like? The fullest account comes in Revelation 21—22. There we read that there will be no more pain, sorrow or death: 'He will wipe away every tear from their eyes, and death shall be no more, neither shall there be mourning nor crying nor pain any more, for the former things have passed away' (21:4). We will be able to recognize each other – otherwise we would be less human than we are now. There will be no more sin, otherwise the final state would prove not to be final after all. We will be unable to sin – not in the way that an addict deprived of cigarettes is unable to smoke, but in the sense that those who are perfectly good have no desire to do evil. The time of trial and testing will be over. The coming kingdom will be God's reign of justice in which all evil is overcome.[3] This refers not just to the evil that we have ourselves done but also to the wrongs that we might have suffered, such as bullying, sexual abuse or persecution.

What will we be doing? Playing harps? Gardening? Will there be animals there? Will there be dogs to foul the pathways and bite the postmen?[4] We simply do not know. 'Beloved, we are God's children now, and what we will be has not yet appeared' (1 John 3:2). Or, as *Luther graphically put it, 'We know no more about eternal life than children in the womb of their mother know about the world they are about to enter.'[5] This is a slight exaggeration, but his basic point is correct. Although what we know is very imprecise, it is enough to give us confidence and hope for the future. We would like to know more, but we know what we need to know at this stage.

How much continuity will there be between this age and the Age to Come? The New Testament points to elements of both continuity and discontinuity:

1 After Jesus rose from the dead, his disciples recognized him, but not straight away. This happened more than once. 'When he was at table with them, he took the bread and blessed and broke it and gave it to them. And their eyes were opened, and they recognized him' (Luke 24:30–31). He was the same (his wounds remained) but different (they did not recognize him at once).

2 In 1 Corinthians 15:35–54, Paul compares the relation between our present bodies and our resurrection bodies to that between a seed and what emerges:

What you sow does not come to life unless it dies. And what you sow is not the body that is to be, but a bare seed, perhaps of wheat or of some other grain . . . So is it with the resurrection of the dead. What is sown is perishable; what is raised is imperishable. It is sown in dishonour; it is raised in glory. It is sown in weakness; it is raised in power. (15:36–37, 42–43)

This points to continuity, and to considerable discontinuity. Compare an acorn with an oak tree!

3 Revelation 21:1 refers to a 'new earth' but we also read that 'the kings of the earth will bring their glory into it . . . they will bring into it the glory and honour of the nations' (21:24, 26). It is not, as some have claimed, like the sinking of the *Titanic*, where all that can be rescued is individual people. To some extent the fruits of our efforts in this world will be carried over into the next.

What do you think? My answer

According to the New Testament and the ancient creeds our Christian hope is for the resurrection of the body and the coming of God's kingdom. So does this mean that the churches' emphasis on going to heaven when we die is wrong? Yes and no. The Church has been wrong to ignore and marginalize the New Testament hope of the resurrection body and of new heavens and a new earth. The Church is, however, not wrong to answer the question: what happens when we die? Christians on their deathbed want to know where they will be tomorrow. When they have died their loved ones want to know where they are *now*, not just where they will be at some unspecified time in the future. We turn our attention, therefore, to the issue of the 'intermediate state' between death and resurrection.

The New Age will not be totally new, but nor will it just be the old one patched up. The truth lies somewhere in between, which leaves a huge scope for legitimate difference about how much continuity or discontinuity there will be. It will not be totally new (like buying a new pair of shoes and discarding the old) but nor will it just be the old one cleaned up (like polishing one's shoes). It will be *somewhere* in between. Exactly where, no one knows.

THE INTERMEDIATE STATE

What happens when we die? The prime emphasis in Scripture is on the End, rather than the intermediate state between death and resurrection. Scripture says *not much* about this, but *not nothing*.

- The Old Testament speaks 65 times of 'Sheol' as where the dead go. Sheol is not extinction but nor is it particularly desirable – it is a shadowy existence.
- The Greek equivalent of Sheol in the New Testament is Hades. In his Pentecost sermon Peter quotes Psalm 16 and comments that David 'foresaw and spoke about the resurrection of the Christ, that he was not abandoned to Hades, nor did his flesh see corruption' (Acts 2:31).
- In both Old and New Testaments, death is referred to as 'sleep'. For example, Job 14:12: 'Till the heavens are no more he will not awake or be roused out of his sleep'; John 11:11: 'Our friend Lazarus has fallen asleep, but I go to awaken him'; Acts 13:36: 'David, after he had served the purpose of God in his own generation, fell asleep.' It is uncertain whether 'sleep' here is merely a euphemism for death or is intended to tell us something about the state of the departed. It is interesting that our word

'cemetery' comes from the Greek word for 'dormitory', a place where people sleep.

- In 1 Samuel 28:5–20 the prophet Samuel was brought back by the witch of Endor to speak to Saul. This implies that Samuel was not extinct but available to be summoned back. The Old Testament does not portray the dead as extinct, but also recognizes that their present existence is shadowy compared with life on earth.
- In Mark 9:2–7 Moses and Elijah appear with the transfigured Jesus: 'There appeared to them Elijah with Moses, and they were talking with Jesus' (9:4). As with 1 Samuel 28, the appearance of Moses and Elijah implies they must be available to appear from somewhere.
- Luke 16:19–31:

  The poor man died and was carried by the angels to Abraham's side. The rich man also died and was buried, and in Hades, being in torment, he lifted up his eyes and saw Abraham far off and Lazarus at his side. (16:22–23)

Hades refers not to Hell, but to an intermediate state between death and resurrection, because the rich man asks for Lazarus to be sent back to his brothers who are still alive. In the first century it was believed Hades was divided into two sections, good and bad.

- Luke 23:43: 'Truly, I say to you, today you will be with me in Paradise.' This is often taken to mean that the criminal would that day have a new body in an earthly paradise like the Garden of Eden, but in the first century Paradise was seen as a heavenly realm. This can be seen from Paul's comment in 2 Corinthians 12:3: 'I know that this man was caught up into paradise – whether in the body or

out of the body I do not know.' So Jesus was promising the criminal that he would go to a heavenly realm, not to an earthly paradise for which a resurrection body would be necessary.

- 1 Peter 3:18–20: Christ was 'put to death in the flesh but made alive in the spirit, in which he went and proclaimed to the spirits in prison, because they formerly did not obey, when God's patience waited in the days of Noah.' The *Apostles'

Errors to avoid

How to tie together all these statements about the intermediate state is a complex issue, but there are two erroneous views which, in my opinion, can clearly be excluded on the basis of this evidence. The first is the view that we are extinct between physical death and resurrection – a view that is held by some Christians today. The second is the view that we receive full salvation at death, despite having no body and no brain. The image of being 'asleep' in Christ brings out the idea of peace and rest. But sleep should not be confused with unconsciousness; it is what the medics call an *altered* state of consciousness. The difference between sleep and unconsciousness can be observed very easily by sticking a pin into someone who is prone. If he does not react he is unconscious; if he gets up and hits you he was only asleep.

Reducing salvation to 'going to heaven when we die' is like responding to the question 'Where are you going on holiday?' with 'Heathrow, Terminal Three', when your final destination is Hawaii. Terminal Three doubtless has its attractions, but as a holiday destination it does not compare with Hawaii! At Terminal Three one leaves behind the stresses of everyday life and begins to enter holiday mode, but the holiday does not really begin until one reaches Hawaii.

Creed states that Christ 'descended to the underworld', i.e. to Hades.

- 2 Corinthians 5:1–10: 'For while we are still in this tent, we groan, being burdened – not that we would be unclothed, but that we would be further clothed, so that what is mortal may be swallowed up by life' (5:4). Paul talks of a time of being unclothed between two clothed states; the naked stage is in an intermediate state.[6]
- In Philippians 1:20–24 Paul greets the prospect of martyrdom with the statement that his desire was 'to depart and be with Christ, for that is far better' (1:23).
- Revelation 6:9–11: 'I saw under the altar the souls of those who had been slain for the word of God and for the witness they had borne' (6:9).

Sceptic's corner

Surely modern brain science excludes the need or the possibility of any soul that transcends the body or survives its death.

Answer: This was discussed briefly in Chapter 6. Brain science is a young discipline and not all of its practitioners would agree with the claim made. It is certainly true that many of the activities of the mind can be observed as physical events in the brain. To argue therefore that they are nothing but physical events in the brain is a classic example of 'nothing buttery', of reductionism. Even if every mental activity could be explained in physical terms (which is far from true at the moment) that would not prove that there is nothing in human nature that transcends the body, nothing that can survive death. It is true, however, that the findings of brain science undermine the view of those who treat the resurrection of the body as unimportant, who regard a bodiless existence as a satisfactory destiny.

What about out-of-body or near-death experiences? These clearly argue against a reductionist view, but must be handled with caution. While we should not disregard such experiences (especially if talking with those who have had them) and it is an important area for research, the basis for our future hope is the work of Christ and the witness of Scripture. We should not allow people's experiences to determine our doctrine – e.g. by suggesting that there is no judgement beyond death. Nor should we base our confidence on them.

WHO WILL BE SAVED? (CCC 1033, 1037)

If not all are saved, who will be? There are a number of criteria for salvation given in the New Testament:

- Faith, repentance, baptism and receiving the Spirit, as we saw in Chapter 18.
- Bearing the fruit of repentance:
  - Matthew 3:8: 'Bear fruit in keeping with repentance.'
  - Matthew 7:21: 'Not everyone who says to me, "Lord, Lord", will enter the kingdom of heaven, but the one who does the will of my Father who is in heaven.'
- Forgiving others:
  - Matthew 6:15, 'If you do not forgive others their trespasses, neither will your Father forgive your trespasses.'
  - Matthew 18:21–35: 'And in anger his master delivered him to the jailers, until he should pay all his debt. So also my heavenly Father will do to every one of you, if you do not forgive your brother from your heart' (18:34–35).
- Caring for the needy:
  - Matthew 25:35–36: 'I was hungry and you gave me food, I was thirsty and you gave me drink, I was a stranger

and you welcomed me, I was naked
and you clothed me, I was sick and
you visited me, I was in prison and
you came to me.'
  - 1 John 3:17: 'If anyone has the world's
    goods and sees his brother in need, yet
    closes his heart against him, how does
    God's love abide in him?'
• Works:
  - James 2:14, 20: 'What good is it, my
    brothers, if someone says he has faith
    but does not have works? Can that
    faith save him? . . . Faith apart from
    works is useless.'
• Love:
  - 1 John 4:7–8: 'Beloved, let us love
    one another, for love is from God, and
    whoever loves has been born of God
    and knows God. Anyone who does not
    love does not know God, because God
    is love.'
  - 1 John 4:16: 'God is love, and whoever
    abides in love abides in God, and God
    abides in him.'

These criteria are to be seen as the symptoms,
the marks of a Christian, as described in
Chapter 20. But how rigorously should
these criteria be applied? Mark Twain
describes one approach:

> The minister gave out his text and
> droned along monotonously through
> an argument . . . that dealt in limitless
> fire and brimstone and thinned the
> predestined elect down to a company
> so small as to be hardly worth the saving.
> (*The Adventures of Tom Sawyer*, 40)

Fortunately the standard required is not
perfection – otherwise the number of
the elect would be small indeed and
God would have condemned himself
to a lonely eternity!

WHAT OF THOSE WHO NEVER HEAR?[7]

The most important criterion for salvation
is response to Christ: 'Whoever believes in
him is not condemned, but whoever does
not believe is condemned already, because
he has not believed in the name of the only
Son of God' (John 3:18). This immediately
creates a problem. It is all very well to say
that we are saved through faith in Christ,
but what about those who never have the
opportunity to respond to him? This is
the great majority of the human race. It
includes all who die in infancy (who for
much of human history were the majority)
and all who die without hearing about
Christ (who for most if not all of human
history have been the majority of adults). Is
there a way that they can be saved? *Cyprian
argued that there is no salvation outside the
(Catholic) Church, but very few would take
such a hard line today. So, for example, the
*Second Vatican Council states:

> Those also can attain to salvation who
> through no fault of their own do not know
> the Gospel of Christ or His Church, yet
> sincerely seek God and moved by grace
> strive by their deeds to do His will as it
> is known to them through the dictates
> of conscience. (*Lumen Gentium* 2:16)

As we saw in Chapter 14, the work of Christ
is the only basis for salvation. But is it
necessary to *know* of that in order to benefit
from it? There is some biblical evidence
for answering 'No'. The Old Testament
believers did not know specifically about
Jesus, but were saved by him through their
faith in God's promise. This is spelt out in
Hebrews 11. Again, if one accepts that it
is possible for those dying in infancy to be
saved we have another example of salvation
without hearing about Christ.[8] Paul in his

preaching to pagans seems to suggest that their ancestors could be saved: 'In past generations [God] allowed all the nations to walk in their own ways' (Acts 14:16). 'The times of ignorance God overlooked, but now he commands all people everywhere to repent' (Acts 17:30).

A number of ways have been suggested in which those who have no opportunity can be saved.

OPPORTUNITY AFTER DEATH
A few passages suggest it is possible to have an opportunity to respond to Christ after death:

- 1 Peter 3:18–20: Christ was 'put to death in the flesh but made alive in the spirit, in which he went and proclaimed to the spirits in prison, because they formerly did not obey, when God's patience waited in the days of Noah.'
- 1 Peter 4:6: 'This is why the gospel was preached even to those who are dead, that though judged in the flesh the way people are, they might live in the spirit the way God does.'

However, other passages suggest it is only what happens in *this* life that counts:

- Luke 16:26: 'Between us and you a great chasm has been fixed, in order that those who would pass from here to you may not do so, and none may cross from there to us.'
- 2 Corinthians 5:10: 'We must all appear before the judgement seat of Christ, so that each one may receive what is due for what he has done in the body, whether good or evil.'
- Hebrews 9:27: 'It is appointed for man to die once, and after that comes judgement.'

'ANONYMOUS CHRISTIANITY'
This is the idea that those who have not heard can be anonymous or implicit Christians without knowing it. It was popularized by the Roman Catholic theologian *Karl Rahner and is widely accepted in the Roman Catholic Church. It is also held by many Protestants. We have hints of this idea in the New Testament. Jesus stated that 'Abraham rejoiced that he would see my day. He saw it and was glad' (John 8:56). Hebrews states that Moses 'considered the reproach of Christ greater wealth than the treasures of Egypt, for he was looking to the reward' (11:26). This is tantamount to describing Moses as an 'anonymous Christian'.

The opposite of believing in Jesus is not ignorance of him but rejecting him: 'Whoever believes in the Son has eternal life, but whoever *rejects* the Son will not see life' (John 3:36, TNIV).

JUDGEMENT ACCORDING TO THE LIGHT RECEIVED
Another possibility for the salvation of those who have never had the opportunity to respond to Christ is that they will be judged according to the light that they have received. *John Wesley taught that all people receive prevenient grace and are judged by their response to this. Hebrews 11:6 could be seen as giving the logical minimum for faith: 'Without faith it is impossible to please him, for whoever would draw near to God must believe that he exists and that he rewards those who seek him.'

This raises the question of whether God can be known through conscience, nature and the created world. A number of passages can be taken to suggest that he can:

- John 1:9: 'The true light, which enlightens everyone, was coming into the world.'
- Romans 10:14–21 starts with need for a preacher, but possibly suggests that creation can serve that role: 'But I ask, have they not heard? Indeed they have, for "Their voice has gone out to all the earth, and their words to the ends of the world"' (10:18). Paul is quoting from Psalm 19:4, which follows on from 19:1: 'The heavens declare the glory of God, and the sky above proclaims his handiwork.' Is Paul saying that all have indeed heard, through nature? This ties in with Romans 1:20: 'For his invisible attributes, namely, his eternal power and divine nature, have been clearly perceived, ever since the creation of the world, in the things that have been made. So they are without excuse.'

The expression 'God only knows' is used flippantly by many people, but on this topic it is strictly true! We need to leave this in God's hands. As Abraham put it, 'Shall not the Judge of all the earth do what is just?' (Gen. 18:25). We should approach those who have not responded to the gospel as lost, not as already anonymous Christians – but that does not entitle us to pronounce judgement upon them. It is God who reads people's hearts and God who is able to work in the heart of whomever he will. If past precedent is anything to go by, the End will probably bring many surprises: 'I tell you, many will come from east and west and recline at table with Abraham, Isaac, and Jacob in the kingdom of heaven, while the sons of the kingdom will be thrown into the outer darkness' (Matt. 8:11–12).

© Miriam Kendrick 2013 www.miriamkendrick.co.uk

Worship

There's a wideness in God's mercy
like the wideness of the sea;
there's a kindness in his justice,
which is more than liberty.

For the love of God is broader
than the measures of man's mind,
and the heart of the Eternal
is most wonderfully kind.
(Frederick W. Faber, 'Souls of men, why will ye scatter')

PRAYER

Merciful God, you have prepared for those who love you such good things as pass our understanding: pour into our hearts such love toward you that we, loving you in all things and above all things, may obtain your promises, which exceed all that we can desire; through Jesus Christ your Son our Lord. (*Common Worship*: Collect for Sixth Sunday after Trinity)

NOTES

1 This was written while Margaret Clarkson was in hospital recuperating from orthopaedic surgery. I am not dogmatically stating that *no* traditional hymns refer to the resurrection body, only that a modest search failed to yield one.

2 M. J. Erickson *Christian Theology*. Grand Rapids: Baker, 1985, 1227.

3 Contrary to an unfortunate typo in a recent book on Revelation which states that 'evil cannot not last forever'!

4 It is noteworthy that in the *Left Behind* films the dogs have clearly been 'left behind' but there is no sign of any cats, which have presumably all been raptured with the saints!

5 In his *Table Talk*, cited by Paul Althaus, *The Theology of Martin Luther*. Philadelphia: Fortress, 1966, 425.

6 The interpretation of this passage has been a subject of controversy.

7 ATS ch. 12/11.

8 ATS Appendix 7 (second edn).

RESOURCES FOR CHAPTER 29

D. L. Okholm and T. Phillips (eds) *Four Views on Salvation in a Pluralistic World*. Grand Rapids: Zondervan, 1996.

J. Sanders (ed.) *What About Those Who Have Never Heard? Three Views*. Downers Grove: IVP, 1995.

S. S. Smalley *Hope for Ever: The Christian View of Life and Death*. Milton Keynes: Paternoster, 2005.

N. T. Wright *New Heavens, New Earth: The Biblical Picture of Christian Hope*. Cambridge: Grove Books (Biblical Series 11), 1999.

QUESTIONS TO ANSWER

Numbers refer to chapters; some chapters have more than one question. Questions should be answered in *no more than 100 words*.

1 What role do reason, tradition and experience have in theology?

2 Who is/are the author(s) of the Bible? *Why* should we regard the Bible as God's word?

3 How can finite human beings speak about God?

4 What are the implications of the doctrine of creation? How should theology relate to modern science?

5 What did God create apart from the physical universe? What place should the spirit world hold in our beliefs?

6 What is the image of God in which we are created?

7 What are the effects of sin?

8 What is original sin? Does Genesis 3 describe an actual event?

9 Is God in control of human history?

10 If God is all good and all powerful, why is there evil?

11 What is the role of law in the Christian life? How does the New Testament relate to the Old?

12 What did Christ come to do for us?

13 Who is Christ?

14 Is Christ the only way to God?

15 Who (or what) is the Holy Spirit? What does the Holy Spirit do in us?

16 What three truths does the doctrine of the Trinity affirm against heresies?

17 Does God change? Does God know the future?

18 How does one become a Christian according to the New Testament?

19 What does baptism do?

20 On what basis does God accept us? Can we be sure of our salvation?

21 What is sanctification?

22 Can converted Christians lose their salvation? What role is there for reward in the Christian life?

23 Does God choose who will be saved, or do we?

24 What is the Church?

25 Describe the four traditional marks of the Church.

26 What is the meaning and purpose of Holy Communion?

27 How will this age end?

28 What is Hell?

29 What is the Christian hope for those who have died in Christ?

GLOSSARY

Italics in the definitions refers to other terms in this list.

accommodation God limits or accommodates himself to our capacity in revealing himself.

Adoptionism Christ was a human being who was 'adopted' as God's Son.

agape love feast held by early Christians (Jude 12).

Age to Come the everlasting age that will follow the return of Christ.

Amillennialism doctrine that there is to be no literal *Millennium*.

analogy God loves, is good, is Father, etc., in a way that is similar but not identical to us.

annihilationism doctrine that the ultimate fate of the lost is annihilation or extinction.

anonymous Christian someone who is an implicit Christian without having heard of Christ.

anthropomorphism speaking of God in human terms, as Father, as loving, etc.

Antinomianism Christians can live as they please (or) Christians do not need the written law.

apophatic the *negative way* of speaking about God by saying what he is not.

apostasy/apostate abandoning or renouncing one's faith/one who does this.

asceticism leading a life of voluntary austerity – celibacy, poverty, etc.

atonement the work of Christ in reconciling us to God.

baptism in/with/of the Holy Spirit the initial reception of the Holy Spirit.

Binitarianism Father and Son are God but the Holy Spirit is not.

canon of Scripture the list of which books belong in the Bible.

cataphatic the *positive way* of speaking about God by saying what he is.

Catechism a treatise for instruction in the faith, usually composed of questions and answers.

Christendom where Christianity is the official religion of the state.

Christology doctrine of the person of Christ.

Christus Victor 'Christ the Victor' over Satan and death.

collect a prayer appointed for use on a particular day.

compatibilist free will is compatible with being predictable – e.g. God is always good.

concursus 'running together' – of the relation between divine and human authorship of the Bible.

contextualization translating the biblical message into a different context/culture.

Copernican Revolution shift from seeing the earth to seeing the sun as the centre of the universe.

covenant mutually binding relationship established by God with people, with terms and conditions.

Credobaptism the doctrine that only conscious, consenting believers may be baptized.

deification the doctrine that God enables us to partake in his divine nature.

Deism the doctrine that after God created the universe he left it to run on its own.

demon a fallen angel.

dichotomy (of human nature) the doctrine that we are twofold – body and soul.

Docetism doctrine that Christ only appeared to have a body/suffer/be human.

dual outcome the *Last Judgement* results in some being lost as well as some being saved.

dualism with reference to human nature, see *dichotomy*.

Early Church the Church of the first five centuries.

ecclesiology doctrine of the Church.

effectual calling an inner call by the Spirit that infallibly achieves the result of winning us round.

efficacious grace *grace* that infallibly achieves the result of winning us round.

election God's choice of who will be saved.

Enlightenment nineteenth-century movement that set reason against superstition and questioned *revelation*.

entire sanctification Wesleyan doctrine that we can achieve perfection in this life.

equivocal having different unrelated meanings (of uses of a word, like a dog's and a tree's bark).

eschatology doctrine of the last things and their impact on the present age.

Eucharist a name for the service instituted by Christ at the Last Supper.

Evangelical Revival the eighteenth-century revival that gave birth to modern Evangelicalism.

ex nihilo doctrine that God created the universe 'out of nothing'.

exegesis the scholarly interpretation of the original meaning of a text.

Fall the introduction of sin into the human race by the sin of Adam and Eve.

filioque Holy Spirit proceeds from the Father 'and from the Son' ('filioque' in Latin).

foreknowledge God's knowledge of future events.

free choice we choose freely even though our choices may be totally predictable.

free will this has a variety of meanings, including both *free choice* and the idea of unpredictability.

gathered church a church composed of those who have freely chosen to belong.

General Councils seven councils recognized by the Catholic Church of East and West.

general revelation God's *revelation* through creation and reason.

Gnosticism a major movement of radical heresy in the second century.

grace God's favour towards us and, in particular, the inner working of the Holy Spirit.

Great Exchange on the cross Christ made our sin his own, and his righteousness became ours.

Hades Greek term for the abode of the dead, equivalent to *Sheol* in the Old Testament.

Hell the fate of those who are finally lost.

hermeneutical spiral progressive interaction between received views and the Bible.

Holy Communion a name for the service instituted by Christ at the Last Supper.

image of God human beings are created in God's image and likeness.

immutability (of God) God's unchangeability, which can have many different meanings.

impassibility (of God) God's immunity from all suffering.

Incarnation doctrine that Jesus is the eternal Word of God become flesh.

inerrancy the Bible contains no errors or mistakes.

infallibility the Bible's reliability does not extend to matters like science or historical details.

initiation the process of becoming a Christian.

Inner Light direct *revelation* from the Holy Spirit as an alternative to Scripture.

inspiration the work of the Holy Spirit in inspiring the text of Scripture.

intermediate state the state of the faithful departed between death and the *Parousia*.

invisible Church the true Church, the company of the elect, whose boundaries are known only to God.

irresistible grace term used by some Calvinists to describe *efficacious grace*.

Judaeo-Christian revelation specific *revelation* to Israel from Abraham on, culminating in Christ.

justification acquittal, not-guilty declaration, reckoning of us as righteous.

Last Days period between the First and Second Comings of Christ.

Last Judgement the final judgement when Christ returns at the *Parousia*.

legalism belief that we need to earn our acceptance by works of the law.

Liberal theology nineteenth-century theology that questioned many of the beliefs of biblical *revelation*.

libertarian free will free will which is unpredictable, unlike *compatibilist free will*.

liturgy set pattern of worship.

Lord's Supper the meal described in 1 Corinthians 11 at which *Holy Communion* took place.

Middle Ages the period between the *Early Church* and the *Reformation* (AD 500–1500).

Millennium 1,000-year reign of Christ on earth, as described in Revelation 20:1–7.

Modalism/Monarchianism Father, Son and Spirit are three manifestations of the one God.

Monism with reference to human nature, view that the soul does not exist separately from the body.

Natural Theology theology based on nature and reason, without *special revelation*.

naturalist philosophy philosophy claiming that nothing exists apart from the material universe.

negative way the method of describing God by saying what he is not, also called *apophatic*

omnipotence (of God) God's ability to do anything.

original guilt   we share in the guilt of Adam and are not born totally innocent.

original sin   the bias towards sin (? and guilt) with which we are born.

pantheism   the doctrine that identifies God with the universe.

paedobaptism   the doctrine that (some) babies are to be baptized.

Parousia   the 'presence' or 'arrival' of Jesus Christ, his *Second Coming*.

Penal Substitution   the doctrine that Christ on the cross bore our punishment in our place.

penance   discipline imposed on a Christian who commits a serious sin.

Pentateuch   the first five books of the Bible, the 'books of Moses'.

perseverance   endurance in the Christian way to the end of life.

perseverance of the saints   doctrine that God preserves all true Christians from *apostasy*.

pluralism   no one religion can claim uniqueness and finality.

positive way   the method of describing God by saying what he is, also called *cataphatic*.

Postmillennialism   doctrine that Christ will return after (post) the *Millennium*.

predestination   God determines in advance the destiny of all people.

pre-incarnate Christ   the eternal Word before his *Incarnation*.

Premillennialism   doctrine that Christ will return before (pre) the *Millennium*.

prevenient grace   inner working of the Holy Spirit that draws us to faith in Christ.

primary cause   idea that God's will is the ultimate cause of what happens.

providence   God's rule/control of human history, working out his purposes.

recapitulation   Christ sums up the human race and introduces a new redeemed humanity.

Reformation   sixteenth-century reform of the Roman Catholic Church leading to Protestantism.

Reformers   the leaders of the sixteenth-century *Reformation*.

regeneration   the process of being 'born again'.

reprobate   those whom God has not elected for salvation.

revelation   God's revealing himself/making himself known to his people.

rigorism   those guilty of serious sin should be permanently excluded from the Church.

Sabbath   the seventh day of the week (Saturday) on which the Jews were commanded not to work.

Sabellianism   doctrine that Father = Son = Holy Spirit – three manifestations of one God.

sacraments   baptism and *Holy Communion* – divinely instituted effective signs, 'visible words'.

sanctification   God's work delivering us from sin and making us like Christ.

Satan   leading angel who fell into sin and heads up the company of *demon*s.

schism   a split in the Church leading to a breakaway group.

Second Adam   Christ as the one who puts right what Adam got wrong, introducing a new humanity.

second blessing   a specific blessing after conversion that should be sought by all Christians.

Second Coming   the return of Christ at the end of this age in the *Parousia*.

secondary cause immediate cause (human choices, etc.) of that which God purposes.

Septuagint (LXX) Greek translation of the Old Testament, used by the New Testament authors.

Sheol Hebrew term for the abode of the dead, equivalent to *Hades* in Greek thought.

sola fide we are justified 'by faith alone' (see *justification*).

sola scriptura 'Scripture alone', a slogan that postdates the *Reformation*.

special revelation specifically *Judaeo-Christian revelation* – as in OT, NT, Christ.

sufficient grace *grace* that enables someone to convert, without making it inevitable.

syncretism mixing together of two or more religions.

theodicy 'the justification of God' in the light of evil and suffering.

theotokos Mary as 'Mother of God', her baby being God the Son, made flesh.

total depravity every part of fallen human nature is to some extent spoiled and tainted by sin.

tradition our Christian heritage, the Christian faith as handed down from the past.

transubstantiation substance of bread/wine is converted into substance of Christ's body/blood.

trichotomy (of human nature) the doctrine that we are threefold – body, soul and spirit.

Tritheism doctrine that Father, Son and Holy Spirit are three Gods.

universalism doctrine that all will be saved, regardless of what they do.

univocal having the identical meaning (of different uses of a word or statement).

verbal inspiration doctrine that it is the actual text of Scripture that is inspired by God (see *inspiration*).

Virgin Birth Jesus was conceived without a human father (strictly, virginal conception).

visible Church the Church that we see on earth, comprising false as well as genuine Christians.

Wesleyan Quadrilateral Scripture to be interpreted with reason, tradition and experience.

COPYRIGHT ACKNOWLEDGEMENTS

CARTOONS

INDEX OF BIBLICAL REFERENCES

INDEX OF NAMES AND SUBJECTS

Lightning Source UK Ltd.
Milton Keynes UK
UKHW031847240820
368748UK00008B/1839

'What does the Church believe? What does the Church's faith have to do with prayer and worship, and life in the everyday world? Why don't all churches believe the same thing? Tony Lane addresses these basic questions and more . . . Students, especially, will find this a welcome guide.'

Joel B. Green, *Associate Dean for the Center for Advanced Theological Studies, Fuller Theological Seminary, California*

'Tony Lane is a masterful teacher . . . He has a knack of writing epigrammatic sentences that instantly clarify an issue. He has a gift for accurately apt illustrations. Just when things might be getting a little dull, he throws in a joke or even a cartoon. Ideal for anyone who wants to understand the basics.'

Richard Bauckham, *Emeritus Professor of New Testament Studies, University of St Andrews, Scotland*

'Engaging in style, evangelical in spirit, ecumenical in atmosphere, and eclectic in its use of resources . . . *Exploring Christian Doctrine* will delight students looking for a textbook that is clear and informative, never overbearing but always challenging.'

Sinclair B. Ferguson, *Professor of Systematic Theology Redeemer Theological Seminary, Dallas, Texas*

'Tony Lane's survey of Christian belief is accessible and engaging. Alive to historical debates and to contemporary challenges, his focus nonetheless remains on offering a clear and thorough account of the essential points of Christian doctrine from a broadly evangelical perspective . . . Anyone wanting to understand what Christians believe and why will find this an extremely helpful guide.'

Steve Holmes, *Senior Lecturer in Theology University of St Andrews, Scotland*

'The book's structure is appetizingly laid out in a series of initial questions, positions taken, objections raised, errors to avoid and Lane's own succinct answers – all framed by credal and confessional bounds and set within the context of worship.'

Kevin J. Vanhoozer, *Research Professor of Systematic Theology Trinity Evangelical Divinity School, Illinois*

'This is a simply outstanding introduction to doctrine . . . The product of decades of classroom experience, it is rooted in the Bible, answers a barrage of questions and objections, and is enlivened by cartoons and humour. If you think doctrine is dull and boring, think again.'

Robert Letham, *Director of Research and Senior Tutor in Systematic and Historical Theology Wales Evangelical School of Theology*

www.spckpublishing.co.uk

ISBN 978-0-281-06449-6

9 780281 064496

Cover image: *Trinity* by Andrei Rublev. Tempera on wood, Tretyakov Gallery, Moscow. Anatoly Sapronenkov/SuperStock